Investing in America's Workforce

Volume 3

Investing in America's Workforce

Improving Outcomes for Workers and Employers

Volume 3
Investing in Systems for Employment Opportunity

Stuart Andrcason
Todd Greene
Heath Prince
Carl E. Van Horn
Editors

2018

W.E. Upjohn Institute for Employment Research
Kalamazoo, Michigan

Library of Congress Cataloging-in-Publication Data

Names: Van Horn, Carl E., editor.
Title: Investing in America's workforce : improving outcomes for workers and
  employers / Carl Van Horn [and three others], editors.
Description: Kalamazoo, Michigan : W.E. Upjohn Institute for Employment Research,
  [2018] | Includes bibliographical references and index.
  Contents: Volume 1. Investing in workers — Volume 2. Investing in work —
  Volume 3. Investing in systems for employment opportunity.
Identifiers: LCCN 2018044491 | ISBN 9780692163184 (vol. 3 : pbk. : alk. paper)
Subjects: LCSH: Manpower policy—United States. | Manpower planning—United
  States. | Labor supply—Effect of education on—United States. | Human capital—
  United States.
Classification: LCC HD6724 .I568 2018 | DDC331.12/0420973—dc23 LC record
  available at https://lccn.loc.gov/2018044491

Editors:
Stuart Andreason, Federal Reserve Bank of Atlanta
Todd Greene, Atlanta University Center Consortium
Heath Prince, The University of Texas at Austin
Carl E. Van Horn, Rutgers University, The State University of New Jersey

Contributing Editors:

Ashley Bozarth	Rob Grunewald	Alexander Ruder
Janet Boguslaw	Richard A. Hobbie	Jennifer Schramm
Maureen Conway	Kathy Krepcio	Robb C. Sewell
Stephen Crawford	Karen Leone de Nie	Chris Shannon
Brian Dabson	Emily Mitchell	Steven Shepelwich
Nancey Green Leigh	Edison Reyes	

The facts, observations, and viewpoints expressed in this book are the sole responsibility of the authors. They do not necessarily represent positions of the Federal Reserve Bank of Atlanta, the Federal Reserve System, the John J. Heldrich Center for Workforce Development, the Ray Marshall Center for the Study of Human Resources, or the W.E. Upjohn Institute for Employment Research.

Cover design by Andrew Giannelli and Gregory Famularo.
Printed in the United States of America.

Contents

Introduction

Investing in Systems for Employment Opportunity

Stuart Andreason and Alexander Ruder

As the economy has changed over the past several decades, many different organizations have developed programs to support workers, help businesses enhance productivity and solve human resource challenges, reemploy workers who have lost their jobs, and move people from precarious positions on public support to positions of employment and self-sufficiency, among many other unique and targeted approaches to supporting employment and economic opportunity. Collectively, this array of programs and policies makes up the workforce development system, and more broadly a system that supports employment opportunity. While many of the programs have been incredibly effective, businesses and job seekers report challenges in understanding and navigating the workforce development system. And, with many smaller organizations involved in the system, it is constantly evolving and changing; the sustainability of programs and policies also presents a challenge. Policies that support these efforts need to be updated and made more modern, given the quickly changing economy and labor market (Van Horn, Edwards, and Greene 2015).

Chapters in this volume discuss promising practices in workforce development and policies and actions that elected officials can take to expand upon those successes. Central to these efforts is building stronger partnerships across regional workforce organizations and creating a foundation for stronger collective impact. Strong partnerships are likely better positioned to organize services that workers need to be available and ready to work, no matter their skill level—services like transportation, housing, and child care, to name a few. In addition to policy and coordination, there are a number of changes to programmatic systems that could enhance the scope and scale of workforce development programs—particularly in financing, technology, and credentialing.

Financial investment in workforce development presents a number of important considerations. New financial tools and models for contracting services in workforce development can structure funding toward paying for outcomes rather than outputs. Ultimately, workforce development programs need to ensure they are creating opportunities for job seekers and developing productive workers for firms—and there should be little dogma in the interventions that accomplish these goals. New financial tools can help organizations move toward this funding strategy and potentially engage new investors in workforce development. These models may help attract socially minded investors who are seeking returns and social benefits for communities of investment. This is an underutilized source of capital. These models also likely can help grant-making organizations and governments focus their giving on programs that are creating greater social benefits.

Technology is changing the way workforce partners build data systems to evaluate programs, deliver training, and inform stakeholders about various aspects of the labor market. Technology enhances the reach of workforce development programs to more people and helps expose workers and businesses to new ideas and models. Similarly, technological advances in data collection, data sharing across workforce system partners, and research capacity can help organizations evaluate the effectiveness of workforce development programs.

Technology is not just allowing workforce partners to build data systems for evaluation and accountability, but also to use it as a learning tool—to expand workforce programs to broader audiences, often in remote areas, and deliver new learning content quickly and efficiently. To support these new systems, organizations need to ensure equitable access to broadband Internet for individuals and businesses. As technology becomes more ubiquitous in learning environments, communities without fast and reliable broadband Internet will disadvantage businesses, learners, and community members. The infrastructure that supports technological utilization is critical.

Related to new technology, several organizations have invested considerable effort to build systems that improve transparency of the large credentialing marketplace. Many educational institutions have looked for ways to offer credentials that serve as strong signals for skills demanded by the labor market. However, with the rapid growth in the number of credentials, employers and students may struggle to determine the value of a given credential. The purpose of these new credentialing systems is to allow businesses and students to access comparable information about various credentials, from badges to doctoral degrees. With this information, employers can more clearly assess the skills of applicants, and students can make more informed decisions when choosing among different credential programs.

Employment opportunity reaches beyond skill development. There are critical parts of the infrastructure that will create a stronger and broader workforce system, including not only new financial models, technology, and credentialing systems, but also connections to services that support individuals through training and various stages of employment. As noted above, these services include many housing, community, and human services. The concept of "spatial mismatch" refers to the extent to which these supportive services, job training, and employment are located away from the areas where individuals live. How the broader workforce systems address the impact of this spatial mismatch on workforce outcomes is a major concern. Providing workers with ways to access these services is a part of addressing the workforce needs of workers, employers, and the community.

Finally, the workforce development field has long emphasized the need for strong partnerships at the local and regional level. Today, rapid economic and technical change create an even greater need for diverse stakeholders to collaborate. Collaborative partnerships that extend across geographic and institutional boundaries form the foundation of a workforce system that can respond to rapid shifts in workforce demand, establish shared strategic priorities, and frame workforce development as a model of lifelong learning. This collaborative approach enables workforce partners to address more efficiently the systems-level opportunities discussed in this volume.

SCALING AND SUSTAINING PROGRAMS

While the model for measuring costs and benefits of workforce programs may be very different across communities or even among partnerships in the same community, it is critical to understand and evaluate how these programs may affect longer-term community goals, including economic growth. Evaluation requires different perspectives on how to understand the interventions—it is not adequate to measure social service costs alone. Workforce development must be considered an investment in worker opportunity, business competitive advantage, economic development, or other community-defined goals for programs to reach the scale or maintain the sustainability necessary to reach those goals. These considerations are critical in striving for broad systems to create opportunity for workers and employers.

Scale and sustainability have long been a challenge for workforce development programs. Many successful programs serve several hundred people a year, and, while this is not to diminish their success, their scale could be much greater with increased partnerships and financial investment. It is critical to explore how these models may align with programs of significant scale already in operation, such as the federal workforce development system and educational system, potentially aided by technology and finance.

The workforce development community increasingly understands the types of policies and programs that create opportunities for workers and employers, but it is essential to expand these effective programs. A first step is to develop ways to assess the quality and effectiveness of programs and communicate them to outside partners. Throughout the book, you will see how different organizations, partnerships, and communities have developed an investment framework to make these assessments. They aim to instruct how this might happen in your organization, partnership, or community, but they do not include the full range of possibilities. There is room for continued innovation in driving financial investment and new partners to workforce development. We hope this volume will help spark new ideas that continue to grow these partnerships.

BUILDING AN INVESTING FRAMEWORK

The term *investment* is used in this book in a number of different ways. In one sense, it means actual financial investment in workforce development programs—the act of expanding programs requires additional monetary resources—but this is far from the only type of investment. Workforce development programs need partners that are invested in the success of the program, which includes businesses and economic development organizations as well as community development and social support organizations. Community organizations also can help address existing labor market disparities and challenges that are not completely skill based. It is also critical that future evaluations of workforce programs include cost-benefit analyses that show the benefits to workers, businesses, and society.

Investing in America's Workforce: Improving Outcomes for Workers and Employers offers research, best practices, and resources for workforce development practitioners from more than 100 contributing authors. The book aims to reframe workforce development efforts as investments that can result in better economic outcomes for individuals, businesses, and regions. In the three volumes, we focus discussions of investments on three areas: 1) investing in workers, 2) investing in work, and 3) investing in systems for employment opportunity. Within each volume are discrete sections made up of chapters that identify specific workforce development programs and policies that provide positive returns to society, to employers, and to job seekers.

Investing in Workers, the first volume, means regarding all job seekers—and particularly disadvantaged workers—as opportunities and assets rather than deficits. Workers left out of the recovery, such as the long-term unemployed or chronically unemployed youth, are important sources of new talent in a tight labor market. These workers also bring new and different perspectives at any point of the business cycle and can help drive innovation. Seeing these workers as opportunities to build new ideas and competitive advantage is important; it is also important for workers who are mired in poverty. It is vital to invest in core literacy and technical skills so these workers can create wealth and build assets. Several chapters in Volume 1 explore both skill development and supporting workers who have particular barriers to work and economic opportunity.

Investing in Work, the second volume, explores the extent to which firms are able to address human resource challenges and difficulties for their workers by investing in the jobs, fringe benefits, and structure of employment that workers encounter with employers. Many firms have found that offering enhanced quality of work and benefits helps attract more productive workers, boosts the productivity of current workers, and produces other tangible benefits, such as reduced turnover. Investments in work structure also include considering how changes to the employee-employer relationship help build wealth, such as through different models of employee ownership of firms and planned succession of ownership. Finally, investing in work includes place-based and job creation efforts. Volume 2 explores these issues broadly and specifically in rural areas in an effort to better align workforce development and economic development efforts. Considering both the supply of and demand for labor likely will improve the effectiveness of both efforts.

Investing in Systems for Employment Opportunity, the third volume, explores the different ways organizations and policymakers deliver training and support worker and business productivity. The stakeholders involved in these efforts are multiple and varied, including governmental entities, businesses, philanthropies, and nonprofits. Finding ways to coordinate across these different sectors for collective impact is critical. In addition, several important factors and trends could influence the strategies of these programs, individually or collectively. Innovations in technology may change the type of work people do and the products firms create, while also providing a new and different delivery system for training. Access to these technologies is also vital, since many communities are not well connected. New finance models may help attract new players and investors in workforce development and help drive investments toward the most effective interventions. Aligning efforts and aiding them with new innovations and business models could significantly increase the scale and scope of workforce development programs.

As you read this book, we hope you find information that helps you advance initiatives, policies, and worker and employer opportunities in your community or state. Please reach out to the authors and editors if you wish to learn more. We hope that you will see the need to understand workforce development as an investment, and that you discover strategies that will help you make progress in your own organization or in your efforts on workforce policy. We believe this mind-set and further engagement and investment in the workforce development system are necessary to expand opportunity for workers and employers and to promote economic growth in the country.

Reference

Van Horn, Carl, Tammy Edwards, and Todd Greene, eds. 2015. *Transforming Workforce Development Policies for the 21st Century.* Kalamazoo, MI: W.E. Upjohn Institute for Employment Research.

Part 1

Financial Innovations
in Workforce Development

1
Rebalancing the Risk

Innovation in Funding Human
Capital Development

Heath Prince

Much attention of late has been given to the importance for workers to continually maintain and upgrade their skills in order to remain competitive in the labor market. Whether one regards this observation as socially just, it is an accepted fact that wages tend to rise with education and skill level, and that failing to maintain education and skill levels is a prescription for falling behind either at an individual or a national level. Maintaining and expanding skill levels, however, comes at a cost, and this cost is increasingly shifted onto the shoulders of workers themselves, particularly those at the lower end of the skills ladders, and arguably the ones who need assistance the most. Restoring some equity in terms of sharing the costs of training is the subject of this set of chapters.

BACKGROUND

Jessop (1993) described the then emerging shift in the global economy as moving from a "Keynesian welfare state" to a "Schumpetarian workfare state," characterized by a movement from a focus on full employment to a focus on economic competitiveness and the dictates of the private sector. Jessop also described this shift toward a workfare state as moving from one that encourages mass consumption through the expansion of welfare rights to one that reduces social policy to simply meet the ever-shifting requirements of the labor market and its need for flexibility in the workforce. Along with these trends, he argued, comes a "hollowing out" of the state, in which we observe an emptying of any content that is not directly or indirectly in service to the market. What Jessop described in 1993 as a "thought experiment prompted by observation of some general trends" (p. 35) has turned out to read like a blueprint for the creation of the modern labor market.

Wartzman (2017) notes several troubling data points in *The End of Loyalty*, including, for example, that "nearly half the nation's work-force earns less than fifteen dollars an hour [and] a third of men in their prime don't make enough to keep a family of four out of poverty or are altogether unemployed—double what it was thirty years ago" (p. 3).

Our current workforce development system—this collection of sometimes connected and coordinated, and sometimes duplicative and competing, set of federal, state, and local policies, programs, and funding sources—is, implicitly and explicitly, a vehicle for exactly this sort of flexibility and entrepreneurialism about which Jessop warned and to which Wartzman writes. The system is flexible in that it is premised on the need for constant retraining, and entrepreneurial in that it assumes an acceptance on the part of the worker that the social contract is defunct and that her success depends, in large part, on whatever resources she can muster to the task.

The time is quickly approaching when the workforce development system, as it currently operates, may struggle to defend its existence. As the burden continues to shift to the individual workers to ensure that they possess the skills required to succeed in the labor market, the need for a formal system may diminish to the point of vanishing. Whereas organized labor used to provide the countervailing power to offset the drive toward placing the needs of shareholders above workers, and union apprenticeships could provide stable careers in family-supporting occupations, we now have the growth of the "gig economy" and the rising membership in the "precariat," both of which limit paths to the American dream, and both of which harshly punish failure.[1]

As the workforce development and economic growth literature commonly note, success in this new economy depends on, above all other factors, the ability to adapt and expand skills as needed—exactly the sort of premium placed on flexibility that Jessop (1993) predicted. This need for further skills training, however, has paralleled steady declines in public support for it alongside growing numbers of workers who require it. Formula funding to states for adult, dislocated worker, and youth programs have fallen steadily since 2000, from approximately $5.1 billion to $2.8 billion in 2017, providing assistance to approximately 450,000 of the 165 million individuals who would benefit from training, according to the National Skills Coalition.[2] At the same time, student loan debt has steadily increased over the past 15 years (even while other types of debt have begun to decline), as youth and adults turn to postsecondary educational certificates and credentials with the hope that these will help secure them a spot in a shrinking middle class.

TOWARD ALTERNATIVE FINANCING STRATEGIES

The chapters in this section describe several funding strategies for education and training that have emerged in response to the shifts described above. Taken together, these strategies represent alternatives to the increasing tendency for the cost of training to be borne by the individual alone—an issue of critical importance at a time when being adequately skilled may mean the difference between employment and poverty.

The following chapters can be categorized as those that analyze legislative and philanthropic strategies for closing the funding gap, those that recruit private investors to help ensure better performance, and those that avoid the up-front costs of education and training by tying repayment to future earnings.

LEGISLATIVE AND PHILANTHROPIC STRATEGIES

Sobel Blum and Shepelwich highlight several partnerships that have emerged between banks and training providers as a result of a 2016 clarification regarding the Community Reinvestment Act (CRA) of 1977. The CRA requires banks to meet the credit needs of all segments of the communities that they serve, and it stipulates that banks will be evaluated for compliance by the Federal Reserve, the Office of the Comptroller of the Currency, and the Federal Deposit Insurance

Corporation. The clarification permits banks' investments in workforce development programs serving low- and moderate-income individuals to be an allowable activity toward satisfying CRA requirements. Through lessons from several existing case studies, Sobel Blum and Shepelwich illustrate how these investments not only potentially increase the number of workers with skills required in the local economy, but also benefit individual financial institutions by raising their profile as responsible community members. The authors describe several strategies through which training providers might partner with banks in order to leverage CRA training resources.

Wardrip and de Zeeuw analyze recent trends in philanthropic support for workforce development, which has long been a source of flexible funding, permitting the sorts of experimentation and piloting that other funding sources, particularly public ones, do not. While it is undoubtedly essential for these reasons, Wardrip and de Zeeuw find that over one-third of philanthropic support is concentrated in only three metro areas, pointing toward severe limitations in the current distribution of these resources.

RECRUITING PRIVATE INVESTORS TO THE CAUSE

So-called pay-for-performance contracts have received a good deal of attention in recent years, as funders and practitioners attempt to derive methods for financing workforce development that break with the traditional models by reimbursing costs only when successful outcomes are achieved. Richie's chapter on the pay-for-performance provisions contained in the Workforce Innovation and Opportunity Act calls attention to several applications of this provision. She highlights three successful workforce development board–led, pay-for-performance programs in Austin, San Diego, and northern Virginia. Each jurisdiction has adopted outcomes-based programming to upend traditional contracting approaches so that payments are linked to successful outcomes as opposed to the cost-reimbursement status quo. Richie draws lessons from these case studies, including the criticality of access to reliable data on participant outcomes.

Nirav Shah notes weaknesses in workforce development programming, evident from the relatively few rigorous studies to demonstrate beneficial outcomes in recent decades, coupled with the continuing emphasis placed on evidence-based programming and the perennial need for flexible and stable funding. Shah describes how "social impact bonds" (SIBS)—one type of pay-for-performance contract—raise capital from private investors for publicly backed skill development. In the process, social impact bonds demonstrate the potential for shifting the risk for success from low-income individuals and the public sector to investors interested in social, as well as financial, returns. As noted in Richie's essay, access to reliable data is central to the success of social impact bonds. Drawing from successful SIB projects, including a Jewish Vocational Services project in Boston and a Department of Veterans Affairs project targeting employment outcomes, Shah provides insight into the potential for pay-for-success models to more efficiently and effectively meet the education and training needs of the workforce.

A VARIATION ON THE PAY-FOR-SUCCESS THEME

Palacios, like Richie and Shah, focuses on the emergence of funding strategies that suggest a radically new paradigm in how workforce development financing is conceptualized. Palacios examines the potential for "income share agreements" as an alternative to traditional agreements. In essence, these agreements between training providers, employers, and workers avoid the up-front costs associated with training by requiring workers to repay the cost of training out of a share of future income. Unlike student loans, which increase the risk exposure of the trainee, income share agreements make repayment for training proportional to posttraining earnings and, in the process, reduce the risk on the trainee's posttraining income. Significant advances in the past decade in the ability to track income over time make possible the growth of income-contingent repayments for education and training. This, in turn, has the potential to solve a fundamental weakness in the current method for funding human capital—namely, that the risk is almost entirely borne by the individual, while the benefits accrue not only to her but also to her employer and community.

Closing the widening gap between the ever-increasing need for human capital development and the funding required for it is no small task. A theme that runs across each of the chapters in this section relates to rebalancing the risk borne by each of the three primary beneficiaries of a well-trained, well-educated workforce—employers, individuals, and society. Each chapter suggests approaches to this problem, and each merits serious consideration.

Notes

1. The precariat is a social class characterized by its economically precarious, unpredictable, and unsecure sources of livelihood.
2. Information downloaded from National Skills Coalition's Interactive Federal Funding Tool, 2017. https://www.nationalskillscoalition.org/federal-policy/federal-funding-tool (accessed May 3, 2018).

References

Jessop, Bob. 1993. "Toward a Schumpeterian Welfare State: Political Remarks on a Post-Fordist Political Economy." *Studies in Political Economy* 40(1): 7–39.

Wartzman, Rick. 2017. *The End of Loyalty: The Rise and Fall of Good Jobs in America.* Philadelphia: Perseus Books.

2

Partnering with Banks in Workforce Development

Elizabeth Sobel Blum
Steven Shepelwich

Four decades ago, the federal government enacted the Community Reinvestment Act (CRA), which requires banks to meet the credit needs of all segments of the communities that they serve, including low- and moderate-income (LMI) neighborhoods.[1] Under this regulation, banks can get CRA credit by engaging in economic development, community services that target LMI individuals, affordable housing for LMI individuals, and "activities that revitalize or stabilize LMI geographies, designated disaster areas, and distressed or underserved non-metropolitan middle-income geographies" (Federal Reserve Bank of Dallas 2005, p. 1).

In July 2016, federal banking regulators clarified that banks can get CRA credit for "creating or improving access by low- and moderate-income persons to jobs or to job training or workforce development programs" and access to day care operations and other supportive services (Department of the Treasury 2016).[2] This official clarification is important because it encourages banks to engage in workforce development and specifies to bank examiners that workforce development can count as a CRA-creditworthy activity.

HOW PARTNERING WITH WORKFORCE DEVELOPMENT ENTITIES CAN BENEFIT BANKS

By participating in workforce development, banks can partner with entities that help improve the talent pipeline for their bank and the financial sector more generally; identify new opportunities for their community development work; provide expertise, knowledge, and leadership to the workforce system, which could also strengthen a bank's social capital and reputation in its markets; and improve the financial stability of low- and moderate-income individuals by increasing their access to full-time job opportunities.

Banks also can expand their marketing and outreach by offering financial services, education, and training as a tenant or through planned events at a local comprehensive workforce center. Banks can provide value to existing and potential business customers by demonstrating their understanding of the importance of workforce needs. In addition, banks can align their educational outreach with the regional workforce system's strategies and programs to improve their effectiveness in providing financial education and services to students.

Banks have a CRA public file that includes their current plans and programs and is available at their branches upon request. Their understanding of local low- and moderate-income communities' needs is built through relationships with community organizations. If they are not already working with workforce boards, community and technical colleges, economic developers, and others involved in workforce development, then they could benefit from such a relationship. For example, each state's strategic and operational workforce development plan can inform banks about relevant labor market data, regional economic development areas, key industries, potential partner organizations, and the use of funding sources.

ABOUT THE COMMUNITY REINVESTMENT ACT

In 1977, the CRA was enacted to ensure that banks help meet the credit needs of all segments of the communities that they were chartered to serve, including low- and moderate-income neighborhoods.

The CRA requires the three bank regulators, the Federal Reserve, Office of the Comptroller of the Currency, and the Federal Deposit Insurance Corporation, to evaluate the performance of the banks they supervise in helping meet those credit needs, assign one of four statutory ratings to that performance, and make the rating and underlying evaluation public. These four ratings are Outstanding, Satisfactory, Needs to Improve, and Substantial Noncompliance.

The implementing regulation provides for banks of different sizes (small, intermediate small, and large) to have different requirements under the CRA. CRA asset-size threshold adjustments are annual. The most recent adjustments are as follows: "large" banks had assets equal to or greater than $1.252 billion as of December 31 in 2017 or 2016; "intermediate small" banks had assets of at least $313 million as of December 31 in 2017 and 2016 and less than $1.252 billion as of December 31 in 2017 or 2016; and "small" banks had assets less than $313 million as of December 31 in 2017 or 2016.[3] The CRA requirements of banks differ based on their size. The Federal Reserve Bank of Dallas's (2005) publication, "A Banker's Quick Reference Guide to CRA," outlines these requirements.[4]

When banks get a Needs to Improve or Substantial Noncompliance rating, they increase their reputational risk. In addition, their primary federal regulators may reject their requests for a merger or acquisition.[5]

DETERMINING IF A WORKFORCE DEVELOPMENT ACTIVITY QUALIFIES FOR CRA PURPOSES

When a bank would like to earn CRA consideration for a workforce development activity, it must determine if the program qualifies as a community development loan, investment, or service.

If a bank offers a loan, it must be reportable under the Home Mortgage Disclosure Act (HMDA) guidelines[6] or reported as a commercial real estate, farmland, agricultural, or commercial/industrial loan.[7] For an intermediate small bank, it has to report to its bank examiner that it wants the loan to be considered as a community development activity and then explain how the loan meets at least one of the CRA's four community development purposes: affordable housing, community services targeting low- and moderate-income individuals, economic development (which includes workforce development), or revitalization or stabilization of low- or moderate-income communities in its assessment area or regional area that includes the assessment area.

Under the CRA, a bank's assessment area(s) "must, in general, consist of one or more metropolitan statistical areas (MSAs) or metropolitan divisions or one or more contiguous political subdivisions, such as counties, cities or towns. It must include geographies in which the bank has its main office, branches and deposit-taking ATMs, as well as the surrounding geographies in which the bank has originated or purchased a substantial portion of its loans" (Federal Reserve Bank of Dallas 2005, p. 1).

If the bank offers an investment or service, it must explain how it meets at least one of the CRA's four community development purposes.

INFORMATION BANKS NEED TO TELL THEIR "WORKFORCE DEVELOPMENT AND THE CRA" STORY

To help banks identify workforce programs that may fit within their CRA strategies and programs, they need to know not only how workforce programming could assist the bank in meeting its CRA objectives, but also how it could help them meet their business development goals and organizational development needs. For example, they need to know how their loan, service, or investment in workforce development could help them expand their customer base and local talent pool.

A bank's CRA/compliance officer needs to be able to explain—to its internal management, customers, community partners, target communities, and bank examiners—why the bank is involved in workforce development. The amount of this information to be shared depends on the audience. Nonetheless, when an entity involved in workforce development is interested in exploring potential partnerships with banks, it is important to come equipped with the following information:

- The program/initiative/partnership's target clientele

- The goal/objective of this program/initiative/partnership, such as increasing the availability of apprenticeships, job shadowing opportunities, and other learn-and-earn opportunities; increasing the availability of transportation, child care, or other support services; or increasing/verifying the skills, knowledge, competencies, or work functions employers require for certain occupations for use in an educational or job training program

- The industries/occupations targeted by the program/initiative/ partnership
- The biggest successes and challenges of the program/initiative/ partnership
- What the program/initiative/partnership needs to significantly increase its impact, scalability, and sustainability
- How the bank could be most helpful to the program initiative (e.g., giving grants, sitting on the board, mentoring, conducting mock interviews, or providing financial education)

All this information is important for banks to assess what type of loan, service, or investment would be most helpful to the workforce development entity.

BANKS ENGAGING IN WORKFORCE DEVELOPMENT

There are a variety of ways for banks to engage in workforce development. For example, they can serve on the board of directors and provide a loan or grant to a community-based organization that supports workforce development. They can conduct mock interviews and help with résumé writing. They also can provide financial education and learn-and-earn opportunities for individuals who meet the CRA's low- and moderate-income criteria at the beginning of the workforce development activity. Such opportunities include internships, apprenticeships, summer employment opportunities for youth or young adults, college work-study positions outside the college, job-shadowing opportunities, and transitional jobs programs.

As banks engage in workforce development, they must be able to clearly and concisely tell their workforce development story to internal and external stakeholders. Therefore, when organizations invite banks to the table, they must be prepared to outline the costs and benefits, return on investment, and financial and social impact to the bank, community partners, and target community. It would also be helpful to include the impact of workforce development on the health of the target community.

EXAMPLES OF HOW BANKS ARE PARTNERING WITH WORKFORCE DEVELOPMENT ENTITIES[8]

CAP Tulsa

CAP Tulsa is a community action agency that employs two-generation strategies to break the cycle of poverty for low-income families with young children. One of its programs is CareerAdvance, a parent-centered work-readiness program that offers training and job placement in high-demand health care occupations to parents of young children. Certifications offered include certified nursing assistant, pharmacy technician, and dental assistant, all of which have an average starting wage of $10–$15 per hour. CareerAdvance provides support such as tuition assistance, financial coaching, and peer networking opportunities. Its business-development team works with local health care employers to understand their needs and connect participants with job opportunities.

CAP Tulsa partners with many local and national organizations, including banks. Their support comes in the form of grants and volunteerism. Bank employees serve on the CAP Tulsa board in the roles of president, vice president, and general board vice president members. The organization's bank partners include global and local financial institutions, the Federal Home Loan Bank (FHLB) of Topeka, and a bank foundation. Specifically, a local bank submitted a proposal to the FHLB of Topeka's JOBS program for support of CareerAdvance in March 2015, from which CAP Tulsa received $25,000 to support staff salaries. CAP Tulsa also received awards from a bank foundation for $10,000 and a global financial institution for $20,000 to support participant incentives, child care, and other expenses.

Mi Casa

Denver-based nonprofit Mi Casa serves 18-to-55-year-olds in low-income households whose goal is to obtain middle-skill jobs that offer a career pathway with upward mobility. Mi Casa offers job training programs, one-to-one coaching on resume writing, cover letter preparation, negotiation skills, career assessment, and bilingual business development services. It also has middle- and high school–based neighborhood centers that offer youth development programs. For its clients seeking extensive training, Mi Casa provides four to six weeks of technical- and soft-skills classroom training (including certifications and industry-recognized credentials), customized job search support and job placement services in growth sectors (financial services, retail, hospitality, and health care), and support services that promote job retention and stability.

Mi Casa partners with community, regional, national, and global financial institutions, credit unions, and nonbank financial services providers. Over 130 employer partners support Mi Casa by providing guest speakers, leading tours, networking, holding interview days, and serving on its Employer Advisory Councils. These councils are composed of representatives from diverse employers and are organized by industry, such as financial services, or role, such as customer service representative. According to Mi Casa, members of its advisory councils play a vital role in shaping its Career Development Training programs by advising staff on talent needs, hiring practices, training needs, and industry trends.

Per Scholas

Nonprofit Per Scholas provides full-time, tuition-free information technology training to individuals who are unemployed or in low-wage jobs. It operates in Atlanta, Cincinnati, Columbus (Ohio), Dallas, New York, and the national capital region (Washington, DC, Maryland, and Virginia). Per Scholas works directly with employer partners to assess their talent needs and hiring challenges for entry- to mid-level information technology jobs and then designs its training in response to these needs. At the same time, its coaches and volunteers guide students on job search strategies, resume writing, interview preparation, and career development and soft skills: communication, conflict resolution, agility, adaptability, and emotional intelligence.

To help ensure its students' success, Per Scholas and its community partners provide them with support services such as financial management, behavioral health support, and child care. Graduates can continue to obtain career coaching and tuition-free education for up to two years after completion.

Several banks partner with Per Scholas. For example, a global financial institution invested over $800,000 to expand Per Scholas's reach to Brooklyn, New York. This expansion will enable Per Scholas to serve an additional 140 New Yorkers annually and train them on cybersecurity, a high-demand role in information technology. Per Scholas also partners with a national bank in the National Capital Region that is helping Per Scholas design cybersecurity training curricula (e.g., agile data analytics, virtualization, and cloud computing) so that students will be qualified to work in a securities operations center. The financial contributions of Per Scholas's bank partners since 2014 range widely: from $5,000 to $1.4 million.

Skill QUEST

The nonprofit Skill QUEST is an outgrowth of the community organizing efforts of Dallas Area Interfaith, a network of more than 30 faith-based institutions and community organizations. Skill QUEST's clients enter its program making an income of less than $10,000 per year. It monitors clients' academic attendance and performance and supports their career readiness by connecting them to support services, including child care, counseling, fitness training, financial education, tutoring and exam preparation, and career counseling. Once they graduate, it monitors their job satisfaction and performance.

Skill QUEST is part of a Texas network of organizations that have the same mission—to lift working adults out of poverty and into living-wage careers through education. The organizations use the same business model and help each other improve by sharing data and best practices. Skill QUEST was founded in 2010, and its network colleagues were established earlier: Project QUEST in San Antonio was launched in 1992, Capital IDEA in Austin started in 1998, and Capital IDEA in Houston was founded in 2009.

Skill QUEST has two banking partners. Both provide financial contributions, but one also provides volunteers and financial education. The bank uses the Federal Deposit Insurance Corporation curriculum Money Smart as a starting point and customizes training to meet participants' needs.

Year Up

National nonprofit Year Up provides low-income adults aged 18–24 and without a college degree opportunities to build technical skills (through courses where they earn college credits and corporate internships) and receive professional training (including public speaking, professional attire, and business communication). According to New York–based program and policy evaluator Economic Mobility Corporation, Year Up reports that it boosted a young adult's annual earnings by an average of 30 percent compared to a randomized control group.

Over a dozen banks partner with Year Up and contribute $24,700 for each Year Up intern they host. Partners include regional, national, and global financial institutions. In addition to this core support of Year Up's internship program, banks have partnered in the following ways:

- A national bank has provided more than $1.2 million to Year Up over the life of its partnership. Support has included regional resources for the organization's core programming in key markets, and national support for the organization to track, engage, and measure its alumni as they professionally progress.

- A global bank awarded Year Up $5 million through its foundation over five years to support program expansion in up to six cities where the bank has a strong footprint. Funding also supports program quality initiatives that strengthen the curriculum, outcome metrics, and alumni support.

- A global bank sponsors and hosts an annual leadership forum, which convenes top financial services employers to share best practices in establishing pathways to corporate employment for Opportunity Youth.

ENGAGING WITH BANKERS TO IDENTIFY PARTNERSHIP OPPORTUNITIES

Partnerships with banks are best considered as long-term relationships based on mutual interests and benefits. While banks do have obligations to serve community interests under the CRA, specific activities and goals are not prescribed. Organizations that can help identify, shape, and realize opportunities for banks to meet community needs in innovative ways will lay the groundwork for lasting partnerships.

Following are four initial steps to help organizations identify and approach banks in ways that focus on building productive relationships:

1) Identify bankers that your organization has a relationship with now. They may be board members, provide support for other programs, or provide banking services for your organization. Discuss with them how their CRA obligations factor into their current activities.

2) Consider opportunities for expanding collaboration with existing bank partners to help them better meet their CRA goals. Discuss potential opportunities in terms of services, investments (including grants), and loans.

3) Identify other banks with assessment areas that overlap your service area(s) and their contacts. The person in charge of community outreach and CRA compliance may work in different areas within a bank, depending on its size and structure. Try to get a referral from a community partner.

   • Learn as much about the bank as possible through reviewing its activities in the community and its online CRA Performance Evaluation. Each bank also has a CRA Public File available for review at each of its branches.

4) Approach the bank as a community partner. A transactional relationship is inadequate; seek to develop relationships that can provide benefits to both the bank and the organization.

CONCLUSION

Examples across the country like those described above show potential connections between workforce development organizations and financial institutions. Currently there are many ways that financial institutions may be interested in partnering with these organizations in order to meet CRA obligations. More information on these numerous potential opportunities for financial institutions and workforce development efforts to partner are noted in Blum and Shepelwich (2017). This guide has tools and resources to help banks and workforce development entities start the conversation about potential partnership opportunities.

Notes

1. In this publication, *bank* refers to financial institutions that are subject to the CRA.
2. For the complete definition of community development, see Department of the Treasury (2016, p. 48506). https://www.ffiec.gov/cra/qnadoc.htm (accessed May 16, 2018).
3. Technically, "intermediate small" banks are a subset of "small" banks, so, by definition, "small" banks had assets less than $1.252 billion as of December 31 in 2017 or 2016. Asset thresholds determine the procedures under which the banks are examined. For more information, see "Explanation of the Community Reinvestment Act Asset-Size Threshold Change Applying the January 1, 2018, CRA Definitions," https://www.ffiec.gov/cra/pdf/AssetThreshold2018.pdf (accessed May 16, 2018).
4. For specific exam procedures, see https://www.ffiec.gov/cra/examinations.htm #EX_PROCEDURES (accessed March 8, 2018).
5. For more information, see https://www.ffiec.gov/cra/qnadoc.htm, p. 44 (accessed March 8, 2018).
6. See "Home Mortgage Disclosure Act," https://www.ffiec.gov/hmda/ (accessed March 8, 2018).
7. See "Chart 1: Community Development Decision Flow Chart," Federal Reserve Bank of Dallas. https://www.dallasfed.org/~/media/microsites/cd/epersp/2007/4 _3.aspx (accessed March 8, 2018).
8. The case studies in this section were written based on interviews conducted in 2016 for the development of Blum and Shepelwich (2017).

References

Blum, Elizabeth Sobel, and Steven Shepelwich. 2017. *Engaging Workforce Development: A Framework for Meeting CRA Obligations.* Dallas, TX, and Kansas City, MO: Federal Reserve Bank of Dallas and Federal Reserve Bank of Kansas City.

Department of the Treasury. 2016. *Federal Register* 81(142): 48526. Washington, DC: Department of the Treasury. https://www.ffiec.gov/cra/qnadoc.htm (accessed May 16, 2018).

Federal Financial Institutions Examination Council. 2017. "Explanation of the

Community Reinvestment Act Asset-Size Threshold Change." Arlington, VA: Federal Financial Institutions Examination Council. https://www.ffiec .gov/cra/pdf/AssetThreshold2017.pdf (accessed March 8, 2018).

Federal Reserve Bank of Dallas. 2005. "A Banker's Quick Reference Guide to CRA." Dallas: Federal Reserve Bank of Dallas. https://www.dallasfed .org/~/media/documents/cd/pubs/quickref.pdf (accessed March 8, 2018).

3

Nimble Capital for an Agile Workforce

Keith Wardrip
Mels de Zeeuw

Foundations represent a significant source of capital that can be deployed—either through grantmaking or through the strategic investment of their endowments—in a variety of charitable ways, including for workforce development initiatives. In 2014, the nearly 87,000 foundations operating in the United States drew on assets of more than $865 billion to distribute in excess of $60 billion in grants (Foundation Center 2014). However, we could find no recent, comprehensive analysis regarding how these institutions contribute to job skills training, entreprencurship, vocational education, microfinance, and similar activities that constitute the field of workforce development. In this chapter, we examine the funding provided by the nation's largest foundations (as measured by their level of grantmaking) to support workforce development efforts.

PHILANTHROPY'S NICHE

Philanthropic funding is a critical source of capital in the community and economic development field generally, and the qualities that make it invaluable to the broader nonprofit sector also apply to those putting the "work" into workforce development. First, foundations can seed innovation and test promising solutions in an effort "to figure out what strategies work best to solve social problems" (Merisotis 2015). Foundations can take risks that other sources of capital, such as the government and the private market, cannot (Abramson, Soskis, and Toepler 2014), provided it is not prohibited by the organization's mission or board. For an issue as complex and multifaceted as workforce development, flexible funding could be the difference between a good idea in theory and a good idea in practice. Once put into practice, foundations often have the resources to assess how effective an idea truly was, and some then fund its advocacy should it stand up to rigorous evaluation (Hacke, Wood, and Urquilla 2014; Markley et al. 2016).

In a less tangible but equally important way, foundation support can also lend legitimacy to workforce development efforts. Mosley and Galaskiewicz (2015) note that "philanthropic foundations play important symbolic and leadership roles in public policy debates by conferring legitimacy upon specific social problems and policy solutions" (p. 1225). Attention paid by the philanthropic sector to workforce issues can thus have a validating effect on efforts more broadly. Biswas (2007) believes that program-related investments can serve as a "stamp of approval" that can be used by an individual recipient to leverage additional investments. In essence, philanthropic backing provides "street credibility" on both a macro- and a micro-level.

Apart from providing legitimacy and their ability to innovate, foundations are also known for convening across sectors—public, private, nonprofit, and philanthropic (Department of Housing and Urban Development 2016; Hacke, Wood, and Urquilla 2014). Cross-sector collaboration can be pivotal for the success of workforce development efforts, as these can involve employers, training providers, academic institutions, and social service agencies. Equally important may be foundations' ability to provide opportunities for intrasector conversations. For example, industry partnerships, through which employers in the same industry communicate their local training needs to inform worker training in a region, depend heavily on such within-sector cooperation.[1]

PHILANTHROPY'S INVOLVEMENT IN WORKFORCE DEVELOPMENT

Foundations and government agencies (local, state, and federal) collaborate on workforce development initiatives in many instances. Abramson, Soskis, and Toepler (2014) apply several of the roles mentioned above to public-philanthropic partnerships when they suggest that foundations can pilot new government programs or help fund exist-ing ones, build public-sector capacity, capitalize on their cross-sector convening power, fund research and analysis of government programs, and evaluate public policy. Foundation support has jump-started both large and small workforce development efforts, and some, such as the National Fund for Workforce Solutions (Clark 2016), have taken on lives of their own. A recent report by the Department of Housing and Urban Development (2016) notes that "philanthropy and the govern-ment sector have the potential to be extremely effective partners, with each bringing a unique skill set that complements the other. By working together, the public sector can accelerate and support the innovative practices that philanthropy often leads and help communities adapt to new challenges and opportunities" (p. 56). As providers of capital that can take risks, foundations are well positioned to provide first-in money, but the public sector might be better resourced to provide continuing financial support for proven solutions.

An alternative to collaboration is substitution. Abramson, Sos-kis, and Toepler (2014) note that during the recent recession, govern-ment officials "often quite explicitly claimed that philanthropic dollars should fill the gaps left by government retrenchment" (p. 60). However, the substitution of philanthropic for public-sector capital could dimin-ish resources for the workforce development system as a whole, and efforts would not benefit from the unique advantages that both sectors bring to the table.

Employers play an important role in workforce development, but corporate capital is not always deployed to improve outcomes for dis-advantaged workers. In their review of surveys conducted in the mid-1990s, Lerman, McKernan, and Riegg (2004) find that less-educated workers are less likely to receive employer-provided training than their more-educated counterparts. The same is true for those earning the lowest wages, and—when employer-provided educational assistance is excluded—workers 25 and younger and 55 and over. Carnevale, Strohl, and Gulish (2015) suggest that because the majority of employer-provided formal training is directed toward workers with at least a bachelor's degree, it "typically complements, rather than substitutes for, a traditional college education" (p. 5).

Whether acting as a partner or as a substitute for public or private capital, philanthropy's greatest contribution to workforce development funding might be as a guarantor of social equity. Funding from foundations can target those underserved by the employer-provided training ecosystem or with access to fewer publicly funded opportunities in an era of waning federal support. Philanthropic investment can target both the labor force (i.e., supply-side solutions) and employers (i.e., demand-side practices). Regarding the former, foundations can support programs that directly connect workers to jobs, educational systems that lay the foundation for skills development, or programs that tackle issues — unrelated to skills — that nonetheless act as barriers to employment (e.g., transportation, child care) (St.Clair 2017). They might also support specific populations that have not historically experienced equitable labor market outcomes. Demand-side efforts can include encouraging industry agreement on the skills workers need to succeed in a given field, providing a road map for educators and workforce development practitioners (Ross et al. 2016). They may also include promoting a shift in hiring practices from a focus on educational attainment to skills and competencies. This could provide employment opportunities to segments of the labor force often overlooked by employers today (Blivin and Wallerstein 2016; Canner et al. 2015; Ross et al. 2016). Foundation grants can help employers test the effectiveness of these new hiring practices and, if they stand up to rigorous evaluation, encourage their widespread adoption (Ross et al. 2016).

Philanthropic capital deployed to support workforce development efforts can change the economic trajectory of low-income or less-educated workers and their families. Markley et al. (2016) write that place-rooted foundations can be motivated to promote equitable economic development not only by their vision of an economy that works for everyone but also because such work has downstream impacts on program participants and their communities: "Directing the foundation's energy and resources toward improving economic outcomes is viewed as a way to address root causes rather than repeatedly treating the symptoms of a desultory economy" (p. 96). By supporting workforce development efforts, both place-based foundations and those with a broader scope can improve the economic health of employers and workers alike.

DEFINING WORKFORCE DEVELOPMENT

The results presented in this chapter are based on an analysis of a grant-level database acquired from the Foundation Center. The database used in this study is drawn from the Foundation Center's FC 1000 data set, which includes grants of at least $10,000 made by the 1,000 largest U.S. foundations in any given year, as determined by their grant-making volume, between 2008 and 2014. Included are grants from independent and corporate foundations, operating foundations that make grants, and, where available, grants from community foundations' unrestricted and donor-advised funds.[2] In addition to identifying the grant maker and the grant recipient, the database includes fields with a short description of the grant and one or more codes that specify the primary subjects of the grant and its recipient.

For this study, the definition offered by Sobel Blum and Shepelwich (2017) is probably the most in line with how we approached our analysis: "Workforce development consists of a range of strategies to develop talent and skills, connect employers and workers, and facilitate career mobility" (p. 4). Guided by this definition, we used a grant's codes and description to determine whether it should be classified as supporting workforce development. After a review of the 850 subject codes used by the Foundation Center to characterize grants and recipients,[3] we selected the 19 that best align with what we consider workforce development activities. They cover topics such as job training and retraining, job counseling, entrepreneurship, microfinance,[4] vocational and adult education, ESL and second language acquisition, vocational rehabilitation, and sheltered employment.[5] We also developed a list of roughly 40 terms that we associate with workforce development, including apprenticeship, internship, summer job, work study, skills gap, training program, job search, microenterprise, and adult literacy. Because we followed a fairly strict conception of workforce development, we excluded grants with subject codes or keywords associated with job quality and conditions, labor standards, labor rights, organized labor, paid leave, unemployment insurance, antidiscrimination, and legal services. Through experimentation and subsequent validation using random samples of grants, we developed a systematic way to use the subject(s) of the grant, the subject(s) of the recipient, and the presence of keywords in the description to determine whether the grant should be included in this analysis.[6] We additionally reviewed all grants of $1 million or more that we considered only peripherally related to our definition of workforce development, and we manually reclassified these large grants as appropriate.

No research is without its limitations, and a few are worth noting here. First, the overall data set from which workforce development–related grants are drawn captures 40–50 percent of all philanthropic giving.[7] Notably absent are grants made by small foundations and grants under $10,000 from large foundations. Also missing are grants that are not funneled through corporate foundations but are made directly by corporations themselves. For these reasons, the estimates that follow should be considered conservative and representative of giving from the largest domestic foundations only. Second, while used intensively for this study out of necessity, the grant and recipient subject codes are not always consistently applied. Any grant that is miscoded by the Foundation Center is misclassified in this analysis unless, in some cases, its description includes one of the keywords. Finally, others may have defined workforce development and its associated activities differently; a broader definition than ours might, for example, have included "integrative human service supports" (Giloth 2000, p. 342), and the subsequent analysis using such a definition would have led to quantitatively and qualitatively different conclusions.

FINDINGS

Overall

Between 2008 and 2014, the largest foundations in the United States made 24,633 grants totaling roughly $2.6 billion to support workforce development activities.[8] For grants where information was provided, nearly two-thirds of the volume was directed to specific projects or programs, and another 14 percent provided general support for the recipient organization. Grants for organizational capacity building, continuing support, and capital/infrastructure accounted for another 12 percent in total; little funding was directed toward individual development (e.g., scholarships, internships) or research and evaluation.[9]

With the exception of 2009, a year in which both overall and workforce development grant making from these foundations dipped substantially, philanthropic funding for workforce development occupied a fairly narrow range annually, from roughly $358 million to $419 million (Figure 3.1). Between 2012 and 2014, the number of grants fell sharply, but grant volume remained relatively flat, suggesting a preference for larger grants in recent years; in fact, the median grant size grew from less than $31,000 to more than $38,000 between 2012 and 2014.[10]

By comparing these levels with total grantmaking, we can conclude that workforce development did not represent a top priority for the largest foundations collectively during the study period. Workforce development grants constituted a very small share of total grant volume awarded to U.S.-based recipients by these foundations, ranging from 1.4 to 1.9 percent annually between 2008 and 2014.[11] Using data from the same source, but with a more restrictive definition, Mosley and Galaskiewicz (2015) find that grants related to workforce development represented between 1 and 2 percent of total giving from the largest foundations between 1993 and 2001, providing some support for the magnitude of our findings and suggesting general consistency across decades.

Figure 3.1 Workforce Development Grantmaking by the Largest Foundations

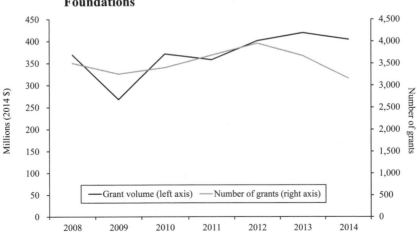

SOURCE: Authors' analysis of FC1000 data from the Foundation Center.

Foundation involvement in workforce development initiatives adds value beyond the dollar values of the grants themselves. With that in mind, our research suggests that the volume of workforce development grants distributed by the philanthropic sector is minimal relative to government spending. Workforce development funding from the federal government is difficult to pin down and depends on the programs included and the years analyzed, but it exceeds foundation funding by a wide margin. The $404 million in 2014 grant volume represents just over 5 percent of the more than $7.5 billion enacted in the 2015 federal budget for various U.S. Department of Labor and U.S. Department of Education programs considered by the National Skills Coalition to represent "investments in the skills of America's workforce."[12] Even if we double the workforce development grant volume analyzed in this research, under the aforementioned assumption that our data set represents only 40–50 percent of total philanthropic grantmaking, the federal government is still a much larger source of funding. However, should federal support continue to decline, as it has in recent years for select programs that support worker training, career and technical education, and adult education (National Skills Coalition, n.d.), foundations may find themselves playing an increasingly important role.

Workforce Development Grantmakers

Roughly 70 percent of workforce development funding came from independent foundations, a level that is in line with this category's contribution to overall charitable giving.[13] Likewise, 11 percent of workforce development grant volume originated with community foundations during the study period, comparable to their 10 percent contribution to overall giving by large foundations. Notable differences arise in the relative contributions by corporate and operating foundations, however. Operating foundations play an important role in overall grantmaking (11 percent) but a negligible one in terms of supporting workforce development (less than 1 percent).[14] Corporate foundations, on the other hand, accounted for roughly 10 percent of overall charitable giving between 2008 and 2014 but contributed over 18 percent of workforce development grant volume during that time. Porter and Kramer (2002) note that corporate philanthropic activity can be strategically directed to improve the "competitive context" in which a cor-

Table 3.1 Leading Workforce Development Grantmakers by Volume: 2008–2014 (2014 $)

Name	Metro area	Grant volume ($ millions)	Number of grants	Median grant-made ($)
James Irvine Foundation	San Francisco-Oakland-Hayward, CA	105.5	183	250,000
Ford Foundation	New York-Newark-Jersey City, NY-NJ-PA	102.8	242	244,000
Bill & Melinda Gates Foundation	Seattle-Tacoma-Bellevue, WA	102.6	91	415,000
W. K. Kellogg Foundation	Battle Creek, MI	100.3	253	250,000
Wal-Mart Foundation, Inc.	Fayetteville-Springdale-Rogers, AR-MO	70.8	261	32,000
Ewing Marion Kauffman Foundation	Kansas City, MO-KS	70.0	302	52,000
JPMorgan Chase Foundation	New York-Newark-Jersey City, NY-NJ-PA	65.2	633	45,000
Harry and Jeanette Weinberg Foundation	Baltimore-Columbia-Towson, MD	63.4	329	65,000
Goldman Sachs Foundation	New York-Newark-Jersey City, NY-NJ-PA	51.8	100	338,000
Annie E. Casey Foundation	Baltimore-Columbia-Towson, MD	47.7	361	63,000
Total		2,591.3	24,633	31,000

SOURCE: Authors' analysis of FC 1000 data from the Foundation Center.

poration operates—for example, by increasing the local availability of skilled labor or by growing the size of the market for its products or services. These considerations for corporate philanthropy could also be related to the disproportionate role corporate foundations play in workforce development funding.

A relatively small number of foundations conduct a large proportion of workforce development grantmaking. In fact, the top 10 foundations listed in Table 3.1 accounted for some 30 percent of all large foundation grantmaking in this space.[15] The top 28 grantmakers by volume distributed more than half of the $2.6 billion granted during the study period. Some, like the Bill & Melinda Gates Foundation, ranked among the top 10 by making few, very large grants. Others, like the JPMorgan Chase Foundation, made significantly more grants for distinctly smaller amounts. Still, workforce development grantmaking is not the purview of a niche group of funders, as 317 large foundations made workforce development grants totaling at least $1 million during the study period.

Grant Recipients

Nonprofit organizations attracted the lion's share of workforce development grant volume (86 percent of the total) during the study period, followed distantly by government agencies (6 percent) and religious institutions (5 percent). Where the target population was specified for the grant recipient, we find that a substantial share of workforce development grant volume was directed at economically disadvantaged populations (25 percent), those involved in academic pursuits (both students and instructors) (21 percent), children and youth (18 percent), specific ethnic and racial groups (13 percent), and people with disabilities (10 percent).[16]

Using subject codes provided in the data set, we can also classify workforce development grants by the primary focal area of the grant recipient. Organizations that fall under the admittedly broad category of "employment" attracted 16 percent of overall workforce development grant volume, followed by organizations that focus on entrepreneurship (10 percent), and universities (6 percent).[17] Recipients primarily classified as providing vocational rehabilitation and job training each received roughly 5 percent.

Table 3.2 Largest Recipients of Workforce Development Grants by Volume: 2008–2014

Recipient	Metro area
Jobs for the Future	Boston-Cambridge-Newton, MA-NH
Year Up	Boston-Cambridge-Newton, MA-NH
Kauffman Laboratories for Enterprise Creation	Kansas City, MO-KS
Goodwill Industries International	Washington-Arlington-Alexandria, DC-VA-MD-WV
YouthBuild USA	Boston-Cambridge-Newton, MA-NH
Center for Employment Opportunities	New York-Newark-Jersey City, NY-NJ-PA
Harvard University	Boston-Cambridge-Newton, MA-NH
ConnectEd: The California Center for College and Career	San Francisco-Oakland-Hayward, CA
Marriott Foundation for People with Disabilities	Washington-Arlington-Alexandria, DC-VA-MD-WV
National Employment Law Project	New York-Newark-Jersey City, NY-NJ-PA

SOURCE: Authors' analysis of FC 1000 data from the Foundation Center.

Nearly 6,900 organizations received a workforce development grant during the study period. The typical recipient secured a single grant and received grant capital of roughly $64,000. Table 3.2 lists the 10 organizations that received the greatest volume of workforce development grant funding during the study period. Relevant grants to these organizations totaled $307 million during the study period, or about 12 percent of the volume captured in this analysis. Eight of these 10 have headquarters in the Boston; New York; or Washington, DC, metro areas, but most operate in a number of additional metro areas or conduct research or policy work with a national reach.

Regional Distribution

Having discussed the scale of workforce development grantmaking, the most active funders, and the characteristics of the recipients, we close by addressing how the grants were distributed across the metropolitan landscape between 2008 and 2014. In recent work on grant-

Table 3.3 Workforce Development Grant Volume by Metro Area of Recipient: 2008–2014 (2014 $)

Rank	Metro area	Grant volume ($ millions)	Number of grants	Median grant received ($)
1	New York-Newark-Jersey City, NY-NJ-PA	379.5	2,652	51,000
2	Washington-Arlington-Alexandria, DC-VA-MD-WV	302.3	1,656	39,000
3	Boston-Cambridge-Newton, MA-NH	266.4	1,402	38,000
4	San Francisco-Oakland-Hayward, CA	167.3	1,939	33,000
5	Chicago-Naperville-Elgin, IL-IN-WI	108.8	1,392	38,000
6	Los Angeles-Long Beach-Anaheim, CA	95.2	900	38,000
7	Detroit-Warren-Dearborn, MI	78.4	286	55,000
8	Minneapolis-St. Paul-Bloomington, MN-WI	63.8	1,246	30,000
9	Pittsburgh, PA	63.5	444	73,000
10	Baltimore-Columbia-Towson, MD	63.3	587	41,000

SOURCE: Authors' analysis of FC 1000 data from the Foundation Center.

making by large foundations for the broader community and economic development field, Wardrip, Lambe, and de Zeeuw (2016) find significant regional variation in grant receipt. Some metro areas received a significantly higher level of grant volume from large foundations than did others. Is the same true for workforce development?

In short, it is. Nearly 37 percent of total workforce development grant volume went to recipients located in just three metro areas: New York; Washington, DC; and Boston. Recipients in six metros accounted for just over half of the total workforce development grant volume: the aforementioned three, along with San Francisco, Chicago, and Los Angeles.

The volume of workforce development grants attracted by recipients in New York, Boston, and other metro areas among the top 10 on this measure (see Table 3.3) is not reflective of the experiences of the typical region. Recipients of workforce development grants were located in 316 metro areas, and the typical metro received 10 grants totaling just over $600,000. Notably, another 65 metros did not directly receive even a single workforce development grant from these large foundations during the study period, and none of these regions had a population over 300,000 in 2014. Additionally, only 3 percent of the funds analyzed in this study flowed directly to nonmetro areas, even though these regions constituted over 14 percent of the nation's population.

There are various reasons that workforce development grant capital from the largest foundations would be more likely to find its way to larger metro areas and less likely to land directly in smaller metros and nonmetro areas. At the risk of stating the obvious, larger regional economies employ more workers and typically have a more robust nonprofit sector, both of which create opportunities for attracting and deploying workforce development grants. Further, as we have shown, the foundations most active in this arena are generally located in major metropolitan areas, where national nonprofits able to capitalize on large grants are also concentrated. Many of these large nonprofits conduct nationally relevant work that benefits the workforce development field broadly; others redistribute grants from their headquarters to other regions where affiliated offices are located. Lastly, workforce development efforts in smaller metro areas surely attract grants from smaller foundations not captured in this analysis. It is clear that the largest foundations distribute a substantial share of their workforce development grants directly to recipients in large metro areas. However, for the aforementioned reasons, we cannot accurately quantify to what extent smaller economies benefit indirectly from this grantmaking activity, nor do we know the level of support they receive from the rest of the philanthropic sector.

IMPLICATIONS AND FUTURE RESEARCH

Large domestic foundations are an important source of support, both financial and otherwise, for local and national workforce development initiatives. Grants from these foundations averaged around $370 million annually between 2008 and 2014. Collectively, workforce development grantmaking does not appear to constitute a top priority for large foundations, nor does it rival the magnitude of public funding. However, foundations engaged in this field play an important role in advancing efforts in communities across the country.

For a number of reasons stated above, the estimates provided in this analysis are likely conservative. The data set we used captures neither grants of less than $10,000 nor grantmaking by small foundations. Further, we used a fairly restrictive definition of workforce development. Lastly, grants that may appear tangential to workforce development efforts can be nonetheless important in improving the odds of success for low- and moderate-income or less-educated participants in the labor market. Traditional workforce development activities may be "an important component of a broader strategy" that includes income supports, services such as child care and transportation, benefits such as health insurance, and high-quality education (Holzer 2008, p. 28). Our analysis is less expansive.

This chapter scratches the surface of foundation involvement in workforce development activities and raises a number of questions that should be answered in future research. First, building on an earlier study of philanthropic support for the broader community and economic development field (Wardrip, Lambe, and de Zeeuw 2016), it would be interesting to know whether the characteristics of metro areas are related to their ability to attract funding. Are places with greater workforce challenges more likely to benefit from philanthropic largesse, or are demand and supply unrelated?

It would also be interesting to investigate whether better-resourced communities experience improved economic or social outcomes relative to lesser-resourced peer regions. It is not clear whether, at current levels, foundation support is sufficient to have impacts that would be observable at the scale of the metropolitan economy.

Lastly, when funders "evaluate, document, and communicate" their successes and failures (Giloth and Gewirtz 2009, p. 118), they lay the foundation for more effective future investments. Research that promotes peer learning and knowledge sharing can only strengthen the field and lead to improved outcomes for workers, employers, and their communities.

Notes

We thank Crystal Bridgeman, Karen Brown, Karen Leone de Nie, Eileen Divringi, Sarah Oldmixon, Keith Rolland, Theresa Singleton, Sarah Steinberg, and Noelle St.Clair for thoughtful feedback on an early draft of this chapter; and Reina Mukai at the Foundation Center for assisting with data use and interpretation. Their comments led only to improvements in this piece, and we take responsibility for any remaining errors. The views expressed in this chapter are ours and do not necessarily reflect the views of the Federal Reserve Banks of Philadelphia or Atlanta or the Federal Reserve System.

1. See the National Fund for Workforce Solution's discussion of industry partnerships at https://nationalfund.org/initiatives/industry-partnerships/.
2. More information on Foundation Center data is available at http://data.foundation center.org/about.html.
3. More information on the Philanthropy Classification System used by the Foundation Center is available at http://taxonomy.foundationcenter.org/subjects.
4. Others may not have included entrepreneurship (and access to associated capital) in the definition of workforce development. We chose to do so because entrepreneurial skills training is listed as an eligible activity in the Workforce Innovation and Opportunity Act, and, though it does not represent a primary focus of the public workforce investment system, we agree that entrepreneurship has the potential to be "an important workforce development (and hence self-sufficiency) option" (Harper-Anderson and Gooden 2016, p. 239).
5. The Philanthropy Classification System defines sheltered employment as employment in a protected environment for workers with disabilities who cannot secure competitive employment, as well as work activity centers that offer personal development for those with limited production capabilities.
6. Nearly 40 percent of the grant volume classified in this study as funding workforce development activities was included because the primary subject of the grant itself

was in our list of relevant subject codes. For another one-third, no information was provided on the subject of the grant, but the primary subject of the recipient was related to workforce development. For most of the remainder, the grant description included one of our terms, and either the grant or the recipient was assigned a secondary subject related to workforce development.

7. Authors' calculations using 2008–2012 data from Foundation Center (2014).
8. The full value of any multiyear grant was assigned to the year in which it was made, so the results reflect the value of large foundation grants committed, but not necessarily distributed, during the study period. Dollar values are adjusted to 2014 using the Personal Consumption Expenditures Price Index produced by the Bureau of Economic Analysis, Table 1.1.4. Price Indexes for Gross Domestic Product.
9. Where more than one grant strategy code was provided, the primary one was used to classify the grant.
10. Correspondence with Foundation Center staff suggests that 2014 grants that were not available when the data set was finalized may be added in the future. Should any meet our criteria for workforce development, both the number and volume of grants in 2014 would increase.
11. Authors' calculations using workforce development grant volume as the numerator and total grantmaking to U.S. recipients as reported in the Foundation Center's FC 1000 data set as the denominator. FC 1000 totals are from Foundation Center (2014) and correspondence with Foundation Center staff.
12. Authors' calculations using data available through the National Skills Coalition's Interactive Federal Funding Tool, available at http://www.nationalskillscoalition .org/federal-policy/federal-funding-tool. We include the Department of Labor and Education programs itemized by the National Skills Coalition with the exception of Pell Grants. Other analyses take a broader view of workforce development and report higher federal funding, albeit in earlier years (Center for Law and Social Policy 2013; GAO 2011).
13. The distribution of overall grantmaking by foundation type was calculated using data from Foundation Center (2014). The Council on Foundations describes an independent foundation as a private foundation that, unlike the family and corporate varieties, is not governed by its benefactor, the benefactor's relations, or a corporation. Definitions of various foundation types are available at www.cof.org/ content/foundation-basics.
14. Operating foundations generally fund their own charitable activities, so these figures include only operating foundations that also make grants. More information on what distinguishes an operating foundation from other private foundations is available from Foundation Source at https://www.foundationsource.com/ learn-about-foundations/what-is-a-private-foundation/.
15. Metro areas used in this study reflect the definitions published by the Office of Management and Budget (2013).
16. The population served by the recipient was unclear for about a quarter of grant volume. Where more than one organization or population code was provided, the primary one was used to classify the grant recipient.

17. Grants to universities are a subset of grants to recipient organizations involved in higher education more broadly, and these grants were included in this analysis as long as the grant was related to workforce development. Nearly 80 percent of the workforce development grant volume to recipients in higher education (including community colleges, four-year institutions, and other universities) was for program development, intended to support specific workforce development–related projects. Research and evaluation and individual development (e.g., internships, scholarships) combined to account for roughly 11 percent of the grant volume directed to recipients involved in higher education.

References

Abramson, Alan, Benjamin Soskis, and Stefan Toepler. 2014. "Public-Philanthropic Partnerships: A Review of Recent Trends." *Foundation Review* 6(2): 52–66.

Biswas, Radha Roy. 2007. "Part V. Program-Related Investments." In *Strategies for Financing Workforce Intermediaries: Working Papers*, Heath Prince, ed. Boston: Jobs for the Future, pp. 145–170.

Blivin, Jamai, and Ben Wallerstein. 2016. *Shift Happens: The Entrepreneurs, Wonks, and Investors Revolutionizing the Learning-to-Employment Landscape.* Santa Fe: Innovate+Educate; Washington, DC: Whiteboard Advisors.

Canner, Niko, Abigail Carlton, Guy Halfteck, and John Irons. 2015. *Impact Hiring: How Data Will Transform Youth Employment.* New York: Incandescent; San Francisco: Knack; New York: Rockefeller Foundation.

Carnevale, Anthony P., Jeff Strohl, and Artem Gulish. 2015. *College Is Just the Beginning: Employers' Role in the $1.1 Trillion Postsecondary Education and Training System.* Washington, DC: Georgetown University, Center on Education and the Workforce, McCourt School of Public Policy.

Center for Law and Social Policy. 2013. *A New Look at the GAO Report on Workforce Funding.* Washington, DC: Center for Law and Social Policy.

Clark, Jacob. 2016. "The National Fund for Workforce Solutions Launches with Expanded Mission." Press release, October 27. Washington, DC: National Fund for Workforce Solutions. https://nationalfund.org/news_post/the-national-fund-for-workforce-solutions-launches-with-expanded-mission/ (accessed June 23, 2017).

Department of Housing and Urban Development. 2016. *Scaling Solutions: A How-To Guide for Unleashing the Potential of Public-Philanthropic Partnerships Based on Lessons Learned from the Sustainable Communities Initiative.* Washington, DC: Department of Housing and Urban Development.

Foundation Center. 2014. *Foundation Stats*. New York: Foundation Center. http://data.foundationcenter.org/ (accessed July 21, 2017).

Giloth, Robert P. 2000. "Learning from the Field: Economic Growth and Workforce Development in the 1990s." *Economic Development Quarterly* 14(4): 340–359.

Giloth, Robert, and Susan Gewirtz. 2009. "Philanthropy and Mistakes: An Untapped Resource." *Foundation Review* 1(1): 115–124.

Government Accountability Office (GAO). 2011. *Multiple Employment and Training Programs: Providing Information on Colocating Services and Consolidating Administrative Structures Could Promote Efficiencies.* Report to Congressional Requesters. GAO-11-92. Washington, DC: GAO.

Hacke, Robin, David Wood, and Marian Urquilla. 2014. *What Can Foundations Do to Foster Community Investment? 10 Roles for Philanthropy.* Troy, MI: Kresge Foundation; Cambridge, MA: Harvard University, Initiative for Responsible Investment, Hauser Institute for Civil Society.

Harper-Anderson, Elsie L., and Susan T. Gooden. 2016. "Integrating Entrepreneurship Services into Local Workforce Development Systems: Who Is Doing It and How." *Journal of Poverty* 20(3): 237–260.

Holzer, Harry J. 2008. "Workforce Development as an Antipoverty Strategy: What Do We Know? What Should We Do?" Discussion Paper No. 3776. Bonn, Germany: IZA.

Lerman, Robert I., Signe-Mary McKernan, and Stephanie Riegg. 2004. "The Scope of Employer-Provided Training in the United States: Who, What, Where, and How Much?" In *Job Training Policy in the United States*, Christopher J. O'Leary, Robert A. Straits, and Stephen A. Wandner, eds. Kalamazoo, MI: W.E. Upjohn Institute for Employment Research, pp. 211–244.

Markley, Deborah, Janet Topolsky, Don Macke, Travis Green, and Kristin Feierabend. 2016. "A New Domain for Place-Rooted Foundations: Economic Development Philanthropy." *Foundation Review* 8(3): 92–105.

Merisotis, Jamie. 2015, October 1. "A 21st Century Call for Philanthropy: Tackle the Talent Gap." Arlington, VA: Council on Foundations. http://www.cof.org/blogs/re-philanthropy/2015-10-01/21st-century-call-philanthropy-tackle-talent-gap (accessed June 4, 2017).

Mosley, Jennifer E., and Joseph Galaskiewicz. 2015. "The Relationship between Philanthropic Foundation Funding and State-Level Policy in the Era of Welfare Reform." *Nonprofit and Voluntary Sector Quarterly* 44(6): 1225–1254.

National Skills Coalition. N.d. "Invest in America's Workforce: We Can't Compete If We Cut." Washington, DC: National Skills Coalition. http://www.nationalskillscoalition.org/resources/publications/file/We-Cant-Compete-if-We-Cut-1.pdf (accessed July 21, 2017).

Office of Management and Budget. 2013. OMB Bulletin No. 13-01. Washington, DC: Office of Management and Budget. https://www.whitehouse.gov/sites/whitehouse.gov/files/omb/bulletins/2013/b13-01.pdf (accessed May 2, 2018).

Porter, Michael E., and Mark R. Kramer. 2002, December. "The Competitive Advantage of Corporate Philanthropy." *Harvard Business Review*. https://hbr.org/2002/12/the-competitive-advantage-of-corporate-philanthropy (accessed July 21, 2017).

Ross, Michaela, Reilly Kiernan, Devin Murphy, and Debby Bielak. 2016. *"Billion Dollar Bets" to Establish Pathways to Careers: Creating Economic Opportunity for Every American.* Boston: Bridgespan Group.

Sobel Blum, Elizabeth, and Steve Shepelwich. 2017. *Engaging Workforce Development: A Framework for Meeting CRA Obligations.* Dallas, TX: Federal Reserve Bank of Dallas; Kansas City, MO: Federal Reserve Bank of Kansas City.

St.Clair, Noelle. 2017. *Investing in America's Workforce: Report on Workforce Development Needs and Opportunities.* Washington, DC: Federal Reserve System.

Wardrip, Keith, William Lambe, and Mels de Zeeuw. 2016. "Following the Money: An Analysis of Foundation Grantmaking for Community and Economic Development." *Foundation Review* 8(3): 51–65.

4

Outcomes-Oriented Contracting

Unlocking Economic Opportunity
for Low-Income Communities

Celeste Richie

The $13 billion public workforce system limits innovation by relying mostly on cost-reimbursement contracts. These contracts often prescribe services and prohibit providers from adapting to population needs. The federal government pours dollars into disconnected services that focus on short-term results that incentivize serving individuals who face fewer barriers to employment. Outcomes contracting is key in transforming the federal agencies that fund workforce programs into engines for economic opportunity by reinventing a vital but widely overlooked link in the workforce funding system—public sector contracts.

At the community level, this directly affects who has access to economic opportunities. In Northern Virginia's Fairfax, Loudoun, and Prince William Counties, for example, the Workforce Investment Act and Workforce Innovation and Opportunity Act (WIOA) Youth programming has enrolled an average of only nine youth each year since 2011 who are involved in the foster care or juvenile justice systems.[1] We know that these youth populations face increased barriers to educational attainment and access to good-paying jobs, so why haven't workforce services prioritized them?

How can we change the system to focus services on those who need it most? This is exactly the question that Northern Virginia is asking—and answering—using the recent Pay-for-Performance (P4P) provisions in WIOA. These counties are using outcomes-based contracts to prioritize youth previously not served by the workforce system. By offering bonus payments linked to achieving workforce outcomes for foster care– and juvenile justice–involved youth, Northern Virginia has aligned contract incentives to ensure that these youths are not left out.

While demand has increased for evidence-based programs that are proven to more effectively achieve outcomes such as wage growth over time and educational attainment, focusing on specific programs does not address the system failure of the current cost-reimbursement status quo. Emphasizing impacts, not specific programs, outcomes-based contracts embed data to provide feedback to improve services and reward providers that achieve results (see Figure 4.1). To enable payments linked to outcomes, these contracts necessitate the linking, sharing, and analyzing of administrative and program data. By changing what government pays for and how, we unlock innovation by enabling workforce organizations to experiment, scale what works, and deliver sustained results. Outcomes-based contracts are making measurable differences in communities from Northern Virginia to San Diego, to Austin, Texas, and it can happen across the country.

Figure 4.1 Continuum of Contracting Methods

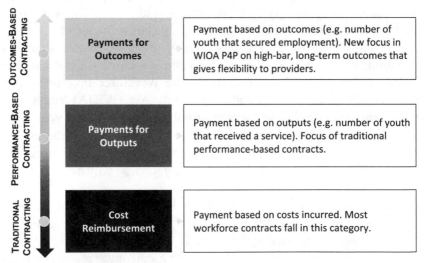

Paying for performance is a continuum of contracting methods

Payments for Outcomes	Payment based on outcomes (e.g. number of youth that secured employment). New focus in WIOA P4P on high-bar, long-term outcomes that gives flexibility to providers.
Payments for Outputs	Payment based on outputs (e.g. number of youth that received a service). Focus of traditional performance-based contracts.
Cost Reimbursement	Payment based on costs incurred. Most workforce contracts fall in this category.

OUTCOMES-BASED CONTRACTING

PERFORMANCE-BASED CONTRACTING

TRADITIONAL CONTRACTING

SOURCE: Third Sector Capital Partners.

COMPONENTS NECESSARY FOR SUCCESS

Policy

Important changes in the 2014 WIOA, including P4P, represent both a new iteration in the long history of performance-based contracting, as well as an evolution in Pay for Success. While the workforce system has benefited from decades of performance-based contracts, those attempts to pay for results tended to define results as inputs, like program enrollment, and outputs, like job placement. Certainly, some outcome measures were tracked, but given the short two-year funding cycle, it was not possible to develop contracts that would link payment directly to high-bar, long-term outcomes for participants, such as wage growth over time or advanced degree attainment. And while some contracts are performance-based, the majority of workforce contracts are still cost-reimbursement.

By contrast, as seen in Figure 4.2, funding made available through the WIOA P4P differs from traditional performance-based contracts in the following ways:

- Focus on long-term outcomes. WIOA performance measures track participant outcomes further out than the Workforce Investment Act did, assessing outcomes at four quarters after the end of a program in addition to the previously required two quarters. With WIOA P4P, jurisdictions can structure contracts in new ways that allow for longer timelines for interventions and payments based on even longer-term outcomes.

- 10 percent set-aside "no-year" funds. By putting payment points well beyond the normal two-year WIOA funding cycle, funders can offer sites the flexibility to focus on long-term outcomes. Local areas can now link payment to long-term success for young people, incentivizing providers to address the needs of participants holistically with comprehensive services, in addition to linking to other resources and programs, such as TANF, SNAP, and career and technical education.

- Additional rigor. The use of P4P requires the development of a contracting strategy that includes third-party data validation, population analysis, and cost modeling.

Figure 4.2 Comparing Performance-Based Contracting to WIOA Pay-for-Performance

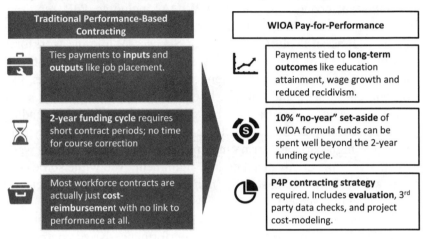

WIOA incentivizes workforce agencies to structure outcomes-oriented Pay-for-Performance contracts to achieve longer-term, high-bar outcomes

Traditional Performance-Based Contracting	WIOA Pay-for-Performance
Ties payments to **inputs** and **outputs** like job placement.	Payments tied to **long-term outcomes** like education attainment, wage growth and reduced recidivism.
2-year funding cycle requires short contract periods; no time for course correction	**10% "no-year" set-aside** of WIOA formula funds can be spent well beyond the 2-year funding cycle.
Most workforce contracts are actually just **cost-reimbursement** with no link to performance at all.	**P4P contracting strategy** required. Includes **evaluation**, 3rd party data checks, and project cost-modeling.

SOURCE: Third Sector Capital Partners.

Local Buy-In and Cooperation

P4P has provided a rallying point for governments, employers, providers, and funders to come together and strategize on how to better serve communities. WIOA allows states to develop combined plans that link funding and services across workforce programs, including TANF, Perkins CTE, and SNAP E&T. Combined plans enable more seamless implementation of systems of services while efficiently using shrinking funds across the many federal workforce programs.

Data Integration and Accessibility

Because outcomes-based contracting requires government agencies to integrate administrative data systems and share data across programs and agencies, these agencies are then better able to target their services to those most in need, correctly price their outcomes of interest, track performance, and develop an ongoing performance feedback loop that allows both government and providers to adjust and improve. This leads to better understanding of population needs, moving toward a seamless experience for the individual service recipient.

THREE CASE STUDIES

In 2016, as part of the Social Innovation Fund grant from the Corporation for National and Community Service, Third Sector partnered with workforce boards in Austin, Boston, Denver, San Diego, and Northern Virginia to leverage outcomes-based contracting models to strengthen youth programming in their communities. The three jurisdictions moving to contract launch in 2017 each developed unique approaches, demonstrating the power of P4P and outcomes-based contracting in a diverse range of communities. Northern Virginia used a model that incentivized stretch goals for serving a new population, leveraging data that was already being collected. San Diego developed a contract that blended output and outcome payments requiring data sharing across workforce and justice systems, as well as access to long-term wage data. Austin leveraged private sector data to develop cost models for employer outcome payments that will allow them to grow their youth employment program.

Northern Virginia

Northern Virginia's use of P4P is a great example of how a simplified outcomes contract, using available data, can bring a focus on equity, serving a high-need population that was previously ignored (see Figure 4.3). With their new P4P contract, Northern Virginia aims to serve 100 youth, about one-third of the total number served, aged 18–24, who have been involved in foster care or juvenile justice. Northern Virginia Team Independence, a new mobile unit, will meet these young adults at nontraditional locations. Their goal is to exceed WIOA Youth Program Measures for this harder-to-reach population, including helping more of these young people get into and stay in school, get and keep jobs, earn more, and learn real skills.

Figure 4.3 Overview of Northern Virginia's Pay-for-Performance Project

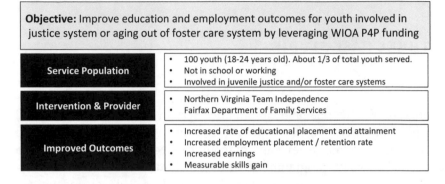

The SkillSource Group, Inc. is focused on justice and foster care involved youth

Objective: Improve education and employment outcomes for youth involved in justice system or aging out of foster care system by leveraging WIOA P4P funding

Service Population	• 100 youth (18-24 years old). About 1/3 of total youth served. • Not in school or working • Involved in juvenile justice and/or foster care systems
Intervention & Provider	• Northern Virginia Team Independence • Fairfax Department of Family Services
Improved Outcomes	• Increased rate of educational placement and attainment • Increased employment placement / retention rate • Increased earnings • Measurable skills gain

SOURCE: Third Sector Capital Partners.

Aside from reaching a new population of youth, this project is unique in that it was framed as a learning opportunity for all the stakeholders. The government partners have the opportunity to learn more about this service population and develop their ability to coordinate services and embed data within a contract. Because the outcomes payments were piloted as bonuses, providers are able to take a risk in serving a new population and increasing their own capacity to use data to adjust programming to meet the ambitious goals. As seen in Figure 4.4, the provider can earn a bonus payment of approximately $712 per youth per outcome for a total bonus payment of $2,848 per youth. These bonuses will be part of a three-year contract addendum with Fairfax Department of Family Services, with $50,000 reserved each year for a total of $150,000 in bonuses. Because the bonus payments are being incorporated by addendum, these provisions will be renewed with the rest of the contract.

Additionally, Northern Virginia stands as an example that helps to dispel the myth that outcomes contracting is inherently complex. First, there is only one data source involved for their initial contract, because they are leveraging WIOA performance data that are already being collected. Second, there is no money loss on the line, thanks to the use of WIOA P4P bonus payments. Providers have the chance to earn more by

Figure 4.4 Northern Virginia's Pay-for-Performance Contracting Strategy Design

Northern Virginia P4P Contracting Strategy Design
• 3-year contract addendum with Fairfax DFS to include contingent WIOA outcome bonus payments • Bonus payments payable upon achievement of 4 WIOA performance measures • $50K reserved each year for bonus payments ($150K total)

WIOA Outcomes	Bonus Payment (Per Youth, Per Outcome)
Measurable Skills Gain During Programming	$712
Youth Placed in Employment, Training or Education (2Q After Exit)	$712
Youth Placed in Employment, Training or Education (4Q After Exit)	$712
Attainment of Degree or Certificate (Within 4Q After Exit)	$712
TOTAL:	$2,848

SOURCE: Third Sector Capital Partners.

serving a harder to reach population but won't lose cost coverage for their services. Northern Virginia was able to take advantage of the fact that they have funds rolling over year to year to set up the bonus payment structure. The next phase of work aims to include justice data and outcomes, advancing the sophistication of the contract model over time as both government and providers learn and respond to data.

San Diego

The San Diego Workforce Partnership (SDWP) is using P4P to measurably improve outcomes for youth involved in the justice system in San Diego County. By combining the P4P provisions with evaluation and performance-driven service provision, SDWP aims to improve employment, education, and recidivism outcomes for these youth (see Figure 4.5).

San Diego's P4P contract will serve up to 300 youth, aged 16–24, who are not in school or working and who have just served a court sentence. The provider, Second Chance, will work with youth to achieve increased rates of educational placement and attainment, increased

Figure 4.5 Overview of San Diego's Pay-for-Performance Project

Objective: Improve education, employment, and recidivism outcomes for justice-involved out-of-school youth	
Service Population	• Up to 300 youth, ages 16-24 • Not in school or working • Post adjudication + true finding + commitment • In Field Services or re-entry from Institutional Services
Provider	• Second Chance
Improved Outcomes	• Increased rate of educational placement and attainment • Increased wages • Increased rate of employment placement and retention • Reduced recidivism rate

SOURCE: Third Sector Capital Partners.

wages, increased rates of employment placement and retention, and reduced recidivism rates.

SDWP will be allocating $1–$2 million of its WIOA youth funds over four years to an outcomes-based contract that will include payments linked to specific short- and long-term outcomes. By using a combination of traditional performance-based contracting and P4P contracting methods, San Diego is able to develop an outcomes orientation focused on long-term impacts while meeting the cash flow needs of the provider through shorter-term output payments (see Figure 4.6).

By including reduced recidivism as a payment point, San Diego could partner with the justice system, working toward shared priorities. Synchronized services across justice and workforce allows for a more seamless and well-coordinated experience for the youth participants. Previously, providers were required to give youth the same types of training in the residential justice facilities and then repeat that training once the youth was being served through WIOA. Now, participants can get the training they need based on their own specific situation, not sitting through mandatory classes on repeat. Providers are freed up from overly prescriptive, compliance-focused contracts, and can use the data feedback loop embedded within the contract to improve services, customizing based on individual needs.

Figure 4.6 Overview of San Diego's Pay-for-Performance Contract

San Diego's payment plan combines performance-based contracting with P4P

Performance Based Contract		Pay for Performance Strategy
Output Payments	**Short-Term Outcome Payments**	**Long-Term Bonus Payments**

• Guaranteed funding is released to provider
  – (a) upon enrollment of each youth who fits the agreed-upon and designated eligibility criteria, and
  – (b) upon submission of monthly performance progress reports
	• Funds are released based on each participant's individual performance, as measured by the ability of each youth served to meet agreed upon short-term WIOA performance measures
	• Final short-term outcome payment are paid out during the standard 2-year WIOA funding cycle
		• "No Year" funds are reserved and released based on the annual performance of each cohort in 4 specified long-term performance areas, as compared to an agreed upon baseline
		• Independent validation of achievement of agreed-upon outcomes prior to payment

SOURCE: Third Sector Capital Partners.

Austin

The exploration of P4P contracting in Austin began with a few unique and competing forces. On one hand, Workforce Solutions Capital Area (WSCA) was extremely satisfied with their youth workforce providers and the outcomes they were able to achieve. On the other hand, only a small fraction of Austin's Opportunity Youth, youth who are not in school and not working, were being served by these high-quality programs. At the same time, the city of Austin is trying to fill 60,000 new jobs in the next few years, which will be challenging if there is a shortage of talented entry-level employees.

The main questions for Austin became how to leverage outside funding to expand the Youth Employment Program (YEP). Working with providers from Goodwill, Lifeworks, American Youthworks, and Communities in Schools, WSCA began to deepen their relationships with private employers to see how an outcomes-based contract might meet the needs of Austin's opportunity youth population and its growing businesses (see Figure 4.7).

Figure 4.7 Overview of Austin's Pay-for-Performance Project

Objective: Improve education and employment outcomes for Opportunity Youth by using P4P concepts to secure more performance-based funding.	

Service Population	• Austin's Opportunity Youth
	  • 16-24-year-olds
	  • Not in school or working

Providers	• Youth Employment Partnership (YEP)
	  • Goodwill
	  • LifeWorks
	  • American Youthworks
	  • Communities in Schools

Improved Outcomes	• Placement of YEP youth into employment • Retention of YEP youth [at 6 months] • Advancement of YEP youth [at 1 year]

SOURCE: Third Sector Capital Partners.

With employers as the end payers, the hypothesis is that youth who have gone through the program will be better workers and will have a positive impact on company culture. We know from more than a decade of data from Gap Inc.'s This Way Ahead program, which targets similar opportunity youth with employment training and work experience, that participants stay with the company twice as long as their coworkers in the same cities and show greater enthusiasm and company loyalty than their peers.[2]

Using employer data by industry, we developed sample cost models for outcomes payments linked to the placement of YEP youth into employment, retention of YEP youth (at least six months), and advancement of YEP youth (at one year). The cost model in Figure 4.8 shows proposed outcomes payments based on employer costs for a certified nurse's aide. The sample payment structure can be refined using employer specific data, and as the value of YEP trained employees is proven, additional outcomes payments may be negotiated.

Austin's approach defies the common assumption that outside investors must provide upfront funding for P4P or PFS contracts. Here, YEP will cycle the employer outcomes payments back into the program to scale services in future years.

Figure 4.8 Austin's Employee Turnover Costing Tool

Employee Turnover Costing Tool
Sample Occupation: Certified Nurses Aide

SOURCE: Third Sector Capital Partners.

Any state or local government can adapt outcomes contracting and P4P models for their own needs and constraints. There is not a one-size-fits-all framework, and the diversity of the above examples is evidence of how different circumstances can lead to different solutions. P4P at first glance might seem too complicated, but each of these sites took a different approach based on the realities of data access, internal and provider capacity, partnerships in the community, and the needs of the service population. It takes effort and commitment to shift to an outcomes orientation for social services, but there is nothing standing in the way of taking that first step.

SUCCESSES AND CHALLENGES

Across these sites, we see benefits and challenges of using P4P to improve workforce outcomes. They can be categorized as follows:

Data, Outcomes, and Evaluation

Just getting individuals around the table to talk about data and outcomes was a huge benefit. For some localities, incorporating evaluators into the discussion was new, as was developing data sharing agreements. Sites need access to justice, tax record, academic, and employment data, which will help improve programs and direct funding where it is most needed. Not all sites were able to access their ideal data sources, and data access continues to be a time-consuming step in developing outcomes-based contracts. Workforce boards should look to state longitudinal data systems as potential partners in creating enhanced data access to support outcomes orientations.

Partnerships and Processes

Each site has also successfully formed new partnerships. Whether it was brain trusts, working groups, or formal collaboratives, getting folks from inside and outside government to collaborate in developing an outcomes-based approach has yielded wins across many topics. However, because P4P is new and runs up against current practices and protocols, some agencies and partners have pushed back against the changes out of risk aversion. Having a strong government champion can help to reassure and motivate partners to stay involved.

Service Provision and Population Served

The partnerships formed through this work have enabled in-depth assessments of target populations, resulting in a deeper understanding of the needs and challenges of typically underserved groups. Through these assessments, locations were able to reach consensus on a very specific target population focus and also prioritize where and how to deliver services to achieve the greatest impact. The ability to focus on populations most in need of service but previously left out, as in Northern Virginia, or the ability to customize services to the individual needs of the youth, as in San Diego, has allowed jurisdictions to enhance the equity of their services while deploying funds effectively and efficiently.

HOW TO GET STARTED?

Every government, provider, funder, or community can begin the journey toward an outcomes orientation, no matter their starting point. First, examine current contracts and procurement opportunities. Every procurement is an opportunity to align resources with results, and outcomes payments can be incorporated into a larger contracting strategy. Starting small is a great way to build outcomes orientation muscles, allowing all parties to learn and grow.

Second, get to know your service population, the interventions in your community, and the data that tell you how they are doing. Partnerships with local community colleges can help with access to outside data and potentially folks who are willing and able to do some initial analysis. Third, turn your data into actionable information by embedding it in contracts, building in governance policies that link data, and sharing it with providers to enable learning over time. Sharing data before linking it directly to payments may be one way to get reluctant partners to the table by reducing the risk while emphasizing the benefit. Finally, seek support and increase your capacity by partnering with intermediary organizations or requesting technical assistance from the Department of Labor (see Figure 4.9).

Figure 4.9 Considerations in Developing an Outcomes Orientation

Developing an Outcomes Orientation
PROCUREMENT POWER: Every procurement is an opportunity to align resources with results – use it! Outcomes payments can be part of a larger contracting strategy, and it is ok to start small.
INVESTIGATE: Get to know your service population, the interventions in your community and the data that tells you how they are doing.
LINK DATA: Turn your data into actionable information by embedding it in contracts. Start small, building in governance policies that link data and share it with providers to enable learning over time.
SEEK SUPPORT: Increase your capacity and the time dedicated to outcomes-oriented contracting by partnering with experts and requesting TA from the Department of Labor.

SOURCE: Third Sector Capital Partners.

In reinventing a vital but widely overlooked link in the workforce funding system—public sector contracts—we can shift government's focus from delivering specific services to achieving measurable outcomes. By holding service providers accountable for results without prescribing interventions, outcomes contracts offer much-needed flexibility to experiment with new approaches and technologies. If workforce systems are contracting for outcomes, evidence-based practices no longer need to advocate for political will—agencies are incentivized to use them through the contracting process. Changing how and what government pays for becomes a systemic way to scale what works and deliver sustained results for communities.

Notes

1. SkillSource participant data.
2. See Gap Inc. https://www.bewhatspossible.com/thiswayahead (accessed April 13, 2018).

5

Improving Workforce Outcomes with Pay for Success

Nirav Shah

"From this training I feel like I can see the light at the end of the tunnel and it feels very promising now."
—Immaculate Nabuule, Jewish Vocational Service participant

Immaculate Nabuule has always dreamed of being a banker. When she moved to the United States from Uganda six years ago, she applied to many banks but was never hired. Finally, in May 2017, Nabuule enrolled in the Bank Teller Training program at Jewish Vocational Service (JVS) in Boston. JVS, one of Greater Boston's largest community-based workforce and adult education providers, assisted with her resume and cover letter, went through practice interviews, and helped her become more familiar with the American banking system. Soon after graduating, Nabuule began working full time as a bank teller in Boston.

Over the next five years, an innovative funding model called Pay for Success (PFS) will allow JVS to serve an additional 2,000 people in Greater Boston, equipping them with the skills they need to advance their careers and providing Greater Boston necessary human capital to fuel its economy.

Launched in 2017, the Massachusetts Pathways to Economic Advancement Pay for Success Project (MA Pathways) is a collaboration between the Commonwealth of Massachusetts, JVS, and 40 impact investors, including financial institutions, donor advised funds, individuals, and foundations. It is the nation's first PFS project to focus exclusively on improving workforce development outcomes and is one example of how governments are using results-based financing tools to advance and accelerate workforce development solutions.

Workforce development policies, strategies, and initiatives aim to achieve two connected objectives: help individuals attain the education and skills necessary to enter the workforce and climb the economic ladder, and improve the productivity and vitality of the economy. Effective workforce development initiatives weave these objectives together to create positive outcomes for individuals, industries, and society.

However, expanding effective programs to dramatically move the needle on workforce development objectives requires persistent and sustained collaboration between the education, economic development, nonprofit, and business sectors. Outcomes-focused financing tools like PFS offer these stakeholders a tool that can align incentives across sectors to achieve meaningful and measureable results.

In this chapter, we will define PFS, explore its increasing popularity as a way to tackle complex social challenges across the United States and around the world, and highlight three examples of our work employing Pay for Success to improve workforce outcomes for individuals in need.

WHAT IS PAY FOR SUCCESS?

Also known as Social Impact Bonds, PFS is an innovative public-private partnership that drives resources toward effective social programs. It unites investors, nonprofit service providers, and payors (often government) around a powerful common goal: improving outcomes for individuals and communities in need (See Figure 5.1).

A PFS project begins with a social challenge the government is trying to address. Government partners with high-performing nonprofits, who scale their services with up-front capital from private investors. An independent evaluator measures the impact of the project on predetermined outcome metrics. If the project successfully improves outcomes, the government repays investors with a modest return. However, the government pays only at the level of outcomes achieved.

There are currently over 100 PFS projects in 24 countries. In the United States, 20 projects are mobilizing over $200 million in capital to tackle a wide range of issues, including adult and juvenile recidivism,

Figure 5.1 Uniting Uncommon Partners through Pay for Success

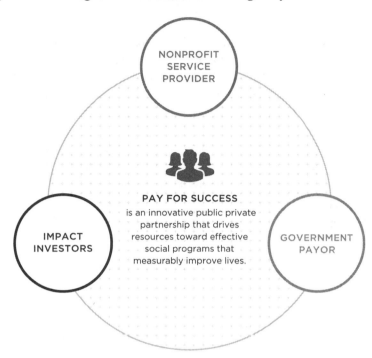

SOURCE: Social Finance.

workforce development, child welfare, the opioid epidemic, and maternal and child health (Social Finance, n.d.).

Globally, over one-third of Social Impact Bonds have focused on workforce development.[1] This includes projects developed in 12 countries across four continents. The applications for PFS in workforce development are diverse and include a cross-border project between Germany and the Netherlands to address a labor shortage in Germany and relatively high unemployment in the Dutch municipality of Enschede and a project supporting cocoa farmers in the Peruvian Amazon.

THE POWER OF PFS

The PFS structure ensures that all stakeholders benefit: governments gain a new level of accountability for taxpayers by paying only for programs that deliver measurable impact; nonprofits secure multiyear, flexible funding, which allows them to grow; and investors can reflect their values in their investment portfolios by receiving financial returns only when projects measurably improve people's lives.

PFS is about systems-level change, a pursuit that at its core is about changing mindsets: government contracts for outcomes instead of services rendered, investor repayments are based on the measurable impact a project generates, and service providers measure and communicate the outcomes their participants achieve. It is about bringing all parties to the table and encouraging them to think outside their traditional silos.

Achieving Positive Outcomes for all Project Stakeholders

In their book *Moneyball for Government* (2014), Peter Orszag and John Bridgeland write that less than 1 percent of programs funded by the federal government are backed by the most basic evidence that the program has worked. PFS helps governments put data to work and scale programs that are supported by evidence to more effectively steer taxpayer dollars toward social service interventions that have measurable results for people.

High-impact nonprofits need flexible, sustainable funding to expand effective programs and generate greater impact. Instead, too many must rely on a patchwork of fee-for-service funding that underfunds, impedes, or even prohibits activities that could generate more impact.

PFS benefits service providers by providing multiyear, flexible, unrestricted funding that service providers can use for critical internal systems such as data systems and analysis, project ramp-up periods, and evaluations.

Finally, more investors are looking to achieve both social and financial returns with their investments. Impact investing is shaking up a bifurcated worldview organized around the bright line between for-profit activities, which should only seek to maximize financial returns; and charity, which traditionally gives money without expecting any back in return. Through models like PFS, the private sector and philanthropy align in their pursuit of outcomes *and* returns.

HOW PFS IS BUILDING MOMENTUM TO TACKLE SOCIAL ISSUES

Shifting the Focus from Outputs to Outcomes

Each year, governments spend hundreds of billions of dollars to provide necessary human services, including providing health care for the sick, supporting vulnerable children, and helping build our workforce. For the most part, government only measures the outputs of these services, such as the number of people served, volunteer engagement, or money distributed.

In answering the big questions about impact and about lives changed, outcomes are what matter: ex-offenders becoming employed and reintegrated into society, students graduating and connecting to the labor force, women delivering healthy babies. However, measuring, tracking, and reporting on outcomes requires a significant investment in resources and a shift in mind sets. PFS provides a way to effectively focus public sector attention and resources on the achievement of these outcomes.

For workforce development, beneficial outcomes like increased earnings and improved postsecondary enrollment have tangible value that accrues to the individual, the community, and the government. PFS helps monetize that value, which is the engine that allows impact investors to fund the expansion of services to people in need and the government to pay only if measurable outcomes are achieved.

Allowing Governments to Invest in Prevention

PFS enables governments to invest early and upstream, focusing on prevention rather than remediation: vaccines are cheaper than treating disease and result in better population health outcomes; job training and housing cost less than incarceration and enable economic mobility. By engaging the private sector to provide up-front capital, government can focus on preventive measures while continuing to provide a needed social safety net, thus reducing costs and avoiding social challenges down the road.

PFS increases governments' capacity to invest in an ounce of prevention today rather than a future pound of cure. This allows governments to direct already limited funds more effectively, improving access to services for people in need over the long term.

Transferring Risk from the Public to the Private Sector

PFS transfers performance risk from government to funders. This risk transfer is meaningful to government: private funders provide upfront working capital to expand a social intervention, and in doing so they take on the performance risk if the project does not deliver positive results. Government repays investors based on the level of outcomes achieved, as measured by an independent evaluator. Outcome metrics are jointly established by the payor, the service provider, and the intermediary. Once these details are finalized, capital is mobilized from project investors.

Transferring performance risk ensures government payment is commensurate to the impact created. PFS is essentially about ensuring value for taxpayers—not only because government pays just for programs that work, but also because it can help governments get more value for every taxpayer dollar spent.

Engaging Stakeholders in Active Performance Management

Through active performance management, which includes project oversight, analyzing programmatic and administrative data, initiating course corrections, and financial management, the service provider and the PFS intermediary are better able to manage outcomes achievement over the life of the project. Active performance management creates a close working partnership between governments and service providers with the singular focus on achieving project goals. In the MA Pathways project, for example, quarterly measurement and payment points provide a rapid flow of information to facilitate continuous improvement of JVS program services.

SOCIAL FINANCE CASE STUDIES: PFS AND WORKFORCE DEVELOPMENT

A well-educated, highly skilled workforce is an essential part of the long-term health of our local, regional, and national economies, which can make economic mobility a reality for individuals in the labor force. The economic benefits of increased employment and improved social outcomes make workforce development a promising fit for PFS.

We know that in today's complex economic landscape there is no one-size-fits-all solution. Different populations have different needs for services that help them improve their career outcomes over the long term, and different geographies present unique opportunities and challenges. Below are three distinct examples of how Social Finance, a non-profit organization that has been pioneering the PFS field in the United States for seven years, is working with nonprofits, governments, and funders to scale effective workforce development programs across the nation with PFS. These projects span the country and will serve veterans, immigrants, and refugees in Massachusetts, and high-need youth in Ohio, Texas, New York, and California.

Massachusetts Pathways to Economic Advancement PFS Project

The long-term vitality of Greater Boston's economy is dependent on its workforce. Immigrants, like Immaculate Nabuule, whose story we highlighted at the beginning of this chapter, make up nearly one-third of the adult working age civilian population in the greater Boston area. However, the potential for this population to contribute to the labor force is not being fully tapped. In 2014 and 2015, the median annual earnings for immigrants was nearly $15,000 lower than that of native Bostonians. Forty percent of the immigrant population does not have more than a high school education, compared to 22 percent of the nonimmigrant population in Boston, and 38 percent of immigrants indicated that they have poor English language skills (Osterman, Kimball, and Riordan 2017).

Advancing career opportunities for the working-age immigrant and refugee population in Boston will allow this community to improve their socioeconomic standing, which will result in improvements in health and greater education opportunities for their children. Better workforce outcomes for individuals and families will further strengthen Boston's economy. Industries will have access to the skills needed to improve productivity and profitability. Increased purchasing power by the immigrant and refugee population will generate more economic activity, which in turn fuels greater growth and more jobs.

In 2015, the Commonwealth of Massachusetts established the Workforce Skills Cabinet with the goal of developing cross-sector solutions "to effectively, efficiently, and equitably promote economic growth through education programs, workforce skills trainings, employment opportunities, and business development services" (Commonwealth of Massachusetts 2015). As one of the first states to utilize PFS to tackle chronic social issues, Massachusetts identified a tool that allowed it to leverage private investments to fund a suite of workforce development services that align with the regional needs of a large and low-income segment of the workforce while supporting the industries that power Boston's economy.

Social Finance raised $12.4 million from 40 impact investors, providing JVS with flexible capital to expand workforce development services to 2,000 additional immigrants and refugees in the Greater Boston community (Commonwealth of Massachusetts 2017). Aligned with JVS's theory of change to deliver the right services to the right people at the right time in their lives, the PFS project will enable the delivery of a multitrack program to ensure that those who seek services are able to fully engage in a program that puts them on a path to success. The Rapid Employment track provides vocational English and job placement services to adults who are looking to secure a first job immediately. English for Advancement is a more intensive program for higher-level English speakers seeking employment or job advancement. Skills training facilitates job placement in the health care or hospitality sector. The Bridges to College track will support individuals with high school equivalency seeking to transition into higher education.

Aligning stakeholders' incentives to focus on meaningful and measurable outcomes has dual advantages. Outcomes-contingent payment ensures accountability of taxpayer resources. For MA Pathways, the Commonwealth's payment to investors will be determined by an independent evaluator's measurement of three outcomes among project participants: 1) earnings, 2) successful transitions to higher education, and 3) program engagement. The active performance management plan developed by the partners creates rapid feedback loops, allowing JVS and the cabinet agencies to continually refine services and continuously improve the training.

Veterans Coordinated Approach to Recovery and Employment (CARE)

Since 2001, the wars in Afghanistan and Iraq have resulted in thousands of service members transitioning out of the military and into the civilian workforce. Many veterans find this to be a challenging experience.

Veterans with posttraumatic stress disorder (PTSD) are especially prone to facing challenges in the transition process, particularly with obtaining and maintaining well-suited, stable employment. Symptoms of PTSD may result in a lack of interest in engaging in tasks and activities, anxiety, depression, feelings of detachment from others, and trouble with concentration. This vast array of symptoms combined with other employment barriers such as limited nonmilitary vocational skills and work experience, lack of resources to assist with preparation for finding a civilian job, and a challenging job market can prevent veterans with PTSD from successfully transitioning into the workforce.

While the Department of Veterans Affairs (VA) and other government organizations, such as the Department of Labor, have programs that assist veterans in seeking employment, there is not currently an employment program that focuses specifically and solely on veterans with PTSD. In 2016, the VA and Corporation for National and Community Service (CNCS) selected Social Finance, in partnership with the Tuscaloosa Research and Education Advancement Corporation (TREAC), to develop a PFS project that improves employment outcomes for approximately 500 unemployed veterans with service-connected PTSD. The resulting project, CARE, will expand the Individual Placement and Support (IPS) program, an evidence-based approach to supported employment that emphasizes rapid job search by matching an individual's needs and preferences and provides integrated mental health care. IPS has been evaluated by randomized controlled trials spanning multiple countries, diagnoses, and contexts, which have shown increased competitive employment for veteran participants.

To evaluate if the project is successful at improving long-term employment outcomes, the CARE project will measure veteran earnings, sustained competitive employment measured by days worked, job satisfaction, and fidelity of implementing the IPS model in new geographies.

Through the CARE project, private funders will provide approximately $5 million in up-front capital to expand IPS in several communities across the United States. The VA, CNCS, and local jurisdictions will then repay the funders based on the success of the program in achieving outcomes for veterans.

Catalyzing Career and Technical Education through PFS

Underserved, high-need youth—including low-income youth and students of color—have the lowest rates of high school graduation and attainment of postsecondary credentials, and, consequently, low employment in jobs providing family-sustaining wages (National Center on Education Statistics 2016). Research shows that well-implemented career and technical education (CTE) programs result in improved student outcomes, such as improved high school graduation, transitions to two- and four-year colleges, persistence in college, accumulation of college credit, and attainment of postsecondary credentials (see, for example, Elliot, Hanser, and Gilroy [2002] and Kemple [2008]).

Social Finance, with support from the U.S. Department of Education's Office of Career, Technical and Adult Education and Google.org, is leading the exploration of PFS financing in support of high-quality CTE models that propel students to postsecondary and career success. In partnership with Jobs for the Future (JFF), Social Finance will develop the nation's first PFS projects focused on CTE programs.

In the spring of 2017, Social Finance and JFF held a national competition to select high-quality CTE programs with the potential to expand via PFS financing. Four sites were selected to receive technical assistance and participate in a PFS feasibility study to determine whether PFS is a good fit to expand their career and technical education programs:

    1) South Bay Community Services, in San Diego County, California, will launch a CTE program designed to support traumatized youth aged 16–24. It will include enriched academic

preparation, support with making college connections, and extended support into the first year of college.

2) NAF, a New York–based group that runs a network of career academies, will expand fully paid internships.

3) Mahoning County Educational Services Center, in northeastern Ohio, will double the reach of its career-focused, early-college programs.

4) Pharr-San Juan-Antonio Independent School District, in the Rio Grande Valley of Texas, will increase enrollment in a new program focusing on agriculture, food, and natural resources.

These sites from across the United States serve diverse populations of underserved, high-need youth through varied types of CTE programs. They will be the first in the country to explore PFS in K–12 education.

For each site, Social Finance and JFF will assess the potential for PFS to launch or expand the proposed CTE model. For up to three applicants, Social Finance and JFF will continue to work with the organization to develop a PFS project and raise capital. Finally, Social Finance will stay involved in all PFS projects once services are launched, providing active performance management to ensure that projects stay on track and that outcomes are met.

CONCLUSION

The nature of work is changing; we know that the twenty-first century workforce will require skill sets that are very different from those in the preceding century. Diverse interventions are needed to prepare individuals to thrive in this new economy. Pay for Success can help scale such interventions, from individualized support for veterans with PTSD to vocational training for immigrants with limited English skills. It can support the expansion of programs that prepare underserved youth for postsecondary education and for careers.

Improving the well-being of our most vulnerable citizens requires a commitment to continuously improving government services. A well-educated, highly skilled workforce, in particular, is an essential part of the long-term health of our local, regional, and national economies.

PFS offers the opportunity to improve employment and career options for our nation's workers and job seekers by mobilizing capital to grow programs that work. In doing so, it supports the development of strong, vibrant communities where people and businesses can thrive.

Note

1. For more information, visit http://www.socialfinance.org.uk/database/.

References

Commonwealth of Massachusetts. 2015. "Executive Order No. 560: Creating the Workforce Skills Cabinet." Boston: Commonwealth of Massachusetts. https://www.mass.gov/executive-orders/no-560-creating-the-workforce -skills-cabinet (accessed May 2, 2018).
―――. 2017. "Baker-Polito Administration Launches Workforce Development Pay for Success Project." Press release. Boston: Commonwealth of Massachusetts.
Elliott, Marc N., Lawrence H. Hanser, and Curtis L. Gilroy. 2002. "Career Academies: Additional Evidence of Positive Student Outcomes." *Journal of Education for Students Placed at Risk* 7(1): 71–90.
Kemple, James J. 2008. *Career Academies: Long-Term Impacts on Work, Education, and Transitions to Adulthood*. New York and Oakland, CA: MDRC.
National Center for Education Statistics. 2016. *The Condition of Education 2016*. Washington, DC: National Center for Education Statistics.
Orszag, Peter, and John Bridgeland. 2014. *Moneyball for Government*. Austin, TX, and New York: Disruption Books.
Osterman, Paul, William Kimball, and Christine Riordan. 2017. *Boston's Immigrants: An Essential Component of a Strong Economy*. Boston, MA: JVS Center for Economic Opportunity.
Social Finance. n.d. "Impact Bond Global Database." London: Social Finance. http://sibdatabase.socialfinance.org.uk/ (accessed September 18, 2018).

6

Financing Human Capital through Income-Contingent Agreements

Miguel Palacios

The second half of the twentieth century saw an explosion in financial innovation. A wide variety of products for savers, institutional investors, and consumers sprung to life, offering better and cheaper mechanisms for achieving the central roles finance plays in an economy: allocating capital and sharing risk. Even after 2008, when some of these innovations were accused of causing a financial meltdown, their use continues in the trillions of dollars in the United States as of 2017.[1] Most of these products, comprising a now well-understood array of contractual arrangements and practices, are available in connection to investments in tangible assets, such as houses and other real estate. A much smaller fraction targets intangible assets, like research and development. This is not because there are fewer opportunities to invest in intangible projects, but because intangible investments face special financing challenges. Chief among intangible investments is human capital.

Human capital development benefited from some financial innovations during the second half of the twentieth century, but it still received comparably small attention when compared to other areas of the economy, such as housing and retail investing. The main innovations that took place were, for the most part, driven by government through widespread student loan programs rather than private initiatives. Government intervention followed from better understanding of the many barriers that prevent human capital from being fully funded.

Since then, changes in the economic environment, notably in information technology, combined with the successful experience of a few public and private initiatives, have opened the door for new alternatives for funding human capital. Several income-contingent products have been tested now for almost 30 years, and they can transform the way human capital is funded.

In this chapter I revisit the obstacles for funding human capital, explain why recent changes improve the potential for funding, and briefly describe income-contingent innovations that were tested in 2017.

WHO SHOULD FUND HUMAN CAPITAL DEVELOPMENT?

The discussion of emerging innovations in financing human capital must first address who should do the funding. The simplest answer starts with an abstract concept: "capital markets." This would be an appropriate answer for the question of who should fund a consumer's car, or who should fund a corporation's expansion. It is also a valid answer for human capital, although relatively incomplete because capital markets do not include the opportunities for funding that can arise from close relationships between the main stakeholders.

The connection between an employer's needs and a worker's training, coupled with a complex interaction between workers, institutions offering training, and employers, provides an answer beyond capital markets. Funding has the potential to achieve better alignment of incentives if it links individuals, training institutions, and employers. Why? Because training providers have information about their own product that trainees do not have, while employers have information about how to use that training. In this circumstance, contracts contingent on outcomes reduce the costs associated with private information by aligning each party's incentives.

Beyond having an incentive for funding training, employers and society profit from trained individuals and therefore have a reason to not only provide funding but also subsidize it. In the case of employers, this means they pay for part of the training. Similarly, the state has a reason to pay for part of the cost of training, as it benefits from the direct taxation of a more productive workforce and, indirectly, from the reduced costs of unemployment, subemployment, and social challenges derived from them.

The analysis below focuses on interactions between private stakeholders. It begins by explaining why, even though they all benefit, stakeholders are reluctant to participate. The emerging alternatives will then be addressed, highlighting the opportunities for funding interactions between them.

HUMAN CAPITAL INVESTMENT: AN INFORMATION AND CONTRACTUAL CHALLENGE

The reasons human capital will not be funded at optimal levels have been described amply elsewhere.[2] Before explaining how financial innovations offer new solutions, it is important to revisit the problem. Here I compare investments in human capital and tangible investments, a comparison that is increasingly relevant in light of recent developments in artificial intelligence and robotic technology.

Consider an investment in the "knowledge and skills" of a new crop of robots. Suppose these robots can learn, for every intent and purpose, to perform the same tasks that people do today. They can follow advanced instructions, analyze complex problems, and provide recommendations. They are capable of writing or devising strategic plans for new businesses, and can interact with humans and inspire emotions in them. However, unlike humans, these robots do not have free will: they do what they are told or, more precisely, programmed to do, and when deciding between different alternatives, they act according to an objective chosen by the robot's programmer according to specific rules.[3] Suppose that these robots can be bought, sold, or rented at will.

Now, say these robots need a new program that will allow them to do a new set of tasks. Even though this investment in "knowledge and skills" is intangible, the effects of that knowledge and those skills are embodied in a tangible object, the robot, which can be rented or sold. Furthermore, because the robots follow objectives given to them, contracts can specify exactly what those objectives should be.

If such robots existed, funding their training would not be different from funding other tangible projects, such as investment in machinery or real estate. Corporations would buy robots, train them, and enjoy their services at a profit. Some robots would be available for rent, in which case funding for their training could be done using the robot as collateral or, similarly, using contracts that specify precisely what the robot will do in certain circumstances.

In such a world, worthwhile opportunities for training—worthwhile in an economic sense, that is, when the lifetime cost of the investment is lower than the lifetime benefits—would be funded by the robot's owner up to the point where additional training would not yield any extra benefits. Lack of capital would be an issue in the same way that funding capital for new machinery is an issue. Financial intermediaries, or other individuals and firms, would provide capital using the typical arrangements and contracts available for other tangible investments. The cost of capital would closely reflect the opportunity cost of the investment and any risk transfer taking place between the parties.

Firms, to the extent that they can profit from training robots, would contribute to the funding, even if not owning the robot outright. Owners would fund training themselves, or would raise capital based on the robot's capacity to produce future income. Training institutions would offer only valuable programs, tailored to the needs of the robot's owners and the firms using them. They would generally be unable to charge tuition fees higher than those justified by the value of the training they offer, and those fees would be partially paid by firms and owners.

In this world, it does not really matter who comes up with the money first—robot owners or the firms who use them—since the possibility of writing contracts between the different parties provides an avenue for ensuring that everyone involved ends up paying some amount and taking a predetermined amount of risk.

FREE WILL

From an economic perspective, investment in human capital is fundamentally different from investing in robots in two important dimensions. First, those acquiring skills and knowledge follow their own objectives, which are generally not known to others, and cannot be forced to work for a particular employer. Second, our robot example supposes that a knowledgeable being, the robot's owner, decides the robot's objectives. In reality, individuals choosing training for themselves do not have the information to fully analyze a specific training choice. If they did, they probably would not need training. The consequences of these differences are profound.

Consider, first, unknown objectives. Employers are unsure about an individual's future behavior within the firm and their future performance, and employees are unsure about how much they will enjoy working for a particular employer. Both sources of uncertainty reduce the willingness of employers to fund, and employees to seek, long-term contracts with their employers. Unlike the robot case, where objectives were clearly known, individuals' intentions and behavior cannot be fully contracted on.

Inability to commit to work for a particular employer leads to the same result: employers who might benefit from a highly skilled workforce, even after paying a market wage, will not be willing to pay for training. They fear that once they pay for training, a competitor will poach workers away. The difference when compared to our robot example is that courts will not enforce contracts that commit individuals to work for someone, as such contracts would be akin to indentured servitude.

If firms will not invest in training, then the onus for funding falls on the individual. This observation, attributed to Arthur Cecil Pigou (see, for instance, Acemoglu and Pischke [1998]), leads to the conclusion that individuals will have to finance most of their development, even if their training greatly benefits their employers and society.

Our second problem, the individual's incomplete information, means that those who would have to shoulder the funding are also the ones who, almost by definition, are unable to assess the benefits of the investment. They perhaps understand that the investment opens doors, but are in a position that makes it difficult to assess which program is worthwhile, which one is not, and which one offers a better fit. It is not surprising that many programs of questionable quality spend significant fractions of their budgets in marketing. In a marketplace with incomplete information, institutions that offer training can profit handsomely by shaping perceptions, no matter how removed from reality.

To summarize, training provides knowledge and skills to individuals who cannot commit to behave in a particular way or work for a particular employer. As a result, employers will limit the investment they make in their employees' training. Instead, individuals will pay for their own training. At the same time, individuals do not have the information they need to make the best decisions regarding their training.

Once one accepts that individuals will need to fund their own train-ing, the inalienability of their investment affects the type of funding they will receive as well. Given that the usefulness of a specific set of skills is uncertain, an investment in training will entail some risk. Financing, therefore, will include some type of risk transfer between the individ-ual and the source of capital. In our robot world, the best arrangement would share risk between the robot's owner and those providing capital. Yet, to share risk effectively, the parties involved need to be able to agree on the activities the robot will perform after the investment—its choice of "occupation" (in robot speak) and the intensity of work, for example—and need to contract on the actions the robot is programmed to take to mitigate (or increase) risk. Since individuals' motivations and actions are largely hidden, and therefore cannot be contracted on, an agreement that shares a lot of the risk will be difficult to implement. The result is funding that *does not* transfer risk. This type of funding is essentially a loan.[4] Because these loans will have no collateral, they will be expensive, rationed, or unavailable.

In conclusion, absent arrangements that overcome the problems outlined above, we should expect human capital development to be funded by individuals using loans. We should also expect that training institutions will attempt to impress individuals with offerings that are not necessarily in their best interest. This is what we observe, with the notable difference of the state's intervention to provide funding. Until quite recently, the state mainly offered this funding through loans.

Economists normally label the problems described above as infor-mation and agency problems. Information problems are those that stem from employees finding it difficult to judge the quality of different pro-grams, or employers finding it difficult to judge the qualities of an indi-vidual. These problems are compounded by agency problems: employ-ers are hesitant to fund an individual's training if they cannot get the employee to commit to work for the employer (which they cannot), and the employee is hesitant to invest in training, given the employer's unwillingness to commit to hire them later at an acceptable wage. These problems are partially addressed by the state's involvement, for in some areas it has an advantage over private funders and providers, but state intervention certainly does not remove all of the obstacles to funding human capital.

The result is insufficient funding, excessive risk taken by individuals, and resources allocated to inappropriate and expensive training.

INNOVATIONS OVERCOMING THE CHALLENGES

The previous discussion paraphrased the standard economic argument explaining limits in the funding of training (and education, more generally). Yet a changing economic environment reduces the previous issues and allows for new arrangements that more closely resemble the efficient investment we witness in tangible assets. The new arrangements are attractive because workers can find funding for their training without taking too much personal risk, and because these arrangements better align the incentives of training institutions and employers with those of employees seeking funding.

A significant change in the economics of human capital investment is the fall in the cost of income-tracking technologies. This is important because whereas it is true that workers cannot commit to work for a particular employer after receiving training, nothing prevents writing a contract contingent on the worker's earnings. In the past such contracting would have been impractical, since reliably tracking an individual's income was virtually impossible. The rise of income taxes during the last 80 years changed this, however, and today high-income economies boast sophisticated income-tracking mechanisms for most of the population. Evasion exists, but it is small enough that governments can reliably count on income taxes to fund their operations. More recently, income information has become even more accessible through information technology that has made income verification a fast and cheap activity.

Better income-tracking technology was a necessary development to enable the use of income-contingent payments around the world. Governments, including that of the United States, have been progressively switching to income-contingent loans for students. New businesses are piggy-backing on this information, creating income-contingent contracts with individuals.

The second, much more recent development, is the growing experience of businesses that enable different types of entities—training institutions, employers, individuals, and a wide variety of investors—to sign income-contingent contracts with individuals, such as App Academy and Learners Guild. The increased availability of these platforms has made it possible for some training institutions to implement, in effect, income-contingent tuition fees with their students. The triggering event for these new institutions was the lack of available funding from the U.S. government and the realization that offering income-contingent contracts allowed them to attract students. The income-contingent contracts used by these institutions are referred to in this nascent industry as Income Share Agreements (ISAs).

INCOME SHARE AGREEMENTS

ISAs are contracts whereby a student agrees to pay a percentage of income for a fixed period upon graduation. They are attractive for funding human capital for three reasons:

1) ISAs reduce risk for the individual. Since payments are income contingent, the probability that those who use them to pay for training would subsequently suffer from a liquidity crisis due to fixed payments goes down. Since the repayment period is fixed, the total value of the trainee's payments will be proportional to the trainee's earnings, reducing risk on the trainee's postpayments income. In contrast, as described above, loans *increase* the riskiness of a graduate's postpayment lifetime income *and* have the potential to induce a liquidity crisis at some point.

2) Institution-funded ISAs align incentives between the institution and students. An institution-funded ISA means training providers have "skin in the game," and the effective tuition paid by the student will be proportional to the institution's capacity to place its graduates in gainful employment situations.

3) Employer-funded ISAs improve both the poaching problem and the information problem. An ISA ensures that an employer obtains a return on the investment in the event the worker decides to leave. In principle, the same result can be obtained

with an employer loan, but the ISA improves the contract in two dimensions. First, an ISA protects the employer from a lemon problem: highly valuable employees leave, whereas those offering marginal value stay. An ISA ensures that the upside from an investment remains with the employer. Second, an employer-funded ISA also helps with the information problem, since employers then have an incentive to pay for training only in institutions that offer the type of training employers need.

ISAs IN TODAY'S ENVIRONMENT

The first modern income-contingent financing of education dates from the mid-1970s, when Yale and other universities pioneered an income-contingent payment scheme for their students. The programs did not last long, as they became redundant following the introduction of the U.S. government's federal loans program. Yet, they inspired income-contingent loan programs in multiple countries. The most notable is Australia's Higher Education Contribution Scheme (HECS), which, packaged with multiple changes in Australia's higher education funding system, has inspired other governments to follow suit. The United States included income-contingent loans as an option in the 1990s, and most recently through its Income-Based Repayment program.

Beyond international public initiatives, and amid concerns in the United States of high tuition fees and increased pressure from labor markets to acquire degrees, a plethora of private initiatives have surfaced in the last decade. These include Purdue's Back-a-Boiler program, as well as funding offers from start-up firms such as Upstart, SOFI, PAVE, Education Investments, Lumni, and Vemo, all of which have funded students using future income potential as criteria for underwriting, rather than immediate credit records, family resources, or other collaterable assets.[5]

From this list, Purdue's Back-a-Boiler program stands out as an institution-based initiative. Purdue's experiment with ISAs is the first undertaken by a large public university in the United States, but multiple smaller initiatives, mostly associated with boot camps, have emerged in recent years. By receiving payments linked to graduate's income, these boot camps in effect link tuition fees with success in the marketplace. An institution that charges tuition only in case of success is broadcasting its quality, making it easier for potential students to evaluate where to go.

At the time of writing, no large-scale involvement of employers with income-contingent funding has taken place. Yet, this is a natural solution for the problem of employers not being willing to invest because of a worker's inability to commit to work for them. For employers to recover their investment even when employees leave, contracts between both must include features beyond the traditional wage for employment contract. One straightforward mechanism for achieving this is to have a finance contract—one where the employee pays the employer who offered funding, even if the employee then works elsewhere—in addition to the employment contract. In other words, the alternative is to have a financing contract independent of the employment relationship.

In principle, a contract between employer and employee could be structured with many contingencies. Two simple ones are to pay a loan conditional on leaving, and the other is to make the contract income contingent. A loan partially solves the problem but would again expose the worker to risk. An income-contingent contract, in contrast, achieves both risk reduction for the individual while solving the employer's problem.

REMAINING CHALLENGES FOR INCOME-CONTINGENT FINANCING

The well-trained economist will point out fairly quickly that income-contingent financing still suffers from high agency costs. Students signing ISAs can choose to earn less income after their training is completed; those with an inclination to "take it easy" will find the contract particularly attractive and will make the contract more expensive for enterprising ones. These costs stem from the private information students have about their intentions and capabilities, and the disincentives created by the contract for inducing high effort. The development of income-based financing hinges on the success that particular implementation settings have in keeping those costs relatively low.[6] Indeed, debt is plausibly the instrument with lowest agency costs, but it is also the instrument that concentrates risk on the individual and, in the case of secured loans, asks from them a preexisting stock of assets, coming from parents or previous endeavors. Thus, the mechanism with lowest frictions is, plausibly, the one worst suited for *fairly* funding human capital investments. Income-based repayment offers a better outcome—less risk for the individual with no collateral—but still with costs.

Further improvements in information technology, and increased familiarity with the income-contingent products currently tested by private initiatives and governments, will plausibly reduce those costs, thereby increasing the availability of capital while simultaneously improving risk sharing. However, as with many other economic issues, time along with further research and experience will tell. At stake is individuals getting the training they need in order to take full advantage of new knowledge and technology.

CONCLUSION

The importance of training cannot be overstated. On a global scale, as long as machines do not develop themselves as humans do, human capital development holds the key for raising productivity growth, ensuring that the economic prosperity of the last few centuries continues uninterrupted. Yet, the fact that owners of human capital cannot write contracts specifying what they will do in the future reduces the amount of funds available for investment and narrows the options for the types of funding available. Concretely, individuals need to look for funding and carry a lot of risk.

Two relatively new developments offer an opportunity for improving this problem. First, better income-tracking and verification technology enables the creation of contracts contingent on income. Second, the emergence of platforms that are facilitating those contracts between training institutions, employers, and individuals, creates an opportunity for a natural economic interaction to take place between the stakeholders involved in training.

Notes

1. Two such products include mortgage-backed securities and over-the-counter derivatives. Just the outstanding value of mortgage-backed securities in the United States at the end of 2017 was $2.952 trillion (Board of Governors of the Federal Reserve System 2018). The largest share of over-the-counter derivatives consists of interest rate contracts. The market value of U.S.-denominated interest rate contracts, including FRAs, swaps, options, and other products, was $1.434 trillion at the end of 2017 (Bank of International Settlements 2018).
2. The literature goes back to Pigou but is discussed extensively as early as 1962 in Becker's (1962) seminal work. More recently, Barr (2001) offers a very accessible discussion.
3. We will not venture in this example on what happens when these robots fail to follow instructions from their programmers and start making decisions based on their own objectives.
4. To the extent that bankruptcy is an option for borrowers, loans do transfer a limited amount of risk. The key word for the context of this essay is *limited*.
5. The author is one of Lumni's cofounders.
6. I have argued elsewhere (Palacios 2014) that these costs have probably been over-emphasized by economists.

References

Acemoglu, Daron, and Jörn-Steffen Pischke. 1998. "Why Do Firms Train? Theory and Evidence." *Quarterly Journal of Economics* 113(1): 79–119.

Bank of International Settlements. 2018. *BIS Statistical Bulletin*, Table D7. Basel, Switzerland: Bank of International Settlements. https://www.bis.org/statistics/d7.pdf (accessed May 15, 2018).

Barr, Nicholas A. 2001. *The Welfare State as Piggy Bank: Information, Risk, Uncertainty, and the Role of the State*. Oxford: Oxford University Press.

Becker, Gary S. 1962. "Investment in Human Capital: A Theoretical Analysis." *Journal of Political Economy* 70(5): 9–49.

Board of Governors of the Federal Reserve System. 2018. "Mortgage Debt Outstanding," Table 1.54. Washington, DC: Board of Governors of the Federal Reserve System. https://www.federalreserve.gov/data/mortoutstand/current.htm (accessed May 15, 2018).

Palacios, Miguel. 2014. "Overemphasized Costs and Underemphasized Benefits of Income Contingent Financing." In *Income Contingent Loans*, Bruce Chapman, Timothy Higgins, and Joseph E. Stiglitz, eds. Basingstoke, Hampshire: Palgrave Macmillan, pp. 207–215.

Part 2

Government Investment in Workforce Development

7
Strategy and Capacity of Public Workforce Systems

Richard A. Hobbie

This section addresses six basic questions about government investment in workforce development:

1) What is government workforce development?

2) What are the benefits and costs of government investment in workforce development?

3) How are decisions on government investment in workforce development made in the face of imperfect information and annual federal budgeting?

4) What is the evidence on government investments in workforce development?

5) What are the capacities of states to evaluate the benefits and costs of workforce development programs?

6) How have states and localities applied evidence and other information on, for example, sector approaches, career pathways and employer involvement to enhance the effectiveness of workforce development programs?

FRAMING THE SECTION

For the purposes of this section, the following terms are used:

- **Government** involves the federal, state, and local governments or some combination of these levels of government. It also can involve nongovernmental organizations such as nonprofit organizations, universities, unions, employers, and research/

consulting firms in partnership with government through grants and contracts.

- **Investment** is spending on a product or service that yields a return in the future. This contrasts with consumption, which only yields utility in the present.

- **Investment in workforce development** increases the productivity of labor. It is measured by increases in remuneration to labor, that is, increases in the earnings and fringe benefits of the beneficiaries of the investment.

The discussion of investment in workforce development is limited by excluding (but not entirely) prekindergarten and elementary, secondary, and postsecondary education. These areas are, however, treated explicitly in other sections. The U.S. Government Accountability Office (GAO) has limited its analyses of such programs to those "that are specifically designed to enhance the specific job skills of individuals in order to increase their employability, identify job opportunities, and/or help job seekers obtain employment" (GAO 2011, p. 2).

The GAO further elaborated that programs excluded from workforce development and funded by the federal government could be grouped into the following categories (GAO 2011):

- Economic development programs that aim to increase job opportunities but do not provide services to individuals to enhance their job skills, identify job opportunities, or find employment

- Programs that aim to achieve broad workforce-related goals, such as increasing educational opportunities for minority individuals in particular fields, or improving the status of and working conditions for wage-earning women, but do not provide employment or training services themselves

- Education programs that fund student loans for educational expenses, initiatives for student recruitment and retention, or other student support services

- Programs that support training for training providers, such as vocational rehabilitation specialists who assist disabled individuals seeking employment

To justify government investment, spending not only should yield a future return, but the present value of current and future benefits should exceed the present value of costs. So, what are the benefits and costs, and how could they best inform government decisions? Government policymakers must consider several investment perspectives to make informed decisions (Hollenbeck and Huang 2016; Hollenbeck and Huang 2017). Table 7.1 summarizes the benefits and costs from the three main perspectives—society, participants, and government.

Society's benefits and costs are most important, but they often are unknown and can only be estimated well through expensive, multi-year longitudinal studies of randomly assigned participants and non-participants in control groups, and many assumptions must be made. The estimates of program impacts look at the experiences of participants compared to estimates of what would have happened if they had not participated in the program. The latter is called the "counterfactual," which must be estimated to determine net program impact. Participants must believe the present value of their benefits will exceed the present value of their costs if they are to participate. I use the word *believe* because they probably will not "know," although they might know some follow-up information on prior graduates of a particular program. Governments cover some of the costs in their budgets and look for budget savings to offset costs, but they also look, at least in a qualitative sense,

Table 7.1 Main Benefits and Costs of Government Investment in Workforce Development for Society, Participants, and Government

Benefits/costs	Society	Participants	Government budget
Increased earnings and fringe benefits	Benefit	Benefit	No effect
Increased taxes	No effect	Cost	Benefit
Reduced income transfer payments	No effect	Cost	Benefit
Foregone earnings and fringe benefits	Cost	Cost	No effect
Program operating costs	Cost	No effect	Cost
Capital costs	Cost	No effect	Cost

SOURCE: McConnell and Glazerman (2001).

for the present value of social benefits to outweigh the present value of social costs.

Depending on the perspective, three benefits are most important to such government decision making: 1) increased earnings and fringe benefits, 2) increased taxes paid by beneficiaries (such as payroll and income taxes), and 3) reduced government transfer payments received by beneficiaries (such as unemployment compensation).

Increased earnings and fringe benefits are the most important benefits, both to society and to the participant. These important benefits, however, are not factored into the government budget. Moreover, they usually are unknown, although they are often mentioned by referencing evaluations of comparable programs or potentially correlated program performance measures.

Increased tax payments by participants are an important benefit to government, but they are a cost to participants. They too are often unknown prospectively and not considered explicitly in government budgetary decision making.

Reduced government income transfer payments to participants also are benefits to government, but a cost to participants. And again, in government budgetary decision making, they are often unknown and not explicitly considered.

Neither increased taxes nor reduced government benefit payments are regarded as benefits or costs to society because they are income transfers from beneficiaries to governments or governments to beneficiaries, respectively. Knowing them, however, would at least help decision makers understand the net budget cost of these investments to governments even though they probably only account for the gross cost in their actual budgets.

Depending on the perspective, three costs are most important to government decision making: 1) foregone earnings and fringe benefits, 2) operating costs, and 3) capital costs.

Foregone earnings and fringe benefits are the important costs to society because they reflect lost productivity while individuals don't work at paid jobs and participate in programs instead. These "opportunity costs" represent the social costs of not working while enrolled in a training program. The costs vary depending on the employability of the beneficiaries during program participation, and they can vary depending on the phases of the economic cycle, with expected foregone earnings likely to be lower during periods of high unemployment. As a result, a recession period can be a good time to invest more in workforce development programs, particularly if there is a realistic possibility of a robust economic recovery and increased job opportunities for program participants after they leave a program.

Operating costs and capital costs are factored into the government budget. Although they are also costs to society, the cost is not incurred by participants.

Although the benefit-cost framework can help government officials make informed decisions, imperfect information and government exigencies lead officials to focus mainly on possible benefits and actual program operating and capital costs.

In government budgeting, officials usually have some estimates of annual cost per participant and total cost, but only vague information on possible benefits stemming from research studies that might be uncertain and outdated or on performance measures that might or might not be good proxies for benefits. The federal government has an annual current budget and no capital budget. Hence, it practically treats all costs as if they represent consumption. State and local governments have current and capital budgets, but their capital budgets deal with physical capital, such as school buildings, not human capital.

Advocates of workforce development investment face several challenges. Among the most important are:

- **Poor information on benefits.** Even with estimates of net impact from controlled longitudinal evaluations with random assignment between treatment and control groups, policymakers still must deal with uncertainty. The estimates might be three or more years old. The estimates might be based on impacts for only two to five years. The estimates might depend on a critical assumption about short-term impacts lasting the remainder of the participants' work careers, as much as 40 or more years, a period for which no data have been collected. Estimates are also sensitive to the discount rate used to calculate the present value of benefits, with a relatively low discount rate yielding positive net benefits but a higher rate yielding lower or possibly even negative net benefits (McConnell and Glazerman 2001).

- **Government treatment of investments as consumption.** As much as advocates assert workforce development spending is an investment, many other programs make the same assertions. Government budgeting probably will continue treating such spending as consumption. Although it will behoove workforce development advocates to continue referencing recent research evaluations and valid performance measures, they need to realize the assessments in government budgeting will most likely continue to emphasize quantitative estimates of costs and qualitative considerations of benefits. Nevertheless, research, evaluations, and performance measures should continue to inform decision making not only about funding, but also about the design and operation of these programs.

- **Uneven state government staff capacity in research and evaluation.** A recent scan of state research and evaluation staff capacity by NASWA's Center for Employment Security Education and Research revealed 22 percent of state workforce agencies reported their staff capacity is "nonexistent" or "inadequate," 44 percent reported staff capacity was "fair," and only 34 percent reported staff capacity was "adequate" or "very adequate" (Chocolaad and Wandner 2017).

To make progress on these challenges, government needs to take several measures. These include:

- **Improve data accessibility.** Quarterly wage data on nearly all workers should be more readily accessible to researchers and evaluators through either the federal database collected mainly for child support enforcement purposes (i.e., the National Directory of New Hires) or the state Wage Record Interchange System (which allows states to share in-state wage data with other states where program participants might have been educated, trained, or employed). This would improve the ability of researchers to estimate changes in wages and key components of benefits and costs. Of course, government and researchers must maintain strict privacy of individual wage records as they are used for research and evaluation.

- **Make wider and more effective use of research and evaluations in government decision making.** Research should be more widely and effectively used in decision making, but we also need to understand that governments tend to focus on measurable costs. This largely depends on staff keeping up with the accumulation of evidence and making appropriate use of it in government budget processes. The government, in turn, should invest in staff that can conduct and use research and evaluations wisely.

- **Make more government investments in research and evaluation.** More research is needed to support evidence-based policymaking. Rigorously evaluated pilot and demonstration programs would help lead the way.

Research and evaluation can seem problematic to workforce development programs if the question is framed as, "Do they work?" If the answer is "no," some would say cut or eliminate investments in the programs. A more constructive question might be, "Do they work under certain circumstances and with certain participants?" or "Can they be improved?" Granted, the evidence on workforce development investments has been mixed to date, but if we focus on the reasons for positive results and improve the programs based on evidence, society could gain additional net benefits beyond our recent experience.

THE FIVE ESSAYS

"Results and Returns from Public Investments in Employment and Training," by Demetra Smith Nightingale and Lauren Eyster, outlines the spending in fiscal year 2016 of 10 federal agencies and 9 major federal programs in some of those agencies. The authors report secondary education yielded net benefits to society and students with training connected to in-demand occupations also benefited society and trainees. They also note mounting evidence that career services also are beneficial to participants (see, for example, Poe-Yamagata et al. [2011]). In addition, the authors say that, even though private investment in workforce development is substantially greater than government investment, the private sector leaves a gap because it focuses on more educated and higher-paid workers. Government helps fill that gap by aiming to help less educated and lower-paid workers.

"Research and Evidence-Building Capacity of State Workforce Agencies," by Yvette Chocolaad and Stephen Wandner, summarizes their USDOL-funded report from the National Association of State Workforce agencies (NASWA) Center for Employment Security, Education and Research (CESER). The authors find many state agencies lack the funding and staff capacity to engage in robust research and evaluation: Half the surveyed states reported they had two or fewer full-time equivalent staff to conduct research and evaluation. And only half the surveyed states reported producing at most three in-house research and evaluation studies during the five years from 2011 through 2015.

"State Sector Strategies for Talent Pipeline Systems," by Michael Bartlett and Martin Simon, discusses the development of state talent pipeline systems in education. In general they observe that states are embedding sector strategies into their talent pipeline systems by aligning their elementary, secondary, and postsecondary educational systems with workforce and economic development. The authors say the Workforce Innovation and Opportunity Act of 2014 (WIOA) reinforced the trend toward sector strategies by requiring state plans to describe these strategies. In addition, the Act set aside 15 percent of WIOA funds that can be used by governors in various ways to expand industry sector partnerships and other purposes, such as research and evaluation. In education, they say the Every Student Succeeds Act (ESSA) requires state plans to specify students be provided with work-based learning opportunities with industry professionals and to promote skills attainment needed to fill in-demand jobs.

"Improving Outcomes for Workers and Employers through Mayoral Leadership," by Kathy Amoroso and Evan Amoroso, summarizes three award-winning city workforce development initiatives in Albuquerque, New Mexico, Birmingham, Alabama, and West Sacramento, California. All three cities provide excellent examples of innovations linking education and workforce development with employers by leveraging the power of partnerships, career pathways, industry clusters, and talent pipelines.

"Employer Engagement Policy: Shifting from Customers to Partnerships," by Andy Van Kleunen, reports on the strong trend in workforce development away from single-employer advisor arrangements to multi-employer partnerships and the related challenges to further progress. The author notes that in 2016, the USDOL proposed pilot measures to address this issue, such as: retention with the same employer, repeat business customers, and employer penetration rate (all of which were incorporated into the system in 2017 (USDOL 2017). A major challenge to employer engagement is the need to mitigate employer risks associated with employing unskilled workers who could become more productive employees worth hiring at relatively high wages. Intermediaries employing such workers initially might be an effective way of helping employers partner with the workforce development system without absorbing undue risk of hiring.

References

Chocolaad, Yvette, and Stephen A. Wandner. 2017. *Evidence-Building Capacity in State Workforce Agencies: Insights from a National Scan and Two State Site Visits.* Washington, DC: National Association of State Workforce Agencies, Center for Employment Security Education and Research.

Hollenbeck, Kevin, and Wei-Jang Huang. 2016. "Net Impact and Benefit-Cost Estimates of the Workforce Development System in Washington State." Upjohn Institute Technical Report No. 16-033. Kalamazoo, MI: W.E. Upjohn Institute for Employment Research. https://doi.org/10.17848/tr16-033 (accessed March 7, 2018).

———. 2017. "Net Impact and Benefit-Cost Estimates of the Workforce Development System in Washington State." *Employment Research* 24(1): 1–4. https://doi.org/10.17848/1075-8445.24(1)-1 (accessed March 7, 2018).

McConnell, Sheena, and Steven Glazerman. 2001. *National Job Corps Study: The Benefits and Costs of Job Corps.* Report submitted to U.S. Department of Labor, Employment and Training Administration, Office of Policy Research. Washington, DC: Mathematica Policy Research.

Poe-Yamagata, Eileen, Jacob Benus, Nicholas, Bill, Hugh Carrington, Marios Michaelides, and Ted Shen. 2011. Impact of the Reemployment and Eligibility Assessment (REA) Initiative. Columbia, MD: IMPAQ International.

U.S. Government Accountability Office (GAO). 2011. *Multiple Employment and Training Programs: Providing Information on Colocating Service and Consolidating Administrative Structures Could Promote Efficiencies.* Report to Congressional Requesters. GAO-11-92, Washington, DC: GAO.

U.S. Department of Labor (USDOL), Employment and Training Administration. 2017. *Beyond 101: WIOA Performance Accountability.* Continuing Conversation, 2017 WIOA National Convenings. Washington, DC: USDOL. http://www.futureworksystems.com/docs/wioa/WorkforceGPSResources/Day_2 -1030am_and_3pm_Beyond_101.pdf (accessed September 19, 2018).

8
Results and Returns from Public Investments in Employment and Training

Demetra Smith Nightingale
Lauren Eyster

The nation's public workforce development system is a partnership of federal, state, and local governments charged with providing employment-related services to two customer groups: workers and employers.

Job training is just one of many activities in the nation's workforce development system. Through more than 2,000 local American Job Centers (formerly One-Stop Career Centers), the system operates a free nationwide labor exchange, offers job search and job matching services, and provides access to a range of services to improve the employability of Americans, including training. The goal of the system is to help anyone find a job, especially the unemployed and underemployed, dislocated workers, and veterans. Veterans and their spouses must be given priority for all services. Employment services and job training are also provided to workers with disabilities, older workers, younger and other new workers entering the job market, and people lacking skills that employers in their community demand.

In addition, since 1933, when Congress initially enacted the Wagner-Peyser Act, which provided for "the establishment and maintenance of a national system of public employment offices" (U.S. Department of Labor, Employment and Training Administration, n.d.), the workforce development system has been regularly called upon to mobilize during national economic recessions and in local areas where unemployment rates or economic dislocation is particularly high. The system also facilitates the processing of unemployment insurance claims; administers transitional or subsidized jobs when authorized; arranges to retrain workers whose regular occupations or industries have disappeared; and assists workers, communities, and regions affected by disasters.

The Workforce Investment and Opportunity Act (WIOA) of 2014 is the latest statutory enhancement of the public workforce development system. The new law includes provisions to improve the system overall and to increase the emphasis on and quality of job training. For example, the law intends the workforce development system to be more responsive to businesses, increase access to training, better align training and education programs, expand public access to information about training programs to allow workers to make more informed decisions about possible career options, and increase services to individuals with barriers to employment.

This essay focuses on job training as part of the public workforce development system and how research and evaluation can inform workforce development policy, especially WIOA implementation. The next section provides a brief summary of how the federal government funds job training and highlights evaluation results on the effects of job training on individuals' employment, earnings, and other outcomes that are informing policy discussions.

HOW THE FEDERAL GOVERNMENT FUNDS JOB TRAINING

Across the federal government, 10 agencies support job training programs, with more than 95 percent of the funding coming from four agencies: the U.S. Departments of Labor (45 percent), Education (30 percent), Health and Human Services (13 percent), and Veterans Affairs (8 percent) (Biden 2014). The programs include those funded through WIOA, which serves dislocated workers, adults, youth, persons with disabilities, and individuals with low basic skills, among others. Additional programs, through other legislative authority, also provide funding that can be used for job training as well as other services and activities, such as Temporary Assistance for Needy Families (TANF), Veterans Vocational Rehabilitation and Employment, Supplemental

Nutrition Assistance Program Employment and Training, and Career and Technical Education.

Table 8.1 highlights the major federal funding sources that support these programs, as identified by Barnow and Smith (2015). Not all the activities that comprise these programs are job training because they also include activities such as employment and job placement services that help individuals find and keep a job, rather than learn new skills or receive credentials.

Another way the federal government funds job training is through federal student financial aid, namely the Pell Grant program. Pell Grants, which are needs-based grants to low-income college students, can be used to pay tuition and related college expenses for attendance at two- and four-year institutions for recipients to earn degrees and certificates from eligible programs of study (U.S. Department of Education 2015). The 2015–2016 annual limit for Pell Grants was $5,775 (U.S. Department of Education 2015), but the amount the student receives depends on financial need, costs of attendance, status as a full-time or part-time student, and plans to attend school for a full academic year or less. Barnow and Smith (2015) estimate that over $8 billion in Pell Grants annually go toward funding individuals to earn occupational degrees and certificates, making it the largest means-tested source of funding for job training programs.

WIOA also governs the "public" workforce system, where local boards of representatives of employers, government, nonprofit organizations, education and training, unions, and other organizations administer employment and training programs funded under WIOA. These boards also coordinate with other federally funded programs present in local employment offices—referred to as One-Stop Centers or American Job Centers—such as TANF and Vocational Rehabilitation (Eyster et al. 2016).

The enactment of WIOA complemented the Obama administration's increased focus on skills training. In 2014, Vice President Joe Biden spearheaded a review of job training in the United States to promote strategies that meet the needs of businesses and industry. Although there was little new federal funding, the intent was to shift the available funding through WIOA and the largest discretionary grant programs (such as the 2015 H-1B TechHire Partnership grants) administered by the Department of Labor more toward developing training programs for

Table 8.1 Annual Federal Funding for Major Workforce Development, Education, and Training Programs

Funding source or program	Federal agency	Fiscal year 2016 appropriation
Workforce Innovation and Opportunity Act Title I-A programs	U.S. Department of Labor	$813 million (adult), $1.2 billion (dislocated worker), and $871 million (youth)
Workforce Innovation and Opportunity Act Title II programs	U.S. Department of Education	$596 million
Carl D. Perkins Career and Technical Education Act of 2006 (Perkins IV) (Title I) program	U.S. Department of Education	$1.1 billion
Pell Grant program	U.S. Department of Education	$34.5 billion
Senior Community Service Employment Program (SCSEP)	U.S. Department of Labor	$433 million
Trade Adjustment Assistance (TAA) program	U.S. Department of Labor	$391 million
H1-B Job Training Grants	U.S. Department of Labor	$127 million
Temporary Assistance for Needy Families (TANF) (the share of total funding that is for work-related activities only)	U.S. Department of Health and Human Services	$1.6 billion (FY2015)
Supplemental Nutrition Assistance Program Employment and Training (SNAP-ED only) (allocations to states)	U.S. Department of Agriculture	$408 million

NOTES: Federal programs listed are those with more than $100 million in annual funding, and some (but not all) of the funding can be used for job training as well as for other benefits and services. The TANF amount is 6.7 percent of total TANF spending, which is the most recent estimate of spending that goes to work-related activities; thus, it is based on FY2015 expenditures rather than appropriations.

SOURCES: U.S. Department of Agriculture, Food and Nutrition Services (2015); U.S. Department of Education (2016); U.S. Department of Health and Human Services (2016); U.S. Department of Labor, Employment and Training Administration (2016).

in-demand jobs. The resulting report on "job-driven" training (Biden 2014) highlights a range of ways education and training can be appropriately aligned with labor market needs to assure "workers have the skills they need to secure good jobs that are ready to be filled" (p. 2). The report called for a "Job-Driven Checklist" that uses evidence-based practices to ensure that federally funded job training adheres to the following principles:

- Engaging employers upfront
- Offering work-based learning opportunities
- Making better use of data for accountability
- Measuring and evaluating employment and earnings outcomes
- Promoting a seamless progression from one educational step to another
- Breaking down barriers to access to training and hiring through support services
- Creating regional partnerships to provide a network for employer, training, and related services (Biden 2014, pp. 8–10)

These principles were intended to send a message to the field to focus on job training and to improve the design, implementation, and coordination of federal programs that fund job training.

WHAT WORKS IN JOB TRAINING?

Over the past four decades many evaluations have been conducted to determine the impact of job training and other employment services. The evaluation evidence suggests four job training strategies that can work well.

Training Connected to Work Has the Most Positive Impact for Workers

Not all training is the same, and not all training, whether publicly funded or privately provided, is effective. However, a cross-departmental report that accompanied the job-driven skills principles synthesized considerable evidence from evaluations over many years. The evidence shows that the most effective type of job training is connected directly to work, rather than "stand-alone" training not aligned with jobs in demand (U.S. Departments of Labor, Commerce, Education, and Health and Human Services 2014). Several formal evaluations have found positive impacts on earnings and employment from work-based and work-integrated training models, including registered apprenticeships with particular employers, sectoral and industry-specific training, career pathways, and on-the-job training where a subsidy is offered to employers for a portion of wages for a set period (e.g., 50 percent of salary for six or nine months). Findings from more recent evaluations of integrated education and occupational instruction also show promise, where students are taught basic education skills such as mathematics or English composition, in the context of a particular occupation and skills required on the job.

Training by Postsecondary Institutions Has Positive Returns to Workers and Society

It is common wisdom that postsecondary education, on average, yields positive returns for students as compared to those who do not attend (Card 1999). Much of the federal investment in job training is directed to postsecondary institutions, particularly community colleges. For example, the U.S. Department of Labor invested $2 billion beginning in 2011, through the Trade Adjustment Assistance Community College and Career Training (TAACCCT) grant program, to help community colleges build their capacity to provide innovative programming, services, and partnerships to accelerate learning, improve students' completion of programs, and support labor market success for adult learners (Mikelson et al. 2017).

Research suggests these types of approaches can have positive labor market returns for students, but not all postsecondary degrees and certificates have the same ultimate effect on earnings. For example, students in some fields, such as health and business, appear to achieve substantial increases in earnings, particularly if they receive an associate's degree rather than just a nondegree certificate. Overall, earnings gains are greatest for those studying math and technical fields of study at community colleges and obtaining bachelor or higher degrees in science, engineering, and information technology (Carnevale, Strohl, and Melton 2014; Goldin and Katz 2008; Jacobson, LaLonde, and Sullivan 2005; Jepsen, Troske, and Coomes 2014; Stevens, Kurlaender, and Grosz 2015).

Few studies, however, have examined whether community job training provided by colleges is cost beneficial to society. One recent study showed that federal investments in job training at community colleges, such as from a large grant program like TAACCCT, could begin to yield positive returns to society as soon as the eighth year after the initial investment (Eyster 2017). More cost-benefit studies of actual investments are needed, however, to show which types of community college yield the greatest returns to society.

Counseling and Customer-Focused Career Services Are Important

Several evaluations suggest that the types of intensive services offered in One-Stop Career Centers are important for job seekers and trainees. Veterans who receive assistance from specialized staff have better employment outcomes than veterans who receive general core services (U.S. Department of Labor, Chief Evaluation Office 2015). Trainees who receive assistance in selecting their training do better than those who make their own choices without any career coaching (Mathematica Policy Research 2012). In addition, interim results from the evaluation of Workforce Investment Act programs indicate that individuals who have staff-supported services, such as workshops and counseling, available to them do better than those who have access to only basic self-service resources (McConnell et al. 2016). Similar findings about the importance of student supports have been seen in evaluations of community college programs (Anderson et al. 2016).

Comprehensive and Integrated Models Work for Youth

Youth, especially those out of school and not working, are much more challenging to serve than adults. Fewer formal evaluations of job training for youth have been done than for adults. However, growing evidence indicates that the programs showing the most positive outcomes for youth have a comprehensive set of integrated services, including education, occupational training, counseling, and support services. Residential models such as Job Corps (Schochet, Burghardt, and McConnell 2008) and National Guard Youth Challenge (Millenky et al. 2011) have been found to increase employment outcomes. Comprehensive programs, though, are costly, limiting the number of young people who can be served. As with adults, there is evidence that industry-focused training is important for youth. Career academies, for example, where high schools prepare students for particular industries and sectors, have positive and long-lasting impacts on labor market outcomes, particularly for young men (Kemple 2008). Recent reports from an evaluation of the YouthBuild program document positive impacts of that construction industry-based comprehensive model (MDRC 2012).

Public Investment in Training Fills a "Gap"

Most job training in the United States is provided by employers. Public funding for training comes mainly from the federal government, although some states invest considerable resources in training, usually in tandem with the federal funding. The private sector spends 8 to 10 times as much as the public sector (federal and state combined) each year on training (Carnevale, Strohl, and Gulish 2015; Mikelson and Nightingale 2004). Training at work is clearly important, especially for company-specific purposes (Lerman, McKernan, and Riegg 2004). Surveys indicate, though, that employer-provided training is more likely to go to more-educated and higher-level workers. More highly educated and highly paid employees are twice as likely to receive employer-provided training as lower-level and less-educated workers. The 2016 Training Industry Report's recent survey suggests more than 60 percent of those receiving training by employers are executives, managers, and other "exempt" employees (*Training Magazine* 2016).

The public workforce system's very limited funding only allows serving a small fraction of the 150 million or so workers in the nation. The public system also tends to serve smaller businesses and newer businesses by identifying available workers and training them, because many of those businesses do not have the same level of resources that larger, established companies have. Thus, the public system is training workers who might not otherwise receive it—namely, those with middle and lower skills and wages, and providing training for businesses that might not have the resources to do it on their own. However, the system is constrained by very limited funding in reaching all workers and businesses that could use the services.

HOW MIGHT WIOA CHANGE THE SYSTEM TO IMPROVE PARTICIPANT OUTCOMES?

WIOA is the latest congressional legislation regarding the workforce development and training system. It reinforces many of the evidence-based approaches just mentioned. WIOA continues some of the basic parameters of the Workforce Investment Act, such as the emphasis on universal services to both job seekers and employers, and requiring that veterans and eligible spouses receive priority of service. The law also includes the following provisions and changes that should improve the workforce development system and continue to build evidence about "what works":

More demand-driven. The full range of work-related evidence-based training noted previously is allowable under WIOA. Local workforce boards are now required to develop industry or sector partnerships to improve the connection between the job training provided and the skills that are in demand by employers. WIOA also explicitly endorses the most evidence-based approach by recognizing the importance of workplace training, including endorsing registered apprenticeships with specific employers, increasing the subsidy amount employers can receive through their participation in on-the-job training, and expanding the support of work experience for youth.

More flexibility in service delivery. Rather than requiring a sequence of services before offering training as was the case under WIA, WIOA allows staff to work with customers to develop the most appropriate plans, including training. The redefinition of core and intensive services also reinforces the importance of the client-focused services and assistance, while allowing states and local boards to use sophisticated electronic information tools for those preferring self-directed services.

Alignment of workforce development and other systems. WIOA aligns workforce development, employment services, adult education, economic development, and vocational rehabilitation. The joint federal guidance is sending a clear message about the importance of alignment and partnerships.

Revised performance accountability requirements to improve results. The new performance measures apply to the entire WIOA system: workforce development, adult education, employment services, and vocational rehabilitation.

Expanded public access to data about the performance of training programs. The latest federal guidance indicates new consumer tools will be available to compare training programs so workers can make more informed decisions about their options. In addition, WIOA calls for federal funding to states to create and improve longitudinal data systems, an investment that is critical to better track program performance and outcomes over time.

Increased services to individuals with barriers to employment. WIOA increases the emphasis on both job training and serving those with barriers to employment, who often require supportive services such as child care, transportation, and referrals to other services in order to succeed in training. WIOA shifts youth funding to devote more focus on out-of-school youth than on in-school youth, who may have other programs and resources available to help them. The shift is in keeping with the WIOA priority on those with barriers to employment.

Increased emphasis on evaluation and evidence. Several provisions in WIOA specifically require formal evaluations so federal agencies and states can test the effectiveness of strategies and approaches, including career pathways models that can train workers in health care and early childhood education occupations, strategies for expanding gender equity in occupations, including nontraditional job training, and tests of other promising approaches to improve outcomes. Adding to the knowledge about effective programming is critical, and WIOA's future evaluations can make a major contribution about what works.

The challenge under WIOA will be how to achieve better participant outcomes and program performance, increase services to those with barriers to employment, strengthen performance accountability, increase cross-agency integration, and meet the skills needs demanded by employers. The law provides the framework for doing so, but current appropriations may not be enough to support these goals. Federal funding for job training, through WIOA and other grants, is helping to fill in the gaps and direct training priorities, such as recent grants for building apprenticeships. However, state and local implementers may need to build partnerships beyond WIOA to gradually recalibrate the system to meet the mandates in the new law.

References

Anderson, Theresa, Lauren Eyster, Robert I. Lerman, Maureen Conway, Ranita Jain, and Marcela Montes. 2016. *Implementation of Accelerating Opportunity: Final Implementation Findings with Lessons from the Field*. Washington, DC: Urban Institute.

Barnow, Burt S., and Jeffrey A. Smith. 2015. "Employment and Training Programs." NBER Working Paper No. 21659. Cambridge, MA: National Bureau of Economic Research.

Biden, Joe. 2014. *Ready to Work: Job-Driven Training and American Opportunity*. Report to the President of the United States. Washington, DC: The White House.

Card, David. 1999. "The Causal Effect of Education on Earnings." In *Handbook of Labor Economics, Vol. 3, Part A*, Orley Ashenfelter and David Card, eds. Amsterdam: Elsevier, pp. 1802–1863.

Carnevale, Anthony P., Jeff Strohl, and Artem Gulish. 2015. *College Is Just the Beginning: Employers' Role in the $1.1 Trillion Education and Training System*. Washington, DC: Georgetown University, Center on Education and the Workforce.

Carnevale, Anthony P., Jeff Strohl, and Michelle Melton. 2014. *What's It Worth? The Economic Value of College Majors*. Washington, DC: Georgetown University, Center on Education and the Workforce.

Eyster, Lauren. 2017. "A Cost-Benefit Analysis of Federal Investments in Job Training at Community Colleges." PhD diss., George Washington University.

Eyster, Lauren, Christin Durham, Michelle Van Noy, and Neil Damron. 2016. *Understanding Local Workforce Systems*. Washington, DC: The Urban Institute.

Goldin, Claudia, and Lawrence F. Katz. 2008. *The Race between Education and Technology*. Cambridge, MA: Belknap Press of the Harvard University Press.

Jacobson, Louis, Robert LaLonde, and Daniel G. Sullivan. 2005. "Estimating the Returns to Community College Schooling for Displaced Workers." *Journal of Econometrics* 125(1–2): 271–304.

Jepsen, Christopher, Kenneth Troske, and Paul Coomes. 2014. "The Labor-Market Returns to Community College Degrees, Diplomas, and Certificates." *Journal of Labor Economics* 32(1): 95–121.

Kemple, James J. (with Cynthia J. Willmer). 2008. *Career Academies: Long-Term Impacts on Labor Market Outcomes, Educational Attainment, and Transitions to Adulthood*. New York: MDRC.

Lerman, Robert I., Signe-Mary McKernan, and Stephanie Riegg. 2004. "The Scope of Employer-Provided Training in the United States: Who, What, Where, and How Much?" In *Job Training Policy in the United States*, Christopher J. O'Leary, Robert A. Straits, and Stephen A. Wandner, eds. Kalamazoo, MI: W.E. Upjohn Institute for Employment Research, pp. 211–244.

Mathematica Policy Research. 2012. "Larger Training Awards and Counseling Improve Cost Effectiveness, Long Term Impacts of Individual Training Accounts." *In Focus*. Washington, DC: Mathematica Policy Research.

McConnell, Sheena, Kenneth Fortson, Dana Rotz, Peter Schochet, Paul Burkander, Linda Rosenberg, Annalisa Mastri, and Ronald D'Amico. 2016. *Providing Public Workforce Services to Job Seekers: 15-Month Findings on the WIA Adult and Dislocated Worker Programs*. Princeton, NJ: Mathematica Policy Research.

MDRC. 2012. *Building a Future: Interim Impact Findings from the YouthBuild Evaluation*. New York: MDRC.

Mikelson, Kelly, Lauren Eyster, Christin Durham, and Elissa Cohen. 2017. *TAACCCT Goals, Designs, and Evaluation*. Washington, DC: The Urban Institute.

Mikelson, Kelly, and Demetra Smith Nightingale. 2004. *Estimating Public and Private Expenditures on Occupational Training in the United States*. Washington, DC: The Urban Institute.

Millenky, Megan, Dan Bloom, Sara Muller-Ravet, and Joseph Broadus. 2011. *Staying on Course: Three Year Results of the National Guard Youth Challenge Evaluation*. New York: MDRC.

Schochet, Peter Z., John Burghardt, and Sheena McConnell. 2008. "Does Job Corps Work? Impact Findings from the National Job Corps Study." *American Economic Review* 98(5): 1864–1866.

Stevens, Ann Huff, Michal Kurlaender, and Michel Grosz, M. 2015. "Career and Technical Education and Labor Market Outcomes: Evidence from California Community Colleges." NBER Working Paper No. 21137. Cambridge, MA: National Bureau of Economic Research.

Training Magazine. 2016. "2016 Training Industry Report." November/December. https://trainingmag.com/trgmag-article/2o16-training-industry-report (accessed March 7, 2018).

U.S. Department of Agriculture, Food and Nutrition Services. 2015. "SNAP-ED FY2016 Allocations." Washington, DC: U.S. Department of Agriculture. https://snaped.fns.usda.gov/administration/funding-allocations (accessed March 23, 2018).

U.S. Department of Education. 2015. *Federal Pell Grant Program.* Washington, DC: U.S. Department of Education. http://www2.ed.gov/programs/fpg/index.html (accessed March 7, 2018).

———. 2016. *FY16 Congressional Action.* Washington, DC: U.S. Department of Education. https://www2.ed.gov/about/overview/budget/budget16/16action.pdf (accessed March 7, 2018).

U.S. Department of Health and Human Services. 2016. "FY2016 Budget in Brief." Administration for Children and Families. Washington, DC: U.S. Department of Health and Human Services. https://www.hhs.gov/about/budget/budget-in-brief/acf/mandatory/index.html (accessed March 23, 2018).

U.S. Department of Labor, Chief Evaluation Office. 2015. "Women Veterans Who Get Employment Services from Veterans Specialists Earn More." *Evaluation Snapshot.* Washington, DC: U.S. Department of Labor. https://www.dol.gov/asp/evaluation/snapshots/20150428VeteransStudySnapshot.pdf (accessed March 7, 2018).

U.S. Department of Labor, Employment and Training Administration, Office of Adult Services. n.d. *Wagner-Peyser Act of 1933 as Amended by the Workforce Investment Act of 1998.* Washington, DC: U.S. Department of Labor. https://www.doleta.gov/programs/w-pact_amended98.cfm (accessed March 7, 2018).

U.S. Department of Labor, Employment and Training Administration. 2016. "Summary of Appropriation Budget Authority, Fiscal Year 2016." Updated 6/27/2016. Washington, DC: U.S. Department of Labor. https://www.doleta.gov/budget/docs/16app$_160627.pdf (accessed March 23, 2018).

U.S. Departments of Labor, Commerce, Education, and Health and Human Services. 2014. "What Works in Job Training: A Synthesis of the Evidence." https://www.dol.gov/asp/evaluation/jdt/jdt.pdf (accessed March 7, 2018).

9
Research and Evidence-Building Capacity of State Workforce Agencies

Yvette Chocolaad
Stephen Wandner

With support from the U.S. Department of Labor and federal funds, state workforce agencies and their local partners administer workforce development and unemployment insurance programs that are designed to reduce labor market friction, ensure better matching of workers with jobs, provide temporary income support during certain periods of unemployment, and increase job-seeker skills to the ultimate benefit of both employers and job seekers. New federal workforce development legislation enacted in 2014, the Workforce Innovation and Opportunity Act (WIOA), emphasizes the use of labor market and other workforce information by state policymakers and program managers to drive customer and frontline staff decision making, to hold state workforce agencies and local workforce entities accountable for outcomes, and to inform program and policy development. That statute includes a requirement that state agencies use set-aside funds to conduct evaluations of their workforce development activities. The U.S. Department of Labor has interpreted this requirement as supportive of a broad array of evaluation types.

State workforce programs are among the few federally funded grant programs with a history of using administrative data sets to implement performance accountability systems, and state workforce agencies have long been involved in rigorous research and evaluations focused on reemployment services, job search assistance, and training (Wandner 2010). Despite this history, systematic national information on the capacity of state workforce agencies to conduct research and evaluations did not exist at the time of WIOA's passage. Although a few agencies appeared to have significant research capacity, funding and staffing limitations impeded or even stalled research and evaluation activities in many others. The U.S. Department of Labor funded the Center for Employment Security Education and Research, the technical assistance and research arm of the National Association of State Workforce Agencies (NASWA), to help fill the knowledge gap by capturing information, through a national scan, on the current capacity of state workforce agencies to conduct research and evaluations and on recent state research and evaluation products. As part of the effort, NASWA researchers also developed two state case studies, based on in-depth, semistructured interviews in Ohio and Washington, to help illuminate factors and practices that enable their higher volume and broader range of workforce research and evaluation activity. The goals were not only to document existing capacity in the state agencies, but also to help agencies learn from other agencies' experiences and practices, and to identify mechanisms likely to enhance research and evaluation activity at the state and cross-state levels aligned with the new workforce legislation.[1]

The scan was released in June 2016 to the 50 state workforce agencies plus the agencies in D.C., Guam, and Puerto Rico; 41 jurisdictions responded with details on their agencies' recent research and evaluation efforts. On the demand side, state workforce agencies reported that policymakers in their states are asking important questions that workforce agency research and evaluations could help answer. On the supply side, however, the results from the national scan demonstrate that many agencies lack the staff capacity and funding to implement a robust research agenda necessary to be learning organizations that can develop customized, evidence-based approaches to service provision. Ohio and Washington are among the minority of agencies with ongoing significant workforce research and evaluation activity, backed by longitudinal administrative data sets. Although their models differ, both states have achieved substantial research accomplishments based on a long history of using evidence to support policy development, critical federal and state funding support, buy-in from agency heads and state leaders, and access to well-led, high-capacity research units.

NATIONAL SCAN: FINDINGS ON EVIDENCE-BUILDING CAPACITY

Of the 41 state workforce agencies participating in the national scan, all but one reports that there is demand—from the governor's office, the legislature, or within the agency—for the kinds of information workforce research and evaluations can yield. We asked the agencies to list the most pressing workforce development research questions their states are facing. The agency responses include some questions related to improving program administration and understanding customers and their barriers, but they are heavily weighted toward understanding labor markets, measuring program performance and outcomes, and measuring program impacts and effectiveness (Table 9.1).

What is the capacity in the agencies to address this demand for information? Organizationally, three-quarters of the agencies report that there is at least one unit in the agency that initiates and advances research and evaluation efforts. Also, 80 percent of the agencies report having partnered with or having relied on outside researchers to conduct at least one research or evaluation effort from 2011 through 2015. We collected information on these internal research units and outside research partners, and present it in the full report (Chocolaad and Wandner 2017).

Findings on staff capacity and funding (the inputs), research and evaluation activity, and research and evaluation methods used (the products) were less encouraging. Evidence-building capacity varies tremendously by state, and while some states published a large number of research products, half reported producing three or fewer in-house research and evaluation studies over the five-year period from 2011 through 2015. Looking at research and evaluation conducted with outside contractors or other partners, the median reported output was two research and evaluation products over this same period. In establishing a baseline, it is also worth noting that only a small number of agencies reported employing (directly or through contracts or partnerships) quasi-experimental (14 agencies) or experimental (7 agencies) research methods for one or more studies. To help create a database of recent research products, the state workforce agencies provided short summaries of their research and evaluation products, a Web link to their online research publications, or a combination of these.

Table 9.1 Examples of States' Most Pressing Questions for Workforce Agency Research and Evaluation

Program impacts/effectiveness	• Are the educational programs provided to offenders by the state prison helpful in obtaining employment after release?
	• What is the effectiveness of UI profiling?
	• What are optimal policies or incentive mechanisms that encourage greatest return on investment?
	• What is the relationship of TANF participation to successful workforce outcomes?
	• What is the effectiveness of refugee training services?
Program performance/outcomes	• Are participants making family-sustaining wages?
	• What are the workforce outcomes from training programs?
	• What are the employment and wage outcomes of degree and certificate program completers?
	• What are the outcomes of Department of Labor and Department of Public Health and Human Services workforce programs (WIOA, RESEA, TANF)?
	• What are the wage and employment outcomes of apprentices? Does the increase in wages result in sufficient tax revenue to justify an employer tax credit?
Development of labor market data	• How are demographic changes impacting the labor force?
	• What are the demographics of minimum wage workers?
	• Where can employers find qualified workers?
	• What are the new industry clusters (e.g., advanced manufacturing)?
	• Who are the long-term unemployed?

Customers and their barriers

- What can be done to encourage higher labor force participation rates in targeted populations?
- What tools should we create to evaluate client education and skills gaps?
- Why are participants not successful, or why do they drop out?
- What are the barriers to changing jobs for those currently employed?
- What can be done to improve commuter transportation issues?

Program administration/operations

- What is the accuracy and utility value of WIOA performance measures?
- How do we address declining research budgets but increasing demand for data and insight?
- How can we build on programs that are working?
- Are we maximizing services across programs, particularly across multiple agencies?
- How can we increase the number of apprenticeships?

NOTE: TANF is the Temporary Assistance to Needy Families program; WIOA is the Workforce Innovation and Opportunity Act program; RESEA is the Reemployment Services and Eligibility Assessment program.
SOURCE: Chocolaad and Wandner (2017).

We asked the state workforce agencies to describe their current internal research and evaluation staff capacity, taking into account not only staffing levels but also staff experience and research skills. Twenty percent of the agencies reported that their staff capacity was "inadequate"; 44 percent reported capacity was "fair"; 29 percent reported capacity was "adequate"; and the remaining states were at either end of the spectrum, reporting "nonexistent" (2 percent) or "very adequate" (5 percent) research staff capacity.

We collected information on the research and evaluation skill areas for which agencies reported having sufficient capacity or a need for technical assistance or additional capacity. This information will help enable the U.S. Department of Labor to design and deliver support and technical assistance to state agencies, and also help state agencies share practices and strategies with their peers. Across 15 skill areas, a minority of agencies (ranging from 10 to 44 percent) report having sufficient capacity. For example, 32 percent reported sufficient capacity to access and analyze large databases, and 19 percent reported sufficient capacity to employ quasi-experimental evaluation or demonstration designs. Depending on the skill area, at least 40 percent and up to 78 percent of the agencies reported that they would like some assistance or capacity (in the case of agencies with zero capacity) or more assistance or capacity (in the case of states with some but insufficient capacity). For example, 46 percent reported that they would like some or more capacity performing regression analyses; 63 percent reported that they would like some or more capacity communicating research results in a way administrators, policymakers, or customers can understand and use; and 78 percent reported that they would like some or more capacity conducting research using qualitative methods (e.g., interviews and field studies).

Focusing on two research skill areas most often associated with evidence-based policymaking—conducting experiments and employing quasi-experimental designs—only a handful of the agencies reported having sufficient capacity, and about half the agencies reported that they either had zero capacity or did not know if they had capacity.[2]

Looking more narrowly at staffing levels, most of the agencies were able to provide an estimate of the number of full-time equivalent agency staff currently working on research and evaluation projects:

- Several agencies reported that they had zero research staff.
- A quarter of the agencies reported less than one full-time equivalent staff.
- Half the agencies reported two or fewer full-time equivalent staff.

We recognize that these numbers do not paint a complete picture of staff capacity for agencies that rely on outside research partners or contractors to support their research activity. Outside partners can be an important supplement to internal capacity. At the same time, there are different benefits to having experts on staff, such as more opportunities to leverage the combination of institutional knowledge and research and data expertise.

Considering federal, state, and private funding sources, 20 percent of the 41 agencies reported that they spent zero dollars on research and evaluations in calendar year 2015. Another 20 percent reported that they spent less than $100,000, and 37 percent report spending more than $100,000. The remaining quarter of the agencies reported spending some funds on research and evaluation in calendar year 2015, but they did not provide an estimated spending level. The responses to this and other questions show agency funding sources varied, and some agencies drew upon a range of funding sources. The site visits and scan data, however, also demonstrated that an important source of funding has been the U.S. Department of Labor's Workforce Data Quality Initiative grants, but some states have not received these grants and others have exhausted their funds.

Almost 30 percent of agencies report that they consider their research and evaluation funding adequate. From the majority that report inadequate funding levels, we collected insights on the consequences of inadequate funding for their ability to be learning organizations to the benefit of their customers and the workforce system more generally. Examples of these insights include the following:

- "The system is less able to anticipate changes in trends and therefore remains reactionary. It reduces the ability to fulfill requests and for customers to make timely data-driven decisions."
- ". . . harder to make sound policy decisions without proper research."

- ". . . limited knowledge, unknown effectiveness, limited transparency, reduced consumer choice."

- "The extent of our research is limited by resources available; [we need] more resources."

- ". . . would lead to more analysis, more innovation, and more robust 'evidence-based' decision-making."

Looking across all state workforce agency responses regarding staff capacity, funding, and research output from calendar year 2011 through 2015, the authors estimate that roughly one-third of the agencies appear to have had adequate or fair staff capacity and funding, and fairly active data development and research efforts.

FINDINGS FROM THE OHIO AND WASHINGTON SITE VISITS

Ohio and Washington are among the state workforce agencies that report substantial research and evaluation capacity, and they are interesting case studies because their models differ. The Ohio Department of Job and Family Services works in partnership with Ohio State University, which oversees the longitudinal administrative data set of their agency, and other Ohio agencies, to produce research and evaluation products. Washington's Employment Security Department collaborates with an internal state entity, housed in the governor's office, which oversees the state's longitudinal administrative data set. Washington's workforce board, the Workforce Education and Training Coordinating Board, also conducts research and evaluations. Washington also received crucial funding support from the Department of Labor's Workforce Data Quality Initiative and the Department of Education's State Longitudinal Data Systems grants, which seeded the development of the data infrastructure necessary to make research activity possible and efficient, and supported research activity.

Common factors contributing to the substantial workforce research activity evident in Ohio and Washington include a history and culture in the government of using workforce research to inform policy and practice. These states have buy-in, leadership, and support from the office of the governor and agency heads. Both states have developed a cross-agency longitudinal administrative data set covering a range of public programs, including Unemployment Insurance wage record data, and have a long history of sharing data between the state workforce development and education agencies. They also rely on a neutral administrative entity to collect data across agencies and govern the longitudinal administrative data set, and this entity employs staff with great knowledge of the individual agency data sets (e.g., former agency staff who have worked with the data for a long time). Data governance, data access procedures, and security standards have been addressed and maintained as high priorities.

Both states also employ strategies to develop and maintain trust and information sharing among state agencies and their staff; have data and research staff work environments that are mission driven, collegial, and allow research staff room to innovate, thus retaining talented staff; and produce objective research products, in a politically neutral environment, upon which policymakers can rely for information to inform decisions.

Finally, Washington has enacted legislation to institutionalize its cross-agency longitudinal administrative data set and the key roles and responsibilities for the entities engaged in data and research efforts. Legislation is being pursued in Ohio to help institutionalize its model.

INSIGHTS

For the many state workforce agencies that desire to be learning organizations using evidence to drive decisions but need assistance with seed funding and technical know-how, getting to the same point as Ohio and Washington will be difficult. Federal leadership and support will be key to success, given declining funding in the workforce system,[3] research staff skills training needs, and the many new demands the WIOA creates for labor market and workforce information. Providing additional rounds of Workforce Data Quality Initiative and State Longitudinal Data Systems grants, and supporting other targeted funding such as Workforce Information Grants, would greatly assist the development and maintenance of longitudinal data sets and agency research capacity. State workforce agencies also seek training and technical assistance.

Beyond funding and technical assistance, consideration should be given to the question of how to both supplement and leverage individual state efforts. Even in many of the workforce agencies with greater evidence-building capacity, various limitations were often noted. Research output alone is not adequate to address all information needs, especially for impact and effectiveness studies, much less to ensure routine replication. Our interpretation is that many, if not all, states would benefit from opportunities to work in multistate environments that can efficiently support not only the needs of individual state workforce agencies but also cross-state research and evaluation efforts and a national research agenda.

While the development of evidence-building capacity and a longitudinal administrative data set in Ohio and Washington relied on a state history of using research to inform policy, staff from both states do not believe such a history is a necessary condition. They emphasized that state workforce agencies in states that do not have a strong history of using research to inform policy can learn and borrow from the practices, experiences, and successes of Ohio, Washington, and other states with strong research and evaluation capacity.

Agencies should focus on demonstrating data "wins" that draw the support and engagement of key staff in the governor's office and legislature, thus creating a stronger culture in the state for workforce research and evaluation, one success at a time. As the benefits of research and evaluation products become more obvious to policymakers, ongoing funding to maintain a longitudinal administrative data set and research staff capacity will also need to be addressed.

Notes

1. For additional details, see Chocolaad and Wandner (2017), the full report upon which this essay is based.
2. Although a great number of experimental and quasi-experimental evaluations and demonstrations have been conducted for public workforce programs, the great majority of them have been funded by the U.S. Department of Labor and conducted by outside research organizations.
3. Federal funding for major workforce development grants has fallen by 30 percent or more in inflation-adjusted terms over the past 15 years. The more targeted U.S. Department of Labor core grants to states for the development of labor market information, tools, and analysis have also experienced reductions in inflation-

adjusted terms. The Bureau of Labor Statistics' Federal/State Cooperative Statistics Program grant was funded at $263 million in fiscal year 2016, compared to its $286 million value in fiscal year 2003 (in 2016 $). Similarly, the Employment and Training Administration's Workforce Information Grants were funded at $32 million in fiscal year 2016, compared to $50 million in fiscal year 2003 (in 2016 $). In this budget environment, the State Longitudinal Data Systems and Workforce Data Quality Initiative grants have been important sources of support for the development of longitudinal administrative data sets and research and analysis.

References

Chocolaad, Yvette, and Stephen A. Wandner. 2017. *Evidence-Building Capacity in State Workforce Agencies: Insights from a National Scan and Two State Site Visits.* Washington, DC: National Association of State Workforce Agencies, Center for Employment Security Education and Research. https://www.naswa.org/assets/utilities/serve.cfm?gid=938B2045-5E83-45AC-BEAA-80AAD19725D0 (accessed March 14, 2018).
Wandner, Stephen. 2010. *Solving the Reemployment Puzzle: From Research to Policy.* Kalamazoo, MI: W.E. Upjohn Institute for Employment Research.

10
State Sector Strategies for Talent Pipeline Systems

Michael Bartlett
Martin Simon

As state economies continue to experience low overall levels of unemployment, the greatest challenge facing many American businesses seeking to grow and remain competitive is finding the talent they need. Although estimates of the size and severity of the skills gap vary and arguments persist about the existence of a skills gap or mismatch, there is consensus that there is a long-term need to focus on ensuring that state systems for education and training meet the needs of their state's industries and ensure that workers can access good careers across their lifetimes. Governors, state legislators, and policy leaders have had a clear focus on a variety of strategies that build these "talent pipeline" systems. Sector strategies are a group of approaches being implemented by many states to build their talent pipeline systems through supporting regional industry sector partnerships.

Although they go by many names, the core focus of industry sector partnerships is to bring together businesses at scale to align education and training to broader economic needs. Sector partnerships serve as proven, successful vehicles for communicating the needs of industry to the public sector, ultimately serving both workers and industry. States play a key role in supporting industry sector partnerships by providing an environment in which local and regional efforts can grow and be sustained. States are increasingly working to embed sector strategies into their broader talent pipeline ecosystem by aligning K–12 and postsecondary education, workforce development, and economic development.

This chapter briefly summarizes the larger trends driving the need for these partnerships, outlines the core capabilities of high-quality state systems to guide states in scaling industry sector partnerships, and posits a new opportunity and common language to connect sector strategies, career pathways, and industry clusters as the core of states' broader talent pipeline systems.

LABOR MARKET FORCES ACCELERATE THE IMPORTANCE OF SECTOR STRATEGIES

Several intersecting labor market forces are increasing the importance of industry sector partnerships across states. As state economies improved after the Great Recession, record-low levels of unemployment leading to a tight labor market threaten to constrain the ability of businesses to grow. Although several states hope to increase their rates of workforce participation to address this threat, they are constrained because the levels and types of educational attainment among their populations do not match projected workforce demands. For example, the Georgetown University Center on Education and the Workforce has estimated that more than 65 percent of jobs will require some postsecondary education by 2020 (Carnevale, Smith, and Strohl 2013), but only 45.8 percent of Americans currently have a certificate, associate's degree, bachelor's degree, or above (Lumina Foundation 2017). Although predictions vary, this mismatch could lead to a shortage of more than five million workers with postsecondary credentials by 2020 (Carnevale, Smith, and Strohl 2013). As jobs increasingly require higher levels of education and training, industry engagement strategies will need to be more focused on supporting long-term educational attainment.

Compounding these changes are the retirements of baby boomers (people born between 1946 and 1964). In 2002 baby boomers made up 60 percent of workers across all industries, and while the Great Recession caused some workers to postpone retirement, that pent-up demand is now accelerating the retirement rate—by 2013, baby boomers comprised only 46 percent of the labor market (Deloitte 2015). These retirements seem likely to exacerbate educational attainment gaps because the workers filling these positions are more likely to be from populations that have lower levels of educational attainment, including immigrants and racial and ethnic minorities. In fact, employers are already experiencing the impact of this and other trends, with routine surveys of employers consistently citing difficulties finding skilled workers as a primary concern for CEOs and even as a constraint on growth (Manpower Group 2015). Deloitte's *2016 Global Manufacturing Competitiveness Index*, a survey of manufacturing executives, indicates that talent remains the top-ranked driver of a country's competitiveness (Deloitte 2016).

Considering these challenges, state government and business leaders have worked to think differently about how the public and private sectors can partner to meet their common goals. Industry sector partnerships have a track record of addressing these challenges by bringing together leading employers in specific sectors with education, training, and economic development organizations to find solutions. Furthermore, states have more opportunities today to support such approaches with new flexibility under the Workforce Innovation and Opportunity Act (WIOA), as well as the opportunity to make connections to K–12 education through the flexibility of the Every Student Succeeds Act (ESSA).

OPPORTUNITIES THROUGH FEDERAL LEGISLATION

In addition to state actions to support and expand industry sector partnerships, the passage of WIOA codified support for industry sector partnerships as a key state strategy to address current and future workforce challenges. WIOA offers state (and local) leaders an opportunity to think across systems about strategies to address existing workforce challenges and position such efforts to address future challenges. By requiring states to describe their sector strategies in their state plans, WIOA has given them an opportunity to develop a consensus on strategies that support industry sector partnerships throughout the state. WIOA encourages states to make coordinated investments in industry sector partnerships and provides governors and state workforce development boards a chance to ensure their industry sector partnerships have the components and partners necessary for success. Washington State used the WIOA state planning process to set definitions and goals for its sector partnerships across the state as a collaboration of the business, education, and workforce and economic development sectors (Bartlett 2018).

Another example is Colorado where they launched the "Next Generation of Sector Partnerships." It is a new model for increasing the depth and scope of expanding and scaling sector partnerships championed by the state's workforce development board (Colorado Workforce Development Council), which serves as an industry-led, cross-agency coalition charged with implementing the governor's economic development plan, the "Colorado Blueprint,"[1] particularly, the core objective "to educate and train the workforce of the future." Since launching the Next Generation of Sector Partnerships, Colorado has used state and local WIOA funds to grow its sector partnerships to include 23 partnerships representing almost every geographic area in the state and seven different industries.

One of the important tools available to governors under WIOA is each governor's 15 percent set-aside funding. These funds can be used strategically in a variety of ways to scale up the formation of industry sector partnerships. One way is to provide incentive funds through competitive grants to support pilot efforts. Another is to provide technical assistance and professional development to build regional capacity to scale partnerships that can include opportunities among regional stakeholders to gain a mutual understanding of the sector partnership model and learn about effective industry analysis and employer engagement approaches. States can also use the funds to identify best practices and share them across regions. With the set-aside fully restored under WIOA, more states are investing these funds in support of industry sector partnerships. An example of several of these strategies being put into action is taking place in New Jersey. New Jersey is using a part of their WIOA set-aside to support the creation of Talent Networks across the state, including $8.4 million in grants to create regional Talent Development Centers that will serve as clearing houses for strategies to develop and implement career pathways in a specific industry (New Jersey Department of Labor and Workforce Development, n.d.). Talent Networks will be tasked with working with partners across education, the private sector, and workforce development professions to develop new industry partnerships to meet employer demand.

In addition to WIOA, passage of the ESSA has given states an opportunity to develop stronger alignment between K–12 education and the workforce, as well as require states to provide connections to employers and the world of work. For example, state ESSA plans must promote skills attainment important to in-demand occupations or industries in the state as well as demonstrate that the state will provide work-based learning opportunities that provide students in-depth interaction with industry professionals. While many state plans have yet to be finalized, more than a dozen states have discussed building various measures of career readiness into their school accountability systems.

HIGH-QUALITY STATE SYSTEMS TO BRING SECTOR PARTNERSHIPS TO SCALE

As industry sector strategies have evolved, they provide an important connection between workforce development, education, and economic development by directly addressing the needs of employers in becoming more productive and competitive and aligning the education and training efforts with those needs. The most effective state strategies in support of regional industry sector partnerships are coordinated across state agencies to align policy, integrate resources, and define and agree on performance metrics. High-quality industry sector partnerships cannot be sustained without measuring their impact for employers, workers, and the community, and they require a systemic approach that embeds funding in existing funding streams and moves beyond pilot funding. States are best positioned to drive this systemic change and move from supporting transactional activities to transformative strategies.[2]

The state role in industry sector partnerships has evolved from one of providing general policy guidance and funds for pilot projects to embedding sector strategies as a key component of their talent pipeline and economic competitiveness strategy, all in recognition of the fact that businesses must drive the conversation and determine their needs. In this evolved role, states create an ecosystem in which regional industry sector partnerships can take root, grow, and be sustained over time. A good example is the Commonwealth of Pennsylvania where successful industry-focused models evolved by integrating the economic development model of "cluster partnerships" that address the comprehensive needs of the industry with the workforce development model of "sector initiatives" into the "Next Generation of Industry Sector Partnerships"[3] model that puts business at the center. Pennsylvania is making annual targeted investments in regional industry partnerships as part of building a pipeline of talent that business needs to grow and prosper.

As the state role has evolved, six core capabilities have emerged as important to scaling up statewide efforts. These capabilities are identified in an "action guide" by the Employment and Training Administration (ETA) and described below (U.S. Department of Labor 2016):

1) **Shared Vision and Goals**: Develop a shared vision, across key agencies, of sector strategies that focus on serving and positively impacting the state's economy, businesses, and job seekers.

2) **Industry Data Analysis and Tools**: Provide rigorous labor market data and effective tools to help local and regional sector partnerships make informed decisions about target sectors and investments.

3) **Training and Capacity Building**: Provide technical assistance to local and regional areas to expand their capacity to build quality sector partnerships.

4) **Awareness and Industry Outreach**: Effectively promote the value of sector partnerships and actively recruit industry champions to participate at a local level.

5) **Administrative and Legislative Policy**: Ensure there are necessary policies and funding mechanisms in place that help establish, sustain, and scale local sector partnerships.

6) **Performance Measurement**: Measure the success of sector strategies, and use that information to drive policy and practice.

These six capabilities provide a framework to guide states in launching and scaling up industry sector partnerships.[4] They are gleaned from successful practices by states over more than a decade. Although each state may differ in how these capabilities manifest, they represent the common elements of high-quality state systems. It is important that states assess their effectiveness in implementing these capacities and make continuous improvements along the way.

Shared Vision and Goals

In developing a shared vision and goals, it is important that the vision and goals are adopted across state agencies and organizations that are directly involved in talent development and engagement with industry, including the governor's office, workforce and economic development agencies, and postsecondary and K–12 education agencies. In many states, the state workforce development board authorized under WIOA plays an important coordination role in developing the vision and overseeing its implementation. Other states have established a special advisory committee or board to guide the direction and implementation of partnerships. The vision and goals can take a variety of forms, from a formal or informal agreement to an executive order or legislative policy. Governors can, and often do, play a critical role in this coordination and integration.

Industry Data Analysis and Tools

Across state agencies there is often a significant amount of labor market data that can be packaged to inform local decisions in establishing regional industry partnerships. A key role for states is to identify leading growth industries across the state and specific to its regions, which helps regional collaboratives coalesce around target industries. States can also provide industry diagnostic tools to create profiles of regional industries. In addition, states can help local governments map supply-side data to better understand the makeup of their workforce to determine potential skill mismatches with industry needs.

Training and Capacity Building

States can support the launch and success of industry sector partnerships by providing training and capacity building for local regions. One important activity is peer-to-peer sharing of lessons learned from both successes and failures. Several states also conduct regional and local training to ensure that the conveners of industry sector partnerships are well equipped to enable industry to lead the conversation. This support has proven to be critical in ensuring that the industry partnerships have the knowledge tools they need to be effective and to achieve desired outcomes.

Awareness and Industry Outreach

States are well positioned to raise the profile and build awareness of the value of industry sector partnerships with both internal and external audiences. Externally, states can communicate the importance of industry sector partnerships as a key element of educational attainment to parents, businesses, students, local governments, and educators. Internally, states must communicate across agencies and with staff and practitioners on the connections between all their programmatic work as part of the larger goal of creating economic opportunity. Governors can play a key role by using the "bully pulpit," and their convening authority and relationships with business and local officials.

Performance Measurement

For industry sector partnerships to be sustainable and meaningful for state policymakers and businesses, progress in meeting the needs of employers and in connecting students and workers to good jobs must be measured. Performance metrics set the benchmark for quality and performance to ensure consistency and inform continuous improvement. While states are beginning to make progress in this area, considerable effort, including research and policy development, is still needed.

Administrative and Legislative Policy

Legislative and administrative policies can play a critical role in scaling up and sustaining industry sector partnerships. They are most effective when the policies are combined to support cross-system coordination and systemic change. At least 18 states have legislation that supports sector partnerships to connect industry with education and training systems to address the talent needs of businesses (U.S. Department of Labor 2016).

By taking a comprehensive approach to implementing these core capacities, states can help businesses meet their talent needs, be more competitive, and provide students and workers with paths toward good jobs and successful careers.

INTEGRATING PARALLEL INDUSTRY-ENGAGEMENT STRATEGIES: THE TALENT PIPELINE APPROACH

The model of local business-led partnerships embedded in and supported by state structures need not be confined narrowly to the workforce development system as defined by WIOA. In fact, there is a strong case to be made for such state strategies to become embedded as a permanent component of larger state systems for talent development, beyond meeting the needs of specific local groups of employers at specific points in time.

By integrating the sector strategy core concept of letting the needs of the economy and businesses inform state decision making, the broader talent pipeline approach recognizes the critical need for states to think of their current disparate systems for education (K–12 and postsecondary), workforce development, and economic development as facets of the same overarching core state mission: to ensure economic vitality for businesses and provide access to meaningful choices and economic prosperity for citizens. This thinking requires moving beyond the traditional silos of state government and asking questions about the basic functions of state government. More than simply better aligning existing program or vision statements (although this is a necessary initial step), there is a clear need to move to integrate these state functions.

Several state systems have been independently moving in this direction. An important evolution of state sector strategies has been their work to connect career pathway systems into industry sector partnership strategies. From the education perspective, the career pathway movement represents the same underlying forces—state supports for local partnerships that more strongly connect individuals to an industry with long-term career prospects. Each of these approaches is oriented to align with the needs of industry. Industry sector partnerships by design engage with employers within a single industry with a focus on their talent needs. Career pathways provide a clear sequence of courses, work experiences, support services, and stackable credentials aligned with employment opportunities in an industry and advancement to higher education levels. Successful career pathway approaches include regular engagement with employers to ensure that credentials and courses of study align with industry skill needs.

These approaches evolved on parallel paths—with workforce development policymakers implementing sector approaches focused on meeting employer needs, and education policymakers implementing career pathway partnerships to meet student needs. Given their complementary goals, this is an opportunity for states to develop an overall strategy to build a skilled workforce that weds these two strategies and creates a stronger state response overall.

WIOA and ESSA integrate these approaches and call on local workforce development boards and schools and colleges to integrate their efforts to engage employers. The integration of these approaches provides a real opportunity for systemic change to strengthen a community's ability to grow its economy through the preparation of a skilled workforce aligned with industry needs.

Another level of integration of industry-engagement strategies is occurring in many states, with the alignment of career pathway systems, sector strategies, and industry clusters. Industry clusters are networks of firms related to common markets, supply chains, infrastructure, innovation and technology, and labor pools and have been an important feature of many states' economic development strategies for years (NGA, Corporation for a Skilled Workforce, and National Skills Coalition 2013). Historical examples include the wine industry in Napa Valley, the automotive industry in Detroit, and the fashion industry in New York City. One of the most important factors contributing to industry growth and economic competitiveness is a skilled workforce. By integrating their career pathway systems with sector strategies aligned with relevant industry clusters, states are better able to communicate the interests and needs of employers to education and training providers and provide paths to good jobs for students and job seekers.

COMMON LANGUAGE: CORE ELEMENTS OF STATE TALENT PIPELINE SYSTEMS

In addition to the roles states play to support strong sector-based industry partnerships and develop career pathways, states can make stronger connections across education and workforce and economic development. Increasingly, states are working to fully integrate these systems as core elements of a broader talent pipeline system. *America Works: Education and Training for Tomorrow's Jobs*[5] outlines several common elements across these systems, emphasizing cross-system integration to expand postsecondary credential attainment as the "new minimum" for workers to achieve middle class status and meet the future skill needs of employers (National Governors Association 2014). These elements, identified by states, represent a common language across state government for building talent, bringing complementary approaches under one roof. Four core elements for building an integrated Talent Pipeline System have been identified as priorities by states (National Governors Association, forthcoming):

1) Set a vision with common goals.

2) Support sector-based industry partnerships.

3) Align resources and incentives to meet the goals.

4) Harness data resources to measure success.

These elements are drawn from the core capacities for scaling and sustaining sector strategies discussed earlier and form a common framework for building a broader talent pipeline system.

Beyond a single program or initiative, many states have recognized that the talent pipeline approach, including support for industry sector partnerships, must be the foundation for how communities build their talent pipelines to meet the new minimum of postsecondary education. Recognizing that a variety of state and local entities including K–12 and postsecondary educational institutions, state and local workforce development boards, economic development organizations, and others have developed and will continue to develop multiple strategies to engage industry, a talent pipeline approach can create a clearer understanding of the terminology for both policymakers and practitioners. This common language must answer both what the purpose of integrated efforts are, and how working together will lead to stronger outcomes for every partner. To overcome existing barriers, there must be a clear reason for action that benefits all stakeholders, as well as a clear path forward, or road map, to help both practitioners and policymakers see how they can drive change that meets their needs.

Governors and other state leaders can have a significant influence on the direction of the education, training, and economic development systems in their state. By establishing a vision and measurable goals, they provide a framework to guide policy across the state. At least nine states have established goals for postsecondary attainment, for example, Tennessee's "Drive to 55 Alliance," which calls for 55 percent of Tennesseans to be equipped with a postsecondary credential by 2025 (Drive to 55 Alliance 2018). Another example is the "Future Ready Iowa" goal of 70 percent of Iowans achieving some form of postsecondary credential by 2020 (Office of the Governor of Iowa 2014).

In addition to setting policy and guidance for the local level, states also make significant and continual investments in those systems. By engaging stakeholders to identify and map the existing resources and funding that currently support a broader talent pipeline system, states can develop comprehensive asset maps of their talent pipeline systems and create trust in an unbiased process that allows stakeholders to imagine new ways to braid and integrate resources. States that perform such asset mapping are in a stronger position to analyze the way existing resources have been used across agencies and programs and critically examine outcome measurement, accountability mechanisms, and alignment with strategic plans across state agencies.

For states to have clear evidence that their efforts to align education and workforce and economic development have moved their state closer to meeting their vision and goals, they must have plans for collecting and analyzing relevant data to demonstrate results and keep partners accountable. States can work to leverage the wealth of available data to build and strengthen their state longitudinal data systems to provide better information on how individuals enter and move through the state talent pipeline systems. Governors and state leaders can harness these data resources by defining a set of key policy questions they want answered about the state's talent needs. Having a clear set of policy questions helps signal what is important and provides a comprehensive picture of the overall talent pipeline system rather than outcomes for specific programs or individual agencies.

CONCLUSION

State sector strategies have evolved as a key element of state talent pipeline systems integrated with career pathways and economic development strategies to address the current and future workforce challenges faced by states. In building their talent pipeline systems, an increasing number of governors are setting postsecondary attainment goals in line with projected growth in jobs requiring postsecondary credentials. To achieve these goals, states are coordinating strategies across their education and workforce and economic development systems, capitalizing on available data across these systems to measure success and inform policy and investment decisions. The ultimate vision is to provide paths to good jobs and careers for students and workers and to ensure that employers across industries have the talent they need to be competitive and grow.

Notes

1. https://choosecolorado.com/programs-initiatives/colorado-blueprint/ (accessed March 7, 2018).
2. The NGA Center for Best Practices, in partnership with the Corporation for a Skilled Workforce and the National Network of Sector Partners, conducted a four-year policy academy on accelerating the adoption of sector strategies working with policy teams from 12 states. Lessons from that project informed a second project with cross-system teams from 14 states focused on building their talent pipeline systems by integrating education, workforce, and economic development systems.
3. Next Generation Industry Partnerships put businesses at the center of a coordinated workforce and economic development system that reacts to businesses' defined opportunities and priorities for action.
4. These core capacities have been embedded and refined in the "Next Generation Sector Partnerships" academies and technical assistance provided by the Woolsey Group, LLC and other associates for states and local governments on implementing sector partnerships.
5. *America Works: Education and Training for Tomorrow's Jobs* was the culminating report from Oklahoma Governor Mary Fallin's initiative as chair of the NGA. The initiative emphasized cross-system integration to expand postsecondary credential attainment as the "new minimum" for workers to achieve middle-class status and meet future skill needs of employers. The initiative led to a three-year NGA project with cross-system teams from 14 states focused on building their talent pipelines.

References

Bartlett, Michael. 2018. *Paving the Way to Meet the Economy's Talent Needs: A Roadmap for States*. Washington, DC: National Governors Association, Center for Best Practices.

Carnevale, Anthony P., Nicole Smith, and Jeff Strohl. 2013. *Recovery: Job Growth and Education Requirements through 2020*. Washington, DC: Georgetown University, Georgetown Public Policy Institute, Center for Education and the Workforce.

Deloitte Development LLC and Manufacturing Institute. 2015. *The Skills Gap in U.S. Manufacturing: 2015 and Beyond*. Washington, DC: Deloitte Development LLC.

Deloitte Touche Tohmatsu Limited and Council on Competitiveness. 2016. *2016 Global Manufacturing Competitiveness Index*. New York: Deloitte Touche Tohmatsu Limited.

Drive to 55 Alliance. 2018. http://driveto55.org/ (accessed March 7, 2018).

Lumina Foundation. 2017. *A Stronger Nation: Learning beyond High School Builds American Talent*. Indianapolis, IN: Lumina Foundation. http://strongernation.luminafoundation.org/report/2017/#nation (accessed March 7, 2018).

Manpower Group. 2015. *2015 Talent Shortage Report*. 10th Annual Talent Shortage Survey. Milwaukee, WI: Manpower Group.

New Jersey Department of Labor and Workforce Development. n.d. *New Jersey Career Connections*. Trenton, NJ: New Jersey Department of Labor and WorkforceDevelopment.http://careerconnections.nj.gov/careerconnections/partners/talent/talent_networks.shtml (accessed March 7, 2018).

National Governors Association. 2014. *America Works: Education and Training for Tomorrow's Jobs*. 2014. Washington, DC: National Governors Association.

———. Forthcoming. "Paving the Way to Meet the Talent Needs of the Economy: A Roadmap for States." Working paper. Washington, DC: National Governors Association.

National Governors Association, Corporation for a Skilled Workforce, and National Skills Coalition. 2013. *Sector Strategies Coming of Age: Implications for State Workforce Policymakers*. Washington, DC: National Governors Association.

Office of the Governor of Iowa. 2014. Future Ready Iowa Fact Sheet. Des Moines, IA: Office of the Governor of Iowa. https://governor.iowa.gov/sites/default/files/documents/FutureReadyIowa-FactSheet.pdf (accessed March 7, 2018).

U.S. Department of Labor, Employment and Training Administration. 2016. *State Support for Sector Partnerships: A Guide for Action*. ETA Sector Strategies Technical Assistance Initiative. Washington, DC: USDOL.

11
Improving Outcomes for Workers and Employers through Mayoral Leadership

Kathy Amoroso
Evan Amoroso

The United States is leading an innovation revolution, transforming the world's products and how we make them. We have a productive workforce, with abundant energy and unparalleled capability. Yet as our nation strives to create new jobs and put people to work in new and burgeoning industries, the growing skills gap—the lack of trained workers—leaves many employers scrambling for talent. The nation's mayors are continually looking for new ways to make strategic investments in education and training to close that gap. Among their most critical priorities are supporting economic growth and preparing a skilled workforce poised to meet the challenges of an ever-changing global marketplace. With the world's growing complexity and the increasing demands on the twenty-first century workforce, it is crucial that all students graduate from high school fully prepared for college and careers.

City leaders know that many of their constituents won't be able to gain a foothold in the middle class unless they earn a postsecondary credential that is valued by local employers. Although mayors may lack the direct authority to improve local community colleges or even a public mandate to take charge of training programs, they can pull a number of levers to bolster the talent pipeline in their cities.

For example, they can:

- encourage local colleges, particularly community colleges, to conduct return-on-investment surveys of their graduates by program and to make those reports widely available;

- encourage community-based organizations to adopt programs that support the connection between education and work;

- engage with employers to help educators meet local labor market needs;

- engage with college and workforce boards to create policies to align supply and demand for talent; and

- assign a staff person in City Hall to connect education and workforce issues programs.

Economic prosperity will favor cities that support a highly qualified talent pipeline and a robust education and workforce system aligned to meet the needs of employers. A mayor's leadership can make a real difference in building a more purposeful path to and through college and on to rewarding careers.

This essay acknowledges and recognizes three mayors who have successfully navigated this arena, established successful programs to provide education pathways with the purposes of completion and entry into the workplace, and calculated the measurable results of that success.

RUNNING START FOR CAREERS—ALBUQUERQUE MAYOR RICHARD BERRY

Running Start for Careers (Running Start) is a public-private, multi-partner initiative launched in 2011 by the City of Albuquerque, New Mexico. It represents a strong and enduring collaboration between education systems (primarily local high schools and the public community college) and employers (in an ever-expanding set of locally relevant industries) to address college preparation and long-term career success. Mayor Richard Berry paved the way for Running Start during his tenure in the state legislature between 2006 and 2009. The original intent of his proposed measure reflected the great local need to advance college and career readiness among students and support better alignment with workforce needs; to help young people learn valued, industry-driven job skills; and to give them increased motivation to stay in school, graduate, and pursue gainful employment and/or higher education.

Running Start engages high school students in viable and in-demand career pathways while at the same time providing workforce development opportunities to employers through dual-credit, industry-led instruction in well-paying, locally in-demand fields. Participants take courses in career disciplines in 12 industries, and earn an industry recognized certificate, life/workforce skills training, and dual credit (high school/college). Students opt in to the program and receive advising, attend weekly off-campus classes, and are placed in internships or pre-apprenticeships (most of which are paid) with industry partners. The program is open to all, but it focuses on students in low-income, disadvantaged neighborhoods who are at risk of not graduating. Running Start closes the gap for these students, creating relevance to core subjects and providing career mentoring, in many cases bilingually. By leveraging resources in Albuquerque schools and community, Running Start builds on New Mexico's investment in students and is increasing retention, graduation, access to higher education, and workforce development in New Mexico. The program has expanded its reach and impact each year: over 230 students participated in 2017 in 12 industry areas, with more than 1,240 students in 70 schools in the Albuquerque area having participated since the program's inception (Albuquerque School District is one of the 30 largest school districts in the country).[1] The program goal is to reach 500 Albuquerque area students in 2017–2018, place 60 students in internships, become a permanent program as one of the City of Albuquerque's public-private partnerships, and to serve as a model for statewide expansion and beyond.

The motivation behind Running Start stems from the scale and scope of the challenges that Albuquerque and New Mexico are facing. Coupled with Albuquerque's low high school graduation rate (66 percent in 2016, an increase from the previous year but still lagging well behind the 83 percent national rate), 20 percent of youth in Albuquerque are considered disconnected (defined as 16- to 24-year-olds who are neither working nor in school), which is higher than the national average of 7.6 percent (New Mexico Public Education Department 2017; Ross and Svajlenka 2016). These factors illustrate the importance of developing supports that retain and motivate students, training them for careers and/or postsecondary education. It is critical to support the struggling students who are most likely to drop out of school and miss the mark for a possible middle- or high-skilled job. Running Start is designed to meet the needs of the most disadvantaged students, while also being open to all other high school students. Running Start also emphasizes the importance of training for middle-skills jobs—those that require a high school diploma and some postsecondary education, but not a four-year degree. These jobs are important to local labor markets across the country, particularly in New Mexico, where they comprise 48 percent of the state's employment projections for 2024 (National Skills Coalition 2017). Yet, there is a skills gap: only 47 percent of the state's workers have the appropriate training for these jobs, and this skill/job mismatch is reflected in metropolitan areas across the country (National Skills Coalition 2017; Sommers and Osborne 2009).

Running Start was operational in 24 schools during the spring 2017 semester, and generally operates in 25 to 30 Albuquerque Public Schools each semester. Currently, schools in Bernalillo, Torrance, Valencia, and Sandoval counties of central New Mexico are part of the program, but statewide expansion is planned in the coming years. The program is open to any New Mexico junior or senior student at an in-district high school (public, charter, alternative, ancillary, or private) offering elective credit in career pathways, provided there is a school representative to document and monitor progress and arrange pre-apprenticeships. Students opt in to the program and receive placement testing and advice free of charge. Class sessions are scheduled on a once- or twice-weekly basis and are typically held at union halls, training facilities, worksites, or one of the community college's applied technology departments. Running Start currently supports courses related to more than 65 career disciplines in 12 industries identified as critical career clusters: Construction, Drone Mapping and Surveying, Electrical Field Services, Film, Health Care, Hospitality and Tourism, Financial Services, Information Technology and Coding, Medical Laboratory Sciences, Pipefitting and Plumbing, Public Safety, and Veterinary Administrative Support. Industry partners also place students in internships or pre-apprenticeships, most of which are paid. Each course is tailored to the discipline and structured to give high school students the opportunity to explore pathways while learning skills in industry internships, job shadowing, and other hands-on activities that are directly transferable to the workplace. Bilingual participants can earn additional wages or stipends.

As previously mentioned, Running Start is open to all high school students, but focuses on those in low-income, disadvantaged neighborhoods. The majority of active Running Start students live in poverty (67 percent), and most are Hispanic (63 percent) and female (58 percent;

the majority had been male until 2017).[2] As the program expands into more schools beyond the Albuquerque School District, it will continue to serve a majority of low-income communities and schools. Running Start for Careers defines low and moderate income by the standards applied by the New Mexico Public Education Department (NMPED). The majority (68 percent) of New Mexico's K–12 students qualify under NMPED terms as economically disadvantaged (NMPED 2017). The program closes academic and career gaps for participating students, creating relevance to core subjects such as applied math and science, while providing bilingual and impactful career mentoring.

Results to date include increased graduation rates, improved student outcomes and access to higher education, and a newly established pipeline of talent to fill jobs in high demand. More than 1,240 students have participated in the program since its inception in 2012.[3] In terms of aligning workforce needs and education, and enhancing student persistence and entry to employment in high-value occupations or postsecondary education, the results have been stunning. Running Start is an overall economic driver because the supported career pathways are critical to Albuquerque's infrastructure and include the fields of construction, health care, financial services, energy, transportation, production, and public safety. They are selected from New Mexico's 30 fastest growing industries, and 21 include middle-skill jobs.

A full 98 percent of participants graduate on time; 86 percent maintain industry employment and/or enter college; 358 program and high school graduates have enrolled in Central New Mexico Community College (CNM), and 61 of those students have received either a degree or certificate from CNM.[4] About 86 percent of Running Start participants identify as students of color, indicating the program has increased access to these opportunities for a population often not well represented in the talent pipeline. Furthermore, graduation rates have risen from 4 to 12 percent among schools with Running Start.[5]

This groundbreaking program knits together the public sector, private sector, and higher education anchor institutions to deliver instruction outside the classroom, using state-of-the-art technology and equipment. Unlike traditional vocational training, Running Start is not bound by campus infrastructure, relevant faculty, the domain of specialty schools, or specific industry types.

INNOVATE BIRMINGHAM—BIRMINGHAM
MAYOR WILLIAM A. BELL, SR.

Designated a TechHire city by the White House in the fall of 2015, Birmingham's tech industry was experiencing the second fastest growth rate in the country during the first half of 2016, with over 5,300 new IT jobs posted on hiring websites.[6] At the time, there were just over 14,600 IT professionals in the Birmingham metro area. The demand for new IT talent called for innovative new models to develop the workforce and stimulate the local economy.

Accordingly, in 2016, Birmingham Mayor William A. Bell, Sr., established the Innovate Birmingham Workforce Partnership and secured nearly $6 million in a prestigious America's Promise Grant to help establish a sustainable pipeline of local talent to fuel inclusive innovation for local employers. Led by the mayor and the University of Alabama at Birmingham (UAB), the network of partners from the public, education, and tech sectors joined forces to create Innovate Birmingham to offer new paths for traditional and accelerated demand-driven educational opportunities for Birmingham youth. Innovate Birmingham is the overall effort underway to create an innovation district in Birmingham to attract and retain high-caliber companies and talent, cluster startup and entrepreneurial activity, and connect surrounding Birmingham neighborhoods with technology training and job opportunities. Financial assistance in the form of grants and scholarships are now used to help ease the financial burden of pursuing education or training endeavors, breaking down barriers to increase completion rates.

The broad coalition of leaders who comprise the Innovate Birmingham partnership team are committed to fostering economic growth for the region and offering better opportunities for young adults. The coalition includes the City of Birmingham, UAB, Lawson State Community College, Jefferson State Community College, Jefferson County's Alabama Career Centers, the Central Six Workforce Development Council, and Tech Birmingham. In addition, more than 30 employer partners, including many of the region's largest employers, have signed on to support Innovate Birmingham programs by interviewing candidates, offering positions, providing mentorship opportunities, or delivering feedback on the course material.

Students are selected for the program via a rigorous interview and screening process that assesses their motivation, competency, and career vision. They complete 12 weeks of full-time intensive technical and professional training at Innovation Depot, a business incubator that's home to more than 100 startups, to prepare them for immediate entry into the IT workforce. Classes are the product of partnerships with McKinsey Social Initiative and Covalence, which have built strategic and rigorous curricula for industry-driven needs in hardware support and software development.

The Innovate Birmingham Workforce program aims to prepare Birmingham-area young adults to obtain 925 high-paying IT jobs by 2021. Many of the 18 graduates of the first class—all from the Birmingham area—have already received job offers with enterprises such as Blue Cross and Blue Shield of Alabama, Brasfield & Gorrie, Regions, and UAB.

The Innovate Birmingham program is administered in the UAB Innovation Lab (UAB iLab) at Innovation Depot. The depot then connects participants in the program with its tenants and other partner businesses. The program uses Tech Hire data, in combination with local resources, to align education and training providers with regional employers, ensuring industry-aligned skill development for workers.

Sustaining this great source of skilled workers makes the Birmingham region far more attractive when recruiting new employers. The program targets nine high-demand IT occupations, identified using data from the Alabama Department of Labor. With Birmingham's rapid IT job growth, demand has greatly surpassed supply for two primary reasons. First, current training programs fail to adequately align skill development with corresponding workforce needs. Second, disconnected youth frequently fail to complete available training options because of the barriers they confront, including tuition prices, transportation, and other associated costs. A pillar of Innovate Birmingham is to establish career pathways for people who do not have the resources to obtain a four-year degree, or even a two-year degree. Creating fast-track training programs, such as coding boot camps and apprenticeship programs is vital to the sustainability of the IT industry. Consequently, the Innovate Birmingham model is designed to offer industry-aligned, job-seeker-centered, flexible training options to fill this gap in workforce supply. These training pathways enable skill-building opportunities from secondary school through a bachelor's degree or alternative training at low or no cost to participants.

Innovate Birmingham serves the City of Birmingham, the largest municipality in the state, along with surrounding municipalities in Jefferson County. The service area was chosen because of the economic need, supply of disconnected youth, IT demand, and close proximity of education and training. Two critical barriers that restrain employment of disconnected youth in Birmingham are poverty and insufficient education or training. Over 30 percent of Birmingham residents and 42 percent of families with children live at or below the poverty threshold (U.S. Census Bureau 2017). Approximately 20 percent of Birmingham City School students failed to graduate with their peers during the last school year, and over 35,000 high school graduates are without a postsecondary degree or credential.[7] Nearly 90,000 Jefferson County residents are unemployed or underemployed, including a disproportionate number of young people (U.S. Census Bureau 2017). Furthermore, Birmingham is home to more than 26,000 disconnected youth, and Innovate Birmingham expects that approximately 85 percent of program participants will be disconnected youth (ages 17 to 26), and additional participants will be economically disadvantaged service-area residents over the age of 26.

Innovate Birmingham expects to serve 925 participants throughout the duration of the grant period (four years). Based on past completion rates from project education and training providers—a 95 percent completion rate from Depot/U, 85 percent from Generation's IT curriculum, and graduation rates near 60 percent from two-year and four-year institutional partners—Innovate Birmingham estimates that nearly 80 percent of participants will complete training. Additionally, because of the program's direct alignment of curriculum to IT workforce needs, consistent employer engagement, and job placement mechanisms, the city anticipates 75 percent of the participants will advance to new employment positions as a result of credentials acquired.

KIDS' HOME RUN—WEST SACRAMENTO
MAYOR CHRISTOPHER CABALDON

West Sacramento is one of the largest employers in the six-county Sacramento region, but it also recently had one of the highest unemployment rates (Civic Dashboards, n.d.). Since its incorporation in 1987, West Sacramento has been a regional leader for infill housing and economic development. The city's workforce development activities, however, took time to mature with the changing economic landscape. Once a blue-collar city across the river from Sacramento, West Sacramento has developed tremendously in the past 30 years into a hub of research and development, advanced manufacturing, food processing, and logistics. However, the education system has yet to fully respond to the altered business environment. Many residents who had the financial ability to do so sent their children to private schools. Upon assuming office in 2004, Mayor Christopher Cabaldon committed to improving the quality of education in the community. In spite of the high levels of poverty in the city, West Sacramento had the lowest percentage of subsidized preschool spaces of all the municipalities in Yolo County. Approximately 70 percent of the three- and four-year-olds in the city who qualified for Head Start or State Preschool were not being served.[8] The few private centers that did exist did not have the resources and workforce to support high quality preschool. Additionally, while the Washington Unified School District identified seven regionally relevant, high wage, high growth industry sectors (Agriculture and Natural Resources; Art Media and Entertainment; Building and Construction Trades; Engineering and Architecture; Health Science and Medical Technology; Hospitality, Tourism, and Recreation; and Information and Communication Technology) for which they have created 10 career pathways inside River City High School, they had yet to outline an effective work-based learning component in the career pathway system. As students exited high school, there was no direct connection to student supports at the local community college that brought them to and through a postsecondary education and back into the local workforce.

In 2016, Mayor Christopher Cabaldon took action to address these issues. To start, under his leadership and through a partnership with FutureReady, the City of West Sacramento became one of 12 cities to be part of the national LRNG network, a digital badging platform used to create, host, and validate online badges (virtual credentials that validate learning experiences). The digital badges allow student success in school and the workforce to be displayed to employers and institutions of higher education while also tracking progress. Mayor Cabaldon then announced the creation of the Kids' Home Run during his 2016 state of the city address. Kids' Home Run incorporates elements of the mayor's signature education programs (e.g., Universal Preschool for West Sacramento [UP4WS] and FutureReady) with internships for students in career pathways and digital badging, and combines them with new initiatives to create a seamless cradle to college and career experience for young people, families, and communities in the City of West Sacramento. Additionally, in November 2016, West Sacramento voters approved Measure E, a mayor-led ballot initiative endorsed by the entire City Council, that added a quarter of a percentage point to the city's portion of the local transactions tax (sales tax) rate to fund the Kids' Home Run.

The Kids' Home Run initiative was designed to be a data-driven means of ensuring that, from cradle to college and career, programs within the initiative would be available to provide students and families with meaningful educational opportunities while helping employers, policymakers, and educational institutions make better workforce and education decisions.

The goal of the Kids' Home Run initiative is to change the culture of the City of West Sacramento into one where every young person is prepared for college and career while creating a more robust workforce for local employers and enhancing the City's economic development capacity and competitiveness. Kids' Home Run is organized temporally, so that one can envision the journey of a West Sacramento youth, starting at age four and continuing on through age 18, when they enter college or begin an entry-level career with a local employer. Kids' Home Run begins with a youth's enrollment in UP4WS to receive a high-quality preschool education. Once a youth has graduated from a UP4WS preschool, they will then have access to a guaranteed college savings account when entering kindergarten within the Washington Unified School District, with the goal of a match for family deposits. High-school-aged youth within the Washington Unified School District will have access to paid internships in a relevant industry sector or job type if they are enrolled in an integrated college and career pathway and making satisfactory progress in school. Finally, through the Kids' Home Run program, every West Sacramento student graduating from high school and directly enrolling full time in a program of study at the Sacramento City College Campus can enroll fee free and have access to a points-based scholarship of up to $1,000. A system of digital badges, virtual credentials that can unlock opportunities for young people, will be used to track young people's progress and motivate them to work their way through the Kids' Home Run program. The initiative was implemented in 2017 for all youth and is designed so that someday in the future, a West Sacramento young person would be enrolled in every program at some point in their life.

There have been dramatic results from the programs that are a part of the Kids' Home Run, particularly the program that has existed for the longest time, UP4WS. Before the UP4WS program, parents did not have access to high quality preschool within the city limits, nor did they know where their children could attend a high quality preschool. The program has increased the number of preschool spaces within the city from 210 to 780, largely due to the growth of the UP4WS program and improvement in access to child care and preschool. Whether a child is cared for in a home-based child care or a licensed child development preschool, the City of West Sacramento is committed to making sure that all learning environments are safe and nurturing. The varied learning environments all actively promote the acceptance of differences in children and embrace diversity among the many cultures of the children, families, and teachers in the programs. One of the goals of UP4WS has been to improve the well-being of children and their families through supporting and promoting the provision of high quality preschool education for low-income and at-risk children in West Sacramento. Mayor Cabaldon has ensured that every child enrolled in UP4WS child care programs receives an extraordinary educational program that prepares him or her for active learning and success in school.

All children in UP4WS are assessed using the Desired Results Developmental Profile at least twice yearly. Quality rating scales consistently place UP4WS classrooms at between six and seven on a seven-point rating scale, with 7 being the highest possible score. In a state where the current monitoring of centers by Community Care and Licensing is rated among the lowest in the nation, this quality monitoring is not just a good idea, it is vital to preserve the integrity of licensed programs.

CONCLUSION

There is no better job creation or wealth creation strategy than a trained and educated workforce, and no single issue impacts how a city succeeds and grows more than the quality of its workers. City and mayoral support for and involvement in education and workforce development is not a choice—it is an imperative. Partnerships are key and mayors are well positioned to build the crucial relationships and coalitions that succeed in preparing a strong and skilled workforce. Because of their status as the chief elected local official in their cities, mayors can make significant contributions by bringing visibility to the issue, increasing public participation, enhancing funding and resources, supporting existing priorities, and setting new ones when necessary. The bottom line is simple: mayors can help make education and training opportunities more productive and successful for all residents, and their involvement makes a difference.

Notes

1. Based on confidential data summarized by program staff and provided to the author.
2. Ibid.
3. Ibid.
4. Ibid.
5. Ibid.
6. Ibid.
7. Ibid.
8. Ibid.

References

Civic Dashboards. N.d. "Unemployment Rate for West Sacramento, CA." http://www.civicdashboards.com/city/west-sacramento-ca-16000US0684816/unemployment_rate (accessed September 14, 2018).

National Skills Coalition. 2017. "Middle-Skill Job Fact Sheets." Washington, DC: National Skills Coalition. https://www.nationalskillscoalition.org/state-policy/fact-sheets (accessed March 7, 2018).

New Mexico Public Education Department (NMPED). 2017. "New Mexico Public School Graduation Rates." Santa Fe: New Mexico Public Education Department. https://webnew.ped.state.nm.us/bureaus/accountability/graduation/ (accessed March 7, 2018).

Ross, Martha, and Nicole Prchal Svajlenka. 2016. "Employment and Disconnection among Teens and Young Adults: The Role of Place, Race, and Education." Washington, DC: Brookings Institution. https://www.brookings.edu/research/employment-and-disconnection-among-teens-and-young-adults-the-role-of-place-race-and-education/ (accessed March 7, 2018).

Sommers, Paul, and Drew Osborne. 2017. "Middle-Wage Jobs in Metropolitan America." Washington, DC: Brookings Institution, Metropolitan Policy Program. https://www.brookings.edu/research/middle-wage-jobs-in-metropolitan-america/ (accessed March 7, 2018).

U.S. Census Bureau. 2017. "2011–2015 American Community Survey 5 Year Profiles." Washington, DC: U.S. Census Bureau. https://www.census.gov/acs/www/data/data-tables-and-tools/data-profiles/2015/ (accessed March 7, 2018).

12

Employer Engagement Policy

Shifting from Customers to Partnerships

Andy Van Kleunen

For two decades, a consistent challenge has been posed to our nation's workforce development programs: do a better job of engaging employers, so that your clients land skilled jobs with local companies. With every passage of a new federal law—the new Workforce Investment Act (WIA) in 1998, its reauthorization as the Workforce Innovation and Opportunity Act (WIOA) of 2014, and the revised Perkins Career and Technical Education (CTE) Act in 2006—policymakers have claimed "we got it right this time" in meeting that challenge. Yet 20 years after WIA's initial passage, too many employers are still reportedly dissatisfied with how they are being engaged.

Our coalition of workforce stakeholders is aware of the frustration, having long advocated for more effective employer engagement policies. Today's workforce and CTE programs can point to many exciting local collaborations with industry; indeed, the level of local employer engagement is better than it has ever been. But those achievements are uneven across our nation's 300+ regional labor markets.

This inconsistency arises in part from a continuing lack of clarity about the particular types of employer engagement our federal policies intend to encourage. While most workforce and CTE systems are motivated to be responsive to local industry needs, many focus their energy on the specific types of employer engagement that are mandated, explicitly funded, or captured in government performance metrics. Unfortunately, the type of engagement that local employers are often seeking is not what our policies are effectively prioritizing.

WE'RE WELL PAST "TRAIN AND PRAY"

Former Labor Secretary Tom Perez had a popular, go-to line in his stump speeches: "We just can't 'train and pray' anymore." The line worked because it invoked the still common belief that workforce programs are training clients without talking to prospective employers.

Yet if the proof point of the workforce system's engagement of employers was simply whether clients were finding jobs, then practitioners had long ago put down their prayer books. In 2016, the U.S. Department of Labor (USDOL) reported that more than two-thirds of WIOA adult and dislocated worker participants found jobs. Placement rates were closer to 75 percent for workers served by Trade Adjustment Assistance (TAA) programs, registered apprenticeships, National Emergency Grants issued in response to mass layoffs, and other discretionary grant programs. In addition, retention rates were in the 85 to 95 percent range across most programs (U.S. Department of Labor 2016a).

That quantitative assessment does not change the fact that, qualitatively, many local employers still feel disengaged from local workforce and CTE systems. For some, being approached for purely transactional purposes—that is, to see if they would be willing to hire a local trainee—does not actually feel like engagement. Therein lies the policy challenge: "employer engagement" has many definitions.

Unpacking the Concept of Employer Engagement

"Working to build a high quality sector partnership in my community has added hiring and training capacity to our midsized, family-owned company. Together, we work as a team to address the evolving skill needs of my company, and my industry" (Liza Smitherman, vice president of Professional Development, Jostin Construction Inc., Cincinnati, OH [Business Leaders United 2016]).

The various types of employer engagement required by our workforce and CTE policies can be categorized across two different dimensions (see Table 12.1):

1) **Number of companies engaged (single vs. multi-firm):** At one end of this continuum, local employer engagement focuses

on a single company, perhaps the dominant large firm in a local industry, to inform local workforce programs. One tick up from this would involve one-on-one engagements with a number of individual companies, but pursued independently from each other. Then there are multi-firm engagement strategies, in which companies are addressed as a group, typically as members of a common industry. At its most developed, multi-firm engagement attempts to not just get a group of companies to provide collective input to local workforce or CTE programs, but to get those companies to collaborate with each other on common workforce needs even though they are commercial competitors.

2) **Intensity of company engagement (advisor vs. customer vs. partner):** At its most limited, employer engagement can be episodic with no impact on a company's day-to-day operations, such as serving as a volunteer advisor. Employers can be further engaged as customers, whereby a company is actually hiring clients, perhaps with some basic input to confirm that trainees meet the company's needs. More in-depth is when employers are engaged as partners or co-owners of the workforce or CTE programs. In this context, business leaders are not only communicating their own company's immediate needs, but also working with programs to help them respond to the broader, long-term priorities of their entire industry. At its most developed, these industry partners are not only providing feedback on how workforce and CTE programs could improve, but also adjusting how their companies hire, train, or promote workers to ensure the collaboration's long-term success.

EXAMPLES OF ENGAGEMENT UNDER WORKFORCE POLICIES

Let's apply this rubric to identify different types of employer engagement required or supported by workforce programs administered by USDOL.

Table 12.1 Examples of Employer Engagement under WIA/WIOA

Single firm	One-off calls for advice with a targeted company	Job developer/sales calls with individual companies to facilitate client placements Sample policies: • Performance measurements for client placement, retention	Mutual collaboration/ investment with a targeted company Sample policies: • Customized job training/on-the-job training contracts • Apprenticeship
Multi-firm	Periodically convening group of companies to advise system Sample policies: • Workforce Investment Boards (now Workforce Development Boards)	Same as above, except with more than one company Sample policies: • New "employer effectiveness" measures on repeat customers, etc.	Group of companies given shared authority and investment in local industry-focused strategy Sample policies: • Sector/Industry Partnerships

Employers as Advisors

WIA's creators responded to employer dissatisfaction with the Job Training Partnership Act by mandating that local businesses control the majority of seats, as well as the chair, on the system's newly created Workforce Investment Boards (WIBs). Yet the number of companies that could possibly participate on these WIBs was always going to be finite. What's more, the participating business leaders were being asked to play more of an oversight function over the administration of public workforce systems rather than solve the workforce needs of their own companies. In fact, to this day, many private-sector WIB members are not actual customers hiring clients trained by the workforce system.

Employers as Customers

As noted above, the primary performance metrics for both WIA and WIOA relate to the placement of clients with local companies.[1] However, during the final year of deliberations about WIA's reauthorization, the Obama White House, the Department of Labor, and Congressional authorizers all acknowledged that these measures fell short of documenting deeper employer engagement. A range of organizations were asked to weigh in—workforce boards, training providers, industry intermediaries, business associations, and groups of small employers themselves—regarding the types of practices whereby local business leaders seem most engaged.[2] Yet it proved difficult for authorizers to translate these activities and their qualitative impacts into legislative language with scalable, easy-to-measure metrics. Hence, the final WIOA bill shifted from proposing new measures of "employer engagement" to those that document the workforce system's "employer effectiveness," and instructed USDOL to continue working with the field to develop the specific metrics as part of WIOA's initial implementation.

In 2016, USDOL proposed three pilot measures to be tested for measuring effectiveness in serving employers (U.S. Department of Labor 2016b):

1) **Retention with the Same Employer**, to assess how well programs were providing employers with skilled workers who succeed with or stay at their companies

2) **Repeat Business Customers**, to assess employers' level of satisfaction with provided skilled workers, such that they continue to come back to hire more from the WIOA system

3) **Employer Penetration Rate**, to assess what portions of employers within a state or local economy were being engaged as customers by the WIOA system

These measures will certainly tell us more about relative levels of employer utilization of the workforce system, but they are for the most part just re-categorizations of the types of transactional data already collected about individual company decisions to hire or retain workers. As such, while they may tell us more about whether local systems are more effective in meeting local employer needs, they do not really tell us much—except what some might choose to infer—about the extent to which employers had been engaged in designing or implementing the workforce strategies being funded by the local WIOA system.

Employers as Partners

The additional step taken by WIOA intended to actually spur deeper employer engagement was its requirement that states and localities begin to "develop, convene or implement" sector partnerships as a means to bring more companies into the execution of workforce programs.[3]

Fully implemented, sector partnerships bring together multiple employers with education, training, labor, and community-based organizations to address both the current and anticipated future skill needs of a local industry. Such partnerships can identify common skill and credential standards that are then adopted both by local programs when they train prospective workers, as well as by local companies when they post hiring requirements. Through these partnerships, companies can jointly design training programs and curricula that are then adopted by local high schools, community colleges, labor-management training funds, and other workforce practitioners. Sector partnerships' conveners or "intermediaries" can include local workforce boards, community colleges, chambers of commerce, community-based organizations, funder collaboratives, and economic development organizations (DeRenzis and Wilson 2015).

In many ways, WIOA's inclusion of sector partnerships was Congress's catching up to a practice that had already been tested and adopted by states during the first decade of WIA's implementation. In the final phases of WIA's reauthorization, increasing numbers of local business leaders—particularly those associated with small- and medium-sized enterprises participating in such partnerships—had begun advocating with Congress for the practice's adoption as a required and explicitly funded element of the federal workforce infrastructure (Van Kleunen 2014). Many of these companies advocated for legislation that specified standards for how businesses were to be engaged as part of these multi-stakeholder industry partnerships.[4] Unfortunately, in the end, Congress opted for a much less defined partnership structure in law. Similarly, USDOL chose to provide relatively little additional guidance or regulation on how such partnerships should be structured or function, or on how the agency might assess if claimed partnerships were actually achieving the kinds of employer engagement that had led to the practice's popularity within the business community in the first place.[5]

Hence, while WIOA's inclusion of sector partnerships was an incredibly important step in the right direction, there is likely going to be a continued inconsistency in how 550 workforce investment areas use those partnerships to engage local companies, largely because both the law and resulting regulations are weak compared to those used to enforce the functioning of workforce boards (employers as advisors) or to variously measure client placements (employers as customers).

OTHER POLICY OPTIONS FOR PARTNERSHIP DEVELOPMENT

While we wait to see if WIOA's new sector partnership requirement achieves more broad-based employer engagement, we also need to look at other areas of federal policy where similar issues are being considered.

Sector Partnerships within Perkins CTE

Although the current Perkins Act, as reauthorized in 2006, does not explicitly require high schools and colleges to actively partner with local employers, states and localities are required to at least consult with representatives of business and industry during the development of their Perkins plans.[6] As such, many states have created industry advisory committees, and a smaller subset has actually required active local partnerships with companies and industry associations to design and roll-out CTE programs (National Association of State Directors 2014). To build beyond what Secretary of Education Arne Duncan described as these select "islands of excellence," the Obama administration in 2012 issued a "Blueprint for Transforming Career and Technical Education" (Duncan 2011). Among its more controversial proposals was the recommendation that Perkins funding, rather than being automatically distributed by state and local formula, should be awarded on an application basis only to those "programs of study" that demonstrated an active engagement of industry leaders in its implementation (U.S. Department of Education 2010).

A higher bar for CTE employer engagement was hailed by many. However, some concerns were voiced regarding how this new emphasis could have unintended consequences if it were not thoughtfully aligned with employer partnership requirements being developed for WIA's replacement. Asking willing employers to both help lead their industry's sector partnership and simultaneously sit on their local high school's or community college's Perkins advisory council could potentially burn out engageable business leaders. It could also work against the goal of these sector partnerships, which was to provide a single place where an industry's small- and medium-sized businesses could gather to set common skill standards and then communicate them back to all local programs preparing students and workers for employment in that sector.

One proposed solution to this potential dilemma was to authorize local Perkins programs to use or contribute to the capacity of existing sector partnerships in their region, including those developed under the new WIOA standards. This would allow local companies to use a single industry platform to communicate shared workforce needs to CTE and WIOA programs. To facilitate this alignment, Congress could provide additional Perkins funding to secondary or postsecondary CTE programs that are participating in a WIOA-sponsored or other existing sector partnership. Congress could also require state CTE plans to describe how they would support state efforts to develop and implement sector partnerships, and require postsecondary grant recipients to coordinate with industry or sector partnerships in their area, where appropriate (National Skills Coalition 2015b).

Sector Partnerships and Community Colleges

During the second term of the Obama administration, the most dramatic boost in federal support for sector partnership development came not from the Congressional passage of WIOA, but from administration initiatives right before and after the July 2014 release of the White House's Job-Driven Training plan. The plan was in response to President Obama's call for a government-wide review of all federal job training, CTE, higher education, and other programs that prepared Americans for employment to assess how those programs could be better aligned and more effective at moving people into skilled careers with American companies. The plan outlined seven principles that would be used as evaluative standards to better ensure that all relevant federal policies and grant programs were effectively moving Americans into skilled careers, starting with:

- **Engaging employers**: "Work up-front with employers to determine local or regional hiring needs and design training programs that are responsive to those needs," and ending with

- **Regional partnerships**: "Create regional collaborations among American Job Centers, education institutions, labor, and non-profits" to work with local employers (Offices of the President and Vice-President 2014, p. 10).

Those principles thereafter shaped nearly $2.5 billion worth of discretionary grants subsequently given out by the Departments of Labor, Education, and Commerce, among others. Included among these was the final round of grants issued under the Trade Adjustment Assistance Community College Career Training (TAACCCT) program. TAACCCT was a four-year, $2 billion initiative created by the administration in 2011 with a portion of the savings from the Department of Education's restructuring of the federal subsidized student loan program. Originally conceived as an Education initiative, the program came to be administered by USDOL due to a Congressional rule related to the process of budget reconciliation that required the newly available funding to be used with an already existing program. An unfunded community college grant program authorized during the preceding reauthorization of the USDOL's TAA program thus became the vehicle to spend these Education resources.

While TAACCCT had originally been intended to focus on the retraining and reemployment of workers displaced by the Great Recession, the grant program's requirements that colleges actively engage local industry were relatively loose. This changed with the last round of TAACCCT, the guidelines of which were being developed at the same time the Obama administration was preparing its Job-Driven Training plan. The White House pushed to require that TAACCCT colleges demonstrate collaboration with multi-firm sector partnerships. Recognizing that TAACCCT was coming to an end, the administration also included in its FY2015 budget proposal an even larger, $6 billion "Community College Job-Driven Training Grant" initiative to further build these collaborations between community colleges and local sector partnerships (National Skills Coalition 2014). When Congress failed to take up the President's budget, members of Congress, with the support of the business community, stepped up to propose new legislation, the "Community College to Career Fund Act," to further this effort to support community college collaboration with local sector partnerships. That legislation has since been reintroduced in the 115th Congress, and may be considered as part of the Perkins Act legislation currently being considered for reauthorization by the Senate.[7]

Sector Partnerships, Intermediaries, and Apprenticeships

The workforce development strategy that has received the most new attention in Washington has been apprenticeship. President Obama proposed to double the number of registered apprentices (from 500,000 to 1 million), and President Trump has since gone further to embrace goals of anywhere from 2 million to 5 million apprentices in the next five years. Between 2015 and 2017 nearly $250 million in grants were distributed by USDOL to promote new apprenticeship development, including $90 million appropriated by Congress on a bipartisan basis to promote the concept.

However, the very thing that makes apprenticeship so attractive to policymakers—that is, apprentices are, by definition, employed while training on and off the job—also makes it one of the more difficult workforce strategies to scale. A new apprenticeship slot is not created without an employer first agreeing to hire an untrained worker and thereafter providing time and resources toward his/her development. This poses a significant operational shift for companies not accustomed to taking on that level of financial and legal risk with a new employee, particularly one who is explicitly not qualified to fill a skilled job. As such, broad-based and intensive employer engagement—whether accomplished one-on-one with prospective company sponsors or across a number of companies as a sector—is going to be necessary if millions of new apprentices are going to be placed in the years ahead.

Many federal policies have been proposed to incentivize or compensate individual companies to create new apprenticeship slots, including the use of employer tax credits as well as up-front wage subsidies, the latter particularly for smaller firms (National Skills Coalition 2017). These types of offsets have worked in the past for some companies, including at the state level, and as such, they each play an important role. But the policy option for employer engagement that we feel holds the most promise for this burgeoning apprenticeship renaissance is the use of industry-based intermediaries, which, like the best of sector partnerships, work with multiple employers within the same industry to help those companies quickly take apprenticeship to scale. When it comes to smaller companies, as well as firms in industries unfamiliar to the processes of setting up an apprenticeship, assistance is often more highly prized than financial incentives when taking their first foray into apprenticeship.

Such intermediaries can simultaneously work with multiple companies to develop shared curricula, submit the paperwork for federal or state registration, and connect new apprentices to the necessary pre- and posthire training and support services to ensure their success. Intermediaries in some cases can even serve as the apprentices' employer of record for their first several months of employment, thereby reducing companies' financial and legal exposure until they are sure a new apprentice is a fit for their operation.

A single partnership or intermediary organization working across multiple firms within a regional industry is much better positioned to take apprenticeship to scale than companies attempting to do so one at a time. Intermediary experiences in countries like the United Kingdom, which recently jumped into the apprenticeship pool and quickly outlapped the United States, would seem to confirm this observation (Lerman 2016). The United Kingdom went from 400,000 to over 800,000 apprentices in the space of five years largely through a national infrastructure of private-sector and nonprofit intermediaries that combine both public and private resources in the preparation of apprentices to meet industry-wide skills standards set by industry-led sector councils (Ayres and Gurwitz 2014). A national infrastructure of sector partnerships here in the United States, enabled not only by WIOA but also by support from the CTE and higher education systems, and buttressed by other discretionary grants made by the federal government, could position the United States for the types of apprenticeship expansion enjoyed by our competitors overseas.

CONCLUSION

For decades the United States has sought to increase employer engagement within its workforce and CTE programs, but it is only in recent years that federal policies have invested in engaging local business leaders in meaningful and scalable ways. Policies that have tried to engage employers either as episodic advisors or transactional customers have made their contributions, but they have fallen short of making local companies feel invested in their local workforce and CTE systems. More recent policies focused on employer engagement through multi-firm, sector-based partnerships are where the United States needs to drive all of its employment-related workforce and education programs in the future.

Unfortunately, even with new sector partnership policies such as those included in WIOA, we are concerned that the type of performance measurement required by federal agencies is missing the purpose of these partnerships, and instead is defaulting to a traditional reliance on single-firm, client-focused measures of success. If we do not push beyond that, state and local systems will deliver what they are required, and deeper employer engagement may still be uneven across this rebooted workforce system.

The growing desire for greater employer engagement within newly developing CTE, higher education, and apprenticeship policies offers a singular opportunity to capitalize on the sector partnership reforms in WIOA. Aligning such partnerships across all of these federal programs could serve as a down payment on the development of a truly national infrastructure of industry-based partnerships that could engage tens of thousands of employers in a manner that could in turn help millions more Americans access available skilled jobs.[8] Congress and the federal administration should recognize and act on this opportunity.

Notes

1. Under WIOA, those measures include the percentage of program completers who are employed in the second quarter after program exit, the percentage who are employed in the fourth quarter after program exit, median earnings in the second quarter after exit, and the percentage attaining some form of credential (U.S. Department of Labor 2016b).
2. For an example of the types of recommendations made, see National Fund for Workforce Solutions (2014).
3. WIOA takes several steps to encourage the development and expansion of sector partnerships. WIOA section 101(d)(3)(D) requires state workforce development boards to assist the Governor in the development and expansion of strategies for meeting the needs of employers, workers, and jobseekers, *particularly through industry or sector partnerships* related to in-demand industry sectors and occupations (emphasis added). WIOA section 134(a)(2)(B) provides that states must use a portion of state set-aside funds to assist local areas by providing information on and support for the effective development, convening, and implementation of industry or sector partnerships. Section 134(c)(1)(A)(v) requires that Title I-B funds allocated to local areas must be used to "develop, convene, or implement industry or sector partnerships."
4. For a description of the SECTORS Act, see National Skills Coalition (2013).
5. See comments on sector partnerships in National Skills Coalition (2015a).
6. See Carl D. Perkins Career and Technical Education Act of 2006.
7. See the Community College to Career Fund Act, S.620, introduced March 2017.
8. See the recommendation for a national infrastructure of regional industry workforce partnerships in National Skills Coalition (2016).

References

Ayres, Sarah, and Ethan Gurwitz. 2014. *Apprenticeship Expansion in England: Lessons for the United States*. Washington, DC: Center for American Progress.

Business Leaders United for Workforce Partnerships. 2016. *The Workforce Innovation and Opportunity Act*. Washington, DC: National Skills Coalition.

Carl D. Perkins Career and Technical Education Act of 2006, Pub.L. 109-270 (2006).

Community College to Career Fund Act, S.620 (2017).

DeRenzis, Brooke, and Bryan Wilson. 2015. *Sector Partnership Policies: 50-State Scan*. Washington, DC: National Skills Coalition.

Duncan, Arne. 2011. "The New CTE: Secretary Duncan's Remarks on Career and Technical Education." Speech, February 2, Harvard School of Education, Boston.

Lerman, Robert. 2016. *Let's Help Intermediaries Expand U.S. Apprenticeships.* Washington, DC: Urban Institute.

National Association of State Directors of Career Technical Education Consortium (now Advance CTE). 2014. *The State of Career Technical Education Employer Engagement in CTE.* Washington, DC: Advance CTE.

National Fund for Workforce Solutions. 2014. *Characteristics of a High-Performing Industry Partnership.* Boston: National Fund for Workforce Solutions.

National Skills Coalition. 2013. *The Strengthening Employment Clusters to Organize Regional Success (SECTORS) Act of 2013: Section-by-Section Analysis.* Washington, DC: National Skills Coalition.

———. 2014. "President, VP Announce Job-Driven Grants." Washington, DC: National Skills Coalition.

———. 2015a. *Comments on Workforce Innovation and Opportunity Act (WIOA) Notices of Proposed Rulemaking (NPRMs).* Washington, DC: National Skills Coalition.

———. 2015b. *Carl D. Perkins Career and Technical Education Act: Recommendations for Reauthorization.* Washington, DC: National Skills Coalition.

———. 2016. *Skills for Good Jobs: An Agenda for the Next President.* Washington, DC: National Skills Coalition.

———. 2017. *Getting to 5 Million Apprentices: Federal Options for Expanding Work-Based Learning.* Washington, DC: National Skills Coalition.

Offices of the President and Vice-President, Obama Administration. 2014. *Ready to Work: Job-Driven Training and American Opportunity.* Washington, DC: The White House.

U.S. Department of Education, Office of Career, Technical and Adult Education. 2010. *Investing in America's Future: A Blueprint for Transforming Career and Technical Education.* Washington, DC: U.S. Department of Education.

U.S. Department of Labor, Employment and Training Administration. 2016a. *Workforce System Results: For the Quarter ending June 30, 2016.* Washington, DC: U.S. Department of Labor.

———. December 2016b. "Operating Guidance for the Workforce Innovation and Opportunity Act." Training and Employment Guidance Letter (TEGL) No. 10-16. Washington, DC: U.S. Department of Labor.

Van Kleunen, Andy. 2014. "Will Workforce Policy Finally Catch Up to Sector Practice?" In *Connecting People to Work: Workforce Intermediaries and Sector Strategies*, Maureen Conway and Robert P. Giloth, eds. Washington, DC: Aspen Institute, pp. 349–368.

Workforce Innovation and Opportunity Act of 2014, Pub L. 113-128 (2014).

Part 3

Investing in Technology

13
The Promise and Perils
of the Future of Work

Carl E. Van Horn

The potential impacts of robotics, artificial intelligence, and digital economy technologies on American workers raise alarming questions. Which occupations will survive? Which workers will be the winners, and which the losers? Will jobs disappear? How will workers, employers, educators, and policymakers manage these challenges? As we consider these questions, it is essential to recall lessons from previous cycles of technology-driven worker displacement throughout American history.

In the early twentieth century, the mechanization of farming and the assembly-line production of automobiles and other durable goods eliminated and created job opportunities by the millions. Toward the end of the twentieth century, robots began replacing assembly-line workers, and personal computers wiped out millions of jobs. Today, advanced software, smart phones, the Internet, and cognitive computing are disrupting the retail, media, transportation, education, and health-care industries.

With each wave of technology, from the steam engine to cloud computing, dire predictions about the scope and characteristics of workforce disruptions have often been exaggerated (McAfee and Brynjolfsson 2017). Our crystal balls are cloudy because we cannot estimate the true extent of economic change, how workers and businesses will adapt, and the new opportunities and enterprises that will emerge. As the great baseball player and quipster Yogi Berra said, "The future ain't what it used to be." Recent predictions about the impact of artificial intelligence on worker dislocation range from the Organisation for Economic Co-operation and Development's estimate that 9 percent of jobs will disappear in the next two decades (Overly 2016) to the analysis of Oxford University scholars, who conclude that nearly half of current jobs could be in jeopardy (Frey and Osborne 2017).

169

Regardless of the pace of technological innovation and economic disruptions, unemployment rises during economic downturns. Growth rates, inflation, and the availability of capital create and destroy jobs and companies. The Great Recession, which wiped out trillions of dollars of economic wealth and tossed millions of workers out of their jobs, was brought about by irresponsible lending practices and financial schemes. The global trade, economic competition, mergers, and acquisitions that eliminate jobs are not driven by technology. Hence, the decline of the American-based steel industry was due in large measure to the failure of American companies to invest in new production methods. U.S. textile manufacturing plummeted because companies moved production to countries where workers are paid a small fraction of the wages earned by U.S. workers. It's not technological innovation that typically motivates most mergers and acquisitions in telecommunications, banking, and health care, but rather the desire to maximize profits and grow market shares. Simple business innovations, such as Walmart's decision to move checkout counters to the front of the store, similar to grocery stores, instead of having them scattered throughout the store by department, eliminated legions of sales clerks long before direct delivery by Amazon entered the scene.

We do not know whether the current bundle of technological changes, including artificial intelligence, semiautonomous vehicles, and the Internet of Things, will eliminate more net jobs than previous innovations. However, those who have limited formal education or skills and who are not retrained for new opportunities will likely be at risk of losing jobs and remaining unemployed. Many technology-vulnerable jobs require limited independent judgment; workers rely more upon their strength and stamina than upon their intellect. The enduring negative impacts of economic disruptions, regardless of the cause, are often shouldered by older workers with long tenure in a firm or occupation, because employers replace them with less expensive younger workers. These replaced workers may suffer a double penalty: they may be stigmatized by employers for being unemployed, and they may also be discriminated against because of their age.

U.S. policymakers have been slow to respond to the disruptive impact of technological innovation on workers who must transition from job to job or from career to career. Congress set aside modest funds for workers dislocated by automation in the Manpower Demonstration and Training Act of 1962, but there have been no sustained, large-scale programs since. The United States consistently spends far less than other developed countries on labor force readjustment programs (Bentolila and Jansen 2016). The largest share of U.S. government workforce program funding is distributed through an unemployment insurance system that provides temporary and partial income replacement rather than skill development, job coaching, and placement. In calendar year 2017, the United States spent roughly $30 billion on unemployment insurance (Statista.com 2018), whereas federal spending on adult and dislocated worker retraining programs was just over $2 billion (Employment and Training Administration 2017).

The federal Workforce Innovation and Opportunity Act programs and the Wagner-Peyser Employment Service are chronically underfunded in relation to demand. As such, administrators concentrate their efforts on matching unemployed workers with job openings and short-term training programs. Also as such, better-prepared job applicants are more likely to be served than long-term unemployed job seekers (Van Horn, Krepcio, and Heidkamp 2015). Postsecondary financial aid programs, such as Pell Grants, are mainly designed to aid full-time students pursuing associate's or bachelor's degrees. Laid-off mature workers who need to update their skills or obtain certificates through short-term training courses receive limited federally funded benefits.

PERSPECTIVES ON TECHNOLOGY AND THE FUTURE OF WORK

The five chapters in this section address some of the most pressing issues about how individuals, employers, and policymakers can manage the inevitable disruptive changes affecting the economy and labor market. Taken together, these essays offer a wide array of evidence-based solutions to meeting these challenges.

"Navigating the Future of Work: Can We Point Business, Workers, and Social Institutions in the Same Direction?," by John Hagel, Jeff Schwartz, and Josh Bersin, identifies major labor market transformations that are due in large part to rapid changes in technology. While many of these disruptive forces are already occurring, businesses, policymakers, and individuals have not adjusted to these fundamental changes. According to the authors, "Unless all three of these constituencies manage to align in their understanding and actions to address emerging opportunities and challenges, the road to the future of work will be bumpy at best" (p. 176). The authors provide detailed recommendations for how that alignment can occur.

Chauncy Lennon and Sarah Steinberg, in "From Want Ads to Mobile Apps: Realizing the Promise of Technology in Labor Market Matching," describe how digital technology, including online job postings and the computer algorithms that employers use to sort applicants, have transformed the job search and hiring process. They propose strategies for helping job seekers and employers navigate an increasingly complex labor market. "Technology may ultimately have the potential to transform labor market matching for the better," the authors argue, "but serious challenges in the existing technology remain" (p. 203). Lennon and Steinberg conclude by outlining recommendations for policymakers, businesses, and job seekers.

In "Personalized Education: From Curriculum to Career with Cognitive Systems," Michael King, Richard Cave, Mike Foden, and Matthew Stent present extensive research on the educational opportunities made available through significant advancements in digital education and cognitive systems. These transformative developments enable educators to deliver personalized education and improve educational outcomes. "We believe that education is potentially at the dawn of a new era," the authors write (p. 215). However, they say, "educators will need to evolve by embracing cognitive systems to deliver personalized learning in order to drive improved outcomes for all" (p. 232).

Rachel Zinn and Bryan Wilson, in "All Data Big and Small: Using Information to Guide Workforce Development," review the progress by state governments in linking and analyzing administrative data systems collected by departments of education, higher education, labor, and other social service agencies. Overall, they conclude that while these "big data" initiatives have not reached their full potential, "there are compelling examples of data making a difference in building America's skilled workforce" (p. 234). They cite, as evidence, improved decision making regarding targeting resources to those most in need, better information for job seekers and students when they are choosing academic majors and careers, and improved service delivery by government agencies, educational institutions, and nonprofits.

Finally, Jordana Barton, in "Preparing Workers for the Expanding Digital Economy," emphasizes that without broadband digital access and literacy, rapid technological changes will make lives more difficult for individuals and communities. "Broadband is now a basic infrastructure essential to the well-being of all communities," she writes. Yet "these innovations are not available to all Americans" (p. 251). Fewer than half of households earning $25,000 or less have access to them. Barton reviews initiatives supported by the Federal Reserve System to expand broadband access by encouraging financial institutions to help close the digital divide, including through allocation of Community Reinvestment Act funds to support digital inclusion programs.

References

Bentolila, Samuel, and Marcel Jansen, eds. 2016. *Long-Term Unemployment after the Great Recession: Causes and Remedies*. London: Centre for Economic Policy Research.

Employment and Training Administration. 2017. "Training and Employment Guidance Letter No. 27-16." Washington, DC: U.S. Department of Labor, Employment and Training Administration. https://wdr.doleta.gov/directives/attach/TEGL/TEGL_27-16.pdf (accessed April 3, 2018).

Frey, Carl Benedikt, and Michael A. Osborne. 2017. "The Future of Employment: How Susceptible Are Jobs to Computerisation?" *Technological Forecasting and Social Change* 114(C): 254–280.

McAfee, Andrew, and Eric Brynjolfsson. 2017. "Why 'How Many Jobs Will Be Killed by AI?' Is the Wrong Question." Sunnyvale, CA: LinkedIn. https://www.linkedin.com/pulse/why-how-many-jobs-killed-ai-wrong-question-andrew-mcafee (accessed April 18, 2018).

Overly, Steven. 2016. "Artificial Intelligence Could Cost Millions of Jobs. The White House Says We Need More of It." *Washington Post*, December 20. https://www.washingtonpost.com/news/innovations/wp/2016/12/20/ai-could-cost-millions-of-jobs-the-white-house-says-we-need-more-of-it/ (accessed April 18, 2018).

Statista.com. 2018. *Total Monthly Unemployment Insurance Benefits Paid in the United States between January 2017 and January 2018 (in Billion U.S. Dollars)*. New York: Statista, the Statistics Portal. https://www

.statista.com/statistics/284857/total-unemployment-benefits-paid-in-the
-us/ (accessed April 18, 2018).

Van Horn, Carl E., Kathy Krepcio, and Maria Heidkamp. 2015. *Improving
Education and Training for Older Workers*. Washington, DC: AARP Policy
Institute.

14
Navigating the Future of Work

Can We Point Businesses, Workers, and Social Institutions in the Same Direction?

John Hagel
Jeff Schwartz
Josh Bersin

"THE FUTURE IS ALREADY HERE"

What images does "the future of work" conjure up for you? Keynes (1930), in an essay titled "Economic Possibilities for Our Grandchildren," foretold a future of "technological unemployment" and 15-hour workweeks. We've long since given up on early twentieth-century utopian visions of a leisure society in which machines do almost everything for us, but there's no question that what we do these days is changing fast and will continue to change.

Maybe in your particular future of work you imagine factories full of robots, automating commonplace tasks, while human beings orchestrate the work's ultimate goals and intent. Perhaps you think of the working population's shifting demographics, with the workforce growing older in developed nations, while emerging economies struggle to assimilate record numbers of young workers. Or you may envision a global gig economy in which most individuals work for themselves, lending their labor—physical or intellectual, online or in person—to a variety of employers on their own time and terms.

The future of work could involve all of these scenarios and more, as disparate forces act and interact to drive the way we behave in the pursuit of a comfortable living, a reasonable profit, and a stable and just society.

It's a big subject, and small wonder that pundits in the business and popular press have tended to narrow their focus, studying one or another of the dimensions of the future of work: automation, demographics, the growth of the contingent workforce, or something entirely different. While this narrowing of scope is understandable, the result is that we sometimes lose sight of the connections and interdependencies across all of these dimensions. We can't grasp where we are and where we're headed without seeing the full picture of this transformation in our lives, our businesses, and our society—and we can't see the whole thing unless we take a step back and let all the elements come into view.

The outlines of the picture are already emerging. Indeed, it may be misleading to explore all this under the heading of "the *future* of work," which suggests that the changes are not yet here and will occur in an indeterminate number of years. The truth is that many of these changes are already playing out, driven by forces that have been under way for decades. As science-fiction novelist William Gibson reminded us, "The future is already here—it's just not evenly distributed."

The biggest challenge in understanding the future of work comes in surfacing the implications for three broad constituencies—the individual, businesses and other employers, and social and governmental institutions—and getting all three pointed in the same direction. Unless all three of these constituencies manage to align in their understanding and actions to address emerging opportunities and challenges, the road to the future of work will be bumpy at best.

Under the best of circumstances, everyone—individuals, businesses, and public institutions—will find this fundamental evolution in the nature of work challenging and stressful. But if our organizational and public policy leaders understand more fully how this complex landscape is evolving, they can target their moves in ways that will help workforces around the world—and societies in general—anticipate and prepare for the coming challenges.

A FRAMEWORK FOR UNDERSTANDING THE FUTURE OF WORK

Forces of Change

What are the components that collectively constitute "the future of work"? Based on our experience and research, we have identified three forces that are shaping the nature of future work and the future workforce: technology, demographics, and the power of pull (changing market forces).

Technology: Artificial intelligence, robotics, sensors, and data

Technological advances—for example, in the areas of robotics, artificial intelligence (AI), sensors, and data—have created entirely new ways of getting work done that are, in some cases, upending the way we use and think about our tools and how people and machines can complement and substitute for one another.

Of course, past technological revolutions—mechanization, electrification, computerization—have also radically reshaped work, jobs, and the organization of business and society. The difference now is that today's advances in digital technologies are remaking not just manufacturing and low-skilled labor, the focus of past revolutions, but *every* sector of the economy and society.

Indeed, exponentially improving digital technology and infrastructures are reshaping the economics of work across the spectrum. On the one hand, automation is dramatically lowering the cost of certain routine tasks, as is expanded geographic access to low-wage labor. On the other, organizations can significantly augment the value of other tasks by leveraging technology capabilities and the increased ability to access deep specialization, wherever it is located.

Consider how today's technologies are beginning to augment human workers' capabilities. As just one example, by helping us "see" much more richly the evolving world around us, applications based on augmented reality (AR) can help us focus our curiosity, imagination, and creativity on early signals of the potential changes ahead that really matter (Mariani, Sniderman, and Harr 2017). Already, AR technology is helping workers out in the field, far from their desktop computers, to assess unexpected developments and focus their efforts on the actions that could have the greatest impact (Kaiser and Schatsky 2017). And it is hardly just cognitive technologies such as AR: in the robotics space, prosthetics and other augmentation devices are helping technicians and others perform operations unimaginable a decade ago.

More broadly, an expanding array of technologies, ranging from 3D printing to biosynthesis, are making productive tools accessible to smaller and smaller businesses, thereby eroding some of large companies' traditional advantages in developing and producing new products and services. This has the potential to create more viable job opportunities for workers in smaller enterprises over time.

We also should not lose sight of the impact of the accelerating pace of technology evolution and the proliferation of data on the skills required to do work. More and more knowledge is being created—with other knowledge becoming obsolete—at an accelerating rate, making it necessary to update our skills and job descriptions ever more rapidly to keep up (Bersin 2017).

Demographics: Longer lives, growth of younger and older populations, and greater diversity

The supply of workers is rapidly evolving globally as a result of shifting demographics, enhanced longevity, and increased focus on the inclusion of marginalized segments of the population (Buckley and Bachman 2017).

The workforce in many economies—especially the developed economies and China—is rapidly aging. This demographic trend is amplified by both low birthrates and enhanced longevity made possible by advances in public health and medicine. For a variety of reasons, ranging from financial need to a desire to continue to make a difference, many older workers are extending their careers well beyond traditional retirement age (Gratton and Scott 2016).

The prospect of older generations working for longer periods as their physical capability to remain employed improves could affect the pace at which younger talent and ideas renew organizations—and potentially intensify the intergenerational competition for jobs. It could also lead to a substantial increase in seniors participating in the "gig economy" out of postretirement desire or necessity.

In parallel, developing economies are supplying an increasing share of younger workers to the global workforce. Digital technology infrastructures are making a growing number of these workers accessible— as full-time or gig workers—to developed economies that are confronting an aging population, not to mention accessible to each other across the developing world.

More generally, women and many marginalized population segments are slowly gaining ground in employment spheres around the world. As population growth in developed countries slows, organizations will be under greater pressure to deepen the talent pool by including workers from more backgrounds. There is growing evidence that more diverse work groups and teams generate more creative and higher-impact results (Page 2008; Woolley and Malone 2011)—an even more important reason for organizations to become more aggressive in drawing in diverse segments of the global population. The likely net effect of all of this will be the workforce expanding to historically underrepresented populations, as well as organizations needing to change work practices to accommodate a more diverse employee base.

The power of pull: Customer empowerment and the rise of global talent markets

Largely thanks to digital technologies and long-term public policy shifts, individuals and institutions can exert greater "pull"—the ability to find and access people and resources when and as needed—than ever before. Institutions and prospective workers alike now have access to global talent markets, enabled by networks and platforms creating new possibilities for the way each interacts with the other. The demand for these platforms will likely be enhanced by increasing customer power and accessibility of productive tools and machines, opening up opportunities for more creative work to be done in smaller enterprises and by entrepreneurial ventures.

Market trends will also play a role in shaping the future of work. In responding to both changing customer demand and the ability to address labor needs more flexibly, the power of pull will likely lead to much tighter alignment of work with customer needs.

Why are customers acquiring more power relative to vendors? Because of their new ability to choose from an expanding array of product and service options globally, to access more information about these options, and to switch from one vendor to another if their needs are not being met.

With buying options expanding, customers are becoming less satisfied with standardized, mass-market products and services, instead seeking creative, tailored niche products, services, and experiences. This dynamic is playing out in digital product markets such as music, video, and software, but it has the potential to rapidly extend into physical products and services, as the technology trends outlined above make it far more feasible for niche vendors to access the means of production. The result is likely to be a growing fragmentation of product and service businesses, with small companies employing more of the overall labor force than currently (Hagel et al. 2014).

On the supply side, labor markets are evolving in ways that enhance organizations' ability to access and work with talent when and where needed. The global digital infrastructures discussed earlier are making it possible for employers to connect with, combine, and leverage talent wherever it resides. A growing array of digital platforms is making it easier for potential employers (and customers directly) to find the most appropriate talent anywhere in the world and to pull that talent together to perform specific tasks. Conversely, the same digital platforms are making it possible for workers to exert pull of their own. Online communities such as Glassdoor offer workers a great deal of insight into prospective employers' workings and culture, narrowing employers' historical informational advantage; and individuals operating in the gig economy can find, contract with, and work for employers worldwide using the Internet and other digital technologies.

The "power of pull" forces described above can spur growing demand for more creative work as customers shift away from mass-market products and services, as workers in smaller businesses gain greater access to the means of production, and as platforms help connect niche product and service providers with smaller segments of customers globally.

While there are other forces at play in shaping the future of work, we believe that they are part of the broader economic landscape. For example, globalization is a long-term trend, which is reinforced by the technological, demographic, and "power of pull" forces discussed above.

WORK AND WORKFORCES REDEFINED

These three forces of change are leading to a profound shift in the nature of work. Employers and workers will no doubt find this shift challenging in the near term, but ideally, a growing number of people over time will be able to achieve more of their potential. Routine tasks will be increasingly automated, while technology-aided creative work expands and evolves in response to a growing array of unmet needs (Davenport 2017; Evans-Greenwood, Lewis, and Guszcza 2017). Taken together, these forces are driving two significant transformations on work and the workforce. First, technology is transforming the nature of work and forcing organizations to redesign most jobs. One result, we anticipate, will be the reconfiguration of jobs to leverage uniquely human skills: empathy, social and emotional intelligence, and the ability to set context and define business problems. Another, due to the accelerating rate of technological change, will be the need for individuals to continually learn new skills to remain employable.

Second, the relationship between employer and worker is shifting. Where once most workers were full-time, on balance sheet employees with benefits and defined salaries, employers of the future will also execute a significant proportion of their activities through individuals engaged in alternative work arrangements, from freelancing to crowdsourcing to contract-based work.

Reengineering Work: Technology Reshapes Every Job

The industrial era defined work largely in the form of highly specialized and standardized tasks that became increasingly tightly integrated. This applied not only to factory jobs and manual work but also to a broad range of white-collar and knowledge-worker jobs such as HR staff, legal staff, and even salespeople and marketers. And it is precisely components of these types of work that are vulnerable to disruption by robots and AI. Law firms are beginning to automate a significant number of lawyers' more routine tasks, news websites are beginning to use AI to write news stories, and many of us use intuitive software to complete our taxes.

As technology accelerates its replacement of tasks once executed by humans, will it oust humans from performing work altogether (except for the work needed to build and maintain the machines)? Many conversations about the future of work quickly devolve into discussions of the potential for robotics and AI technology to cut costs, automate tasks, and displace human beings altogether. The anxiety is understandable, given these technologies' continuing exponential performance/price improvement and the impact they are already having on the elimination of jobs.

However, this narrow view misses much of the larger opportunity regarding future work and productivity. While perhaps a useful starting point, disassembling work into a set of tasks and orchestrating capabilities (people and machines) is not necessarily the goal. The greater opportunity to enhance productivity may lie in reinventing and reimagining work around solving business problems, providing new services, and achieving new levels of productivity and worker satisfaction and passion (Evans-Greenwood, Lewis, and Guszcza 2017). The growing availability of cognitive technologies and data also presents an opportunity to radically reengineer business processes leveraging the breadth and unique capabilities of people, machines, and data to achieve desired outcomes. We expect to see multiple approaches to redesigning jobs emerge: from a narrow focus on identifying tasks to automate, to the radical reengineering of business processes, to the reimagining of work around problem solving and human skills.

In this view, employers should become much more focused on exploring opportunities to create work that takes advantage of distinctively human capabilities, such as curiosity, imagination, creativity, and social and emotional intelligence. Research suggests that more than 30 percent of the high-paying new jobs created will be social and "essentially human" in nature (Deloitte 2016). Increasing diversity in the workforce will likely enhance the shift from routine tasks to more creative work, and we will see the emergence of hybrid jobs that increasingly integrate technical skills, design skills, and project management skills. The specific skills will likely come from diverse domains and evolve rapidly, increasing the need to accelerate learning for both individuals and employers to stay ahead of the game.

We are in the early days of integrating industrial and software robots into work—and of understanding their varying impacts and results. Thus far, the picture is blurry. Recent MIT research, for instance, explores industrial robots' negative impact on employment and wages (Acemoglu and Restrepo 2017), while at the same time, a Mercedes-Benz production facility in Germany recently announced plans to reduce the number of robots on its production line and replace them with human labor—with increasing demand for customized auto options, reprogramming and switching out robots was costlier than shifting the line using human workers (King 2016).

Transforming the Workforce: The Growth of Alternative Work Arrangements

Technology is transforming more than the way individual jobs are done—it is changing the way companies source labor. Many global companies already actively use crowdsourcing efforts to generate new ideas, solve problems, and design complex systems. Deloitte's own Center for Health Solutions and Center for Financial Services collaborated with insurance company specialists on an online platform provided by Wikistrat, in four days generating 44 use cases regarding the potential for using blockchain technology in insurance (Chang and Friedman 2016). Online platforms are playing a key role in accelerating the growth of this kind of crowdsourcing.

In the next few years, we are likely to see rapid growth of the gig economy—defined as individual self-employed workers bidding for short-term tasks or projects—driven by three factors. First, as companies face growing performance pressure, they will have more incentive to convert fixed labor costs, in the form of permanent employees, to variable labor costs incurred when there is a surge in business demand. Second, workers will likely increasingly seek work experiences exposing them to more diverse projects and helping them to develop more rapidly than in a single-employer career. (In a 2013 study, 87 percent of students in the United Kingdom with first- or second-class degrees said freelancing is a "highly attractive and lucrative career option" [Elance, n.d.]). And a third factor driving the growth of the gig economy is the desire of workers who are marginalized or underemployed—younger workers in developing economies, older workers in developed economies, and unskilled workers around the world—to find some productive work, even if it may not be full-time employment.

The gig economy already is becoming a significant component of work in the United States. A recent study by Harvard and Princeton economists shows that 94 percent of net job growth from 2005 to 2015 was in "alternative work" (Katz and Krueger 2016), defined as independent contractors and freelancers. The Bureau of Labor Statistics reported that 10.1 percent of the U.S. workforce are "true freelancer—individuals working in the 'gig economy' with no other primary stream of income" (Hipple and Hammond 2016).

Over the longer term, the gig economy may evolve into something quite different. Many of the gigs being done today—for example, drivers of cars in mobility fleets and basic data-gathering tasks—are routine tasks that are likely to be automated over time. Gigs based on human capabilities—emphasizing curiosity, imagination, creativity, social intelligence, and emotional intelligence—will likely grow over time.

As the gig economy shifts to more rapidly evolving creative work, the way that work is done is likely to change, moving from short-term transactions to longer-term relationships that can help accelerate learning and performance improvement. These more creative gigs—if they still qualify as gigs—will likely be increasingly done by small teams or work groups that will collaborate on different projects over extended periods of time (Polanyi 1967; Thomas and Seely Brown 2009; Weick 2009).

IMPLICATIONS FOR INDIVIDUALS, ORGANIZATIONS, AND PUBLIC POLICY

Implications for Individuals

In the new landscape of work, personal success will largely depend on accelerating learning throughout one's lifetime. As a lifelong learning imperative takes hold, we see individuals increasingly focusing on participation in small but diverse work groups that can amplify learning. Workers will need to take action on their own to enhance their potential for success, but the impact of their efforts will be significantly influenced by the willingness and ability of the other two constituencies—businesses and public institutions—to evolve in ways aligned with the shifting nature of work.

Engage in lifelong learning

As rapid technological and marketplace change shrinks the useful lifespan of any given skill set, workers will need to shift from acquiring specific skills and credentials to pursuing enduring and essential skills for lifelong learning. Individuals will need to find others who can help them get better faster—small work groups, organizations, and broader and more diverse social networks. We are likely to see much richer and more diverse forms of collaboration emerge over time.

Shape your own career path

Historically, a career was defined as a relatively stable, predictable set of capabilities that aligned with the needs of an organization and an industry. This included a progressive mastery of a set of predetermined skills required to advance in the corporate hierarchy, with accompanying salary boosts. But the half-life of skills and expertise is becoming shorter, with new, unexpected skills emerging as valuable. This has two implications. With needs constantly shifting, employers are less able to provide employees with well-defined career paths spanning years or decades. And workers, to keep their skills current, must increasingly do whatever is necessary to accelerate their learning, including pursuing a diversity of work experiences or working for multiple "employers" at the same time.

Rather than relying on paternalistic employers to shape careers' nature and progression, workers will need to take the initiative to shape their own personalized careers. And as work evolves, individuals should cultivate a "surfing" mind-set, always alert to emerging, high-value skills and catching the wave at an early stage to capture the most value from these skills (Bersin 2017). To avoid getting stretched too thin and stay motivated, they must filter a growing array of skill opportunities through their personal passions.

Pursue your passion

What are the obstacles to success in work as it transforms? The biggest obstacle may be ourselves. Most of us have an understandably negative reaction to the mounting performance pressure that is already beginning to accompany the transition to new forms of work. With any disruptive transition, we tend to experience fear and stress, generating an impulse to hold on to what has driven success in the past. We must resist that temptation and use the shifts in the nature of work and employment as an opportunity to achieve more of our potential.

What can help us do that? Instead of just viewing a job as a means to a paycheck, we need to find a way to pursue work that we are truly passionate about. In our research into diverse work environments where there is sustained extreme performance improvement—everything from extreme sports to online war games—we identified the one common element as participants having a very specific form of passion—something that we call the "passion of the explorer." This form of passion has three components: a long-term commitment to making an increasing impact in a domain, a questing disposition that actively seeks out new challenges, and a connecting disposition that seeks to find others who can help them get to a better answer faster (Hagel, Seely Brown, and Samoylova 2013a). Tapping into this kind of passion can shift people from the fear of change to excitement about the opportunity to learn something new and to have a greater impact.

Implications for Organizations

Employers can help individuals along this journey by shaping work and work environments and encouraging individuals to learn faster and accelerate performance improvement. One of the major opportunities and challenges for businesses in the coming years will be the strategies and investments they make in employee learning and development— both for assignment-specific and more general employment skills. Employees at all stages of their careers are placing a higher premium on the opportunities to learn on the job and reskill. Employers, especially those who value talent retention, will be reassessing and recalculating their investments and returns on "on-balance" and "off-balance" sheet talent—and likely making new levels of investment in development for the continuum of talent options.

Redesign work for technology and learning

To take effective advantage of technology, organizations will likely need to redesign work itself, moving beyond process optimization to find ways to enhance machine-human collaboration, drawing out the best of both and expanding access to distributed talent. Businesses will be well advised to not just focus on automation but to identify the most promising areas in which digital technology can augment workers' performance as they shift into more creative and value-added work. For example, how can the technology be harnessed to "make the invisible visible" by giving workers richer, real-time views of their work? How can companies use robotics to provide workers with access to environments that would be far too dangerous for humans (Mariani, Sniderman, and Harr 2017)? Below are two examples of the ways in which AI-based technology can complement human judgment and contextual knowledge to achieve better outcomes than either human or machine alone (Guszcza, Lewis, and Evans-Greenwood 2017).

1) **Augmented reality technologies.** For example, glasses that integrate what a technical repair specialist is actually working on supcrimposed on a schematic providing real-time analysis to facilitate troubleshooting and repair while allowing an off-site expert to observe the same machine configuration being repaired and to add a second set of eyes and insights. This solution allows technical repair workers to complete more repairs with more precision in less time (no need to go back to the office to check technical specifications and get a second opinion).

2) **Cognitive databases and algorithms being applied in medicine and finance.** IBM's Watson, as it is being applied to certain medical diagnostic fields, is augmenting the ability of physicians to more efficiently and accurately diagnose client illnesses, allowing doctors to make more diagnoses—faster and more accurately—and providing them more time to spend with patients explaining their conditions and treatments. Similar approaches are being applied in financial and investment management through robo-investment technologies—again, allowing investment professionals to potentially spend more time with clients.

This is perhaps the greatest challenge for businesses in the next decade: how to plan for the redesign and reinvention of work to combine the capabilities of machines and people, create meaningful jobs and careers, and help employees with the learning and support to navigate these rapidly evolving circumstances.

Organizations will not only need to redesign work, they will need to redesign work environments to support this new kind of work. There has been a lot of effort to reshape environments to make them more enjoyable and flexible to accommodate changing worker preferences and needs, but what if we took as our primary design goal to accelerate learning and performance improvement? What would work environments look like then (Hagel, Seely Brown, and Samoylova 2013b)?

Source and integrate talent across networks

As organizations develop a better understanding of the expanding array of talent options available, they will need to design and evolve networks that can access the best talent for specific work. Beyond focusing on acquiring talent to be employed in their own organizations, they will need to develop the capability to access good people wherever they reside. Since this talent will likely evolve rapidly, these networks will have to be flexible and adapt quickly to changing talent markets.

To accelerate learning and performance improvement, organizations will need to decide where they can truly be world-class and where they can access other talent from top global sources. They will need to cultivate a continuum of talent sources—on and off the balance sheet, freelancers, and crowds and competitions—that harness the full potential of the open talent economy and that taps into talent wherever it resides geographically.

Implement new models of organizational structure, leadership, culture, and rewards

Organizational structures are evolving from traditional hierarchical structures to networks of teams that extend well beyond the boundaries of any individual organization. Hierarchical structures are well suited for routine tasks, but as the emphasis shifts to more creative work done by small, diverse work groups connecting with each other in unexpected ways, more flexible network structures will become more important. As the continuum of talent resources expands and becomes more diversi-fied, organizations will need to develop richer relationships in larger business ecosystems and find ways to participate more effectively on scalable platforms to access expertise and enhance the ability to work together to accelerate performance improvement (Hagel, Seely Brown, and Kulasooriya 2012).

Organizations will need to cultivate new leadership and manage-ment approaches that can help build powerful learning cultures and motivate workers to go beyond their comfort zone. Indeed, leadership styles must shift from more authoritarian—appropriate for stable work environments shaped by routine, well-defined tasks and goals—to col-laborative. In the future of work, we expect that the strongest leaders will be those who can frame the most inspiring and high-impact ques-tions and motivate and manage teams.

To foster these new forms of creative work, organizations will need to reassess the rewards they offer to participants. In a world where rou-tine tasks define work, people look to extrinsic rewards such as cash compensation to stay motivated. As the nature of work shifts to more creative work that rapidly evolves, participants are likely to focus more on intrinsic rewards, including the purpose and impact of their work and the opportunity to grow and develop. Organizations may find it increasingly hard to hold on to employees if they focus narrowly on extrinsic rewards.

Implications for Public Policy

Policymakers have an interest in both hastening the emergence of new forms of work—the better to raise citizens' overall standard of liv-ing—and preparing for the stresses of the transition.

Reimagine lifelong education

Policymakers face significant and formidable challenges to rethink education to draw out students' creative capabilities and to establish a framework to help everyone develop their talent more rapidly *through-out* their lives. Our educational institutions were established, decades or even centuries ago, to provide for mass education for stable careers. The short half-life of learned skills and the rapidly evolving technological work landscape raise the need for new models that support ongoing training and education. How can we create educational models and funding that provide employees with three, four, or more opportunities to reskill and pivot to new fields and new careers?

Education and training can and are being provided and made available 24/7 via the Internet, creating significant new channels and modes of delivery. Businesses can work with educational institutions to certify training credentials that will be recognized in their firms and industry and potentially to offer their own "portable" certifications.

This emphasis on lifelong education could have an especially strong impact if it were to include a more effective focus on marginalized populations and older generations who do not want to or cannot transition out of the workforce. Payment structures and incentives could be designed to support this approach to lifelong education: facilitating access to ongoing education and training throughout a working career that might span 50 years and many different types of work.

Transition support for income and health care

What public policies can help in reducing the stresses that workers will likely face when shaping their own careers, learning new skills, and participating in global talent networks? For those caught in challenging and unexpected transitions, how can public policies help shorten the time spent on the unemployment rolls, support necessary retraining, and ensure the provision of basic necessities such as health insurance? Digital technology infrastructures and more accessibility to data about individuals will make it increasingly feasible to tailor transition programs to people's evolving needs. Governments around the world are considering and revisiting basic income guarantees in various forms. In addition, some recent proposals have surfaced to tax robots as one way to provide funding for transition support programs, which will be increasingly required given the pace of technological change disrupting so many careers and jobs in the coming decade (Shiller 2017).

Reassess legal and regulatory policies

What role can all dimensions of public policy play in accelerating broader inclusion in the workforce, talent development, and innovation capability? (See Eggers and Hagel [2012].) Governments should consider updating the definitions of employment to account for freelance and gig economy work and the provision and access to government health, pension, and other social benefits through micropayment programs. Business formation and bankruptcy rules could be updated to make it easier to launch—and exit—a business as an entrepreneur. The future of work will likely involve a higher percentage of start-ups and small businesses. Policymakers will likely find themselves under pressure to update regulations to make starting small ventures easier.

Note

This chapter is reprinted with permission from Deloitte University Press. See Hagel, Schwartz, and Bersin (2017).

References

Acemoglu, Daron, and Pascual Restrepo. 2017. "Robots and Jobs: Evidence from U.S. Labor Markets." NBER Working Paper No. 23285. Cambridge, MA: National Bureau of Economic Research.

Bersin, Josh. 2017. "Catch the Wave: The 21st-Century Career." *Deloitte Review* 21: 62–79.

Buckley, Patricia, and Daniel Bachman. 2017. "Meet the U.S. Workforce of the Future: Older, More Diverse, and More Educated." *Deloitte Review* 21: 46–61.

Chang, Christine D., and Sam Friedman. 2016. "Blockchain in Health and Life Insurance: Turning a Buzzword into a Breakthrough for Health and Life Insurers." Deloitte. https://www2.deloitte.com/us/en/pages/life-sciences -and-health-care/articles/blockchain-in-insurance.html (accessed September 19, 2017).

Davenport, Thomas H. 2017. "The Rise of Cognitive Work (Re)Design." *Deloitte Review* 21: 108–125.

Deloitte. 2016. *Talent for Survival: Essential Skills for Humans Working in the Machine Age.* Deloitte. https://www2.deloitte.com/content/dam/Deloitte/ uk/Documents/Growth/deloitte-uk-talent-for-survival-report.pdf (accessed September 19, 2017).

Eggers, William D., and John Hagel. 2012. "Brawn from Brains: Talent, Policy, and the Future of American Competitiveness." West Lake, TX: Deloitte University Press. https://dupress.deloitte.com/dup-us-en/topics/talent/brawn

-from-brains-talent-policy-and-the-future-of-american-competitiveness. html (accessed September 19, 2017).

Elance. n.d. *Generation Y and the Gigging Economy*. Mountain View, CA: Elance. www.csd.org.uk/content/uploads/2015/07/gen-y-and-the-gigging -economy.pdf (accessed April 20, 2017).

Evans-Greenwood, Peter, Harvey Lewis, and James Guszcza. 2017. "Reconstructing Work: Automation, Artificial Intelligence, and the Essential Role of Humans." *Deloitte Review* 21: 126–145.

Gratton, Lynda, and Andrew Scott. 2016. *The 100-Year Life: Living and Working in an Age of Longevity*. New York: Bloomsbury.

Guszcza, Jim, Harvey Lewis, and Peter Evans-Greenwood. 2017. "Cognitive Collaboration: Why Humans and Computers Think Better Together." *Deloitte Review* 20: 8–29. https://dupress.deloitte.com/dup-us-en/deloitte -review/issue-20/augmented-intelligence-human-computer-collaboration .html (accessed September 19, 2017).

Hagel, John, Jeff Schwartz, and Josh Bersin. 2017. "Navigating the Future of Work: Can We Point Business, Workers, and Social Institutions in the Same Direction?" *Deloitte Review* 21: 27–43.

Hagel, John, John Seely Brown, and Duleesha Kulasooriya. 2012. *Performance Ecosystems: A Decision Framework to Take Performance to the Next Level*. West Lake, TX: Deloitte University Press.

Hagel, John, John Seely Brown, and Tamara Samoylova. 2013a. *Unlocking the Passion of the Explorer*. West Lake, TX: Deloitte University Press.

———. 2013b. *Work Environment Redesign: Accelerating Talent Development and Performance Improvement*. West Lake, TX: Deloitte University Press.

Hagel, John, John Seely Brown, Tamara Samoylova, and Duleesha Kulasooriya. 2014. *The Hero's Journey through the Landscape of the Future*. West Lake, TX: Deloitte University Press.

Hipple, Steven F., and Laurel A. Hammond. 2016. "Self-Employment in the United States." *Spotlight on Statistics*, March. Washington, DC: Bureau of Labor Statistics. https://www.bls.gov/spotlight/2016/self-employment-in -the-united-states/home.htm (accessed September 19, 2017).

Kaiser, Ryan, and David Schatsky. 2017. *For More Companies, New Ways of Seeing: Momentum Is Building for Augmented and Virtual Reality in the Enterprise*. West Lake, TX: Deloitte University Press.

Katz, Lawrence F., and Alan B. Krueger. 2016. "The Rise and Nature of Alternative Work Arrangements in the United States, 1995–2015." NBER Working Paper No. 22667. Washington, DC: National Bureau of Economic Research.

Keynes, John Maynard. 1930. "Economic Possibilities for Our Grandchildren." In *Essays in Persuasion*. New York: W.W. Norton, pp. 358–373.

King, Alanis, 2016. "Mercedes Will Reduce Robots on Production Line, Employ More Actual Humans." *Jalopnik*. http://jalopnik.com/mercedes-will-reduce-robots-on-production-line-employ-1761720298 (accessed September 19, 2017).

Mariani, Joe, Brenna Sniderman, and Cary Harr. 2017. "More Real than Reality: Transforming Work through Augmented Reality." *Deloitte Review* 21: 146–163.

Page, Scott. 2008. *The Difference: How the Power of Diversity Creates Better Groups, Firms, Schools, and Societies*. Princeton, NJ: Princeton University Press.

Polanyi, Michael. 1967. *The Tacit Dimension*. New York: Anchor/Doubleday.

Shiller, Robert. 2017. "Why Robots Should Be Taxed If They Take People's Jobs." *Guardian*, March 22. https://www.theguardian.com/business/2017/mar/22/robots-tax-bill-gates-income-inequality (accessed September 19, 2017).

Thomas, Douglas, and John Seely Brown. 2009. "Learning for a World of Constant Change: Homo Sapiens, Homo Faber & Homo Ludens Revisited." Paper presented in June at the Seventh Glion Colloquium, University of Southern California, Los Angeles.

Weick, Karl. 2009. *Making Sense of the Organization, Volume Two: The Impermanent Organization*. Various locations: Wiley.

Woolley, Anita, and Thomas Malone. 2011 "What Makes a Team Smarter? More Women." *Harvard Business Review*, June. https://hbr.org/2011/06/defend-your-research-what-makes-a-team-smarter-more-women (accessed September 19, 2017).

15

From Want Ads to Mobile Apps

Realizing the Promise of Technology in Labor Market Matching

Chauncy Lennon
Sarah Steinberg

The impact of technology on jobs is an issue that has generated no shortage of column inches in recent years. But while economists, policymakers, and journalists debate important questions on the extent to which technology is changing the characteristics or even reducing the overall number of jobs in the economy, less attention has been directed at another way technology is changing one of the most basic functions of the labor market—how employers and job seekers find each other.

Long gone are the days when a job seeker would scour the Sunday paper for want ads, send paper résumés through the post office, and drop by the reception desk of prospective employers to inquire about openings or request applications. At the very least, most of these basic job search functions have moved online, increasing efficiency for both employers and applicants. Moreover, sophisticated technologies are now even removing the old "job description" and "résumé" formats from the process entirely, relying instead on sophisticated algorithms to determine fit based on skills and interests. Other tools are tackling some of the thorniest issues in labor market matching, such as implicit bias in hiring. Many job matches today are still made through friends and family, as has always been the case, but increasingly even these matches are happening online through social networks like LinkedIn.

Technological change is transforming everything from how individuals learn about career options and job openings to how employers find and assess candidates. This matters because finding the right person for the job is a crucial component of business success, employee well-being, worker productivity, and economic health. The consequences of getting the match wrong are high both for employees and employers. One estimate of the cost of replacing a worker is 60 percent of an employee's annual salary (Allen 2008). In this chapter, we examine the ways in which technology is changing labor market navigation, matching, and the decision making of students, job seekers, and employers.

While holding promise for job seekers and employers alike, many new technologies will need significant improvements to truly transform labor market matching. This chapter explores how the rapid expansion of technological platforms and applications is changing traditional labor market matching interactions, categorizes the five main functionalities of labor market matching technology, and highlights the benefits and limitations of each. Finally, we identify the biggest challenges facing the field and offer some recommendations for how labor market matching technology can create the most benefit for individuals, employers, and economies.

NEW TECHNOLOGY IS CHANGING HOW WORKERS AND EMPLOYERS FIND EACH OTHER

For anyone who has searched for a job in the past decade, it comes as no surprise that the Internet dominates today's hiring landscape. According to a recent Pew survey, the proportion of Americans who used online resources to search for jobs doubled from 26 percent in 2005 to 54 percent in 2015 (Smith 2015). When narrowing down to just those individuals who have sought work in the last two years, 79 percent used the Internet to search for jobs (Smith 2015).

Among employers, particularly large ones, the use of technology-enabled hiring tools is equally ubiquitous. A 2016 survey by the Society for Human Resource Management finds that 84 percent of employers now use social media to recruit job applicants—up from 56 percent in 2011 (Society for Human Resource Management 2016a). And it would be rare today to find a large employer that does not post job openings online or rely on an applicant tracking system to automatically pre-screen incoming résumés.

In many ways, the advantages of this new tech-enabled hiring landscape are clear. Online job boards, such as Monster or Idealist, are often simply the digitization of job listings that used to be placed on physical job boards or in newspapers. Employers now have the ability to reach a wide audience with just one posting instead of placing multiple ads across regional newspapers, and job seekers anywhere in the world can review and apply to jobs from the comfort of their own kitchen tables.

In addition to improving efficiency, new matching technologies can greatly increase and improve the information available to employers and job seekers by providing real-time data on both in-demand jobs and the skills possessed by the local workforce. One study finds that workers who used the Internet as a search tool were 28 percent less likely to exit their jobs than those who did not (Prakash 2014). This could be because job seekers who use the Internet are able to make more informed decisions about potential opportunities than the job seekers who do not.

Labor market matching technologies can also reduce friction and transaction costs in the market. Expanding the geographic range of a search could benefit low- and middle-skilled workers who live in an area of higher unemployment. The Internet has also reduced many of the costs associated with applying for a job. Companies can now receive many more résumés for each position and use sophisticated algorithms to filter those résumés, potentially increasing the chance of a successful match (Weber 2012). In many cases, job seekers face a streamlined application process and potentially more accurate, up-to-date information.

Finally, labor market matching technologies offer new ways to validate job seekers' skills to employers. This validation can range from demonstrating knowledge and skills in online tests to testimonials by coworkers on social networking platforms. These technologies also create a new opportunity to shift employer thinking to a more skills- and competency-based hiring model due to increased information sharing, which could particularly benefit low- and middle-skilled workers who can lack traditional credentials but possess in-demand skills. At the same time, automatic screening technologies can also serve to perpetuate and even exacerbate the barriers to employment that currently face some groups of workers, such as the long-term unemployed and individuals with criminal backgrounds.

JOB MATCHING TECHNOLOGIES VARY WIDELY IN COMPLEXITY AND UTILITY

For all the reasons outlined above, technology has the potential to strengthen labor markets and improve economic outcomes for workers. But for all its promise, the job matching technologies that dominate the market today face limitations in achieving these outcomes, particularly when it comes to improving matching for low- and middle-skilled workers. In this section, we'll describe the five distinct functionalities that make up existing labor market matching platforms, how each works to improve job matching, and some of the limitations of each.

Job Boards

Online job boards—which include the likes of everything from Craigslist to Monster to Idealist—are collections of job listings that occasionally include résumés from job seekers. Users of job boards can search for candidates or positions based on a number of variables or filters. Some job boards encompass multiple fields and industries, while others are narrower, such as those run by colleges and universities, metropolitan areas, and certain industries.

Job boards are one of the most accessible forms of labor market matching technology available. Together with social media platforms, job boards are often the only interaction that many individuals and small or medium-sized businesses will have with matching technology. No special training is needed to understand how to use job boards properly, enabling employers to swiftly post and collect résumés and individuals to search and apply for jobs based on key words or phrases. A recent survey by LinkedIn finds that, after personal referrals, the most common way that users found their new job was through a third-party website or online job board (LinkedIn Talent Solutions 2015).

Although less sophisticated than other matching technologies, job boards have had a powerful impact on the ways that individuals find jobs and that employers source employees. Job boards allow job seekers to find opportunities in their geographic regions and beyond (Prakash 2014) and allow employers to access a broader and more diverse talent pool. Finally, studies have shown that simply by using basic technology such as job boards, individuals are more "content" (Sampson and Obsorn 2013) with their jobs, and experience increased tenure at their place of employment (Mang 2012).

A serious limitation of job boards is that listings can be out-of-date, leading job seekers to waste time applying for roles that have already been filled. Searching through a high volume of listings on job boards can be overwhelming and detract from time that might be better spent engaging in other job search strategies, such as networking. Even knowledgeable job seekers using appropriate search terms or other criteria to sort through listings can be daunted by the quantity of information or miss suitable job openings.

Likewise, employers who post on job boards can be overwhelmed by the number of applicants who apply for a job, leaving them with the challenging task of sorting through more résumés than are feasible to review.

Algorithmic Matching Technologies

Algorithmic matching technologies rely on data science and machine learning to identify potential candidates and make precise matching recommendations (Carroll 2016). While the use of algorithmic matching technology is increasing, it is still far from universal. A study conducted by the Society for Human Resource Management finds that only 26 percent of employers surveyed use automated prescreening tools when assessing candidates (Society for Human Resource Management 2016b).

The majority of the existing platforms in this space focus on identifying individuals with special skills for high-skilled positions, rather than filling low- and middle-skilled openings. One example of an algorithmic matching technology that is attempting to better serve both small employers and middle-skilled workers is WorkFountain, a dynamic matching system that relies on correlated question sets and matching algorithms to connect job seekers and employers based solely on skills, interests, and requirements.[1]

Algorithmic matching technologies are still in the early stages of adoption, and their benefits and risks are still emerging. The use of algorithms has been praised for the potential to diminish implicit bias by recruiters (Feffer 2016) and for resulting in superior matching generally as judged by workers' job performance (Kuncel, Ones, and Klieger 2014). Moreover, algorithmic matching has great potential for businesses seeking candidates with a particular skill set and experience.

At the same time, algorithmic matching technologies have the potential to exacerbate some of the same issues they attempt to ameliorate. Companies may become increasingly focused on finding the ideal candidate to start with, rather than investing in on-the-job training. Furthermore, employers conducting the search may not be aware that their subconscious idea of "perfect" constitutes someone of a particular race, gender, or socioeconomic background (Lam 2015).

Online Skills Assessments

Skills assessments are used by employers and job seekers to assess an individual's suitability for a particular job or career. The focus of these tests can include job skills, cognitive ability, or behavior, and can range in form from straightforward questionnaires to more detailed games (Needleman 2016). For example, Koru is a predictive hiring platform that works with large employers to assess candidates by attempting to predict an individual's performance before he or she is hired. Job seekers take an online assessment that has been tailored to specific employer needs and company culture, and are evaluated on grit, rigor, impact, teamwork, curiosity, ownership, and polish. After completing the assessment, Koru indicates which candidates are the best fit for the employers based on these metrics.[2]

Employers increasingly use online skills assessments during the application process, with some researchers predicting that soon over 88 percent of employers with over 100 employees will use aptitude and personality tests during the hiring process (Chamorro-Premuzic 2015). Technology has made it easier to distribute tests and assess the results quickly and at lower cost (Weber 2015). Accordingly, their use has grown, and this type of assessment takes place earlier in the application process than it did previously. Between 2009 and 2014 alone, the percentage of U.S. workers who underwent testing as part of their application process increased from 30–40 percent to 60–70 percent (Weber and Dwoskin 2014).

Several studies have found that individuals who use skills assessments experience increased "career decidedness and career maturity" and "persistence in majors well aligned with career goals" (Karp 2013). And low- and middle-skilled workers may find online assessments particularly useful in identifying how their current skill set could lead to new training or employment opportunities in more lucrative fields. Several sites devoted to low- and middle-skilled workers feature some form of online skill assessment, either one created in-house or a link to an assessment like the Department of Labor's mySkills myFuture tool.

But there are also pitfalls to these assessments. An individual's responses on an assessment may not be a true indication of his or her interests or abilities. Companies that use such assessments must also be careful to ensure that their tests are not discriminatory. In theory, preemployment tests can reduce discrimination by objectively evaluating all applicants on the same set of job-related measures. In reality, however, some questions on personality tests have been accused of violating the Americans with Disabilities Act (Weber and Dwoskin 2014), and others have been shown to be implicitly biased against different genders (DiBernardo 2015).

Skill Building and Career Development Portals

Individuals are able to build their skill set and learn more about potential career paths or vocational opportunities through online portals. Interest assessments to identify potential career matches are frequently a component of these platforms, and platforms often provide information regarding the credentials that are required to obtain these jobs.

For example, petrochemworks.com is a career exploration and development site that helps users tap into career opportunities in the petrochemical industry.[3] Owned and curated by the East Harris County Manufacturers Association (ECHMA) in Texas, the site was created to inform students and job seekers about the petrochemical industry and help them get the education they need to prepare for a long-term career in the industry. The site features a suite of interactive tools to help users better understand the prospects the industry offers, along with the skills and educational requirements they will need to take advantage of those opportunities. Similarly, bankingonmycareer.com was designed by the financial services industry in New York City to inform students and job seekers about opportunities in the industry and orient them toward training and education that can prepare them for a career in financial services.

LearnUp is another platform that expands on the notion of career exploration by actually connecting users to open jobs.[4] An online recruiting platform that specializes in the retail, food service, hospitality, call center, and customer service industries, LearnUp allows job seekers to take online course modules to learn more about available jobs, build their skills, and receive coaching and support throughout the process. LearnUp provides preinterview training that helps individuals learn more about the job and enables companies like Old Navy and Staples to improve the quality and preparation of their entry-level applicant pool (Cutler 2015).

Skill building and career development portals face many of the same challenges as other technology-enabled labor matching tools. The multitude of platforms and abundance of information can make it challenging for users to determine the best tools for their purposes.

Likewise, platform operators are challenged by a dearth of up-to-date information on employers and the labor market generally, and cannot accurately communicate trends to platform users. Keeping data up to date requires an ongoing investment of time and resources.

Online Social Networks

Online social networks allow individuals to create profiles and build online personal and professional networks. In several respects, they are used differently than other labor market matching technologies. Many users of these platforms are not actively seeking new employment opportunities or potential hires. However, online social networks can have impact when used for labor market matching.

Many individuals still find work through personal connections or referrals (Adler 2015). Despite the increasing prevalence of labor market matching tools, most employers hire from personal networks or employee referrals. Online social networks have the potential to supplement this method of matching.

With these online platforms, individuals can easily find who in their network has connections to a potential employer or field, and employers can search for potential future employees among existing networks. In addition, as a recent World Bank report found, crowdsourced rating systems such as LinkedIn endorsements "help control quality, build trust, and maintain a live 'résumé'" (World Bank Group 2016).

Although online social networks can aid individuals in developing and maintaining their real-world networks, they are limited in their impact. Online social connections are less effective than real-world connections, in part because individuals can maintain a far larger network online with much less effort (Garg and Telang 2011). For example, a survey of LinkedIn users finds that connections on LinkedIn are most useful for securing interviews and job offers if one knows the connector offline (Garg and Telang 2011). This implies that the benefits of these technologies are limited for those who lack strong real-world connections.

Online social network technologies can also silo users based on demographics, further limiting their utility. LinkedIn, despite efforts to expand its base, is predominately used by high-earning individuals who have college degrees. A survey by Pew finds that while 46 percent of people who graduated from college use LinkedIn, only 25 percent of those with some college and 9 percent of those with a high school degree or less use LinkedIn (Duggan 2015). Partially in response, social networks like WorkHands have been designed to focus primarily on those in the skilled trades (Schwartz 2013).

This demographic stratification of online social network users has worrisome implications for social mobility. If low-, middle-, and high-skilled workers lack opportunities to connect with each other professionally, an additional barrier will exist for those who wish to move beyond their current professional sphere, and for employers who wish to improve diversity.

REALIZING THE PROMISE OF JOB MATCHING TECHNOLOGY WILL REQUIRE ADDRESSING ITS CURRENT LIMITATIONS

Technology may ultimately have the potential to transform labor market matching for the better, but serious challenges in the existing technology remain. We've identified four key challenges and provided recommendations for responding to each.

1)   Data Availability, Validity, and Timeliness

As with most technology, job matching tools are only as good as the data on which they rely. And access to quality data on labor market conditions, the nature of skills gaps regionally and nationally, and detailed analyses of occupational data by skill set is currently limited. Many of the technologies we've discussed rely on infrequently updated data libraries derived from federal government sources (like O*NET and the Bureau of Labor Statistics) or state government labor market information data.

In a fluid labor market where the skills needed by employers and the demands of the market shift frequently, stakeholders need to understand both the landscape of the current market and how that landscape will shape the future.

Recommendations:

- Standardize occupational and skills definitions: Stakeholders can ensure accurate and precise data by working collaboratively to improve data collection and standardization. One promising project, led by the University of Chicago with cooperation from the U.S. Department of Labor and other public and private organizations, will create an open-source nationwide database of labor market information and skills definitions. The system will aim to merge public and private data, provide locally relevant and real-time information, and establish the basis for further innovation in labor market matching technology that will benefit all stakeholders.[5]

- Design local tools with local data: Using local data in the design of a labor market matching tool can help ensure that the tool will provide information that is relevant to the local labor market.

- Collect data on long-term outcomes: Documenting job seeker outcomes after using technology tools will help refine tool design and provide further information about the job market, as well as prove the value of these technologies moving forward.

2)   The High Burden of Technological Adoption

For small and medium-sized employers, adopting new technology has real costs, both in money and time. Many small and medium-sized employers rely on human resources generalists to manage operations, or have no designated human resources positions. Moreover, smaller employers may hire only a handful of employees a year. Between limited human resources capacity and a lesser need, these organizations can be slower to adopt innovative technologies like algorithmic matching or human resources information systems. Perhaps it is no surprise then that employee referrals are still the top method for recruitment for businesses with fewer than 500 employees (Society for Human Resource Management 2016b).

Even if new gains are made in the field of labor market matching technology, smaller employers may be reticent to embrace them due to reliance on existing systems, the administrative burden of changing technology, and limited technical expertise. Moreover, technologies can become victims of their own success when unintended consequences lead to negative outcomes.

For example, the comparative ease with which job applications can be submitted electronically after jobs are posted on multiple job boards often means more candidates for open positions. An increased volume of applications, in turn, can push employers to change the minimum requirements for an open position in an effort to narrow the pool of applicants—a phenomenon known as degree inflation. Moreover, due to the ease with which employers can now post positions online, some job seekers find that openings in job boards are not always up to date or may contain other inaccuracies.

Recommendations:

- Intermediaries can help reduce transaction costs: Intermediary organizations that make it easier for employers and job seekers to navigate the labor market can reduce the costs associated with technological adoption. For example, the National Fund for Workforce Solutions supports industry partnerships that gather employers from different sectors to identify needs and provide training for job seekers that will help them meet these needs.[6]

- Platforms should better align and map skills: Technological platforms that better align the skills demanded by employers with the skills job seekers possess would encourage the adoption of skills-based hiring. These platforms make adoption easier for employers by creating a common language for skills and point job seekers toward the right licenses and credentials to demonstrate skills. Moreover, these platforms can provide feedback to companies and job seekers on the effectiveness of their job postings and applications, potentially making the job matching process more effective and efficient.

- Engage users in design process: By involving both employers and job seekers in the technology tool design process, technology tool designers can make sure that their results are helpful and user friendly for all stakeholders.

- Commit to invest in technology tools and definitions over the long term: Once a piece of technology is created, it requires continued refinement and redesign to align with changing technology standards, data, and best practices.

3) Hiring Bias

Implicit bias on the part of employers and hiring managers continues to disproportionately and negatively impact underrepresented groups. Employers still rely overwhelmingly on employee referrals, with approximately 50 percent or more of jobs gained through "informal channels" such as friends and family (Farrell 2012). These referrals often reinforce the benefits of existing social networks and overreliance on generic credentials rather than merit.

While "blind audition" practices like scrubbing résumés of identifiers may help lesson implicit bias in hiring decisions, some warn that algorithms underlying many labor market matching technologies can be just as bad as human filters. Certain variables may serve as unintended proxies for the type of candidate that a human hiring manager would also have filtered.

Moreover, there is often a difference between who a recruiter or human resources professional thinks is a good candidate and who a hiring manager eventually picks. Facebook has sought to create a more diverse workforce by incentivizing recruiters to identify and elevate candidates from underrepresented groups, but recent results show that hiring managers are still hiring candidates with the same demographic backgrounds as before (Seetharaman and Wells 2016).

Recommendations:

- Increase implicit bias training and awareness: To help improve diversity in hiring by reducing the impact of implicit bias, employers should provide bias training to everyone involved in the hiring process, from those conducting interviews to human resources staff to programmers developing matching software.

- Build blind auditioning and diversity metrics into technology: Technology developers can take an active role in reducing implicit bias in labor market matching by introducing blind auditioning practices into their technologies and emphasizing diversity metrics for job seekers. For instance, job matching platform Blendoor removes the identifying information of job seekers from their job applications to facilitate diversity recruiting, while providing job seekers with information on potential employers' employee resources, inclusion programs, and diversity makeup.[7]

4) Lack of digital literacy and access for low- and middle-skilled workers

Low- and middle-skilled workers face distinct challenges in leveraging labor market matching technologies to their greatest benefit. This is evidenced by the correlation between educational attainment and likelihood to go online during the job search: 65 percent of college-educated adults in the United States said they had looked for job information online, while only 44 percent of high school graduates said the same (Smith 2015).

One challenge is that labor market matching technology exists primarily online, and low- and middle-skilled workers, who typically have wages below the median (Tüzemen and Willis 2013), are disproportionately likely to lack access to computers and the Internet at home. Only 63 percent of those with a household income between $20,000 and $50,000 have access to broadband Internet at home, compared to 80 percent of those with a household income between $50,000 and $75,000 (Horrigan and Duggan 2015).

Low- and middle-skilled workers are also more likely to rely on just their cell phones for Internet access and can face digital literacy challenges (Smith 2015). While job seekers with varying degrees of education use their smart phones for job searching at approximately the same rate, job seekers who have not attended college are much more likely to use their smart phones to fill out an online job application and create a résumé or cover letter than those who have graduated from college (Smith 2015). Moreover, low- and middle-skilled workers more frequently lack proficiency in using computers and the Internet, making it difficult to navigate labor market matching technology (Smith 2015).

Low- and middle-skilled job seekers rely on external coaches, counselors, and mentors—such as those at American Job Centers—to navigate labor market matching technologies. Often, however, career coaches are underresourced or have a poor grasp of technology themselves. At community colleges, the ratio of guidance counselors to students can be as high as 1 to 1,500, making it difficult to provide quality services to students (Karp 2013).

Finally, underrepresented communities may have trouble seeing themselves in occupations not typically held by those in their social network. Technology can help expand awareness of the universe of job openings, but individuals may still perceive a barrier to applying for a job they have not seen others in their community holding or of which they have no prior knowledge.

Recommendations:

- Incorporate skill building and career latticing into matching platforms: Labor market matching technologies can improve outcomes for low- and middle-skilled workers by helping job seekers learn which skills are necessary for a given job opening and, if necessary, how to acquire those skills through education and training. For example, LearnUp allows job seekers to both find job openings and take online course models that help them build skills and prepare for an interview.[8]

- Use target-audience language: The language used in job postings should correspond to the language skills of the target job seeker. For example, PostingPro, a tool recently launched by Code for America, assesses the grade level of language in job postings to ensure that they match the academic level necessary to be successful in the position.[9]

- Design for mobile optimization: Low-income individuals are more likely to rely on mobile phones for Internet access, making mobile optimization of labor marketing tools particularly vital for this population.

- Offer in-person assistance: Because human coaches can have the most impact in expanding access to labor market matching technology and improving outcomes for low- and middle-skilled workers, it is vital to invest resources and training for coaches and counselors. Human coaches who are trained to effectively use job matching platforms can amplify the benefits of these tools for their clients.

CONCLUSION

As technological innovations have boosted data collection and processing capabilities in the past decade, new tools and platforms are changing how job seekers and employers find each other. Combined with overall labor market trends that see workers moving jobs more frequently and increasing demand for specialized skills, these matching technologies will continue to play a critical role in the labor market.

It is clear that technology can both help and hinder, depending on how it is designed and implemented. At its best, technology has the potential to increase the efficiency and quality of matches, while reducing information deficits and transaction costs. But without thoughtful design, tools might merely shift what used to be offline into an online world, creating new and higher access limitations and hiring biases. Unfortunately, that may be the case with many existing matching tools—especially if they do not enable skills-based hiring or provide in-person assistance to complement the primarily online tools.

By ensuring that the data that undergirds the technology is as precise, accurate, and timely as possible, outcomes from these technologies can start to match their promise. Moreover, by enhancing assistance and on-ramps to the technology for low- and middle-skilled workers, stakeholders can work to ensure that technological innovation benefits workers at all skill levels.

Notes

The content in this chapter is adapted from research sponsored by JPMorgan Chase & Co. and conducted by Freedman Consulting, LLC. The research is detailed in the report "Swiping Right for the Job: How Tech Is Changing 'Matching' in the Workforce," and draws on interviews with 45 experts and practitioners in labor market matching technology.

1. See https://workfountain.com (accessed November 2, 2017).
2. See http://www.joinkoru.com/koru-7 (accessed November 2, 2017).
3. See https://petrochemworks.com (accessed November 2, 2017).
4. See http://www.learnup.com (accessed November 2, 2017).
5. See Data at Work, "Open Skills Project," http://dataatwork.org/data/ (accessed November 2, 2017).
6. See https://nationalfund.org (accessed November 2, 2017).
7. See http://blendoor.com (accessed November 2, 2017).
8. See Note 4.
9. See https://www.codeforamerica.org/government-partners/new-orleans-la (accessed November 2, 2017).

References

Adler, Lou. 2015. "The Mind-Blowing Reason Behind How the Best Employees Find Jobs." *Inc.*, July 23. https://www.inc.com/lou-adler/how-people-get-jobs-rewriting-your-future-history.html (accessed November 2, 2017).

Allen, David. 2008. *Retaining Talent: A Guide to Analyzing and Managing Employee Turnover*. Alexandria, VA: Society for Human Resource Management Foundation. https://blog.shrm.org/workforce/retaining-talent-a-guide-to-analyzing-and-managing-employee-turnover (accessed November 2, 2017).

Carroll, Robert. 2016. "How OKCupid Changed Hiring Forever." *Recruiting Daily.* http://recruitingdaily.com/how-okcupid-changed-hiring-forever/ (accessed November 2, 2017).

Chamorro-Premuzic, Tomas. 2015. "Ace the Assessment." *Harvard Business Review*, July/August. https://hbr.org/2015/07/ace-the-assessment (accessed November 2, 2017).

Cutler, Kim-Mai. 2015. "LearnUp, a Startup Closing the Skills Gap for Entry-Level Job Seekers, Raises $8m from NEA, Shasta." https://techcrunch.com/2015/09/16/learnup-a-startup-closing-the-skills-gap-for-entry-level-job-seekers-raises-8m-from-nea-shasta/ (accessed November 2, 2017).

DiBernardo, Amanda. 2015. "Pre-employment Personality Testing: A Literature Review." LinkedIn, June 26. https://www.linkedin.com/pulse/pre-employment-personality-testing-literature-amanda-dibernardo (accessed November 2, 2017).

Duggan, Maeve. 2015. "The Demographics of Social Media Users." Washington, DC: Pew Research Center. http://www.pewinternet.org/2015/08/19/the-demographics-of-social-media-users/ (accessed November 2, 2017).

Farrell, Chris. 2012. "The Best Way to Land a Job? It's Still Word of Mouth." *Bloomberg*, May 31. http://www.bloomberg.com/news/articles/2012-05-31/the-best-way-to-land-a-job-its-still-word-of-mouth (accessed November 2, 2017).

Feffer, Mark. 2016. "Algorithms Are Changing the Recruiter's Role." Alexandria, VA: Society for Human Resource Management. https://www.shrm.org/hrdisciplines/staffingmanagement/articles/pages/algorithms-changing-recruiters-role.aspx (accessed November 2, 2017).

Garg, Rajiv, and Rahul Telang. 2011. "To Be or Not to Be on LinkedIn: Job Search Using Online Social Networks by Unemployed Workforce." SSRN. http://papers.ssrn.com/sol3/papers.cfm?abstract_id=1813532 (accessed November 2, 2017).

Horrigan, John, and Maeve Duggan. 2015. "Home Broadband 2015." Washington, DC: Pew Research Center. http://www.pewinternet.org/2015/12/21/home-broadband-2015/ (accessed November 2, 2017).

Karp, Melina M. 2013. "Entering a Program: Helping Students Make Academic and Career Decisions." CCRC Working Paper No. 59. New York: Community College Research Center, Teachers College, Columbia University. http://ccrc.tc.columbia.edu/media/k2/attachments/entering-a-program.pdf (accessed November 2, 2017).

Kuncel, Nathan R., Deniz S. Ones, and David M. Klieger. 2014. "In Hiring, Algorithms Beat Instinct." *Harvard Business Review*, May. https://hbr.org/2014/05/in-hiring-algorithms-beat-instinct (accessed November 2, 2017).

Lam, Bourree. 2015. "For More Workplace Diversity, Should Algorithms Make Hiring Decisions?" *Atlantic*, June 22. http://www.theatlantic.com/business/archive/2015/06/algorithm-hiring-diversity-HR/396374/ (accessed November 2, 2017).

LinkedIn Talent Solutions. 2015. "Why & How People Change Jobs in N. America." Sunnyvale, CA: LinkedIn. http://www.engagedcareers.com/media/2015/09/LinkedIn-Job-Switchers-Report.pdf (accessed November 2, 2017).

Mang, Constantin. 2012. "Online Job Search and Matching Quality," Ifo Working Paper No. 147." Munich: Leibniz Institute for Economic Research at the

University of Munich. http://EconPapers.repec.org/RePEc:ces:ifowps:_147 (accessed November 2, 2017).

Needleman, Sarah. 2016. "Play This Game and Win a Job!" *Wall Street Journal*, March 14. http://www.wsj.com/articles/play-this-game-and-win-a -job-1457921553 (accessed November 2, 2017).

Prakash, Anila. 2014. "Does Internet Job Search Result in Better Matches?" Tucson: University of Arizona. https://econ.arizona.edu/sites/econ/files/ jobmkt_anila_2014nov14.pdf (accessed November 2, 2017).

Sampson, James Jr., and Debra Osborn. 2013. "Using Information and Communication Technology in Delivering Career Interventions." Tallahassee: Florida State University. http://career.fsu.edu/content/download /286610/1986119/201304_UsingICTinDeliveringCareerInterventions_ PPT.pdf (accessed November 2, 2017).

Schwartz, Ariel. 2013. "WorkHands Is a LinkedIn for Blue Collar Jobs." Fast Company, September 10. http://www.fastcoexist.com/3017043/workhands -is-a-linkedin-for-blue-collar-jobs (accessed November 2, 2017).

Seetharaman, Deepa, and Georgia Wells. 2016. "Facebook's Point System Fails to Close Diversity Gap." *Wall Street Journal*, August 16. http:// www.wsj.com/articles/facebooks-point-system-fails-to-close-diversity -gap-1471387288 (accessed November 2, 2017).

Smith, Aaron. 2015. "Searching for Work in the Digital Era." Washington, DC: Pew Research Center. http://pewinternet.org/2015/11/19/searching -for-work-in-the-digital-era/ (accessed November 2, 2017).

Society for Human Resource Management. 2016a. "SHRM Survey Findings: Using Social Media for Talent Acquisition—Recruitment and Screening." Alexandria, VA: Society for Human Resource Management. https://www .shrm.org/hr-today/trends-and-forecasting/research-and-surveys/Pages /Social-Media-Recruiting-Screening-2015.aspx (accessed November 2, 2017).

———. 2016b. "Talent Acquisition: Recruitment." Alexandria, VA: Society for Human Resource Management. https://www.shrm.org/hr-today/trends -and-forecasting/research-and-surveys/Documents/Talent-Acquisition -Recruitment.pdf (accessed November 2, 2017).

Tüzemen, Didem, and Jonathan Willis. 2013. "The Vanishing Middle: Job Polarization and Workers' Response to the Decline in Middle-Skill Jobs." Kansas City, MO: Federal Reserve Bank of Kansas City. https://www.kansascityfed .org/publicat/econrev/pdf/13q1tuzemen-willis.pdf (accessed November 2, 2017).

Weber, Lauren. 2012. "Your Résumé vs. Oblivion." *Wall Street Journal*, January 24. http://www.wsj.com/articles/SB100014240529702046242045771 7 8941034941330 (accessed November 2, 2017).

————. 2015. "Today's Personality Tests Raise the Bar for Job Seekers." *Wall Street Journal.* http://www.wsj.com/articles/a-personality-test-could-stand -in-the-way-of-your-next-job-1429065001 (accessed November 2, 2017).

Weber, Lauren, and Elizabeth Dwoskin. 2014. "Are Workplace Personality Tests Fair?" *Wall Street Journal,* April 14. http://www.wsj.com/articles/ are-workplace-personality-tests-fair-1412044257 (accessed November 2, 2017).

World Bank Group. 2016. "Digital Dividends." *World Development Report 2016.* Washington, DC: World Bank. http://www-wds.worldbank.org /external/default/WDSContentServer/WDSP/IB/2016/01/13/090224b08 405ea05/2_0/Rendered/PDF/World0developm0000digital0dividends.pdf (accessed November 2, 2017).

16
Personalized Education

From Curriculum to Career with Cognitive Systems

Michael King
Richard Cave
Mike Foden
Matthew Stent

In many parts of the world, education is considered to be failing its stakeholders, be they students, educators, or employers. This narrative is rooted in the belief that education is too expensive and fails to provide value for the amount of money paid to acquire it. There is a growing disconnect between what education delivers and the skills being demanded in today's ever-changing global marketplace. The net result is that upon leaving full-time education, many young people are ill prepared for the world of work. At the same time, we are seeing unprecedented levels of change across industries and professions, with digital technologies serving as agents of transformation. Businesses are increasingly faced with a simple proposition: reinvent or die. However, in education, the same sense of pressure and urgency seems to be lacking. This may simply be because educators may be lacking clarity on the correct path to pursue. From our discussions with educators around the world, a harder-working, more dedicated and caring profession would be hard to find.

At IBM, our view is that education's "stakeholder failure narrative" does not have to play out in this way. We believe that education is potentially at the dawn of a new era, and in this chapter we will explain how

- despite challenges, digital education services are being embraced by educators;

- cognitive systems will enable personalized education and, ultimately, the educational experience will be improved when data can be used to benefit students and the entire learning community.

Data-driven cognitive technologies will enable personalized education and improve outcomes for students, educators, and administrators. Ultimately, educational experiences will be improved when data can accompany the student throughout his or her lifelong learning journey.

ABOUT THE RESEARCH

In this research, we set out to discover how educators are using digital education services and cognitive systems to deliver personalized education (a combination of educational programs, learning experiences, instructional approaches, academic-support strategies, and technology that is intended to address the distinct learning needs, interests, aspirations, or cultural backgrounds of individual students). We wanted to cut through the industry hype and understand from early adopters how it worked in real life: What are the challenges, what can we learn from successful implementations, and what are the results? What did vendors think was possible, and what did students actually experience? The chapter is based on four research inputs:

1) In-depth interviews with 47 educational providers and 6 vendors in the United States, India, South Africa, and the United Kingdom (UK)

2) A survey of 126 IBM interns based in the UK

3) Interviews with three IBM Watson partners who are working on cognitive systems for educators

4) Social listening from more than 150,000 tweets relating to conversations around education

TERMINOLOGY

Most countries organize their education systems into three phases:

1) Primary/elementary: < 12 years old

2)   Secondary/high school: 12–18 years old

3)   University/college: > 18 years old

We use the terms *primary* and *elementary* interchangeably, as well as the terms *secondary* and *high* school, except where specifically referencing quotes.

- *Teacher*. We use this term to refer to educators in primary/elementary and secondary/high school.

- *Lecturer/professor*. We use this term for educators in universities/colleges.

- *Education management*. We use this as an aggregate term to cover a range of management roles such as provost, vice chancellor, and head teacher.

IT'S A DIGITAL WORLD

Over the past few decades, the role of technology in education ("EdTech") has continually evolved. In classrooms and lecture halls, "chalk and talk" has increasingly been complemented by digital tools and platforms, which typically vary in scope and sophistication according to where the student is on his or her educational journey.

It is clear that student appetite for digital tools across the whole gamut of education is strong (e.g., Cortez 2017). This fosters a learning environment that is more engaging, more hands-on, more meaningful and memorable, and creates better learning outcomes. In a sense, this is a reflection of how today's students live their lives beyond education. This trend is putting pressure on education professionals as they seek to meet the growing demands of "digital natives." As a primary-school teacher commented, "The kids we're getting now have grown up on technology. They're learning how to use it. . . . They're a lot better than we are, and that's a scary element."

Transformative approaches that may become more widespread include elements of gamification, whereby groups of students can connect and collaborate across different schools and geographical boundaries. Schools are experimenting with innovative "glocal" classrooms (characterized by both "global" and "local" tendencies), in which the lesson is brought to the student to overcome challenges of distance and income found in the developing world. Add to this the potential for virtual-reality field trips, 3-D printing, and foreign-language video conferencing sessions with schools in different countries, all of which point to exciting possibilities for students and educators.

"The kids are very engaged with technology. . . . Any time we can incorporate technology in a lesson, you're adding visual, you're adding audio, you're adding tactile. When they're hands-on with a piece of technology, it sticks better because we are using all modalities of learning," says an educator at a U.S. high school.

CHALLENGES IN ADOPTING THE NEW TECHNOLOGIES

Educators may legitimately ask, "Haven't we been here before?" Many report poor experiences with technology, which they say failed to deliver against expectations and was difficult to use and impossible to integrate with existing and new technologies. Many issues conspire against greater use of digital technologies (see Table 16.1). Furthermore, concepts such as blended learning (an educational program that combines online digital media with traditional classroom methods) and flipped classrooms (a teaching model in which the typical lecture and homework elements of a course are reversed, so that short video lectures are viewed by students at home before the class session, while in-class time is devoted to exercises, projects, and discussions) simply cannot be implemented if students don't have Internet access at home. And this is not just a developing world challenge: the use of digital tools within educational establishments appears to be fairly laissez-faire, rather than strategic. For instance, at a South African university, a source says, "Experience of using digital services really depends on the lecturer. Some lecturers use it widely and some use it very little. There is no one practice in the university."

There are also generational issues to consider. Many teachers never used such tools when they were learning, so they question their pedagogical efficacy. Moreover, educational professionals choose the

Table 16.1 Challenges for the Adoption of Digital Education Today

Market	Extreme competition and fragmentation of digital learning services market leads to information overload and confusion in the mind of the end consumer (educational institutions).
Integration	Lack of integration between current digital learning solutions makes it difficult to track learning outcomes and measure return on investment.
Operational	It is difficult to implement personalized learning pedagogies in classrooms where students are at varying skill levels. Teachers struggle to manage multiple log-ins across platforms.
People	Lack of a dedicated information technology (IT) team to resolve technical issues, causing frustration and a drop in usage among students and faculty. Teachers are not trained to use the technology in the classroom and are resistant to using anything outside their traditional teaching methods.
Economics	Schools have limited budgets, with a pushback for rising tuition costs and reductions in state and federal funding and limited funds to invest in digital learning solutions.

SOURCE: Authors' compilation.

extent to which digital tools are present in their teaching toolbox, if at all. According to a professional education organization from the United Kingdom, "The major challenge is getting professors to deliver content in a digital form. Most professors have been teaching the same content for years and don't want to start delivering audio or video lectures and designing online courses."

There are also risk issues when it comes to adopting new digital technologies. Will new tools integrate with existing IT investments, and will they meet curricular standards? As new vendors arrive on the scene, diversity of choice only adds to these risk factors. As a teacher from a U.S. elementary school responds, "One of the questions we have to answer is: Are these resources meeting common core standards? Are they using state standards, or are they using district standards? My biggest challenge is I don't know what the best apps are out there to support my curriculum."

While such challenges are difficult, they are not insurmountable. We identified a number of leading practices that educational establishments are testing and implementing (Box 16.1).

TRAINING THE TRAINERS

Many teachers are frustrated that training is inadequate, based on our interviews with educators and monitoring of social media discussions on education. Because technology changes so quickly and upgrades are common, the sheer pace of change is difficult to keep up with. The consensus view is that training works best when it is not delivered as a week-long preterm event but is provided continuously, in bite-sized chunks.

Institutions often implement staff mentoring programs such as "digital champions" or "buddy-up schemes" for colleagues to learn from each other. Many report that this often works by having younger, more tech-savvy teachers working with older-generation teachers in a "reverse mentoring" program. Says a source from one high school, "If 'old teacher in Room 30' sees 'new teacher in Room 31' and [the new teacher's] kids are all fired up and excited walking out of that class, he/she's going to ask, 'What are you doing in there?' [The other teacher]

Box 16.1 Digital Leading Practices in Education

- Appoint a formal digital learning leader or team.

- Encourage and reward teacher enthusiasts, champions, and advocates and use them as mentors.

- Employ "reverse mentoring" by having recent graduate teachers advise an older generation of teachers on digital tools.

- Establish focus groups to continually understand student needs.

- Use digital armbands (flash drives) to permit offline working.

- Offer interactive and continuous training for teachers.

SOURCE: Authors' compilation.

will reply, 'I'm doing this. . . . I'll help you.' We try to get the teachers who are excited to be the evangelist for their department."

So rather than a top-down, vendor-led training approach that is often difficult to digest in one go, the leading-practice approaches are piecemeal, ongoing, and informally driven by the staff themselves. As a primary teacher commented, "We have what's called 'Technology Thursdays,' with different things offered each Thursday. It really has to be a gradual, iterative process. There are three of us who are technology-oriented. We've picked three other teachers that we work with."

HOW ARE ANALYTICS HELPING?

The majority of educational establishments we interviewed are using analytics in a limited "rear view" way (descriptive ["What happened?"] instead of predictive ["What will happen?"]; see Figure 16.1). This university's experience is fairly typical of those we spoke with: "On the spectrum of analytics capabilities, we're at the diagnostic level," says the educator from the South African university. "Our system can alert us to students' defaults and would usually tell us which students are at risk of failing. This is what we mostly use it for right now. I am sure it can do a lot more, but this is how we use it for the moment."

Where analytics *are* used, the existing analytics tools are often underutilized. A representative of a UK professional education organization explains that personnel often don't take advantage of the tools because they're not sure how to. "Our university isn't unique in saying our LMS (learning management system) has a lot of analytics within it, but they probably use 10 percent of this," the representative says. "A deeper understanding of analytics is going to be a big trend in the next five years." Such an understanding would make use of the analytics not only of descriptive ("What happened?") and predictive ("What will happen?") but of diagnostic ("Why did it happen?") and prescriptive ("What should I do?"), the four categories shown in Figure 16.1.

We did not find much use of analytics to measure the efficacy of learning. The most cited reason is too many variables, making it impossible to isolate any one thing. "It's not necessarily one technology or two, so it's very hard to measure the impact," the South African

Figure 16.1 Most Educational Establishments Are Only Using Limited Analytics Capabilities

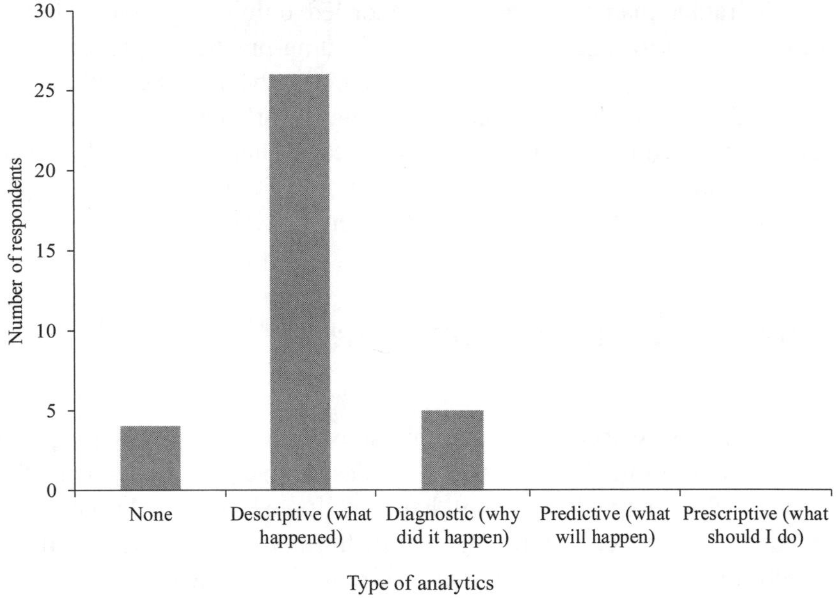

SOURCE: Authors' compilation.

university professor says. "Generally, pass rates have gone up and retention rates have increased, but it would be hard to pinpoint if this is because of a 'flipped classroom'; there are so many reasons."

This in turn may make the return on the investment in digital tools difficult to measure and justify. There is certainly a role here for policy-makers. Recently, in a consultation paper published by the Department for Business, Innovation, and Skills (2015), now called the Department of Business, Energy, and Industrial Strategy, the UK government sought to address the need for institutions to provide more insight on teaching efficacy through deeper analytics. "The government's teaching excellence framework seeks to drive increasing use of analytics, and one of the challenges is to understand student pain," says a representative from a UK professional education organization. "Are students having specific problems? Are they whizzing through stuff and achieving high standards, meaning the course is too easy? These are all questions that can be answered with good analytics" (IBM 2016).

HOW COGNITIVE SYSTEMS CAN ENABLE PERSONALIZED EDUCATION AND IMPROVE OUTCOMES

While the tools and concepts discussed in the previous section have undoubtedly moved education forward, the impact of technology on education as a whole has been evolutionary rather than revolutionary. However, we believe that education is now on the precipice of a transformative next step: the capability to deliver learning on a more individualized basis. New digital tools, coupled with advanced analytics and cognitive systems (more on these later), will eventually facilitate the utopia of teaching—personalized learning.

As observed in other industries, when new digital tools gain traction, this eventually leads to a tipping point of mass adoption, and disruption is caused when the value proposition becomes so overwhelming that it displaces the status quo (think Amazon or Uber). Ultimately, this culminates in the balance of power shifting to the end user, in this case the learner.

As yet, there has not been an "Uber moment" for education. We have, however, seen pockets of disruption taking place. Early successes have served as a postscript to formal education in the form of massive open online courses (MOOCs). In these platforms, learners plug skills gaps with microlevel credentials and pull relevant content on demand rather than being pushed toward completing a one-size-fits-all course: "Rather than going through an entire certification program, users are going through the courses they want to go through," says a representative from a U.S. professional education organization. "We are seeing the balance of power shift to the end user, with more focus on timely training that solves the learning needs and a deemphasis on certifications."

Another possible indicator of early-stage disruption is that 59 percent of IBM's interns say they are discovering digital tools themselves, versus 43 percent who say they discover them as a result of recommendations from faculty.[1] In addition, we are seeing the use of digital tools increase as students climb the rungs of academia. One lecturer observed that "PhD students were very interested in talking about their use of MOOCs, and [they] access experts from all over the world."

Elements of personalization are also taking shape in traditional university settings to deliver a better, more holistic learning experience: "The thing that we're trying to do, particularly in our business school, is to personalise the learning experience," writes a UK university educator. "This supports the students far better in achieving their learning and education goals. I can actually see evidence that this is working at our university. We're trying to understand what is special about each individual so that we can help them meet their potential."

There have often been attempts within education to differentiate across students either through setting (grouping students within a particular subject area based on their having similar abilities in that subject) or streaming (grouping students of similar abilities in a class that stays the same for all subjects rather than regrouping them for each individual subject depending on their ability in that particular subject). Traditionally, teaching capacity limits this to generalized cohorts of students, although in recent years data is increasingly being used to aid educators in this process. However, this process still requires considerable manual data interpretation, making it a complex, time-intensive task. Cognitive systems will "unburden" this task by augmenting and being complementary to the skills of the teacher/tutor. In the long term, through machine learning and natural language processing, there is the promise of a holistic personalized learning that is continuously adapted through life. This marks the beginning of a significant change, moving education from a one-to-many homogenous experience to a one-to-one deeply immersive, personalized learning experience. Forward-thinking establishments see digital tools as part of the answer: "Digital is so obviously the way to go," says a UK primary-school teacher. "Traditional methods lack rigour and the ability to tailor learning to specific needs. Every child will learn at a different pace, and currently we can't support each child. We have to bundle [students] into 'special educational needs' and maybe 'fast learners,' and they get [the] most attention. This is clearly not effective."

A U.S. elementary teacher echoes this thought. "You're teaching to a bell curve," the teacher says. "You've got your gifted kids in there, and you've got your special-ed kids in there. You've got to reach them all, and that's very difficult."

A digital services vendor notes that technology can address this problem by providing a way to teach to this wide range of abilities within a classroom. "With technology, it is easier to send each student down a different learning track," the vendor says. "Once you do that, there are huge levels of possibilities. You are no longer restricted by just having one teacher teach 30 kids the same thing."

And Satya Nitta, director of IBM's Cognitive Sciences and Education Technology, seconds this notion. "Deeply immersive interactive experiences with intelligent tutoring systems can transform how we learn," he says.

In a classroom of 30 students, a teacher typically divides a classroom into three or four cohorts of learners: strugglers; a middle group, which may be subdivided into those above and below average; and a few higher achievers (gifted and talented). The promise of personalized learning is the delivery of a more customized approach, where each and every child is treated uniquely and is always at his or her optimal level of learning.

While some educators are achieving results from deploying digital services, others are not. Of the educational institutions we surveyed that were using digital education services, more than half said they had seen only very little or some impact on learning outcomes. Part of the challenge is that with hundreds of digital services available and a classroom of 30 students, there are too many variables for a teacher to handle.

Could it be that these services are necessary but not sufficient to achieve the utopia of personalized learning? Could some sort of teacher's assistant be required? What if an intelligent (cognitive) system could discover all the available resources, understand where they achieve their best outcomes, and use this to create a personal plan for each student?

What Do We Mean by "Cognitive"?

Until recently, computing was programmable—based on human-defined inputs, instructions (code), and outputs. Cognitive systems are in a wholly different paradigm of systems that understand, reason, and learn. In short, systems that can think. What could this mean for educators? We see cognitive systems as being able to extend the capabilities of educators by providing deep insights into the domain of education and expert assistance through the provision of information in a timely, natural, and usable way. These systems will play the role of an assistant, which is complementary to and not a substitute for the art and craft of teaching. At the heart of cognitive systems are advanced analytic capabilities. In particular, cognitive systems aim to answer the questions "What will happen?" and "What should I do?" (Box 16.2).

The notion of cognitive systems to drive adaptive learning is certainly welcomed by the education professionals we interviewed. A U.S. high school teacher says, "To have some kind of prescriptive/diagnostic program where I could look at the actual question stemming [i.e., the creation of multiple-choice questions] to figure out which questions were most understandable and tailor our teaching to that student would be phenomenal, and every teacher would be in love with that idea."

While establishments can see the value of cognitive systems, many envision the realization as being a long way off. However, the future

---

Box 16.2   Example: A Teacher and Student (Cordelia) Engaging with a Cognitive Teacher's Assistant

Teacher: Cordelia, you did OK on your latest mathematics test; you got 72 percent. It looks as though the algebra questions were areas where you struggled. Is that a fair assessment?

Cordelia: Yes, I'm not sure I really get algebra. Are there any particular areas where I could improve?

Teacher: Well, let's see what my assistant suggests.

Cognitive-enabled teacher's assistant: From an analysis of Cordelia's learning profile and her last five tests, algebra is a relatively weak area for her in mathematics. Based against learning outcomes of 1.2 million similar Year-8 students with matching learning characteristics, her understanding could be improved by either reviewing algebra module 2.3 or looking at instructional video 7.

Teacher: Cordelia, I think you would find the video suits your learning style better. I suggest that you start with that and then we'll see how you get on.

SOURCE: Frase (2016).

may be nearer than we think. For those students in education today, chances are they will still be working 40 years from now. It's a daunting question, but will the skills learned today still be in demand by then?

THE WORLD OF WORK AND EDUCATION IN 2056 IS A REALITY FOR STUDENTS ENTERING THE JOB MARKET TODAY

There is a popular doomsday narrative circulating today, in which many predict significant job losses as technology increasingly usurps people's jobs from the workplace. This is not our view. Across industries and professions, we believe there will be an increasing marriage of man and machine that will be complementary in nature. This man-plus-machine process started with the first industrial revolution, and today we're merely at a different point on that continuum. At IBM, we subscribe to the view that man plus machine is greater than either is alone.

Today's millennial generation sees it this way, too. We asked IBM's UK-based interns what types of skills might be needed in the workplace 40 years from now. They recognize the need for continual skills development—98 percent see a need to keep learning throughout their working lives—and they see a pathway to career longevity by focusing on skills such as communication, leadership, teamwork, problem solving, people management, and critical thinking. These skills underline the rising conflict between traditional education as essentially a memory test culminating in a "paper and pencil" exam, versus modern skills-based learning, which demands teamwork and problem solving.

Cognitive systems are seen as a means to

- improve speed of intervention;
- reduce university dropout rates by creating better candidate selection processes based on more robust data;
- identify students who may need extra help;
- provide a richer analysis of why students fail tests; and
- ensure students are at the optimal level of attainment.

"The benefits of cognitive learning systems and prescriptive analytics are immense," notes a South African professional education organization. "We have students with vastly different backgrounds entering our system, and personalized learning and early intervention would have a positive effect."

A key cause of students dropping out of educational programs is that the pace of a one-size-fits-all course is beyond the capabilities of some students. As one digital provider explains, this can be addressed through systems that are more in step with the learner: "If more students had access to adaptive curriculum material," the digital provider says, "it would make a tremendous difference in solving problems of high dropouts and create better engagement in the classroom. If students were always learning within their level of proximal development, if they were always at the right level, you would have greater success."

For cognitive education services to be effective, they need to be immersive experiences for the student, while being complementary to the art and craft of teaching. They also need to reduce the administrative burden on the teacher, effectively giving time back to the teacher to teach.

We believe that technology will help educators improve student outcomes, but that it must be applied in context and under the auspices of a "caring human." The teacher-to-system relationship does not, in our view, lead to a dystopian future in which the teacher plays second fiddle to an algorithm. The teacher's role changes to a higher-value plane, with less focus on lesson creation or formal lecturing and an increasing focus on facilitating and coaching.

Increasingly, what we will see across teaching, and indeed all professions, is that tasks considered to be of value today will change in terms of how we come to perceive value over time. This is not a new phenomenon but part of a natural evolutionary process. Take, for example, the ability of a machine to assess 100 multiple-choice answers in a matter of milliseconds. It does not get tired, does not need a break, and does not make any errors. We take it for granted today that such a task is ideally suited for a machine. In the future, systems will be capable of analyzing essay-style answers, which will permit teachers to spend more time on higher-value activities. This is a concept that is well articulated in the following quotation: "A lot of teacher time can be taken up by analysing the answers to a long-answer based test," writes a

UK secondary-school teacher. "The insights don't come out very easily. There are things that might have come out of that test in another 10,000 cases clsewhcrc that thcy can't see. Comparing demonstrated answers and abilities and looking for those nuances using AI, you could generate a student profile that would be very helpful indeed for a teacher, who doesn't have the capability to analyse 10,000 tests."

But cognitive systems are only as good as the data available to learn from (what we refer to as the "corpus"). If the corpus is restricted to a single educational establishment or service, this is not as insightful as having access to a wider data pool, such as statewide or countrywide data. In the following section, we explore the concept of electronic data education records to understand whether educators thought this would bring benefits, and what they thought might need to be resolved to make this achievable.

THE EDUCATION EXPERIENCE WILL BE IMPROVED WHEN DATA CAN ACCOMPANY STUDENTS THROUGHOUT THEIR LIFELONG LEARNING JOURNEY

In health care, most developed countries have—to varying degrees of efficacy—a common data record in the form of electronic health care records (EHRs) containing lifelong data for individual people. It is useful to remember that this data serves two scenarios. In one scenario (the doctor/patient discussion) the data is personal to the patient and highly sensitive. In the second scenario (in which the doctor searches all available medical data for a next-best action), the data is rendered anonymous. Similar parallels exist in education, in which a personal record follows the student throughout his or her educational journey, with the anonymized data corpus being used by cognitive assistants to help a teacher choose the best options for that individual student.

We tested the idea of a similar concept for education, whereby education records and digital learning platforms would all join up to offer a lifelong learning data record that could follow the student from primary/elementary, secondary/high school, and college/university onward into education throughout his or her working life. Those records would include more than test scores. They could include data on learning styles and difficulties that could be leveraged by other learning modules for the benefit of the student throughout his or her lifetime.

For the first scenario (a student's personal record), we found that, in the main, the concept is welcome. One U.S. secondary teacher commented, "I lose valuable time working with new students because I have to start all over each year to understand that student, learn how they learn best and what modality fits them. If I had that data, before my students walk in, I could know exactly where I need to start with each one and how I need to present my lesson. It would be incredible."

The idea of a universal digital education record can alleviate the problem exhibited by many education systems, in which each educational stage is siloed and has its own measures of success. Today, such systems in the transition phase (e.g., between primary/ elementary and secondary/high schools) do not work smoothly, with the culminating effect of each failure in transition ultimately resulting in prospective employees saying they see far too many young people without the right skills.

While such a data record has clear benefits to both student and educator, there are some key considerations to be heeded, such as the authenticity, privacy, and security of data, including where and how data is stored. "Control has to be in the hands of the individual or it could lead to inequities," says a U.S. professor. "Say you have children who go to schools that are terrible, and they have these records from their early years. We know these schools have challenges. . . . If you lose all these contextual variables that are impacting students' achievement and if that is not visible in such a record, it could harm people who are already marginalized in our society."

We think that many of the issues raised are resolvable and that solutions are within reach. We have heard about various potential scenarios for addressing control and access to student data:

- Institutions share student records/academic certifications through a distributed database (such as Blockchain).

- Students post their data records (in whole or in part) to a public repository such as Facebook or LinkedIn and retain ownership of who has visibility of their records.

- An industry body or government creates a standardized solution, and users grant access to others (educators, prospective employers) as and when required.
- Users "mash" their own solution based around various digital tools or platforms and provide their education credentials in the form of an e-portfolio.

While most of the issues for the student's personal record are related to privacy and security, these problems disappear when looking at the use of large volumes of anonymized data to help a teacher choose the best personal options. Technically, such a common data platform and the cognitive systems that could drive such a platform are closer than many think, though the precise time line to realizing this is bounded by complex political, economic, and societal differences. "Anything that would provide information concerning how each student best learns would definitely help us in the classroom," says a U.S. primary teacher. "As long as you're in the field of education and in the process of teaching, you have access to it, just like a doctor would. I think it'd be extremely useful."

With such a rich data record, many interesting possibilities start to emerge. One example is a comprehensive career-adviser system enabling the learner to query an adviser as to what he or she might be good at based on a lifelong record of skills and interests. This could uncover career pathways that might not have been immediately obvious to the individual.

Another example could be reciprocal sharing of aggregated and nonidentifiable data between academia and industry. The latter could better understand what student populations are learning and advocate changes to education to better match industry needs. In effect, we create a virtuous circle of real-time data that potentially solves issues relating to student leavers lacking necessary skills.

"While the promise of data-driven decision making is at the heart of enabling personalized education, it is vital that we distinguish the narrow uses of personal data from the broader uses for anonymized data," says Katharine Frase, vice president of IBM's Watson Education unit for business development. "Being clear about this will lay the foundations for all the benefits that cognitive systems can bring."

HOW WE SEE THE JOURNEY FROM CURRICULUM TO CAREER WITH COGNITIVE SYSTEMS

Education as an industry is being challenged (as are the education professionals within it) by the storms of digital disruption to prove its relevance, to maximize value for stakeholders, and to find ways to reinvent itself. Educators will need to evolve by embracing cognitive systems to deliver personalized learning in order to drive improved outcomes for all. The twenty-first-century learner will demand and deserve no less.

Notes

We thank Chalapathy Neti, Katharine Frase, Madalina Irimia, Raluca Dode, and Satya Nitta, who were key contributors to this chapter.

1. In the IBM intern survey, multiple responses were permitted to the question, "Thinking specifically about the MOOCs/apps/digital education platforms that you have used, how did you learn about these services? (Check all that apply.)" It must be noted that, although the results of this survey could be an indicator of an overall shift in the education sector, the sample size is very small at 126 interns who took part in the survey.

References

Cortez, Meghan Bogardus. 2017. "Students Want Laptops, Flexible Digital Tools in the Classroom." *EdTech Magazine*, December 4. https://edtech magazine.com/higher/article/2017/12/students-want-laptops-flexible -digital-tools-classroom (accessed July 10, 2018).

Department for Business, Innovation, and Skills. 2015. *Fulfilling Our Potential: Teaching Excellence, Social Mobility, and Student Choice*. Sheffield, UK: Higher Education Directorate, Department for Business, Innovation, and Skills. https://www.timeshighereducation.com/sites/default/files/breaking _news_files/green_paper.pdf (accessed November 3, 2017).

Frase, Katharine. 2016. "How Cognitive Systems and Personal Digital Records Will Improve Education." Blog entry, July 15. IBM Big Data and Analytics Hub. Armonk, NY: IBM. http://www.ibmbigdatahub.com/blog/how -cognitive-systems-and-personal-digital-records-will-improve-education (accessed July 19, 2018).

IBM Education. 2016. *Personalized Education: From Curriculum to Career with Cognitive Systems*. Portsmouth, UK: IBM.

17
All Data Big and Small

Using Information to Guide Workforce Development

Rachel Zinn
Bryan Wilson

Stakes are high for the workforce development field, as globalization and automation threaten conventional wisdom about what it takes to get a good job. Workers with only a high school diploma have shrinking options for employment, especially in jobs that provide a living wage and benefits. At the same time, education costs are rising, and a college degree is not an automatic ticket to the middle class. Amid this uncertainty, students and job seekers are searching for paths that lead to economic stability. Policy leaders and program managers want to help by investing in workforce development, but tight budgets are creating tremendous pressure to demonstrate that public resources are funding strategies that get results. Now more than ever, data are critical to helping policy leaders, students, job seekers, and program managers make informed choices about workforce development.

Government leaders recognize the need for better information, so they are making significant investments in data analysis to inform decision making. Colorado Governor John Hickenlooper is an advocate for data-driven policy, telling a crowd in 2016 that "in every single agency, if you use data, you're going to get results. . . . American democracy is the greatest form of government on earth, but it is also the most fragile. It's dependent on people believing in their government. If we're not able to begin to use facts more successfully, and make sure people in the entire community are aware of that, then we're putting our very form of government at risk" (Hickenlooper 2016).

In this spirit, the U.S. Departments of Education and Labor have invested about $750 million since 2005 in state longitudinal data systems, which link individual-level data across time and across programs (Clark et al. 2014). In addition, more than a dozen states dedicate part of their annual budgets to their longitudinal data systems (Workforce Data Quality Campaign 2016). These systems allow analysts to match data, including wage records reported quarterly by employers for the Unemployment Insurance (UI) program, to reveal how different cohorts advance through education, workforce programs, and the labor market. Multiple technological and procedural safeguards keep confidential data private and secure, while enabling the use of aggregate or non-identified individual data. Federal and state governments also invest in surveys directed by the U.S. Census Bureau, Bureau of Labor Statistics, and other public agencies to generate labor market information, and local workforce leaders purchase online job ads analysis from private vendors. Several companies now offer analytics packages that scrape information from online job ads to help community colleges, workforce development boards, and state agencies identify types of training that might lead to good jobs in their communities. There are limitations to online job ads data, including a bias toward high-skilled occupations (Carnevale, Jayasundera, and Repnikov 2014), but many workforce development experts are investing in it to supplement traditional survey-based information.

Are these investments in data analysis paying off in ways that help students, workers, and businesses thrive in our nation's changing economy? While the workforce development field is not yet using data to their full potential, there are compelling examples of data making a difference in building America's skilled workforce. The remainder of this chapter, summarized in Table 17.1, describes how data are helping to improve human capital development policy and practice. It describes how data are being effectively used by three different groups: 1) policymakers, 2) students and job seekers, and 3) program managers.

POLICYMAKERS: TARGETING RESOURCES

Officials at all levels of government rely on data to help them decide how to invest limited resources and provide assurance that those investments are getting results. Over the past two years, the nonprofit organization National Skills Coalition worked with four states—California, Mississippi, Ohio, and Rhode Island—to develop specific data tools

Table 17.1 Data Use in Workforce Development

Data user	Objective	Examples
Policymakers	Target public resources to effective workforce development strategies	• Rhode Island is using labor supply/demand analysis to identify high-demand occupations, such as jobs related to finance and computers, and award bonus funding to colleges preparing students for these occupations. • Mississippi's state plan for workforce development calls for using career pathway data analysis to direct job seekers to training with a track record of success.
Students and job seekers	Choose education and training programs that help achieve their goals	• Data about postcollege earnings, like the information published in the Department of Education's College Scorecard, can influence student choices about school and major. • Washington State's Career Bridge website, which displays employment outcomes for education and training programs, is viewed yearly by more than 190,000 students, unemployed job seekers, and workers looking to change careers.
Program managers	Improve services and address equity gaps	• Data revealed that adult students at Oakton Community College had lower persistence and completion rates than their younger peers, prompting the school to create new opportunities for work-based learning to help them succeed. • New York City's workforce board uses customized performance metrics for priorities like employer collaboration, leading to shorter bouts of unemployment and increased earnings for program participants. • Academy of Hope Charter School in Washington, DC, regularly monitors data dashboards to accelerate progress for students close to getting a GED.

to help policymakers make better decisions about workforce development. The State Workforce and Education Alignment Project (SWEAP) awarded small grants to the states for tool development, and provided technical assistance from National Skills Coalition staff and consultants. All four states engaged policymakers in designing their tools. The following section highlights how Rhode Island and Mississippi have already integrated their tools into statewide visions for workforce development.

Labor Supply/Demand Analysis in Rhode Island

In Rhode Island, SWEAP work fit neatly into the vision of newly elected Governor Gina Raimando. She prioritized the creation of a data-driven, business-led workforce development system, exemplified in her Real Jobs Rhode Island initiative to align workforce and education programs with employer skill needs. To identify those occupations most likely to face shortages of skilled workers, Rhode Island officials developed reports (see Figure 17.1) that compare the number of recent postsecondary graduates in specific programs of study with occupational projections from the state's labor market information division (National Skills Coalition 2017a). The labor market information division worked with the office of the postsecondary commissioner to create a crosswalk between programs of study and relevant occupations, so state reports could show the supply of recent graduates versus the predicted job openings by occupation (National Skills Coalition 2017b).

This supply/demand tool is already helping Rhode Island's higher education system select which programs will be used to measure institutional performance under a new funding formula. The formula, mandated by state law in August 2016, awards additional funding to institutions that meet targets for numbers of graduates in high-demand, high-wage fields (National Skills Coalition 2017a). The data are also producing some key takeaways for workforce development leaders, including the need for more workers trained in computer-related occupations, and evidence for the labor market value of associate's degrees and certificates in middle-skill occupations (DataSpark 2016).

In addition to using tools developed through SWEAP, policymakers in Rhode Island are applying data in new ways to determine program eligibility for dislocated workers. States receive federal funding through

Figure 17.1 Rhode Island Labor Supply/Demand Report

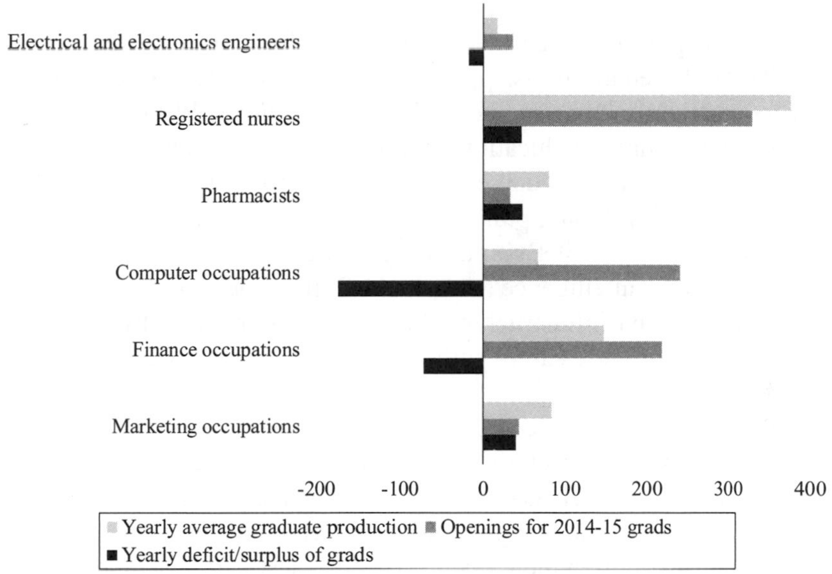

SOURCE: DataSpark (2016).

the Workforce Innovation and Opportunity Act (WIOA) to provide services to workers who lose their jobs due to economic shifts, such as plant closures or declines in particular occupations or industries. Rhode Island faced challenges in verifying eligibility for dislocated worker status, largely due to participants having difficulty providing complete and detailed information about their work histories. The state passed a new policy on eligibility determinations in December 2016, so the state's workforce agency now uses UI wage data and labor market statistics to compare laid-off workers' recent salaries with the projected earnings from their occupation. Individuals with earnings below the projected amount are designated as "dislocated workers" and may be served with federal funds. State officials estimate that the new methodology will make about twice as many dislocated workers eligible for services (Leventoff 2017a).

Pathway Evaluators in Mississippi

Mississippi has a strong state longitudinal data system called LifeTracks based at Mississippi State University. LifeTracks links data across multiple sectors, including PK–12 education, WIOA programs, career and technical education, and public colleges and universities. "Data has become a valuable asset for promoting economic development and for developing policy that matters to our citizens," said Mississippi Governor Phil Bryant. "Data has real value when converted into actionable intelligence" (National Skills Coalition 2017c). With its advanced data infrastructure, Mississippi is building two SWEAP tools that can analyze career pathways to customize services for different populations.

With Mississippi's new Career Pathway Analyzer tool, a user can define the starting characteristics for a cohort such as demographics and prior education, as well as exit conditions such as target occupation and earnings. For example, a user could query which pathways to advanced manufacturing employment result in the highest earnings, and the tool would show multiple pathways in descending order of earnings. In another example, the tool can show the portion of a cohort that followed a specified pathway (e.g., associate's degree) and their credential attainment. A similar tool, the Career Pathway Constructor, will enable users to design a custom pathway for a particular population and discover the actual outcomes for program participants with the selected characteristics who previously followed that pathway. For example, the head of a veterans' employment program could use the tool to decide whether to help clients enter health professions by investing in apprenticeships or in certificate programs (National Skills Coalition 2017a).

Mississippi embedded the concept of customized career pathways into its WIOA Combined Plan, which sets goals for collaboration between One-Stop Centers, adult education programs, Temporary Assistance for Needy Families (TANF) services, and other workforce development programs. The plan calls for all partnering programs to collect the same basic information on new clients, and to create an Individualized Success Plan that identifies cross-program services and referrals needed to help the client move toward unsubsidized employment. The Success Plans are updated as participants receive services, such as basic education or technical training, and become ready for work (State of Mississippi 2016). Program managers may use the SWEAP tools to help design Success Plans based on which services have a track record of success for clients with particular barriers to employment. State officials note in a report that "the SWEAP tools will provide strong support for Mississippi's new streamlined workforce model" (National Skills Coalition 2017c).

The state also anticipates using the Career Pathway Analyzer and Constructor in emerging policy areas, including identifying credentials of value and performance-based budgeting. An increasing number of states are setting up processes to use outcome data, business input, labor market information, and other factors to create lists of credentials that have value in the workforce. These lists help states decide which credentials count in their postsecondary attainment goals, and implement accountability requirements for WIOA and other programs (Leventoff 2017b). Mississippi's state workforce board is considering ways of vetting credentials and expects that the SWEAP tools will be helpful in this process. At the same time, state legislators are taking an interest in performance-based budgeting, which directs resources to those programs that demonstrate positive results. SWEAP tools "could be leveraged by the legislature to evaluate the performance of various training programs, and these evaluations could help the legislators ensure that effective programs continue to receive adequate funding" (National Skills Coalition 2017c).

STUDENTS AND JOB SEEKERS: PICKING THEIR PATHS

Postsecondary education is more important than ever. Through 2024, an estimated 80 percent of all U.S. job openings will require some kind of postsecondary education (National Skills Coalition 2017d). But for students and job seekers, the proliferation of programs and credentials, combined with a swiftly evolving economy, makes it challenging to choose an education and career path. Federal and state leaders, as well as foundations and private sector companies, are investing in efforts to make data more accessible to these audiences. Scorecards showing postsecondary program outcomes and career information are becoming more widely available, and there is some early evidence that these tools influence decisions, particularly by making students more aware of potential labor market outcomes.

College Scorecard

In 2015, the U.S. Department of Education launched a redesigned College Scorecard website. The College Scorecard displays key metrics for every institution in the country that is eligible for federal Title IV aid, commonly known as Pell Grants and student loans. The College Scorecard includes more than 7,500 schools (Hurwitz and Smith 2016). Table 17.2 shows the breakdown of institutions included in the College Scorecard, by both portion of students and portion of schools (U.S. Department of Education 2017). For each institution, the College Scorecard contains metrics on costs, average debt amounts and repayment rates, and graduation rates, as well as two measures of earnings for each postsecondary institution: 1) the percentage of former students earning above $25,000 annually, which is the average salary of a high school graduate six years after enrollment; and 2) the median earnings of former students who were employed 10 years after enrollment. The earnings measures are calculated by linking student data from the U.S. Department of Education with tax data managed by the Social Security Administration. And because earnings outcomes vary significantly within institutions based on program of study, the College Scorecard could be improved by showing metrics by program, not just institution (Zinn 2016).

A few research studies examine how the College Scorecard, and postcollege earnings information more generally, influence student decisions about colleges and majors. One report analyzes data about where students send their SAT scores, often considered a proxy for college applications, and compares college selection before and after the College Scorecard release. The researchers do not have information on whether students in their data set actually used the College Scorecard, but they do try to isolate the effects of the College Scorecard release using statistical methodology. The study concludes that earnings information is the only part of the College Scorecard that influences student behavior, and estimates that "each 10 percent increase in reported earnings results in a 2.4 percent increase in score sends. The impact is driven almost entirely by well-resourced high schools and students" (Hurwitz and Smith 2016). Another report surveys California community col-

Table 17.2 College Scorecard Distribution of Students and Schools

	% of students	% of schools
Public < 2 year	8.2	8.9
	0.2	
Private nonprofit < 2 year	0.2	2.9
	3.6	
Private for-profit < 2 year	3.6	35.7
Public 2 year	30.2	11.3
Private nonprofit 2 year	0.8	2.3
Private for-profit 2 year	2.3	8.5
Public 4 year	34.9	8.3
Private nonprofit 4 year	15.3	17.9
Private for-profit 4 year	4.4	4.3

SOURCE: U.S. Department of Education (2017).

lege students about choosing a major and provides them with randomly assigned versions of information about salaries and the probability of employment in particular industries. This research suggests that labor market outcomes have a significant effect on a student's choice of major, and the impact grows when students are confident about the information's accuracy (Baker et al. 2017). Other studies are consistent with these findings and note that different metrics for employment outcomes can significantly change student decisions on their programs of study (Ruder and Van Noy 2014). Taken together, the literature suggests that using the College Scorecard can make real impacts on student choices. For disadvantaged students with fewer alternative sources of information, the College Scorecard has the potential to help them be more confident in their knowledge of likely earnings outcomes, and therefore consider job prospects more heavily when selecting a school or major.

State Scorecard

Many states are developing their own scorecards to help students and workers select education and training programs that have demonstrated strong outcomes. Instead of using income tax data to calculate programs' employment outcomes like the federal College Scorecard, states use UI wage records housed at state workforce agencies. More than half of states report measuring outcomes for a broad array of workforce and education programs, and most of those states publicize the information on some type of scorecard aimed at students and workers (Workforce Data Quality Campaign 2016). Some of the scorecards only have information on certificates and degree programs at the state's public colleges and universities, while others show outcomes for training providers eligible for WIOA funding, which includes for-profit career schools.

Washington and New Jersey are two states that have comprehensive scorecards. They include all types of education and training providers, and a variety of education and employment outcome metrics. Washington's Career Bridge website has descriptions for more than 6,000 programs at four-year colleges, private vocational schools, and community and technical colleges, as well as apprenticeships and training programs run by nonprofit organizations like Goodwill Industries. About 1,600 of the program descriptions include data about completion rates and postprogram employment rates, industry of employment, and average earnings, as illustrated in Table 17.3. According to a 2014 report, Career Bridge had more than 190,000 unique views that year. Of those views, 46 percent of users were students, 30 percent were unemployed workers, and 13 percent were workers searching for new careers. New Jersey has legislation that supports its scorecard website by requiring all education and training providers to submit student data to the state, which then matches that data to wage records to determine employment outcomes. A 2013 amendment to the law expanded the requirement to for-profit career schools licensed to operate in the state (Davis, Jacobson, and Wandner 2014).

While academic studies do not specifically address the effects of state scorecards on education and training program selection, state leaders and scorecard users report that these tools are influencing decisions. In New Jersey, local workforce development boards staff and American Job Centers career counselors use the state scorecard to help job seekers select training programs (Smith and Fichtner 2015). Minnesota officials have done extensive outreach to high schools to demonstrate its Graduate Employment Outcomes website for students and guidance counselors. According to state leaders, the data help counselors talk to students about career and technical education paths that don't require a bachelor's degree, but lead to jobs with good salaries. "The data that we're displaying is of unprecedented comprehensiveness and unprecedented volume," said one Minnesota official. "The data gives power to

Table 17.3 Sample of Washington State's Career Bridge Website Performance Data

School	Program	Completion rate (%)	Employment rate (%)	Median annual earnings ($)
Bates Technical College	Welding AAS	47	66	39,264
Green River College	Welding Technology AAS	43	77	36,196
Renton Technical College	Precision Machining Technologies AAS	73	93	48,097
Renton Technical College	Welding AAS	38	89	38,739
Shoreline Community College	Manufacturing/ Machinist Technology AAS	70	82	37,294

SOURCE: careerbridge.wa.gov.

users, and it's a new tool that career counselors can use to sit down with their students and jumpstart the conversation" (National Skills Coalition 2015). Similarly, in focus groups with students selecting colleges and majors, the new Launch My Career website in Texas helped students understand their likely future earnings for different programs of study, and influenced some to pick majors aligned with their career and earnings goals (U.S. Chamber of Commerce Foundation 2017).

PROGRAM MANAGERS: IMPROVING SERVICES

Education and workforce program administrators are increasingly relying on data analysis to improve results. They use data to identify areas with low performance and devise strategies to boost overall student and job seeker success, as well as close equity gaps in achievement.

Community Colleges

Data analysis was critical to helping Oakton Community College in Illinois more effectively serve adult students. Following consultations with area businesses that revealed a need for skilled workers in the manufacturing industry, Oakton Community College in Illinois developed a program of study in the field. The program attracted about 100 recent high school graduates, as well as about 80 students older than 23. But after reviewing data on course success, persistence, and completion, the college discovered that adult students were getting worse outcomes. Officials then made it a priority to develop strategies to serve these students and conducted surveys and focus groups to identify challenges. Based on the results, Oakton developed work-based learning components and expanded opportunities to earn credit for prior learning. The college also enhanced its performance reports for department heads to include noncredit students, since many returning adults entered the manufacturing program by taking noncredit courses. The data are disaggregated by race/ethnicity, age, and gender to highlight additional equity gaps moving forward (McCambly 2016).

Miami Dade College is working to scale this type of data analysis across the institution. College leaders monitor a handful of key metrics on persistence, completion, and postgraduation employment. In addition, the college produces more granular data analysis that is useful in adapting specific programs and policies. Administrators track the progress of student cohorts over several years, allowing them to target support services to students falling behind or make program changes to help all students do better. "For example, they can use the insights gained from the data to identify the highest-risk courses in a program of study and offer extra supports, like tutoring or group projects for students enrolled in those courses" (Association of Public and Land Grant Universities 2017). The college is building data literacy among faculty and staff with a noncredit professional development course, to ensure that information is being used for continuous improvement at all levels.

Community colleges also use labor market information to align their offerings with in-demand jobs. California Community Colleges are committed to organizing their programs around regional industry demand through the Doing What Matters initiative. The colleges use a variety of labor market information sources, including federal and state survey data. Cerritos College in Los Angeles County found information from online job ads particularly helpful when researching regional skills gaps in the advanced manufacturing industry. Although the manufacturing industry was declining overall, the detailed data revealed specialized occupations that needed more trained workers. The college was then able to focus its new programs on these in-demand skills (Dorrer 2016).

Local Service Organizations

Community colleges aren't the only entities using student data to improve programs. Many local workforce development boards are working harder to make data-driven decisions about how to serve job seekers. SCPa Works, a workforce board serving southern Pennsylvania, uses labor market information from the state and economic development research from private vendors to guide their outreach to businesses. When data suggest skills gaps in the regional workforce, SCPa Works consults with business leaders to confirm these findings and develop sector-based strategies to train unemployed or underemployed workers for these industries. New York City's workforce board uses performance data to push for continuous improvement. Using customized performance metrics for priorities like service to veterans and closer collaboration with employers, the organization increased the average earnings of program participants and is helping them find jobs more quickly (Prince, King, and Oldmixon 2017).

Some adult education providers also integrate data review into their strategic planning. The Academy of Hope adult charter school in Washington, D.C., works with more than 300 adult learners each year to help them earn a high school credential. The Academy of Hope regularly produces data dashboards to guide teaching strategies and ensure that the school meets required performance targets. The school is particularly focused on helping students at varied literacy levels to make measurable progress. Data disaggregated by literacy level, like Table 17.4, showed that higher-level students were stalling on progress. In response, the Academy of Hope revised the curriculum, increased class frequency,

Table 17.4 Percent of Academy of Hope Students Showing Measurable Skill Gains

Literacy level (from low to high)	Semester	
	Fall 2016	Spring 2017
1	67	71
2	41	56
3	40	56
4	16	22

SOURCE: Lotas (2017).

and added support from volunteer tutors. These strategies are improving progression rates for higher-level student cohorts.

NEXT STEPS: EMBEDDING DATA IN WORKFORCE DEVELOPMENT POLICY

This chapter provides examples of ways that data are influencing policy and practice in workforce development, but stakeholders are not yet using data to their fullest potential. Additional public investments are needed to:

- Build system infrastructure to improve data quality, privacy, and security. Much of the government data relevant to workforce development is being collected and managed using old technology. Upgrades could increase public confidence in data security, and provide more automated safeguards to verify data quality and ensure that a limited number of trained personnel can access confidential data.

- Enhance capacity to analyze data and present it in accessible formats. Public agencies often lack in-house experience with communicating complex data to nonexpert audiences like legislators and job seekers. Over time, more agencies are building these skill sets or hiring consultants to add capacity.

- Create partnerships with skilled researchers, such as those at universities or research centers, who can conduct program impact evaluations that present compelling evidence about what strategies are effective. Government leaders should adopt policies that enable data sharing between different agencies and facilitate use of data by external researchers, while protecting individual privacy.

- Provide data literacy training for program managers and policy leaders so they better understand how information can aid in decision making. This also provides an opportunity for data producers to build deeper relationships with these groups in order to understand what types of actionable information are needed.

Investments in data use are critical for maintaining public support for workforce development. For example, a recent executive order from the Trump administration includes a mandate for federal agencies to review data available on their workforce programs, recommend program improvements, and propose elimination of ineffective or redundant programs (White House 2017). In addition to using data to advocate for workforce development programs, the field will increasingly need to advocate for investments in data itself. We must be able to clearly articulate how data are helping to improve decision making, and ideally be able to quantify the benefits of data use in terms of improved outcomes and return on investment.

As the workforce development field expands data use, we must also ensure that data are being used ethically to help individuals and businesses succeed. Predictive analytics, which uses historical data to predict future behavior, can be useful in targeting services to individuals most likely to face challenges completing programs or obtaining employment. On the other hand, predictive analytics can be used to restrict access to services for people deemed unlikely to succeed, which is especially problematic when it perpetuates racial or socioeconomic inequity (Ekowo and Palmer 2016). If leaders are thoughtful about using data to expand rather than limit opportunities, then investments in data will help our nation build a competitive workforce that allows all individuals to find paths to success.

Notes

1. In the interest of full disclosure, note that author Rachel Zinn serves on the Academy of Hope Board of Directors.
2. Author email interview with Sasha Lotas, coordinator of research, Academy of Hope, July 5, 2017.

References

Association of Public & Land Grant Universities and Institute for Higher Education Policy (APLU). 2017. "Building Institutional Capacity to Use Data for Student Success." Washington, DC: APLU. http://www.aplu .org/projects-and-initiatives/accountability-and-transparency/using-data -to-increase-student-success/APLU_WhitePaper_MIAMIDADE_C.pdf (accessed July 3, 2017).

Baker, Rachel, Eric Bettinger, Brian Jacob, and Ioana Marinescu. 2017. "The Effect of Labor Market Information on Community College Students' Major Choice." Washington, DC: National Bureau of Economic Research. http://conference.iza.org/conference_files/EcoEdu_2016/marinescu_i1517 .pdf (accessed June 25, 2017)

Carnevale, Anthony P., Tamara Jayasundera, and Dmitri Repnikov. 2014. *Understanding Online Job Ads Data: A Technical Report.* Washington, DC: Georgetown University Center for Education and the Workforce. https:// cew.georgetown.edu/wp-content/uploads/2014/11/OCLM.Tech_.Web_.pdf (accessed June 17, 2017).

Clark, Mika, Deanna Khemani, Jill Leufgen, and Melissa Mack. 2014. *A Guide to Building Longitudinal Data Systems from a Workforce Perspective.* Prepared for U.S. Department of Labor, Employment and Training Administration. http://www.spra.com/wordpress2/wp-content/uploads/2016/08/ Putting-Data-To-Work.pdf (accessed July 2, 2017).

DataSpark. September 2016. "Preparing Workers for RI's High-Demand Occupations." http://ridatahub.org/datastories/occupations/1/ (accessed June 19, 2017).

Davis, Scott, Louis Jacobson, and Stephen Wandner. 2014. *Using Workforce Data Quality Initiative Databases to Develop and Improve Consumer Report Card Systems.* Washington, DC: IMPAQ International. https:// www.dol.gov/asp/evaluation/completed-studies/IMPAQ_Scorecards_ Report_2014-06-02.pdf (accessed June 25, 2017).

Dorrer, John. 2016. *Using Real-Time Labor Market Information to Achieve Better Labor Market Outcomes.* Washington, DC: Georgetown Center for Education and the Workforce. https://www.luminafoundation.org/files/ resources/using-real-time-labor-market-information-full.pdf (accessed July 3, 2017).

Ekowo, Manuela, and Iris Palmer. 2016. *The Promise and Peril of Predictive Analytics in Higher Education.* Washington, DC: New America. https:// na-production.s3.amazonaws.com/documents/Promise-and-Peril_4.pdf (accessed July 5, 2017).

Hickenlooper, John. 2016. "Data-Driven Decision-Making at the State and Local Level, Pew Charitable Trusts and Route Fifty." Keynote address, October 14. Denver, CO: History Colorado Center. http://www.pewtrusts .org/en/about/events/2016/governing-by-the-numbers (accessed August 10, 2017).

Hurwitz, Michael, and Jonathan Smith. 2016. *Student Responsiveness to Earnings Data in the College Scorecard.* https://papers.ssrn.com/sol3/papers .cfm?abstract_id=2768157 (accessed June 25, 2017).

Leventoff, Jenna. 2017a. "RI Uses UI Records and LMI to Make Dislocated Worker Determination" (blog). Washington, DC: Workforce Data Quality Campaign. http://www.workforcedqc.org/news/blog/ri-uses-ui-records -and-lmi-make-dislocated-worker-determination (accessed June 17, 2017).

———. 2017b. *Programs That Work: Quality Assurance for Short-Term Occupational Programs.* Washington, DC: Workforce Data Quality Campaign. http://www.workforcedqc.org/sites/default/files/images/WDQC -ProgramsThatWork-web.pdf (accessed June 19, 2017).

McCambly, Heather. 2016. *Pathways to Results: Implementation Partnerships Strategy Brief.* Champaign, IL: Office of Community College Research and Leadership at University of Illinois. http://occrl.illinois.edu/docs/ librariesprovider4/ptr/oakton-implementation-brief.pdf (accessed July 3, 2017).

National Skills Coalition. 2015. "Workforce Data Explained: Data Empowers Students in Minnesota." 2015. YouTube video. https://www.youtube.com/ watch?v=sqojJ2R_ZnI (accessed July 5, 2017).

———. 2017a. *State Workforce and Education Project (SWEAP) Phase Two Report.* Washington, DC: National Skills Coalition. http://www.national skillscoalition.org/state-policy/body/SWEAP-Phase-Two-Report.pdf (accessed June 17, 2017).

———. 2017b. Rhode Island State Report. Washington, DC: National Skills Coalition. http://www.nationalskillscoalition.org/state-policy/state -workforce-and-education-alignment-project/body/Rhode-Island-SWEAP -State-Report.pdf (accessed June 19, 2017).

———. 2017c. Mississippi SWEAP Project Final Report. Starkville, MS: Mississippi State University. http://www.nationalskillscoalition.org/state -policy/state-workforce-and-education-alignment-project/body/Mississippi -SWEAP-State-Report.pdf (accessed June 19, 2017).

———. 2017d. United States' Forgotten Middle. Washington, DC: National Skills Coalition. http://www.nationalskillscoalition.org/resources/publications/ 2017-middle-skills-fact-sheets/file/United-States-MiddleSkills.pdf (accessed June 25, 2017).

Prince, Heath, Chris King, and Sarah Oldmixon. 2017. *Promoting the Adop-*

tion of Sector Strategies by Workforce Development Boards under the Workforce Innovation and Opportunity Act. Austin, TX: Ray Marshall Center. https://raymarshallcenter.org/files/2017/05/Sector_Strategy_Final_Report _March_2017.pdf (accessed July 5, 2017).

Ruder, Alex, and Michelle Van Noy. 2014. *The Influence of Labor Market Outcomes Data on Major Choice: Evidence from a Survey Experiment.* John J. Heldrich Center for Workforce Development. http://www.heldrich.rutgers .edu/sites/default/files/products/uploads/Labor_Market_Outcomes_Major _Choice.pdf (accessed June 25, 2017).

Smith, Tiffany L., and Aaron R. Fichtner. 2015. "Scorecards for Postsecondary Education and Training Programs." In *Transforming U.S. Workforce Development Policies for the 21st Century,* Carl Van Horn, Tammy Edwards, and Todd Greene, eds. Kalamazoo, MI: W.E. Upjohn Institute for Employment Research, pp. 497–504.

State of Mississippi. 2016. *WIOA State Plan for the State of Mississippi.* Jackson: State of Mississippi. https://www2.ed.gov/about/offices/list/osers/rsa/ wioa/state-plans/ms.pdf (accessed June 19, 2017).

U.S. Chamber of Commerce Foundation. 2017. "Launch My Career TX: Student Version." Online video. https://www.dropbox.com/sh/s126gke5a 2b9o4h/AAAAWqKPgeN1KT8ii3hFYZ3Ra?dl=0&preview=Launch+My +Career+TX+Student+Version.mp4 (accessed July 3, 2017).

U.S. Department of Education. 2017. *Using Federal Data to Measure and Improve the Performance of U.S. Institutions of Higher Education.* Washington, DC: U.S. Department of Education. https://collegescorecard .ed.gov/assets/UsingFederalDataToMeasureAndImprovePerformance.pdf (accessed June 25, 2017).

White House. 2017. "Presidential Executive Order on Expanding Apprenticeships in America," June 15. https://www.whitehouse.gov/the-press -office/2017/06/15/presidential-executive-order-expanding-apprenticeships -america (accessed July 5, 2017).

Workforce Data Quality Campaign. 2016. *2016 Mastering the Blueprint: State Progress on Workforce Data.* Washington, DC: Workforce Data Quality Campaign. http://www.workforcedqc.org/sites/default/files/ images/12.2%20NSC%20WD%20Blueprint%202016%20FINAL.pdf (accessed June 17, 2017).

Zinn, Rachel. 2016. *Classroom to Career: Leveraging Employment Data to Measure Labor Market Outcomes.* Washington, DC: Institute for Higher Education Policy. http://www.ihep.org/sites/default/files/uploads/postsecdata/ docs/resources/leveraging_employment_data_0.pdf (accessed June 20, 2017).

18

Preparing Workers for the Expanding Digital Economy

Jordana Barton

Technology is advancing so rapidly that . . . it is always going to outpace the law, the government or the public's capacity to fully understand its ramifications. The genie is never going back into its flip phone. . . . Future startups are going to make decisions that will impact the lives of millions, defining the world the way religions and empires used to. iPhones and tweets and more convenient taxis were one thing. But the wave on the horizon now— artificial intelligence, genetic engineering, nanotechnology—will be something else entirely.

–Steinmetz and Vella (2017, p. 28)

The digital revolution has led to a rise in e-commerce, the gig economy, automation, artificial intelligence, and other digital technologies that have disrupted traditional economic sectors such as manufacturing and retail. Broadband—high-speed Internet access that is always on— is one of the most transformative technologies to emerge. The Internet and the digital innovations it has enabled have dramatically changed the nature of work, education, health care, public safety, and access to government and financial services.

Broadband is now a basic infrastructure essential to the well-being of all communities (Barton 2016). Despite incredible advancements in broadband technology, these innovations are not available to all Americans. According to the Federal Communication Commission's (FCC) *2016 Broadband Progress Report*, 34 million Americans lack access to fixed broadband at speeds of at least 25 megabits per second (Mbps) for downloads and 3 Mbps for uploads (FCC 2016).[1] U.S. households making $25,000 or less have a broadband adoption rate of 47 percent, while those making more than $100,000 have an adoption rate of 92 percent

(U.S. Census Bureau 2013). The digital divide is the gap between people who have access to broadband services and know how to use the Internet and those who do not have such access or knowledge (Levin and Linn 2015). Those who find themselves on the wrong side of the digital divide—including low-income people, those with less formal education, rural populations, the elderly and older workers, and minorities—suffer further economic, social, health, and political disparities resulting from disconnection.

WORKFORCE DEVELOPMENT

Workforce development is a valuable tool for lifting people out of poverty and for creating upward mobility. Closing the digital divide is an essential step toward capturing the economic benefits of a skilled workforce. Workforce opportunities are hindered when low- and moderate-income (LMI) communities lack broadband access. According to Smith (2015) of the Pew Research Center, 79 percent of Americans used the Internet in their most recent job search. Smith further finds that "37 percent of nonbroadband adopters indicate that it would *not* be easy for them to create a professional resume if they needed to do so; 30 percent would find it difficult to contact an employer via email, or fill out an online job application; and 27 percent would have a hard time finding online lists of available jobs in their area" (p. 4). Additionally, many education and job training programs are offered only online. For individuals who live in areas without workforce development centers or community colleges, or who lack transportation or experience barriers due to long distances, Internet access could help them participate in training and certification programs and work from their homes for companies that employ a remote workforce.

Kang (2016b) highlights the impact of the digital divide in Detroit, which has "the worst rate of Internet access of any big American city, with four in 10 of its 689,000 residents lacking broadband. . . . The consequences appear in the daily grind of finding connectivity, with people unable to apply for jobs online, research new opportunities, connect with health insurance, get college financial aid or do homework." Public libraries are often looked upon as replacements for broadband in the home; however, this solution has limitations. Time limits on computer use and long wait times at public libraries and community centers can prevent those most in need from accessing the Internet for these basic services (Kang 2016b). Even if someone goes to the library to apply for a job online, he may not be able to return to the library every day to check email to see if he has been granted an interview.

Education and the Homework Gap

Internet access and skills effectively have become essential for educational and economic opportunity. File and Ryan (2013) of the Census Bureau report that education and broadband adoption are positively related, meaning that households with less educational attainment have lower rates of broadband adoption. Only 43 percent of individuals without a high school diploma use the Internet, compared with 90 percent of those with a college degree (File and Ryan 2013). To provide a curriculum that is relevant and prepares students for the job market, teachers are increasingly assigning homework that requires Internet access. Low-income students are at a distinct disadvantage. It is common to hear stories of students doing their homework in fast-food restaurants or outside school buildings after hours to access free Wi-Fi hot spots (Kang 2016a).

The digital divide is growing in classrooms because of unequal access to essential learning technology resources at home. Horrigan (2015) of the Pew Research Center explains that "roughly one-third (31.4 percent) of households whose incomes fall below $50,000 and with children ages 6–17 do not have a high-speed Internet connection at home. This low-income group makes up about 40 percent of all families with school-age children in the United States. . . . By comparison, only 8.4 percent of households with annual incomes over $50,000 lack a broadband Internet connection at home. In other words, low-income homes with children are four times more likely to be without broadband than their middle or upper-income counterparts" (Horrigan 2015). This is referred to as the "homework gap."

Digital Skills Gap

Computer and Internet skills are critical in today's job market. A report by Burning Glass Technologies (2015, p. 1) notes, "As the nation has recovered from the Great Recession, growth for digital-intensive middle-skill jobs has been equivalent to the growth of high-skilled positions over the same period (4.8 percent for digital middle skills and 4.7 percent for high-skill positions from 2010–2013)." According to this report, middle-skill jobs are those with less than 80 percent of postings calling for a bachelor's degree and with a median hourly wage above the national living wage of $15. The report notes that almost 8 in 10 middle-skill jobs require digital skills. Word processing and spreadsheet proficiencies in particular have become a basic requirement for most middle-skill occupations. Middle-skill jobs with intensive digital requirements have grown more than twice as fast as other middle-skill jobs in the past decade, and pay wages, on average, 18 percent higher than middle-skill jobs without a digital component. Indeed, middle-skill jobs without major digital requirements—which are often in transportation, construction, and installation/repair—have grown less than even low-skill positions. Between 2004 and 2013, nondigital middle-skill jobs grew by 1.9 percent compared to low-skill jobs, which grew by 2.9 percent (Burning Glass 2015, pp. 1–2).

"New collar" is a term coined by IBM CEO Ginni Rometty to describe middle-skill jobs that don't require a traditional four-year degree but do require digital skills. Some of these new-collar jobs include cloud administrator, cybersecurity architect, software developer, technology support technician, and diagnostic medical sonographer. IBM created the New Collar program, which focuses on finding more employees without four-year college degrees—but with tech skills that meet their hiring needs. According to Sam Ladah, vice president of human resources at IBM, "About half a million technology jobs go unfilled in the U. S., and it's because employers can't find what they're looking for. The country is only producing about 50,000 computer science grads each year, and that's the skills gap" (Ryssdal, Bodnar, and Henderson 2017). IBM and Microsoft are supporting tech skills training programs to create new pathways to digital-intensive middle-skills jobs to close the tech job gap. Skillful, an organization that provides training in the areas of technology, advanced manufacturing, and health care, is working with 90 companies to refine and clarify their job descriptions and skills. Lohr (2017) quotes Zoe Baird of the Markle Foundation (which supports Skillful): "We're trying to use the very forces that are disrupting the economy—technology and data—to drive a labor market that helps all Americans." Many cities, such as San Antonio, are seeing a rise in new-collar training programs such as Codeup and the Rackspace Open Cloud Academy. Also emerging are programs such as Youth Code Jam and the U.S. Department of Housing and Urban Development and San Antonio Housing Authority Connect-Home digital skills training program (in partnership with Goodwill), which can directly lead to tech jobs or prepare LMI people to qualify for the more advanced new-collar training certification programs. In addition, long-standing workforce development programs such as Project Quest have added career tracks in cybersecurity, health information technology, computer programming, and software development, to name a few. Figure 18.1 shows the relationship between digital skills training programs and the ability to participate in the Internet economy.

Figure 18.1   The Relationship between Digital Literacy Training and the Internet Economy

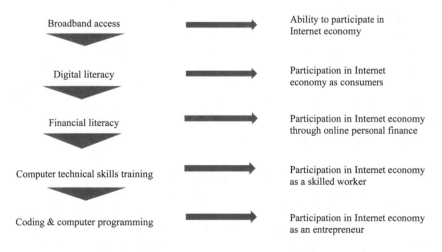

SOURCE: Federal Reserve Bank of Dallas.

MANUFACTURING AND RETAIL JOBS

A significant decline in traditional manufacturing and retail jobs has resulted in unemployment for large segments of the population who lack postsecondary education credentials or digital skills and/or who live in rural communities. In a report analyzing their top demand occupations, the San Antonio Manufacturer's Association finds that the growth of automation and technological complexity within the San Antonio manufacturing industry is increasingly requiring digital workforce skills (Dewey 2015). Moreover, as reported by the Brookings Institution, "the rise of cognitive computing systems [artificial intelligence] brings a potentially massive shift in the way that work is done, which could lead to an equally massive displacement of the workforce" (Desouza, Dawson, and Santiago 2017). Machines are affecting low- and medium-skill jobs by augmenting or completely replacing human labor. Researchers from the University of Oxford report that 47 percent of total U.S. employment is at high risk because of significant automation across a wide variety of blue-collar and white-collar professions (Frey and Osborne 2013).

Automation and globalization have transformed manufacturing and resulted in plant closings in small cities across the United States. Abrams and Gebeloff (2017) describe the effect of this disruptive workforce transformation. Additionally, they examine the subsequent closing of retail stores caused by the proliferation of e-commerce. For example, "Johnstown [Pa] . . . eventually became prosperous from its steel [mills] and offered a clear path to the middle class. For generations, people could walk out of high school and into a steady factory job. But today, the area bears the marks of a struggling town. Its population has dwindled, and addiction treatment centers and Dollar Generals stand in place of corner grocers and department stores. . . ." The authors detail the experience of workers who are facing unemployment nationwide "as the retail industry struggles to adapt to online shopping." The monumental change in retail is evidenced by the decline of the shopping mall. In the past, malls were not only places to shop, but they served as town centers and social gathering places. With the rise in e-commerce between 2010 and 2013, mall visits declined by 50 percent (Sanburn 2017). Malls are closing at a rapid pace, and new malls are not being built.

The country is losing retail jobs due to e-commerce; however, "growth in e-commerce jobs like marketing and engineering, while strong, is clustered around larger cities far away. Rural counties and small metropolitan areas account for about 23 percent of traditional American retail employment, but they are home to just 13 percent of e-commerce positions" (Abrams and Gebeloff 2017). For example, in September 2017 e-commerce giant Amazon announced that it is planning a second headquarters in the United States and made a formal request for proposals from cities. Among Amazon's requirements: a city with a diverse population of one million or more, good schools, evidence of fiber optic Internet connections and a coverage map showing strong cellular phone service at the location, and lists of universities and statistics on the qualifications of local workers (Wingfield and Cohen 2017).

BUSINESS DEVELOPMENT IN LOW-INCOME AND RURAL AREAS

Broadband infrastructure and workers who have digital skills are necessary to attract business and industry (i.e., jobs) to underserved communities. Of the 7.75 million businesses in the United States, 97 percent are considered small business (U.S. Census Bureau/American FactFinder 2016). The Small Business Administration (2016) defines small business as "an independent business having fewer than 500 employees." In terms of net job creation small business has been responsible for about 65 percent of job gains over the past 25 years (Bureau of Labor Statistics 2017). Furthermore, small businesses employ nearly half of private sector workers (Federal Reserve System 2018).

The digital divide limits business development in low-income areas of cities and in rural areas. Businesses need high-speed Internet access so that they can thrive. Broadband infrastructure is a critical component of creating an ecosystem that supports entrepreneurship, enabling businesses to expand market reach and customer bases. It also allows the emergence of tech-related start-ups. Therefore, broadband infrastructure is important for the creation of jobs and the revitalization of underserved areas, as well as for unleashing the potential for LMI people to become entrepreneurs through the Internet economy.

A paper by the International Telecommunication Union (ITU), prepared for a special session of the Broadband Commission for Sustainable Development (Philbeck 2016), analyzes a significant body of international research on the economic impact of broadband and concludes that broadband has a beneficial impact on economic growth. The paper notes that the impact of broadband includes direct effects through large-scale infrastructure investments that lead to increased economic activity in the investment area, indirect or long-term effects that spur innovation and productivity through improved broadband speeds, and induced effects such as spillover into other economic sectors. From the analysis, the author holds that "a 10% increase in broadband penetration is likely to have a positive impact, and could raise economic growth by between 0.25% –1.4%. If broadband speed is doubled, GDP may increase, potentially up to 0.3%" (p. 3).

Communities in the United States with high-speed broadband infrastructure provide an environment that promotes small-business development. In a study by Sosa (2014), he notes that "communities where gigabit broadband was widely available enjoyed higher gross domestic product [GDP], relative to similar communities where gigabit broadband was not widely available" (p. 1). The 14 communities in the study "enjoyed over $1 billion in additional GDP when gigabit broadband became widely available" (p. 1). The study refers to the Chattanooga, Tennessee, municipal-owned gigabit broadband service that has attributed "1,000 new jobs, increased investments, and 'a new population of computer programmers, entrepreneurs and investors'" (p. 6).

A study by the Boston Consulting Group (Dean et al. 2012) finds that the impact of the Internet on GDP in the United States is 4.7 percent; that is, the Internet accounted for $684 billion, or 4.7 percent of all U.S. economic activity in 2010. The study further reports that "the Internet economy in the developed markets of the G20 will grow at an annual rate of 8 percent over the next five years, far outpacing just about every traditional economic sector, producing wealth and jobs" (p. 6). Membership in the G20 includes 20 of the world's largest advanced and emerging economies "representing about two-thirds of the world's population, 85 percent of global gross domestic product and over 75 percent of global trade" (G20 2015).

The key to growing entrepreneurship in the Internet economy is to promote the expansion of broadband networks. Consider that before the advent of the Internet, telecommunications and information technology innovations happened at the center of the network and were created by the engineers working in the industry. The Internet, however, makes unbounded innovation possible on the periphery of the network; that is, with people and their computers (Fransman 2001). Closing the digital divide for budding and established entrepreneurs makes it possible for them to have Internet access to realize their innovative business ideas.

The implication for rural communities is significant because access to high-speed broadband can help businesses thrive and no longer be dependent on physical proximity to a broad customer base. Having broadband infrastructure has the potential to make geography irrelevant for some types of businesses. Furthermore, broadband infrastructure will help curb the "brain drain" of young people from rural areas since it allows them to return to their hometowns to open businesses or work remotely for companies in larger cities.

THE DIGITAL ECONOMY AND THE SHRINKING MIDDLE CLASS

Bonvillian (2016), of the Massachusetts Institute of Technology, discusses how "technological advances in industry require an ever-increasing level of technological skill in the workforce." He argues, "Higher education since the Industrial Revolution has become increasingly tied to economic well-being. . . . For more than a hundred years, the education curve stayed ahead of the technology implementation curve, but starting in the 1970s, the higher education graduation rate began to stagnate while the required workforce skills continued to rise." This dynamic in educational attainment, and the decline in traditional middle-skills occupations in manufacturing and retail discussed previously, has led to a shrinking middle class and job polarization. The phenomenon helps explain the growing economic inequality in the United States. Recent research reveals that between 1979 and 2015, high-skill occupations increased from 25 to 39 percent. However, traditional middle-skill occupations declined from 61 percent to 43 percent, while low-skill occupations increased from 14 percent to 18 percent (Blum and Groves 2016, p. 4).

It is imperative that workforce development programs and higher education systems respond to the ever-increasing level of technological skill required in the workforce by providing timely and relevant content and experiences to meet present and future workforce demands. The skills-based training for new-collar digital-intensive jobs represents an on-ramp to the middle class for people without a four-year college degree the way traditional manufacturing provided in the past. Alternative pathways to the middle class and beyond are important for creating a strong economy where everyone can participate.

Furthermore, as Kaplan (2015) notes in *Humans Need Not Apply*, "The . . . mistake is the tacit assumption that first you go to school, and when you are done, you go get a job. This made sense when jobs and skills changed on a generational timescale, but it does not in today's fast-moving labor markets. These two phases of life need to be strongly interleaved, or at least the opportunity for new skill acquisition must be explicit and omnipresent" (p. 153). The pace of change has dramatically increased; thus, educational institutions and workforce development agencies will be ever more important in helping workers become lifelong learners and competitive participants in the digital economy.

STEPS FORWARD

Increasingly, digital inclusion represents economic inclusion. Thus, the Federal Reserve System and the Federal Reserve Bank of Dallas have taken steps to provide evidence-based research and serve as a resource to help financial institutions and communities close the digital divide and thereby create a more inclusive economy.

The Federal Reserve Board, the Office of the Comptroller of the Currency, and the Federal Deposit Insurance Corporation published updated guidance on the Community Reinvestment Act (CRA), the 2016 Question and Answer (Q&A). The CRA is a law that encourages banks to make loans, investments, and provide services to LMI communities. In the 2016 update, broadband is included as a form of infrastructure investment, and the agencies identify communications infrastructure as an essential community service and describe how investing in new or rehabilitated communications infrastructure is consistent with the CRA regulatory definition of community development.

The 2016 update also provides guidance on the CRA service test and notes that banks should provide evidence that their "alternative delivery systems" using online banking and financial technology are being used/adopted and are effective in providing services to LMI individuals. This was an important update that recognizes that banking has become increasingly digital. It is also a recognition that the industry may develop innovations in fintech, or financial technology, and online and mobile banking; however, if the financial services industry does not reach LMI people with these innovations, the country may have increasingly more people unbanked and underbanked and outside the financial mainstream.

In recent years, Banks across the Federal Reserve System have published research highlighting uneven access to broadband. The Dallas Fed published a how-to guide or framework to be used across the country to accompany the 2016 Q&A, "Closing the Digital Divide: A Framework for Meeting CRA Obligations" (Barton 2016). In addition, the New York Fed published "Investing in Our Communities: A Case Study on Closing the Digital Divide" (Franco, Cruz, and Long 2017) to accompany the framework and serve as an interactive teaching tool to help banks and their community partners understand how to close the digital divide in their communities and support digital inclusion programs. In a similar effort, the Cleveland Fed published "Broadband and High-Speed Internet Access in the Fourth District" (Arvind and Fee 2016), and the Minneapolis Fed published "Border-to-Border Dreams" (Davies and Harrington 2017), an account of how Minnesota's Border-to-Border grants have not reached many rural areas of the state.

Furthermore, the Dallas Fed is working with local governments and partners to map broadband access and adoption in cities and counties and help them create their digital inclusion plans as a part of their economic development plans. The communities are using the "Closing the Digital Divide" publication (Barton 2016) as a guide. And, in South Texas border communities, the Dallas Fed convened a collective impact demonstration project, Digital Opportunity for the Rio Grande Valley, to close the digital divide in an area of concentrated poverty that has one of the lowest rates of broadband connection in the country.

CONCLUSION

This chapter documents how technological disruptions call for new approaches to developing a workforce that has the skills to participate fully in the Internet economy and prepare for jobs that increasingly require digital skills. Broadband infrastructure and access are essential to support both workers (on the supply side) and to attract and sustain business and jobs (on the demand side).

As basic services and tools that are fundamental to upward mobility become increasingly digitized, the digital divide creates a structural barrier to closing the income and wealth gaps in the United States. Income and wealth inequality are at the highest levels since the Great Depression. The Survey of Consumer Finances (SCF) issued by the Board of Governors of the Federal Reserve System (2017) finds that "the distribution of income and wealth has grown increasingly unequal in recent years" (p. 10). For example, according to the SCF, "The share of income received by the top 1 percent of families was 20.3 percent in 2013 and rose to 23.8 percent in 2016. . . . Correspondingly, the rising income share of the top 1 percent mirrors the declining income share of the bottom 90 percent of the distribution, which fell to 49.7 percent in 2016" (p. 10). As Fry and Kochhar (2014) of the Pew Research Center note, "America's upper-income families have a median net worth that is nearly 70 times that of the country's lower-income families, also the widest wealth gap between these families in 30 years." The digital divide creates a barrier to LMI individuals' ability to move up the economic ladder through education, workforce development programs, employment, and entrepreneurship. Indeed, to prevent downward mobility for LMI families, the investment in broadband infrastructure and digital inclusion programs is essential.

Note

1. The Federal Communications Commission defines broadband as a download speed of 25 Mbps (megabits per second) and an upload speed of 3 Mbps.

References

Abrams, Rachel, and Gebeloff, Robert. 2017. "In Towns Already Hit by Steel Mill Closings, a New Casualty: Retail Jobs." *New York Times*, June 25. http://www.nytimes.com/2017/06/25/business/economy/amazon-retail -jobs-pennsylvania.html?smprod=nytcore-iphone&smid=nytcore-iphone -share (accessed September 14, 2017).

Arvind, Shruthi, and Kyle Fee. 2016. "Broadband and High-Speed Internet Access in the Fourth District. A Look behind the Numbers." Cleveland: Federal Reserve Bank of Cleveland. https://www.clevelandfed.org/ newsroom-and-events/publications/a-look-behind-the-numbers/albtn -20161208-broadband-and-high-speed-internet-access.aspx (accessed September 14, 2017).

Barton, Jordana. 2016. "Closing the Digital Divide: A Framework for Meeting CRA Obligations." Dallas: Federal Reserve Bank of Dallas. https://www .dallasfed.org/cd/pubs/digitaldivide.aspx (accessed September 14, 2017).

Blum, Elizabeth Sobel, and Garrett C. Groves. 2016. "Regional Talent Pipelines: Collaborating with Industry to Build Opportunities in Texas." Dallas: Federal Reserve Bank of Dallas. https://www.dallasfed.org/-/media/ Documents/cd/pubs/pipelines.pdf (accessed May 1, 2018).

Board of Governors of the Federal Reserve System. 2017. "Changes in U.S. Family Finances from 2013 to 2016: Evidence from the Survey of Consumer Finances." *Federal Reserve Bulletin* 103(3). Washington, DC: Board of Governors of the Federal Reserve System. https://www.federalreserve .gov/publications/files/scf17.pdf (accessed August 3, 2018).

Bonvillian, William B. 2016. "Donald Trump's Voters and the Decline of American Manufacturing." *Issues in Science and Technology* 32(4): 27–39. http://issues.org/32-4/donald-trumps-voters-and-the-decline-of-american -manufacturing/ (accessed September 14, 2017).

Burning Glass Technologies. 2015. *Crunched by the Numbers: The Digital Skills Gap in the Workforce*. Boston: Burning Glass Technologies. www .burning-glass.com/wp-content/uploads/2015/06/Digital_Skills_Gap.pdf (accessed September 14, 2017).

Davies, Phil, and Ann Harrington. 2017. "Border-to-Border Dreams." *Fedgazette*, August 15. Minneapolis: Federal Reserve Bank of Minneapolis. https://www.minneapolisfed.org/publications/fedgazette/border-to-border -dreams (accessed September 14, 2017).

Dean, David, Sebastian DiGrande, Dominic Field, Andreas Lundmark, James O'Day, John Pineda, and Paul Zwillenberg. 2012. *The Internet Economy in the G20: The $4.2 Trillion Growth Opportunity*. Boston: Boston Consulting Group.

Desouza, Kevin C., Gregory S. Dawson, Bryce A. Santiago. 2017. "Disrupting Work and Workers in the Age of Cognitive Computing Systems." *Techtank* (blog), Brookings Institution, April 26. http://www.brookings.edu/blog/techtank/2017/04/26/disrupting-work-and-workers-in-the-age-of-cognitive-computing-systems/ (accessed September 14, 2017).

Dewey, John. 2015. *San Antonio Manufacturers Association (SAMA) Alamo Region Manufacturing Workforce Assessment Report*. San Antonio: SAMA. http://www.sama-tx.org/wp-content/uploads/2016/08/SAMA_Workforce _Assessment_Report-Final-120115.pdf (accessed September 14, 2017).

Federal Communications Commission (FCC). 2016. *2016 Broadband Progress Report*. Washington, DC: FCC. http://apps.fcc.gov/edocs_public/attachmatch/FCC-16-6A1.pdf (accessed September 14, 2017).

Federal Reserve System. 2018. https://www.fedsmallbusiness.org (accessed April 10, 2018).

File, Thom, and Camille Ryan. 2013. "Computer and Internet Use in the United States: 2013; American Community Survey Reports." Washington, DC: Census Bureau. www.census.gov/content/dam/Census/library/publications/2014/acs/acs-28.pdf (accessed September 14, 2017).

Franco, Adrian, Chelsea Cruz, and Graham Long. 2017. "Investing in Our Communities: A Case Study on Closing the Digital Divide." New York: Federal Reserve Bank of New York. https://www.newyorkfed.org/medialibrary/media/outreach-and-education/cra/reports/DallasFed-Closing -the-Digital-Divide.pdf (accessed October 5, 2017).

Fransman, Martin. 2001. "Evolution of the Telecommunications Industry into the Internet Age." *Communications & Strategies* 43: 57–113.

Frey, Carl Benedikt, and Michael A. Osborne. 2013. "The Future of Employment: How Susceptible Are Jobs to Computerisation?" Oxford: University of Oxford.

Fry, Richard, and Rakesh Kochhar. 2014. "America's Wealth Gap between Middle-Income and Upper-Income Families Is the Widest on Record." Washington, DC: Pew Research Center. http://www.pewresearch.org/fact -tank/2014/12/17/wealth-gap-upper-middle-income (accessed August 1, 2018).

G20. 2015. "G20 Members." www.g20.org.tr/aboutg20/g20-members (accessed August 2, 2018).

Horrigan, John B. 2015. "The Numbers behind the Broadband 'Homework Gap.'" Washington, DC: Pew Research Center. http://www.pewresearch .org/fact-tank/2015/04/20/the-numbers-behind-the-broadband-homework -gap/ (accessed April 11, 2018).

Kang, Cecilia. 2016a. "Bridging a Digital Divide That Leaves School-children Behind." *New York Times*, February 22. https://www.nytimes

.com/2016/02/23/technology/fcc-internet-access-school.html?_r=0 (accessed September 13, 2017).

———. 2016b. "Unemployed Detroit Residents Are Trapped by a Digital Divide." *New York Times*, May 22. https://www.nytimes.com/2016/05/23/technology/unemployed-detroit-residents-are-trapped-by-a-digital-divide.html (accessed September 13, 2017).

Kaplan, Jerry. 2015. *Humans Need Not Apply.* New Haven, CT: Yale University Press.

Levin, Blair, and Denise Linn. 2015. *The Next Generation Network Connectivity Handbook: A Guide for Community Leaders Seeking Affordable, Abundant Bandwidth.* Vol 1.0. Benton Foundation. Evanston, IL: Benton Foundation. http://www.gig-u.org/cms/assets/uploads/2015/07/Val-NexGen_design_7.9_v2.pdf (accessed September 13, 2017).

Lohr, Steve. 2017. "A New Kind of Tech Job Emphasizes Skills, Not a College Degree." *New York Times*, June 28. http://www.nytimes.com/2017/06/28/technology/tech-jobs-skills-college-degree.html (accessed September 13, 2017).

Philbeck, Imme. 2016. "Working Together to Connect the World by 2020: Reinforcing Connectivity Initiatives for Universal and Affordable Access." Geneva: International Telecommunication Union.

Ryssdal, Kai, Bridget Bodnar, and Emily Henderson. 2017. "You Don't Need to Be a College Grad to Work in Tech." *Marketplace*, National Public Radio. August 1. http://www.marketplace.org/2017/08/01/tech/you-dont-need-be-college-grad-work-tech (accessed September 13, 2017).

Sanburn, Josh. 2017. "The Death and Life of the Shopping Mall." *Time* 190(5): 40–45.

Small Business Administration (SBA) Office of Advocacy. 2016. *Frequently Asked Questions about Small Business.* Washington, DC: SBA. www.sba.gov (accessed September 13, 2017).

Smith, Aaron. 2015. "Lack of Broadband Can Be Key Obstacle, Especially for Job Seekers." Washington, DC: Pew Research Center.

Sosa, David. 2014. *Early Evidence Suggests Gigabit Broadband Drives GDP.* Various locations: Analysis Group. www.ftthcouncil.org/d/do/1686 (accessed September 13, 2017).

Steinmetz, Katy, and Matt Vella. 2017. "Uber Fail: Upheaval at the World's Most Valuable Startup Is a Wake-up Call for Silicon Valley." *Time* 189(24): 22–28.

U.S. Census Bureau. 2013. "American Community Survey." Washington, DC: Census Bureau.

U.S. Census Bureau/American FactFinder. 2016. https://factfinder.census.gov/faces/nav/jsf/pages/searchresults.xhtml?refresh=t, (accessed May 1, 2018).

U.S. Bureau of Labor Statistics. 2017. "Table D. Average Percentage Share (1) of Gross Job Gains and Gross Job Losses by Firm Size, Third Quarter 1992–Fourth Quarter 2017, Seasonally Adjusted." Washington, DC: Bureau of Labor Statistics. https://www.bls.gov/web/cewbd/table_d.txt (accessed May 1, 2018).

Wingfield, Nick, and Patricia Cohen. 2017. "Amazon Plans Second Headquarters, Opening a Bidding War among Cities." *New York Times*, September 7. https://www.nytimes.com/2017/09/07/technology/amazon-headquarters-north-america.html (accessed October 2, 2017).

Part 4

Investing in Skills and Credentials

19
Creative Solutions to the Credentialing Chaos

Stephen Crawford

In the 1950s and 1960s, skilled workers, whether factory workers, white-collar employees, or managers and salaried professionals, tended to work for the same firm for many years—often their entire careers.[1] In the words of economist Paul Osterman (2004, p.155), "The typical American worker averaged the same number of years at their employer as did the average Japanese employee, who lived under a system dubbed 'lifetime employment.'" That meant that firms filled many job vacancies from their existing workforce—the "internal labor market"— and promoted existing employees to fill higher-level openings that arose because of turnover, retirements, or business expansion. In doing so, employers did not need credentials to tell them what these workers knew and could do, since they already had years of experience supervising them. Lower-skilled workers labored in the much more volatile "external labor market" but by definition lacked the kinds of marketable skills to which credentials typically attest. Thus, workforce credentials played a much smaller role in the labor market than they do today.[2]

That stable labor market has long since given way to one characterized by considerable volatility for most skilled as well as unskilled employees. Moreover, the skill needs of firms have increased dramatically, as evidenced by both the large expansion in the ranks of technical and managerial employees and the "upskilling" of many occupations. One result is that employers need many more skilled and highly skilled workers than in the past, yet rely far more on the external labor market for them.

In addition, much occupational knowledge has been codified, and educational institutions have emerged to transmit it to those who aspire to enter knowledge-based occupations. These schools and programs award credentials that presumably strengthen their holders' position in the labor market, which in turn reinforces a "credentials competition" among both workers and the institutions that award them. That is, more workers seek higher-level credentials to distinguish themselves on the labor market, and more schools and programs offer their own distinctive credentials in an effort to stand out from their peers and attract more students.

These developments have vastly increased the labor market's dependence on credentials as attestations of their holders' knowledge and skills. Unfortunately, the credentials themselves perform this function badly. To begin with, there is a confusing variety of credentials offered, ranging from academic degrees, for-credit certificates and noncredit certificates to industry certifications, state and federal occupational licenses, apprenticeships, and badges. Degrees and certificates attest to the successful completion of a certain program of study, but they say little about what its holder can actually do in a particular work setting.

By contrast, certifications attest to the demonstrated possession of industry- or occupation-relevant skills, require periodic renewal, and can be taken away for unethical behavior or proven incompetency. Accredited certification programs go further, requiring that the assessments to demonstrate skills are carefully derived from job analyses and that these assessments are fair, valid, and reliable. However, according to Workcred (2018), only about 10 percent of certifications are accredited by either of the two main bodies, the American National Standards Institute (ANSI) and the Institute for Credentialing Excellence (ICE), and the quality of the unaccredited ones varies widely, so that some so-called certifications are in reality just certificates.

Adding to the confusion created by the different types of credentials is the sheer number of them. According to a recent report from Credential Engine (2018), there are 213,913 degree-granting programs (associate's through doctorate) and 66,997 for-credit certificate-granting programs at the nation's Title IV colleges and universities. There are also 13,656 federally registered apprenticeships, 8,864 state-issued occupational licenses, 5,465 certifications, at least 650 coding boot camp certificates, and 47 online MicroMasters and Nanodegrees, for a total of 308,942 credentials in the United States. This tally does not include the growing number of digital badges, nor does it include licenses issued by the federal government, noncredit certificates within and outside higher education, or credentials issued by educational institutions not covered by Title IV, as there is no way to accurately count them.

With such a large and varied assortment of credentials—and many new ones emerging yearly—it is extremely difficult for either employers or those contemplating obtaining a credential to make sense of their options. McCarthy (2014) illustrates the problem well in the case of a Michigan woman seeking to become a medical assistant, an occupation that is a good first step on health-care career paths such as nursing, occupational therapy, and hospital administration. "A certificate in medical assisting," she says, "takes less than a year to complete and, in some cases, can count toward an associate or bachelor's degree" (p. 2). In Michigan, however, there are 59 institutions of higher education that offer certificate programs in medical assisting, and they vary widely in duration, costs, eligibility for federal grants and loans, and whether they provide credit toward a degree, says McCarthy.

In trying to navigate this confusing terrain, the consumers of credentials—students, parents, career counselors, loan agencies, employers, and so forth—often look to the quality assurance bodies that accredit, endorse, recommend, or otherwise approve specific credentials. Yet here too there is confusion about what these stamps of approval mean. Consumers are fairly familiar with the 6 major regional accreditors of higher education institutions,[3] but they are far less familiar with the 10 national accrediting organizations, the more than 100 organizations that accredit specialized and professional programs, and the hundreds of accreditation bodies that are not recognized by the U.S. Department of Education or the Council on Higher Education Accreditation, some of which are "accreditation mills."

The current credentialing landscape makes it virtually impossible for either an employer or a potential student to comprehend and compare what particular credentials represent in terms of competencies, quality of instruction, validity of assessment, relevance to current occupational requirements, market value, and so on. This is a serious problem in an economy whose prosperity depends on the development and deployment of human capital.

Troubled by this situation, policy researchers at think tanks and universities began exploring and discussing possible solutions with representatives of employer associations, higher education associations, and government agencies. This collaborative work resulted in several strategies, one of which was the Credential Transparency Initiative, funded by the Lumina Foundation. This initiative developed a Credential Transparency Description Language for describing the critical features of all credentials and a web-based Credential Registry for aggregating this information and enabling customized searches. These features include costs, competencies, assessments, labor market outcomes, and quality assurance organizations that give recognition to the particular credential involved. Pilot testing showed this system to work so well that in 2016 the Lumina Foundation, with help from the Business Roundtable, created an independent nonprofit called Credential Engine to maintain this system and take it to scale.

In this section, the chapter authored by Ken Sauer and Stephen Crawford describes how Credential Engine works and is addressing the scaling problem of critical mass—of getting enough credentialing organizations to post information on the Credential Registry to make it of interest to potential users. To combat the understandable reluctance of credentialing organizations to be early adopters, Credential Engine is working with a few state governments to build up a critical mass of credentials in one industry. In this chapter's case study, the state is Indiana and the industry is health care. The Indiana Commission on Higher Education is taking the lead, building on existing initiatives—especially those involving transitioning veterans—to successfully engage various stakeholders in the health-care credentialing arena.

Credential Engine exemplifies the potential of a carefully designed digital platform to improve the functioning of the labor market by standardizing supply-side terminology, aggregating information, and enabling easy access to it. Could the same principles be applied to the demand side—the skills that employers seek from potential workers? The U.S. Chamber of Commerce Foundation's Jason A. Tyszko makes a powerful case in his chapter that they can, and he shows how his organization's Talent Pipeline and Jobs Registry initiatives are already doing so. These initiatives are developing processes for signaling at the competency level and in machine-readable ways the skill and credential requirements of local employers within the same industry and for communicating this information to the market, thus enabling job seekers and credential providers to respond more effectively. Tyszko's chapter goes beyond creative ideas to discuss pilots that are well underway in several cities.

Robert Sheets was intimately involved in the creation of Credential Engine and the Chamber initiatives mentioned above. In his chapter, he builds on lessons learned along the way by analyzing the weaknesses of the current system, illustrating the potential inherent in new technologies and recent private-sector innovations, and offering policy recommendations aimed at creating a more flexible, integrated, and effective system—an open-source public-private data infrastructure for labor market information.

The final chapter, by Alejandro Crawford, offers yet one more creative way to improve the credentialing marketplace: by creating a national credential for entrepreneurs. Here, too, much depends on developing satisfactory definitions of key competencies, standardizing the language used to describe them, establishing methods for demonstrating and assessing entrepreneurial skills, and providing a common digital platform for enabling this activity. Creating a credential for entrepreneurs and supplementing it with associated assessment tools is especially challenging because entrepreneurial competency makes sense only in terms of interactions between the entrepreneur and a dynamic ecosystem of investors, markets, talent sources, testing labs, production facilities, and business regulations.

This chapter is a fitting conclusion to the section because, among other things, it points to a curious relationship between the need for an entrepreneurship credential and the growth in the importance of other credentials discussed above (degrees, certificates, licenses, badges, etc.). As more and more Americans have sought and obtained credentials to improve their labor market prospects, those interested in starting their own businesses face additional opportunity costs, especially if they took out loans to acquire a credential. The past few decades have seen a decline in the rate of new business formation (J.D. Harrison 2015), and one reason may be that once a credential is obtained, the temptation to cash in on its labor market value overwhelms any inclination to gamble on an entrepreneurial venture. If that is the case, the rise of credentials makes it all the more desirable to develop a credential for job creators.

All four of this section's chapters are by authors who work directly with the stakeholders involved—colleges, employers, entrepreneurs, and policymakers—and understand their information needs. The authors all build on recent advances in data structuring and the use of digital platforms for aggregating and sharing data.

Most importantly, they recognize and address the challenge of standardizing the terms used to describe skills, assessments, and related information, while still allowing enough flexibility to accommodate desirable variation and adapt to future change. The point is to use standardization not to reduce differences (the way the National Skills Standards Board tried mightily to do in the 1990s), but to make differences more transparent in a rapidly changing marketplace.[4] This bottom-up (vs. top-down) form of standardization enables meaningful comparisons of credentials and thus an effective market where buyers and sellers can make informed choices about the best value for their purposes. Such standardization, combined with sophisticated systems for assembling, verifying, and distributing the relevant information in real time, holds out enormous promise for improving the development and deployment of the nation's talent.

In short, the subsequent chapters offer creative solutions to major problems in today's credentialing marketplace. It remains to be seen whether these visionary solutions will be widely adopted, but given the importance of credentials in our knowledge-based economy, it is vital to consider and build on them.

Notes

1. For this paper, we define a "skilled" worker as any worker who has acquired special skill, training, knowledge, and ability in his or her work, whether gained through college, technical school, or experience on the job.
2. See also Cappelli (1999, 2008).
3. The six regional accreditors are the Middle States Commission on Higher Education, the New England Association of Schools and Colleges, the Northwest Commission on Colleges and Universities, the Higher Learning Commission, the Southern Association of Colleges and Schools, and the Western Association of Schools and Colleges. Additionally, the Board of Regents of the State of New York is recognized as an accreditor for degree-granting institutions of higher education in states that designate the agency as their sole or primary accrediting agency.
4. The National Skills Standards Board was a congressionally chartered federal initiative funded from 1994 to 2003, administered by the U.S. Department of Labor and charged with improving methods for defining and measuring human work performance across multiple industry sectors. When congressional funding ended in 2003, key staff members continued its work through the Global Skills Exchange. See www.skillsdmo.com/who-we-are/.

References

Cappelli, Peter. 1999. *The New Deal at Work: Managing the Market-Driven Workforce*. Boston: Harvard Business School Press.

———. 2008. *Talent on Demand: Managing Talent in an Age of Uncertainty*. Boston: Harvard Business School Press.

Credential Engine. 2018. *Counting U.S. Secondary and Postsecondary Credentials*. Washington, DC: Credential Engine.

Harrison, J.D. 2015. "The Decline of American Entrepreneurship—in Five Charts." February 12, *Washington Post*. https://www.washingtonpost.com/news/on-small-business/wp/2015/02/12/the-decline-of-american-entrepreneurship-in-five-charts/?utm_term=.1e97530d9446 (accessed August 3, 2018).

McCarthy, Mary Alice. 2014. *Beyond the Skills Gap: Making Education Work for Students, Employers, and Communities*. A New America policy report. Washington, DC: New America.

Osterman, Paul. 2004. "Labor Market Intermediaries in the Modern Labor Market." In *Workforce Intermediaries for the Twenty-First Century*, Robert P. Giloth, ed. Philadelphia: Temple University Press, pp. 155–189.

Workcred. 2018. Personal communication from its executive director, Dr. Roy Swift.

20

Fixing the Credentialing Chaos

A National Tool and State Application

Ken Sauer
Stephen Crawford

There is an important race taking place in the world of workforce credentials. On one side are the growing number and variety of unique credentials and the attendant confusion about what they mean, how they relate to each other, and what their value is. On the other side are new tools for creating and communicating comparable information about credentials of all kinds, from certificates and degrees to certifications, licenses, apprenticeships, and badges. At present, the forces of proliferation and chaos are winning, but smart-technology platforms are poised to overtake them. Much depends, however, on whether key stakeholders can overcome classic collective action obstacles and adopt these promising solutions to the credentialing chaos.

This chapter describes one suite of such tools and one state's effort to promote their adoption. It begins by clarifying the nature of the problem, explaining the implications for a solution, and describing a major initiative to build an online platform accordingly. It goes on to discuss in some detail the largely successful efforts of the state of Indiana to promote the population and use of this platform, especially in the health-care sector and in helping veterans transition to civilian careers. It concludes with a brief account of lessons learned and recommendations for leaders in other states who may wish to pursue a similar strategy for improving labor markets, closing skill gaps, and increasing economic growth and social mobility.[1]

THE PROBLEM: LACK OF TRANSPARENCY, TRUST, AND COMPARABILITY

Credentials perform key functions in labor markets. Employers rely on them as a convenient though flawed proxy for the talent, knowledge, and skills of job seekers. Students invest considerable sums to obtain them in the hope they will open doors to desirable jobs and careers. Educational institutions examine their rivals' credentialing programs before making decisions about launching new programs or changing existing ones. Lenders, career counselors, and others use credentials as indicators of value.

Unfortunately, it is extremely difficult for these and other participants in the credentialing marketplace to know or find out exactly what various credentials signify. For students, key uncertainties include how much they will spend in time and money to obtain the credential, what competencies they will have when they graduate, what employment and earnings outcomes to expect, and what doors to further education the credential unlocks. Employers face many of the same uncertainties but are especially concerned about how industry-informed the curriculum is, how relevant and rigorous the assessments are, and exactly what the credential holder knows and can do. Students, employers, and other stakeholders wonder about the meaning of the wide variety of accreditations, endorsements, and approvals that programs claim.

There are several reasons for such confusion. The credentialing marketplace is complex and highly fragmented, with different parts of it using different technical languages and quality criteria to describe and evaluate credentials. The recent increase in the number and kinds of credentials—they have grown to more than 300,000 in the United States alone and now include micromasters and coding camp certificates—is exacerbating the problem.[2] Moreover, there is a growing tendency for students to pursue combinations of educational credentials and industry certifications (or even apprenticeships), often through the same program, thus making evaluations of the value of specific components more difficult.

Complicating matters is the consideration that a credential is not so much a product or service as an attestation that its holders have a specific package of knowledge and skills—or at least have completed a program or test designed to produce or select for them. Yet credentials with the same name—a bachelor of science degree in mechanical engineering, for instance, or an associate of arts degree in criminal justice—often reflect quite different bundles of knowledge and skills, depending on the provider, while those with different names—master of public administration, government administration, or public management—reflect similar ones.

Even when credentialing organizations do provide information about the quality and value of their credentials, they do so in unstandardized ways, which makes comparison difficult at best. And the meaning of claims a credential may make about ensuring quality is often unclear, because there are hundreds of organizations that accredit, endorse, approve, or otherwise recommend credentialing programs, and it is difficult for interested parties to evaluate which of those organizations have higher standards and better methods for assessing conformity with these higher standards.

In short, the credentialing marketplace is characterized by a serious lack of transparency, trustworthiness, and comparability. This is not surprising in a sector as complex and decentralized as that of education, training, and skill assessment. But in a knowledge-based economy, the result is misguided investments, regretted hiring decisions, and serious skills gaps, which in turn weaken workforce quality, economic growth, and social mobility.

THE SOLUTION: A COMMON LANGUAGE AND A SEARCHABLE REGISTRY

To address this market failure, in 2013 concerned stakeholders and experts launched the Credential Transparency Initiative (CTI).[3] The purpose of CTI was to develop and test three things: 1) common terms for describing all kinds of credentials; 2) a web-based registry, modeled on the Learning Registry, for aggregating and sharing the resulting comparable information; and 3) a prototype application that would allow customized searching of the registry. Three years of pilots and stakeholder feedback led to a decision to take the system up to scale, and in 2016, CTI morphed into an independent nonprofit, Credential

Engine, with its own board, staff, and advisory committees. Credential Engine now maintains the key components of the system: the Credential Transparency Description Language, the Credential Registry, and Credential Finder.[4]

The Credential Transparency Description Language is a metadata infrastructure that conforms to the World Wide Web Consortium's specifications and its vision for open Linked Data. The Credential Registry is an open-source, web 3.0–based database that captures, connects, and makes searchable current information about credentials of all kinds, the organizations that award those credentials, and the quality assurance bodies that endorse, approve, accredit, or otherwise recommend them. That information is published voluntarily by participating credentialing and quality assurance organizations.[5]

Credential Finder is Credential Engine's prototype search app. It enables employers, job seekers, students, career counselors, and others (e.g., program operators, policymakers, researchers) to find credentials of interest and compare them along many dimensions—from competencies, assessments, and quality assurances to costs, pathways, and labor-market outcomes. Because it is "open source," other organizations—from commercial vendors to national associations—can develop their own competing or more specialized apps, and some are already doing so.

This system is well designed to provide the transparency, trust, and comparability that the credentialing marketplace desperately needs. However, realizing its potential depends on the registry reaching a critical mass of credentials, and not all credentialing organizations are prepared to provide them. Some imagine that posting the required information takes more time than it does. Some worry about how they will look when compared with others. Nevertheless, a rapidly growing number of credentialing programs is seizing the opportunity to be more visible and "findable" on the Internet, and the registry now contains over 2,200 credentials. Yet, with hundreds of thousands of credentials in the United States alone, there remains a long way to go.

Fortunately, state governments and education commissions are stepping up to this challenge by undertaking to achieve critical mass in their states, industry by industry. Some have signed agreements with Credential Engine, and others are preparing to do so. The first and most advanced of these states is Indiana. There, the Indiana Commission for Higher Education, in collaboration with other state agencies and the governor's office, has launched several initiatives to achieve critical mass within the health care industry. The remainder of this chapter explains these initiatives and the remarkable progress they have made.

INDIANA EMBARKS ON A SCALE-UP OF CREDENTIAL ENGINE

From its first exposure to Credential Engine, the Indiana Commission for Higher Education ("the commission," or ICHE) viewed it as a promising means of better serving the state's residents and workforce needs. This goal could be accomplished by pulling together information, in unprecedented scope and detail, on Indiana credentials of all types, not just college certificates and degree programs, and connecting this information to a wealth of other information on other topics ranging from who can vouch for the quality of these credentials to career pathways and workforce needs.

In March 2017, ICHE, with the support of a grant,[6] began the initial phase of the first, and until recently, the only, statewide scale-up of Credential Engine. Ivy Tech Community College had participated in an early pilot of Credential Engine the previous year by uploading two of its certificate programs to help demonstrate proof of concept. The commission saw value in widespread adoption of this innovative tool. For reasons explained below, the initial efforts focused on health care and the military, with other industries and stakeholders brought into the process in the later months of the effort.

Health care was selected because it is one of Indiana's largest employers. Nine of the top 50 occupations in the state are connected to health care. Moreover, it has been the focus of state government attention. Following Indiana's participation in a Policy Academy sponsored by the National Governors Association, Governor Mike Pence established a three-year Governor's Health Workforce Council in February 2016, which Governor Holcomb has continued. In addition to mobilizing public-sector resources, including the Bowen Center for Health Workforce Research and Policy in the Indiana University School of Medicine, the Council engaged leaders from relevant state agencies, health care employers, professional and industry associations, and non-governmental organizations.

Another important focus of the scale-up has been how military training might be represented on the registry and how veterans might have their training and experience translated into advance standing in certificate and degree programs in Indiana colleges and universities.[7]

Once the scale-up was well underway with respect to health-care and military training, the commission turned to populating the registry with information about non–health credentials, credential providers, and quality assurance entities. In expanding the scale-up beyond health care, the commission sought to focus on a variety of applications that might serve to demonstrate the value and potential of Credential Engine. What follows is a summary of Indiana's progress thus far, organized around 10 "use cases" that illustrate the broad reach of the Credential Engine system.

INDIANA'S INITIAL EMPHASIS ON HEALTH CARE

The work on health care began with entering the more than 350 certificate and degree programs offered by public two-year and four-year institutions. This included certificate programs of any length, even if they required as few as five semester credit hours, as well as all associate-to-doctoral degree programs. Using the commission's Academic Program Inventory, the Indiana Commission on Higher Education's Office of Academic Affairs entered all of the programs on behalf of the public institutions, and it supplemented the basic information about the credential by copying core narratives from the institution's own website.

This approach was taken because the commission did not want its first interaction with an educational institution to be a discussion about the potential benefits of Credential Engine or the mechanics of creating an account and using interactive screens to enter information onto the Credential Registry. Rather, it wanted the first interaction to show how effective the registry could be to a user, such as a prospective student, in seamlessly displaying and connecting a lot of powerful information about the institution's programs. This approach enabled us to immediately engage senior administrative and program leaders about the value of listing information on the registry.

Working in partnership with the Independent Colleges of Indiana (ICI), the commission also contacted two private universities that appeared interested in making use of the registry. By the end of 2017, the University of St. Francis had loaded *all* of its programs onto the registry, not just its health programs, and Indiana Wesleyan University was moving toward that same goal.

Another important component of ICHE's strategy was to work with the leadership of the Indiana Professional Licensing Agency, which licenses 107 health-care professions. This enabled us to gather information about specific licensure boards and to ensure that information about those boards was reviewed by board staff for accuracy.

While it was important to demonstrate the breadth of Indiana's scale-up by entering all of the health-care programs offered by public institutions, it was also important to demonstrate depth. This was accomplished by focusing in greater detail on the nursing profession, behavioral health and human services professionals, and selected allied health fields.

Nursing

Nursing is by far the largest health profession, with some four times as many registered nurses as doctors at the national level—five times as many if you include licensed practical nurses (Penn LDI 2015). This critical health-care profession undergoes frequent cycles of being in significantly short supply. It is also an occupation with career pathways to higher positions. Consequently, many potential students seek information about nursing programs, and the commission gave special attention to getting nursing credentials onto the Credential Registry.

Typical of state boards of nursing, the Indiana State Board of Nursing (ISBN) is both a credential provider (i.e., it issues a license or credential to an individual) and a quality assurance entity (in that it approves nursing education programs that would qualify a graduate of such a program to sit for a nursing licensing examination). Thus, for every ISBN-approved nursing program in the registry, a link was made

between the ISBN and the description of the licensing criteria, procedures, and fees for becoming licensed as an LPN or an RN. Since quality assurance is also provided by one of the two national, specialized
accrediting bodies in nursing (the Commission on Collegiate Nursing
Education [CCNE] and the Accreditation Commission for Education
in Nursing [ACEN]), links were established between these accrediting
bodies and the nursing programs that were accredited by one or the
other of these accrediting bodies.

The nursing profession provides economic and social mobility for
individuals through a well-established career ladder. For this reason,
connections were made in the registry among all of the undergraduate
Indiana nursing programs. One set of connections demonstrates how
a graduate of an 18-month certificate program qualifying someone to
become an LPN could advance his or her career by transferring credits
and achieving advance standing in an Associate of Science in Nursing
(ASN) program, or even a Bachelor of Science in Nursing (BSN) program, preparing that person to become licensed as an RN. Another set
shows how a graduate of an ASN program could transfer and apply his
or her credits toward a BSN program.

RNs can further their careers even more by pursuing a master's or
doctoral degree and becoming an advanced practice registered nurse
(APRN) or, more specifically, a nurse practitioner (NP), a clinical nurse
specialist (CNS), a certified nurse midwife, or a certified RN anesthe-
tist. Becoming an NP or CNS also entails demonstrating expertise in a
specialty area that is signified by the issuance of a professional certification through the American Nurses Credentialing Center (ANCC).
There are about a dozen NP specializations, including acute care NP,
family NP, gerontological NP, and emergency NP. Similarly, there are
almost as many CNS certifications, including adult health CNS, home
health CNS, and public/community health CNS. The Indiana scale-up
of Credential Engine has not yet developed links between such graduate
nursing programs as these APRN specializations, but it soon will.

Behavioral Health and Human Services

Like many other states, Indiana is suffering from a public health
crisis related to having not enough resources to treat mental health and
addiction problems. The Indiana state scale-up of Credential Engine

seemed a good way to address workforce needs in this important area. The Indiana Behavioral Health and Human Services Licensing Board licenses social workers, marriage and family therapists, mental health counselors, addiction counselors, and "associates" of these various professionals. Credential Engine enabled and motivated commission staff to link the related educational programs with the licenses for which they were preparing graduates. Previously, it was possible to draw such connections, but no one had; it took a catalyst like Credential Engine and its platform for storing and retrieving information.

Focusing on mental health and addictions also created an opportunity to better align programmatic preparation with workforce needs. The Indiana scale-up fostered new connections with at least one important group of employers, the Indiana Council of Community Mental Health Centers, whose 25 members employ 8,900 individuals statewide, and led to a discussion of competencies that were missing in new graduates of programs from which these centers often hired. For example, center leaders noted that many new graduates were not well prepared to write collaborative narratives, which document the services provided to a client by a team of health-care providers, and which are needed for a center to be reimbursed for those services. This usually resulted in the inadequate documentation being returned to the center for correction, thus delaying reimbursement, or in the center diverting scarce resources, in the form of an experienced individual's time, to provide on-the-job training for new hires.

Fortuitous circumstances presented an opportunity to address this misalignment of competencies in at least one concrete case. At the time of the discussions with the Indiana Council, one of the public universities proposed a master's degree in mental health counseling, which ICHE must approve. In reviewing the proposal, the feedback from the council regarding the inability of new graduates to draft appropriate documentation needed for reimbursement was articulated, with the result that the program director incorporated a seminar on this topic into the curriculum. As a result of these discussions, for which Credential Engine was a catalyst, ICHE and the Indiana Council of Community Mental Health Centers will be hosting a meeting for all center directors/ HR directors and all directors of relevant university programs to come together to improve the alignment of the competencies that programs produce with those that the centers need.

Allied Health and Military Training

Allied health workers constitute an important, though diversified, part of the health-care industry. In contrast to nursing, social work, mental health counseling, and other fields discussed thus far, there is more variation across the many allied health fields with respect to level of educational preparation or training, who provides the credential, licensure, certification, and accreditation. In addition, allied health fields vary widely regarding the nature of their services, their level of specialization, the number of individuals employed in those positions, and their visibility within the health-care industry. For all these reasons, students with an interest in allied health and other stakeholders stood to benefit greatly from the readily accessible wealth of information that the Credential Registry could provide.

At the December 2017 Indiana rollout of Credential Engine, pharmacy technology, which is offered by both of Indiana's two-year public institutions, Ivy Tech Community College and Vincennes University (VU), was selected as the field to illustrate how allied health could be represented in the registry. Since it is a licensed field, the registry contains connections between the Ivy Tech and VU associate degree programs and the Indiana Board of Pharmacy, housed within the Indiana Professional Licensing Agency, through which one becomes a licensed pharmacy technician. Individuals in this field can also earn the Pharmacy Technician Certification (CPhT) by passing the Exam for the Certification of Pharmacy Technicians (ExCPT exam) given by the National Healthcareer Association or the Pharmacy Technician Certification Exam (PTCE) developed by the Pharmacy Technician Certification Board.

In addition to its importance in the health-care industry, allied health was selected as an area of focus because of the opportunity it represented to illustrate how military training and experience can translate into credits and advanced standing in degree programs, should a veteran prepared in this area wish to follow a career path in allied health. To that end, ICHE worked in partnership with Solutions for Information Design (SOLID)[8] and the leadership of the Medical Education and Training Campus (METC) at Joint Base San Antonio, Fort Sam Houston, Texas, which is where all service members who prepare for a Military Occupational Specialty (MOS) related to allied health do their training.

The Indiana statewide scale-up of Credential Engine provided an opportunity for SOLID and METC to collaborate in populating the Credential Registry with information about all 105 training programs offered at METC, which prepare service members for allied-health-related MOSs. In a number of instances, two or more branches of the armed forces consolidated their training curricula into a single program, although each branch may vary the curriculum in some way, such as the total number of hours of training required. For example, service members preparing to be pharmacy technicians will need to complete 640 hours if they are in the Air Force but 836 hours if they're in the Army and 908 hours if they're in the Navy (U.S. Department of Defense 2017, p. 10).

Once the METC programs were entered into the registry, connections could be made between these programs and degree programs in the civilian sector, indicating the number of credit hours that pharmacy technicians at a particular rank in one of the service branches could expect to be awarded should they enroll in that college or university program.

DUAL CREDIT

Opportunities for high school students to earn college credit—called dual credit or dual enrollment—have become increasingly popular as a way to increase the college-going rate, shorten the time to complete a degree, reduce tuition and other college expenses, and improve graduation rates. These effects tend to be more pronounced for underrepresented groups, including minority students.

Indiana has a very large and successful dual credit program, with some 55 percent of all 2015 high school graduates earning at least some dual credit (Indiana Commission for Higher Education 2017). About 70 percent of the students who took dual credit courses went directly to college, compared with 50 percent who took no College Board Advanced Placement (AP) exams or dual credit, and about 80 percent of dual credit students persisted to the sophomore year, compared to about 60 percent who took no AP exams or dual credit courses. Of the students who took dual credit, 49 percent earned their credit by taking career and technical (CTE) courses (Indiana Commission for Higher Education 2017).

Because of the significant number of dual credit students pursuing CTE courses, the Indiana Credential Engine rollout included a use case that focused on this area. More specifically, the Area 31 Career Center, on the west side of Indianapolis, was entered into the registry, along with one of its CTE programs, pharmacy technician, which is offered in conjunction with its postsecondary partner, Vincennes University. High school students completing this program are eligible to become licensed pharmacy technicians and can earn the Pharmacy Technician Certification. By establishing proof of concept, the Area 31 Career Center paves the way for having all Indiana Career Centers entered into the registry.

APPRENTICESHIPS

Indiana was an early adopter of a model that linked union- and company-based apprenticeship training programs to certificate and associate degree completion opportunities at Ivy Tech Community College and Vincennes University. This model allows an apprentice to achieve recognition as a journeyman when he or she completes a U.S. Department of Labor–approved apprenticeship, but it also provides the individual with an opportunity to earn a postsecondary credential.

For this reason, apprenticeships were included as a use case in the Indiana scale-up of Credential Engine. More specifically, Ivy Tech populated the registry with all of its Associate of Applied Science Apprenticeship Technology programs in some 22 trades, ranging from boilermaker and bricklayer to sheet metal worker and telecommunications technician. Vincennes University apprenticeship programs were added to the registry as well.

Besides demonstrating that one-way workplace/industry training can be represented in Credential Engine, apprenticeships provide another opportunity to incorporate military training into the registry. As a result of collaboration between the U.S. Department of Labor (DOL) and the armed forces, active duty service members in the Navy, Marine Corps, and Coast Guard can participate in apprenticeship programs that are closely related to their MOS/rating or official duty assignment through the United Services Military Apprenticeship Program (USMAP). The U.S. Navy, for example, has more than 100 apprenticeships, including programs such as airframe mechanic, electrician, machinist, pipe fitter, and welder. In partnership with SOLID, the hope is to add as many of these apprenticeships as possible to the registry in the coming months.

Closer to home, the commission has reached out to the Indiana National Guard (INA), which also offers apprenticeship programs throughout the state. A partnership between the U.S. Departments of Labor and Veterans Affairs allows the INA to offer apprenticeship opportunities to Guard members in 17 DOL-approved programs through its Surface Maintenance Apprenticeship Program, which range from a 3,000-hour heavy truck driver program that takes about 1.5 years to complete to 8,000-hour programs in diesel mechanics, logistics engineering, and the sheet metal trade that take about four years to finish (Indiana National Guard, n.d.).

NEXT LEVEL JOBS

In 2017, Governor Eric Holcomb created the Next Level Jobs initiative as part of his Next Level Indiana agenda, which focuses on the high-priority industries and high-demand jobs driving Indiana's twenty-first-century economy forward. In conjunction with Next Level Jobs, the General Assembly approved funding for Indiana's Workforce Ready Grant program to provide free training for Hoosiers without prior college experience who wished to train for these high-demand jobs. The commission and the Indiana Department of Workforce Development (DWD) collaborated on implementing this initiative by identifying the specific jobs and the specific certificate programs at Ivy Tech Community College and Vincennes University for which training opportunities would be supported through this initiative.

Over 100 eligible certificate programs were placed on the registry to demonstrate how it could readily accommodate important new state-level initiatives. Moreover, while lists of these eligible programs were available elsewhere, placing them on the registry demonstrated how Credential Engine could add value. Being on the registry made it easy to draw connections between these certificates and the institutions that were offering these programs, as well as the industry certifications that some of these certificate programs would prepare a graduate to earn, thereby further demonstrating competency through these industry-recognized credentials.

CAREER EXPLORATION AND ROI APPLICATIONS

The Indiana scale-up of Credential Engine explored ways that the open-source software underlying the registry could be utilized to attach applications and other sources of data to Credential Engine, thereby multiplying the value of both the core information in the registry and the companion application/data. As of this writing, integration of the two applications described below with Credential Engine has not yet been achieved, but it has been explored sufficiently to demonstrate the potential and feasibility of doing so, and the two applications remain the object of ongoing activities designed to achieve full integration.

The first application involved how a tool designed to help individuals discover their career interests and explore potential career pathways could be linked to the registry, thus providing a much richer experience to the user. More specifically, the DWD has contracted with Kuder, a career guidance firm, to make Career Explorer available to middle and high schools so students could help define their career interests and develop plans and pathways to realize those ambitions. While the present DWD contract focuses on K–12, the Kuder tool could also help college-age students and adults seeking career changes.

The second application aims to integrate return-on-investment (ROI) data that the commission and DWD have developed by merging data the commission collects on graduates from all public colleges and universities within the state with employment and earnings data collected by DWD. High-level data specific to Indiana have been generated on the earnings associated with graduates of program areas—for example, bachelor's business programs or associate degrees in nursing, one, five, and ten years after graduation. While the data have limitations (e.g., they only track students who stayed in Indiana and exclude individuals who had their own businesses, these data provide important information relevant to the majority of Indiana students who complete postsecondary credentials. The data can even be accessed for specific certificate or degree programs at particular institutions, although smaller programs are left out because of cell size: less than 10 graduates in a given year would create privacy concerns.

Leveraging the capabilities of these two applications with those of Credential Engine would provide a user with an unparalleled opportunity to explore his or her career interests, gain insights on ROI, and then understand what pathway in Indiana can help achieve that career goal.

DIGITAL CREDENTIALS

Indiana's final use case in its rollout of Credential Engine explored the potential for linking the state's well-established eTranscript initiative, powered by its contract with Parchment Inc., to Credential Engine. This last application illustrates how an individual's engagement with Credential Engine can move from a posture of actively navigating a vast information resource, including job postings at some point, to one of response, creating and transmitting personal, verifiable information about one's skills and competencies to an intended recipient, such as a prospective employer, via digital credentials.

The Indiana e-Transcript program began in 2005, when the commission, in collaboration with the Indiana Department of Education (IDOE), contracted with Docufide Inc., which was acquired by Parchment in 2011, to create a web-based mechanism for high school students to request their transcripts be sent to colleges and other destinations throughout the country.

Today, this mature program is based on a statewide common high school transcript, which allows high schools to send their transcripts to colleges as data files consistent with national Postsecondary Electronic Standards Council XML Schema, which describes the structure of an XML document; this, in turn, automates an important element of the admissions process and incorporates the transcript information as data within the college student information system. Indiana is now extending this program to college transcripts and contemplating a transcript supplement that could document experiences, skills, and achievements relevant to potential job performance, which is not captured in conventional academic transcripts.

Parchment has proposed a solution whereby a digitized transcript or credential could be linked to and access other relevant data in the registry. For example, a student graduating from an Indiana institution could have his or her digitized transcript sent to an employer or another college, thereby not only verifying completion of the degree but also permitting the recipient, thanks to the linkages contained in the registry, to find out much more about the institution that conferred the degree, such as who accredits or otherwise endorses it. Similarly accessible would be information about the program from which the student graduated, including the competencies the graduate should have mastered. A transcript supplement could then document how the graduate applied the abstract statement of competencies through actual projects, workplace experiences, achievements, and so on.

LOOKING FORWARD

The 10 use cases discussed above suggest just some of Credential Engine's potential for communicating critical information about workforce credentials and thus improving the performance of labor markets and regional economies. In considering how to realize this potential, it helps to distinguish two challenges: 1) adding sufficient content to the registry and 2) promoting its actual utilization by potential users.

On the first of these, Credential Engine has made impressive progress since its launch in September 2016. As of February 2018, hundreds of "credentialing organizations" had posted information about more than 2,000 credentials on the registry. Many more were in the process of increasing that total—enough that Credential Engine anticipated 50,000 credentials by the end of 2018. Similarly, several national quality assurance bodies had added information about their quality standards and the methods for determining conformity with them. This progress is attributable to strong leadership, advisory panels representing key stakeholders (higher education, certification and licensure, employers, quality assurance bodies), and financial or in-kind support from Lumina

Foundation, the Business Roundtable, JP Morgan Chase Foundation, Microsoft, and others.

State governments are also playing an important role in populating the registry. Thanks to its early start, Indiana has more content on the registry than any other state—all certificates and degrees offered by Indiana's public two-year institutions are now on the registry—but other states are stepping up. New Jersey began an implementation initiative at the end of 2017, other states are exploring similar efforts, and four New England states are contemplating a regional scale-up. Judging from Indiana's success, such state initiatives look to be a particularly promising strategy for achieving a critical mass of credentials on the Credential Registry.

Indiana's experience also offers some lessons that may help other states succeed in any Credential Engine initiative they undertake. One is that it's important to have a "champion"—a governor, state agency, influential employer association—who understands the value and potential of Credential Engine in meeting state needs, and who can provide initial momentum. A second is that it's desirable to achieve consensus on one or two strategic sectors on which the state effort will initially focus and to engage key stakeholders in them. A third is that it's helpful to prepopulate the registry with several relevant credentials, so that a new stakeholder's first encounter with the registry is with a tangible product, not an abstract vision or data entry challenge. Finally, progress will be faster if the lead agency can allocate some modest resources, chiefly in the form of staff time, to help drive awareness and adoption of the registry.

With respect to encouraging use of the registry, the state leadership team should give special attention to career counselors in general (in schools, colleges, job centers, temporary agencies, and community-based organizations that help their clients obtain needed credentials) and to employers in those sectors where the registry has amassed enough relevant credentials to make it useful to human resource directors.

Credential Engine's tools are good news for students, businesses, and educational institutions currently struggling to navigate an increasingly complex and opaque credential system. Students can find out which credentials would serve them best and what opportunities will open up with investments in obtaining credentials. Employers can better determine what a credential holder actually knows and can do. Education and training providers can improve current systems to tackle challenging issues like transfer value, as well as refine their existing programs in ways that strengthen their competitive position, start new ones that take into account the competition, and evaluate the efficiency of their programs. When employers start hiring more of an institution's graduates, there's good reason to expect more and more students will apply.

CONCLUSION

Achieving scale is a challenge for any new information platform like Credential Engine, but states like Indiana are showing how it can be done. Scale is additionally critical to provide stakeholders representative information on the value and effectiveness of credentials. The trick to achieving scale is to focus on attaining critical mass in selected industries, occupations, and regions, and to build from there. State agencies and education commissions can provide crucial leadership with funding, advocacy, and technical assistance. If they do, their state's students, job seekers, and employers will soon find it easier to make sense of the thousands of credentials that mark the path to their goals, and the state will see skill gaps decline, workforce quality improve, and economic growth accelerate.

Notes

1. This chapter brings up to date a story begun in this book's predecessor volume, *Transforming U.S. Workforce Development Policies for the 21st Century*. See its Chapter 7, "Creating and Communicating Critical Information about Workforce Credentials," by Stephen Crawford and Robert Sheets (2015). See also the *New America* blog (Sauer and Crawford 2017), and the many related publications under "Resources" at www.credentialengine.org.
2. See *Counting U.S. Secondary and Postsecondary Credentials, a Credential Engine Report*, April 2018. The 300,000+ figure excludes secondary school credentials and badges, of which Mozilla says there are now more than 1 million.
3. The Credential Transparency Initiative was a project of George Washington Uni-

versity's Institute of Public Policy, in collaboration with Workcred (a subsidiary of the American National Standards Institute that seeks to improve the credentialing system), the Center for Workforce Development at Southern Illinois University at Carbondale, and several distinguished consultants. Funded by the Lumina Foundation, the project's steering committee consisted of senior-level representatives of the American Association of Community Colleges, the American Council on Education, the Business Roundtable, the Committee for Economic Development, the National Association of Manufacturers' Manufacturing Institute, the University Professional and Continuing Education Association, and the U.S. Chamber of Commerce Foundation.

4. For more information about Credential Engine, see "Building an Expanded Public-Private Data Infrastructure for the Credentialing Marketplace" by Robert Sheets in Volume 3 of this book.

5. For a technical explanation of the CTDL and the registry, go to http://www .credreg.net/.

6. The grant came from Credential Engine, utilizing funds from the Lumina Foundation.

7. Like many states, Indiana had legislative mandates and executive orders to accomplish this goal. It also has been and remains a very active member of the 13-state Multi-State Collaborative on Military Credit, a partnership between states and the Midwestern Higher Education Compact.

8. SOLID has contracted with the U.S. Department of Defense to link education, training, and employment opportunities for service members and veterans.

References

Crawford, Stephen, and Robert Sheets. 2015. "Creating and Communicating Critical Information about Workforce Credentials." In *Transforming U.S. Workforce Development Policies for the 21st Century*, Carl Van Horn, Tammy Edwards, and Todd Greene, eds. Kalamazoo, MI: Upjohn Institute, pp. 169–194.

Credential Engine. 2018. *Counting U.S. Secondary and Postsecondary Credentials*. Washington, DC: Credential Engine.

Indiana Commission for Higher Education. 2017. *College Readiness Report Supplement: Dual Credit Taking and College Performance Trends*. Indianapolis: Indiana Commission for Higher Education.

Indiana National Guard. N.d. *Apprenticeship Program, New Student Guide*. Indianapolis: Indiana National Guard.

Penn LDI. 2015. "Nursing in a Transformed Health Care System: New Roles, New Rules." Research brief. Philadelphia: University of Pennsylvania, Leonard Davis Institute of Health Economics. http://www.shepcenter

.unc.edu/wp-content/uploads/2015/07/inqri-ldi-brief-nursing.original.pdf (accessed August 2, 2018).

Sauer, Ken, and Stephen Crawford. 2017. "Indiana Gives Credential Engine a Boost." *New America* (blog), December 13. https://www.newamerica .org/education-policy/edcentral/indiana-gives-credential-engine-boost/ (accessed June 6, 2018).

U.S. Department of Defense. 2017. *Medical Education and Training Campus 2017–2019 Program Catalog.* San Antonio, TX: U.S. Department of Defense.

21
Transforming Employer Signaling in the Talent Marketplace

Jason A. Tyszko

There are competing points of view on the cause and severity of the skills gap, but one point on which most agree is that there is a fundamental disconnect between how employers "signal" (or communicate) their hiring requirements and how students and job seekers communicate what they know and are able to do in relation to those requirements. Many have argued that at least part of the problem is the inability of employers to be consistent in communicating their hiring requirements and preferences in a rapidly changing economy and labor market (Tyszko, Sheets, and Reamer 2017). The result is a perpetual misalignment between education, workforce, and credentialing systems and employer hiring practices, which has stymied education and workforce reform efforts for decades.

Whether it is how employers organize their jobs; determine the skill, competency, and credentialing preferences for those jobs; or identify their most trusted and preferred talent development partners, employer signaling remains elusive and unclear. Unclear signaling contributes toward a persistent and growing skills gap that is negatively affecting employers, students, and workers alike. For businesses, talent-sourcing challenges are reducing their ability to compete and grow, as nearly half of all open positions are going unfilled, and for longer periods of time (Tyszko, Sheets, and Fuller 2014). In addition, nearly 40 percent of companies cannot take on new work because they have an insufficient workforce to meet the demand. For students, the results are no better, as nearly half of all new college graduates are either under-employed or unemployed (Tyszko, Sheets, and Fuller). Past attempts to engage employers and predict employer needs have come up short, especially in an economy that is becoming more dynamic, not less. This signaling challenge has created inefficient labor market transactions in nearly every industry sector, and it will only get worse as the economy becomes more dynamic over time. For example, according to a 2012 Burning Glass Technologies report, there were approximately 1,000 open positions for data scientists in the United States. Within four years, that number had grown to more than 14,000 (Restuccia, Taska, and Bittle 2018). Increased automation is also predicted to rapidly reshape the labor market, affecting blue-collar and white-collar jobs alike across nearly every industry. According to *McKinsey Quarterly*, existing technologies have the potential to automate 45 percent of activities and job tasks found in today's labor market (Chui, Manyika, and Miremadi 2015). Failure to address the challenge of rapidly shifting skill demands will result in the U.S. economy not having the workforce it needs to compete in a global economy. This is a growing economic imperative that requires a solution, one that draws support from both the public and private sectors.

We argue here that the central problem is that existing tools of action are incapable of providing the granular, short-term, dynamic signaling required to keep pace with changing employer needs. However, new organizational models and tools show exciting promise for improving how employers signal their hiring requirements in ways that improve labor market transactions and education and workforce system outcomes, both in terms of employment and in terms of improving the qualifications of job candidates.

This chapter explains these models and tools, and it argues that adoption of them would result in a more efficient talent development system and labor market. Through clearer employer signaling, we can achieve faster and more accurate communication between employers seeking workers with certain skills and job seekers that have those skills. The result will be more Americans transitioning quickly and successfully into the workforce, and more employers having access to a skilled workforce that can improve their ability to grow and compete.

This chapter begins by describing how most employers traditionally communicate the qualities they seek, and how education and workforce systems take these into account. Next, it identifies three new types of employer signaling needed in today's economy, and it examines promising examples of their use. Finally, the chapter makes a series of recommendations for how to improve on these promising practices, while also highlighting key challenges that will need to be overcome by both public- and private-sector stakeholders if improved employer signaling is to become a reality.

PAST ATTEMPTS AT PREDICTING EMPLOYER NEEDS, AND THEIR LIMITATIONS

There have been many attempts to ascertain employer needs. The reasons for this have been both to target education and workforce investments accordingly and to improve job matching and placement services. Many—but not all—of these efforts have been advanced through and supported by public sector initiatives, whether at the local, state, or federal level. The two most common approaches for understanding and validating employer hiring needs and job requirements have involved 1) local advisory boards and other intermediaries, such as workforce boards, and 2) governmental statistical surveys, and more recently the use of real-time labor market information aggregated from online job postings and job boards. Both approaches have met with limited success when it comes to understanding and communicating employer needs.

The Traditional Approach

For decades, the strategy of choice has been to convene employers as advisers and have them communicate their needs to key stakeholders, such as public policy leaders, education and workforce providers, or other interested human service and community stakeholders. They ascertain employer needs through a variety of formal and informal methods, such as going through the process of developing a curriculum or by providing reactions to information presented to them on labor markets to determine its accuracy.

Advisory boards take many shapes and forms. The most prominent advisory boards are local or regional and have input at the program level with colleges and universities as well as other career and technical education providers, such as vocational schools. The workforce system organized under the federal Workforce Innovation and Opportunity Act (WIOA) includes state and local workforce boards that require a majority of employer representatives to make decisions. These boards help set policy, review labor market information, maintain eligible workforce provider lists, and help prioritize education and workforce investments.[1]

While the advisory board strategy is the most common of practices when it comes to attempting to understand employer needs and hiring requirements, it is often quite unreliable. For example, the number of participating employers on non-WIOA advisory boards is often small and not representative of the full breadth and diversity of needs in any given industry sector. Many small to midsize enterprises cannot spare the time that advisory boards require, resulting in low levels of participation, which is doubly problematic because small to midsize enterprises make up the bulk of job creators in the United States.

In addition, it is often unclear what role employers play on advisory boards and whether they are customers of the programs to which they are contributing input, or merely good corporate citizens providing high-level input and validation of information presented to them by others. More often than not, it is the latter. The result is a persistent challenge to keep employers engaged.

Another mechanism for engaging employers is through federal and state grant making. Many education and workforce grants, such as the recent Trade Adjustment Assistance Community College Career Training (TAACCCT) grants, require eligible grant recipients (e.g., community colleges) to organize employer partners to have input on the program design and to assist with its execution.[2] For those workforce systems driven by training grants, it is government's role to manage eligible training provider lists based on criteria set by public workforce policy. When awarding grants and funding, it is government agencies that pick which providers will receive financial support to provide workforce services to a company or industry. These decisions are based on criteria that are most important to the government agency involved, not necessarily based on where employers have historically sourced talent from or where they plan to in the future. Nor are the performance and accountability systems tied to those programs and grants aligned with the performance expectations of employers.

The other widely used source of information about employer job and hiring needs is aggregate data about job vacancies, skill requirements, and occupational growth projections. Generated by government surveys, these data are increasingly supplemented by real-time labor market information provided by private firms. These labor-market information tools are designed to capture employers' job needs by level and qualification, but they have inherent limitations.

The federal government, through the Employment and Training Administration (ETA) at the U.S. Department of Labor (USDOL), in collaboration with the Bureau of Labor Statistics (BLS), produces short-term (2-year) and long-term (10-year) industry and occupation projections for 800-plus federally defined occupations in the Standard Occupational Classification (SOC) system. These resources, and related tools such as the Occupational Information Network (O*NET), the Occupational Requirements Survey (ORS), and many others, create a rich statistical system that attempts to forecast workforce demand by industry, occupation, and skill and credentialing level (Tyszko, Sheets, and Reamer 2017). The occupational projections are released in standardized reports that project current employment levels by occupation, job openings due to growth (new jobs added), and replacement openings due to incumbents retiring or leaving the occupation.

More recently, real-time labor market information vendors have been supplying advisory boards as well as talent development partners with information aggregated from online job postings and job boards. This information is often combined and "cross-walked" with government statistical survey data to gain better insight into employer hiring demand and requirements. Use of real-time labor market information has grown because of the increased availability of online job postings. These services scan thousands of jobs boards and websites to gather the most recent job-posting data available. The reports they provide aggregate data by similar jobs and provide number counts of job openings by occupation as well as an analysis of common skill and credentialing requirements. Whereas government statistical surveys are free to the public, real-time labor market information is a purchasable service provided by data vendors.

While real-time labor market information systems are more current than government labor market information reports, and may provide better details about employer job and hiring needs, they too have limitations. For instance, employers vary in their talent sourcing strategies and the extent to which they use online job ads and postings. Some employers use them only as a complement to other sourcing strategies, such as referral networks, job fairs, internal promotion, etc. Some employers also post positions based on anticipated job openings, not actual ones. These tools are frequently criticized for overrepresenting the number of jobs requiring a college degree and underrepresenting significant vacancies in more blue-collar occupations, such as in construction. When it comes to aggregating employer jobs ads and postings, there is also a challenge with combining different job titles and staffing patterns. The aggregation may result in an industry-wide average but does not reflect the specifics of an actual employer's hiring needs and requirements.[3]

While both government statistical surveys and real-time labor market information provide useful trend data for understanding employer demand in terms of types of jobs, numbers of position openings, and skill and credential requirements, they are not capable of providing all the information needed today by job seekers, students, and the organizations that educate, train, and advise them.

Moving from "Demand-Driven" to "Employer-Led" Education and Workforce Systems

While advisory boards and labor market information may be enough to understand general trends, they do not provide the level of information needed to align with employer demand in a constantly changing labor market and economy. What is needed is a shift from "demand-driven" to "employer led" labor market information. This can be accomplished through new and emerging practices and tools that, if widely adopted, would transform how employers organize and signal their requirements to the market, including job seekers, education and training providers, and workforce intermediary organizations, in ways that can generate a clearer value proposition and return on investment for businesses and workers.

TYPES OF EMPLOYER SIGNALING

It is clear that the strategies and labor market information resources we have today are incapable of providing the granular, short-term, dynamic signaling required to keep pace with changing employer needs.

However, new and emerging organizational models and tools of action suggest new ways of understanding and communicating employer needs and hiring requirements. In this section, we explore three distinct ways in which employers can improve how they do such signaling to boost labor market transactions.

Talent Pipeline Management

Since 2014, the U.S. Chamber of Commerce Foundation, through its Talent Pipeline Management (TPM) initiative, has collaborated with a number of employers and business associations to experiment with new approaches to signaling employer hiring needs and requirements.[4] The TPM initiative is a business-led solution for closing the skills gap by supporting employer-led education and workforce partnerships that are performance driven. A critical component of this movement is organizing employer signaling in ways that support employer-led talent development partnerships and deliver a return on investment for participating employers.

In TPM, employers serve not as advisers but as "end customers" of flexible and responsive performance-based education and workforce partnerships. This contrasts with more traditional public-private partnerships, which convene employer advisory boards and make use of government statistical survey data on jobs and job projections supported by real-time labor market information analytics. Many employers are hesitant to share details regarding their talent-sourcing strategies or hiring requirements for fear of jeopardizing their competitive advantage.

Instead, through TPM, employers are given the space, incentive, and tools to generate their own labor market information, related to their hiring needs and based on their requirements, in ways that protect their competitive advantage and generate a return on investment. The information they produce is then shared with their most trusted and preferred education and workforce partners, whom they rely on for talent. This process ensures that employers are only sharing the information they need to with preferred and trusted partners, which can best help them achieve a better return on investment.

In TPM, employers, through their collaboratives, produce their own labor market information tied directly to their workforce needs. This information sends better, clearer signals about their talent development needs and priorities. In TPM, there are three distinct ways in which employers can improve their signaling around jobs and hiring requirements, resulting in better overall labor market transactions. These signals include how employers: 1) organize their workforce and forecast demand, 2) communicate their hiring requirements, and 3) identify preferred providers of talent.

Organizing Jobs and Forecasting Demand

Employer collaboratives play a critical role for employers and the larger public-private partnerships that they engage in. Through collaboratives, employers go through a systematic process for determining their most critical jobs and competency, credentialing, and other hiring requirements specific to the companies that make up the collaborative.

One of the signals employer collaboratives can send is in identifying the critical jobs that make up their workforce and where there is a shared talent need, shortage, or "pain point." A shared pain point is one where employers cannot successfully locate, hire, and retain sufficient numbers of people to carry out the most critical work inside their companies. This can be measured in terms of the time it takes to fill positions, the cost associated with screening unqualified candidates, the qualifications of applicants, the cost of onboarding and training, and the rate of retention.

Employer collaboratives make use of government statistical surveys and real-time labor market information to help them ascertain where those pain points might be and what the level of need is, but this is no substitute for employers generating their own labor market information tied directly to their company's need. In fact, the most important, trustworthy, and powerful information comes from employers, because it is tied directly to the way they organize and manage work.

Vermilion Advantage, an economic development organization located in Danville, Illinois, is an example of what employer collaboratives look like and how they organize workforce priorities. Vermilion Advantage staffs four sector-based employer collaboratives in: 1) manufacturing, 2) health care, 3) logistics, and 4) technology and services (Tyszko and Sheets 2015). Vermilion Advantage's employer members can opt into one or more collaboratives to address their shared workforce needs. These collaboratives go through a process by which they identify their most critical workforce positions and forecast demand for those positions across each company in the collaborative.

Elevate Virginia, Virginia's state workforce development board, recently led an effort to organize an information technology employer collaborative in northern Virginia. The companies went through a systematic review of government labor market projections and real-time labor market information that were aggregated from job posting data in the region. The business members were able to examine the data and identify specific instances where occupation titles were combined or disaggregated in ways that were inconsistent with how companies organized their workforce. As a result, the participating companies were able to take a half dozen or more job titles and get them down to two core business functions that aligned with their hiring needs. They were then able to project more accurate forecasting data for those two employer-defined business functions based on an agreed-upon set of assumptions, such as whether anticipated government contracts would be included (Tyszko and Sheets 2015).

Communicating Hiring Requirements

When employers organize themselves and use a systematic process to contribute company-specific data related to their jobs, they send better, clearer signals about their workforce priorities, including how they organize jobs, what the level of demand is for those jobs, and the skill sets involved.

In TPM, employer collaboratives organize their own hiring requirements and preferences. This includes employability skills (i.e., soft skills), such as "communication" and "teamwork," as well as technical skills and competencies. It also includes required or preferred credentials and academic level.[5] The goal is not to create common hiring requirements or a skill taxonomy that applies universally to each of the employer members or that aims for the lowest common denominator. Rather, it is to create a shared language for communicating competency and credentialing requirements for the jobs they defined based on their workforce needs. Through this shared language, employer collaborative members can signal competency-based hiring requirements to preferred partners and better delineate similarities and differences in those requirements.

This information is particularly valuable for states, which are now under pressure to develop industry-recognized credential lists that education and workforce systems can integrate into their career pathway programs. The challenge is that there is no consistent and scalable way to produce these lists outside the advisory boards mentioned earlier. What is needed is more dynamic signaling from employers to truly understand which credentials are required or preferred at any given time.

Returning to our Elevate Virginia example, the participating information technology companies were able to respond to a survey of hiring requirements that they cocreated as an employer collaborative. Each company was able to signal how important each skill or competency was and at what level (i.e., entry level, midlevel, or senior level). They were also able to identify required or preferred academic levels as well as which industry credentials were preferred. The collaborative was able to reconvene postsurvey and review where there was consensus on shared hiring requirements, and where there was variance that needed to be discussed, harmonized, or communicated more clearly so that talent development partners were aware of this need for customization.

TPM has demonstrated that, when given the opportunity and tools, employers will provide more comprehensive and actionable information related to their hiring needs and requirements, and they will use a shared language and terminology to signal those requirements. However, this must be a collaborative and bottom-up process based on shared information among employers. It requires open and shared job classification systems and competency frameworks that are available to employers and their talent-sourcing partners. It cannot be accomplished by imposing a predefined occupational classification system using a predetermined language for communicating hiring requirements.

Communicating need is not just an employer engagement challenge; it's also a technological one. It has been argued that the human resource (HR) technologies and services employers rely on for processing job applicants inadvertently pass over otherwise qualified applicants (Cappelli 2015). Much of this can be attributed to the limitations of HR technologies that rely on word searches of résumés and insufficient specifications and descriptions in job profiles.

To address this need, the U.S. Chamber of Commerce Foundation is creating a job registry service for employers and their HR information systems and related HR vendors. This solution can directly address the HR tools, systems, and processes that signal demand for skills and credentials and that are used to review the qualifications of job applicants. This job registry service will focus on the development, benchmarking, and alignment of competency and credentialing requirements using HR open-data standards that are supported by standards organizations such as Schema.org and the HR Open Standards Consortium. The services will also make use of advanced web-based technologies, such as "linked data," which enable companies to dynamically signal a change in hiring requirements.

In practice, this means that HR professionals will be able to select their preferred language for describing competency and credentialing requirements attached to jobs that fit their staffing model. Through a shared technology solution, employers would also be able to more easily signal similarities and differences in competency and credentialing requirements with other employers, even when looking at the same occupation. It would also allow for harmonization of job requirements, whereby employers can select competency descriptions and requirements used by other employers in order to arrive at a common language for describing skill needs for a job or industry. Employers would also be able to more quickly signal their hiring requirements and any changes that occur to those requirements (Tyszko, Sheets, and Reamer 2017).

The result is better, faster, clearer signaling from employers to education and workforce stakeholders. The structured data employers produce for their job profiles can be linked to credentialing data systems and learner record systems in ways that allow for employers to better find and connect with talent suppliers and the most highly qualified talent. It will also provide more accurate, up-to-date labor market information that can be used to improve government statistical systems without increasing the reporting burden and regulatory risk to employers.

Identifying Preferred Providers of Talent

In addition to transforming how to communicate workforce priorities and demand, employer collaboratives can signal where they source their talent from. This information is critical for career guidance systems tasked with informing students and learners about which education or workforce programs deliver the best results.

Employer collaboratives can start by back mapping where they have historically sourced their best talent, including employees they wanted—and were able—to retain. This process identifies which education, training, and credentialing providers were best able to meet the employer's hiring requirements. When employers back map together, they produce better career pathway data and insights.

Collaborative members can go a step further and engage in talent flow analysis to determine what their capture rate is of talent from a particular provider or program and how much talent is being lost to other employers or regions. This analysis allows employers to identify whether existing talent-provider networks are capable of meeting the level of demand forecast by collaborative members or whether new providers need to be accessed in order to meet projected demand.[6] Employers can also signal where they plan to source talent from in the future.[7]

Gateway Community and Technical College provides an example of how a talent provider can improve the quality of its programs and achieve better job placement outcomes for students when employers provide better signals. Gateway was able to take the hiring needs and requirements provided by a newly formed manufacturing collaborative and revamp an underutilized machining program. It rebooted the program as an enhanced operator program, made it competency based, streamlined the learning outcomes, reduced the time it takes to complete, and reduced the cost of delivering the program by half. Since the program was revamped, Gateway has been able to increase recruitment and improve job placement as well as improve the qualifications of those hires (Praiswater 2017).

RECOMMENDATIONS, OPPORTUNITIES, AND CHALLENGES

Improving employer signaling in the ways discussed above will require support and buy-in from both public and private sector partners. There are a number of ways that education and workforce systems can use existing flexibility found in current legislation to both encourage and leverage improved employer signaling. However, employers too must adopt a new role in "pushing" their signals to trusted and preferred partners and not waiting on advisory boards, surveys, and job-posting data analytics to "pull" these signals. Included here are three immediate opportunities.

Recommendations

1) **Activate new employer collaboratives using WIOA resources.** Under WIOA, sector-based partnerships can be rebooted and transformed to become more employer led. State and local workforce boards can use their resources and ability to recognize partnerships in order to seed new employer-led collaboratives that are staffed by business and economic development associations. These collaboratives can produce more granular and actionable labor market information, which can be shared with education and workforce providers to improve curriculum and training alignment. They can also be used to provide feedback on employer results and inform the next generation of employer satisfaction measures based on employer return on investment.

2) **Continue to develop implementation tools, technologies, and supports that help employers organize and send better signals.** This includes expanding the TPM movement and its newly formed TPM Academy to provide training at scale to business and economic development associations. This also includes continued experimentation with structuring employer hiring-requirements data through the proposed job registry service to provide better, clearer, faster signals on changing employer hiring requirements.

3) **Further experimentation is needed with employer-led quality assurance.** Such a process can provide an alternative to higher-education accreditation and workforce-eligible provider lists (Tyszko 2017; Tyszko and Sheets 2016). Such a system can better signal which programs and institutions are best able to meet employer hiring needs. It can also be extended to cover a wider variety of earn-and-learn models, which combine employment with education and training, resulting in documented learning outcomes and credentials. Such models are not presently covered under any quality assurance system.

These recommendations will be successful only if there is broad buy-in and support, both by business and by educational and workforce training partners. This includes employers—particularly small to mid-size companies—engaging in new collaboratives and working together through preferred intermediaries to send better labor market signals. It also requires vendors of HR information systems and application tracking systems to adopt new technologies and standards as part of their existing products and services. Last, it requires workforce and training providers to make use of new employer leadership and signaling as part of their programs, credentials, and career services.

CONCLUSION

Economists and business leaders may debate the severity and causes of the skills gap, but most agree that one major factor driving it is the disconnect between how employers communicate or "signal" their hiring requirements and how students and job seekers communicate their knowledge, skills, and abilities in relation to those requirements. A serious disconnect involves how employers communicate the competency and credentialing requirements tied to their most critical jobs, on which their competitiveness depends. Addressing this problem will only grow in importance as we continue to live in a dynamic, innovation-based economy with constantly changing hiring and skill requirements.

Employer signaling has remained a persistent challenge in aligning education and workforce systems to the needs of the economy. The existing strategies for convening employers and anticipating their workforce requirements are incapable of providing the granular, short-term, dynamic signaling required to keep pace with a rapidly changing economy. However, by leveraging new organizational models and tools, employers can change and improve how they signal their hiring requirements and preferred talent-development partners in ways that bolster outcomes and return on investment for employers, students, and job seekers alike.

Notes

1. For information on the WIOA legislation and how it is implemented at the state and local levels, see USDOL (2018b).
2. For background information on TAACCCT grants, see USDOL (2018a).
3. See Strategy 2 of the TPM Academy curriculum (Tyszko and Sheets 2017).
4. For information on the TPM movement, see U.S. Chamber of Commerce Foundation (2018).
5. See Strategy 3 of the TPM Academy curriculum (Tyszko and Sheets 2017).
6. See Strategy 4 of the TPM Academy curriculum (Tyszko and Sheets 2017).
7. See Strategy 5 of the TPM Academy curriculum (Tyszko and Sheets 2017).

References

Cappelli, Peter. 2015. "Why We Love to Hate HR . . . and What HR Can Do about It." *Harvard Business Review* 93(July–August): 54–61. https://hbr.org/2015/07/why-we-love-to-hate-hr-and-what-hr-can-do-about-it (accessed April 24, 2018).

Chui, Michael, James Manyika, and Mehdi Miremadi. 2015. "Four Fundamentals of Workplace Automation." *McKinsey Quarterly,* November: 50–57. http://www.mckinsey.com/business-functions/digital-mckinsey/our-insights/four-fundamentals-of-workplace-automation (accessed April 24, 2018).

Praiswater, Angela. 2017. *Education Takes a Lesson from Industry*. Washington, DC: U.S. Chamber of Commerce Foundation. https://www.uschamberfoundation.org/blog/post/education-takes-lesson-industry (accessed April 24, 2018).

Restuccia, Dan, Bledi Taska, and Scott Bittle. 2018. *Different Skills, Different Gaps: Measuring and Closing the Skills Gap*. Boston: Burning Glass Technologies; Washington, DC: U.S. Chamber of Commerce Foundation, Center for Education and Workforce. https://www.uschamberfoundation.org/sites/default/files/Skills_Gap_Different_Skills_Different_Gaps_FINAL.pdf (accessed April 24, 2018).

Tyszko, Jason A. 2017. "Employer-Led Quality Assurance." *Change: The Magazine of Higher Learning* 49(1): 26–33.

Tyszko, Jason A., and Robert G. Sheets. 2015. *Building the Talent Pipeline: An Implementation Guide*. Washington, DC: U.S. Chamber of Commerce Foundation, Center for Education and Workforce. https://www.nist.gov/sites/default/files/building_the_talent_pipeline_an_implementation_guide.pdf (accessed April 24, 2018).

————. 2016. *Changing the Debate on Quality Assurance in Higher Education: A Case for Employer Leadership and a Roadmap for Change.* Washington, DC: U.S. Chamber of Commerce Foundation, Center for Education and Workforce. https://www.uschamberfoundation.org/sites/default/files/Changing_the_Debate_Report.pdf (accessed April 24, 2018).

————. 2017. *TPM Curriculum.* Washington, DC: U.S. Chamber of Commerce Foundation. https://www.uschamberfoundation.org/reports/tpm-curriculum (accessed April 24, 2018).

Tyszko, Jason A., Robert G. Sheets, and Joseph B. Fuller. 2014. *Managing the Talent Pipeline: A New Approach to Closing the Skills Gap.* Washington, DC: U.S. Chamber of Commerce Foundation, Center for Education and Workforce. https://www.uschamberfoundation.org/sites/default/files/Managing%20the%20Talent%20Pipeline.pdf (accessed April 24, 2018).

Tyszko, Jason A., Robert G. Sheets, and Andrew Reamer. 2017. *Clearer Signals: Building an Employer-Led Job Registry for Talent Pipeline Management.* Washington, DC: U.S. Chamber of Commerce Foundation.

U.S. Chamber of Commerce Foundation. 2018. *U.S. Chamber of Commerce Foundation Talent Pipeline Management Initiative.* Washington, DC: U.S. Chamber of Commerce Foundation. https://www.uschamberfoundation.org/talent-pipeline-management (accessed April 24, 2018).

U.S. Department of Labor (USDOL). 2018a. *Trade Adjustment Assistance Community College and Career Training Grant Program (TAACCCT): Program Summary.* Washington, DC: U.S. Department of Labor, Employment and Training Administration. https://doleta.gov/taaccct/ (accessed April 24, 2018).

————. 2018b. *The Workforce Innovation and Opportunity Act.* Washington, DC: U.S. Department of Labor, Employment and Training Administration. https://www.doleta.gov/wioa/ (accessed April 24, 2018).

22
Building an Expanded Public-Private Data Infrastructure for the Credentialing Marketplace

Robert Sheets

Federal and state governments historically have played a major role in providing free and widely available information on college degrees and certificates, certifications, licenses, and other types of credentials to improve the functioning of labor markets in the United States. In more recent years, the government also has provided consumer information to students and workers so they can make more informed decisions about investments in credentials. However, the credentialing marketplace is now experiencing significant changes in the demand side (credentials employers seek) and the supply side (credentials available through educational institutions and other credentialing organizations). These changes are creating a growing need for better consumer information and decision-making tools—a need that is now pushing government labor market information (LMI) systems to their limits. At the same time, recent advances in information technology and the rise of new private-sector LMI providers have raised questions about the role of public- and private-sector players in providing labor market information in the United States.

As a result, we are now at a critical crossroads in deciding the future role of government in providing labor market information for the credentialing marketplace. Should government expand its data systems and guidance tools to address new information needs in the changing credentialing marketplace and move into the roles now played by private-sector providers? Or, should government policy move in a different direction and explore how to build an expanded public-private data infrastructure that can be used by both government and private-sector providers?

This chapter explores the second option and its implications for government policy. It delves into the rationale for an expanded public-private data infrastructure that is designed to address changes in the credentialing marketplace and to leverage recent advances in information technology and related private-sector innovations. This paper proposes a new role for government in developing a public-private data infrastructure that can support an "open applications marketplace" that serves employers, students, and workers, as well as education, training, and credentialing service providers.

CHANGING CREDENTIALING MARKETPLACE

Major demand-side and supply-side changes in national, state, and regional credentialing markets, along with new federal and state government policies, are exposing the limitations of the government data infrastructure that currently is used by government LMI systems.

Rapid technological and economic changes in the global innovation-based economy are transforming employer business models, work processes, and related job structures (U.S. Chamber of Commerce Foundation 2017b). The demand for postsecondary education and training is increasing (Carnevale, Smith, and Strohl 2013). At the same time, rapid and continuous skill-set disruptions are reducing the shelf life of worker skill sets (World Economic Forum 2016). These changes will likely drive greater need for continuous learning and credentialing, including more advanced degrees, certificates, certifications, and non-traditional microcredentials that address more specific skill sets.

As described by Cappelli (1999), these economic changes are exposing all major functions of businesses and employees at all levels to market pressures. Employers are increasingly engaging more open talent networks for getting work done. Many employers are outsourcing major business functions and experimenting with new types of employment relationships, including the use of independent contractors—what some have termed the "gig economy." Many of these new employment relationships are developing at the margins or even outside current government regulatory policies and employment reporting systems, making it more difficult to capture information about employment trends. These changing relationships are pushing workers to take more responsibility for making their own career-related investment decisions throughout their working lives.

Demand-side changes will likely raise the stakes for employers, students, and workers in investing in skills and credentials. On the one hand, there will be growing investment opportunities carrying the promise of higher returns for the right investment decisions. On the other, there will be significant downside risks because investors will be placing multiple uncertain bets throughout their working lives, with shorter windows for achieving returns.

On the supply side, education, training, and credentialing organizations such as universities, colleges, and certification bodies are offering more options for students and workers engaged in lifelong learning and credentialing. This large and diverse credentialing marketplace is reflected in the recent inventory of credentials in the United States by Credential Engine (2018).[1] Many of these credentialing options, such as noncredit certificates and industry and professional certifications, are designed to fill gaps between rapidly changing employer hiring needs and the skills of already credentialed workers. In addition, many industry and professional organizations are encouraging higher-level and more specialized licensing requirements, such as health-care professional specializations. Some of these options go well beyond traditional government policy and regulatory boundaries and are not captured in government data systems. Finally, federal and state governments are launching new career and technical education and workforce initiatives that promote industry certifications, apprenticeship credentials, and other types of "industry recognized" credentials. These government initiatives also seek to connect all types of credentials to build better career and education pathways.

These supply-side changes and government initiatives provide growing opportunities to invest in skills and credentialing, but they also contribute to the growing uncertainty and downside risk for students and workers as they decide which education and credentialing options to pursue. Employers may also have difficulty differentiating among credentials as they make investment and hiring decisions.

The United States can be considered a national common market made up of local economic regions (e.g., metropolitan regional economies) that compete in different ways in the global economy (Barnes and Ledebur 1997). These demand-side and supply-side changes, as well as government initiatives, therefore play out differently throughout state and regional labor markets. Major metropolitan areas are competing with other major metro areas for recognition as global centers. Metro and rural regions are transitioning from manufacturing centers to play other roles in the global economy. Similar transformations are happening in rural regions. In recent years, major differences in labor market dynamics have emerged across these metropolitan regional economies (Moretti 2012). As a result, the demand for and return on credentials and skills vary widely across these regional economies. This further complicates the investment decisions of employers, students, and workers, who now must make decisions based on regional labor markets. It also puts more pressures on universities, colleges, and other education, training, and credentialing providers to address skills and credentialing gaps within and across these regional labor markets.

These demand-side and supply-side changes, along with new government initiatives, will create the need for real-time information at a more granular and regional level. These changing information needs likely will push the limits of the traditional public data infrastructure used by government labor market information systems. This is especially true for government systems providing consumer information to students and workers about the potential rewards and risks of pursuing the full range of credentials. To better understand these limitations, the following sections explore the scope and foundations of traditional government systems, as well as innovations among private-sector data providers, including those with implications for building a new public-private data infrastructure in the United States.

OVERVIEW OF GOVERNMENT LABOR MARKET INFORMATION SYSTEMS

Government LMI systems have evolved over the years to address changes in government policy and labor markets. Federal statistical systems have historically focused on providing core economic indicators (e.g., unemployment rates) for macroeconomic policymakers and market analysts (Reamer 2015). Federal and state LMI systems traditionally have been designed to support higher education and workforce planning, program approval, and funding allocations. Through these traditional functions, government systems capture and project information on industries and occupations. These systems also generate high-level occupational demand and supply reports based on occupational projections, as well as federal and state data on graduates of government-funded and regulated postsecondary degree and certificate programs. In addition, they capture high-level summary information on occupational tasks, skills, and requirements for education and credentialing (e.g., O*NET). In recent years, the government has used these systems to provide career and education guidance and consumer information to students and workers to enable them to make better investment decisions in their education and training.

On the demand side, government LMI systems draw on employer data from administrative data systems (e.g., federal and state payroll reporting systems). These data are supplemented with employer surveys and other primary data collection strategies that capture occupational staffing patterns, compensation, and occupational profiles. On the supply side, LMI systems capture data from federal and state postsecondary education reporting systems that mainly cover government-funded and -regulated education and credentialing organizations such as public universities and colleges and federal workforce system providers. For example, new federal and state government individual-level longitudinal data systems provide credential attainment rates and employment rates and earnings of those completing credentials from government-funded and -regulated programs. These longitudinal data systems use administrative data from various federal and state sources, and they draw on employment and earnings data from federal and state employer payroll reporting systems (e.g., unemployment insurance wage records). Government LMI systems also have special data collection efforts to fill information gaps, such as recent efforts to capture data on industry and professional certifications.

PRIVATE SECTOR INNOVATIONS AND LIMITATIONS OF GOVERNMENT SYSTEMS

Leading innovations among private-sector data providers go beyond what government systems have done to address changes in credentialing markets. On the demand side, real-time LMI providers capture and compile online job-posting data from thousands of job boards and websites daily. They use this "real-time LMI" to analyze changing employer hiring requirements, including expected skills and credential requirements. Many of these providers combine government, real-time LMI, and other data sources to provide more comprehensive LMI services. These providers include Burning Glass, Emsi, Geographic Solutions, and Monster.

The U.S. Chamber of Commerce Foundation is establishing a job registry service to build on its Talent Pipeline Management (TPM) initiative and improve employer signaling of changing skill and credentialing requirements (U.S. Chamber of Commerce Foundation 2017a). This job registry service will assist employers and their human resources (HR) technology partners in developing more accurate and comparable job descriptions with competency and credentialing requirements, and to distribute this data through multiple talent-sourcing channels. The registry service can be used by real-time LMI providers and by government LMI systems. It will build on the work of leading global standardization organizations that have developed schemas and standards for online job postings and job data in HR vendor systems (e.g., recruiting and applicant-tracking systems). These include job-related schemas from Schema.org and related standards from the HR Open Standards Consortium.[2] The job registry also will build on leading HR technology advances that promote vendor system interoperability.

On the supply side, Credential Engine is a new nonprofit with a mission to improve transparency in the credentialing marketplace. The organization is pioneering a new approach to gather comparable data on a range of credentials beyond the reach of existing government data systems, such as industry and professional certifications and noncredit certificates.[3] Credential Engine also is developing schemas and standards for defining the major descriptors for credentials and credentialing organizations referred to as the Credential Transparency Description Language (CTDL). These descriptors can be applied to degrees, certificates, certifications, licenses, apprenticeship credentials, badges, microcredentials, and any future credential type offered by public or private credentialing organizations. Credential Engine is developing definitions and vocabularies for these credential descriptors that build on well-established schemas from Schema.org for use by major search engines. Credential Engine descriptors also include important information on credentials not normally found in government data systems, such as competencies, assessments, and quality assurance. In addition, Credential Engine provides guidelines to credentialing organizations on how to publish comparable information about their credentials on the web and on a credential registry—a repository for credential information designed to support an open applications marketplace.

There are also supply-side innovations that allow students and workers to manage, store, publish, and distribute information about their competencies, credentials, and work experience. Private companies such as LinkedIn provide social media platforms for publishing professional profiles and making employer and professional connections. Other companies offer credentialing platforms that can manage and transmit more comprehensive student records, as well as more detailed portfolios and expanded résumés. Some companies also are exploring the use of distributed ledger (e.g., blockchain) technologies to provide secure and verifiable records of transactions. Still others, such as Glassdoor and PayScale, help students and workers better understand employer career opportunities and navigate the job market. These innovations demonstrate how student and worker platforms and data vaults can provide individuals with new services, allowing them to make better investment decisions in skills and credentialing.

As discussed earlier, national and state individual-level longitudinal data systems provide information on the labor market value of credentials, at least for those financed and regulated by government (e.g., public university and college degrees and certificates). The Manufacturing Institute, the National Student Clearinghouse, and the U.S. Census Bureau are exploring how to match a more comprehensive set of student and worker education and credentialing records with employment and earnings information. This would provide data on the labor market outcomes of all types of credentials, including industry and professional certifications and noncredit education certificates. The National

Student Clearinghouse collects and manages individual-level data on the vast majority of credential holders with postsecondary degrees from universities and colleges. The U.S. Census Bureau is exploring how to provide linkages to comprehensive employment and earnings data that go well beyond the unemployment insurance (UI) wage record data used in state longitudinal data systems. The Manufacturing Institute will work with leading industry and professional certification organizations to explore how to provide individual-level data on industry and professional certification holders that can be linked to education, employment, and earnings data.

Federal and state government LMI systems have major limitations in guiding the investment decisions of students and workers in a more complex and dynamic public-private credentialing marketplace. First, these systems were designed to support macroeconomic policy, as well as to be used for long-term government planning, program management, and funding allocation to a government-financed and -regulated credentialing marketplace. On the demand side, public LMI systems were never designed to capture short-term dynamic changes and variations in employer skill and credentialing requirements, especially those outside government regulatory boundaries. They also cannot capture the millions of investment transactions of students and workers as they respond to changing employer requirements and seek new pathways to career advancement and earnings gains. Finally, government LMI systems do not have the capacity to collect complete employment and earnings data across the full spectrum of employment relationships in the new economy, including independent contracting.

BUILDING AN EXPANDED PUBLIC-PRIVATE DATA INFRASTRUCTURE FOR LABOR MARKET INFORMATION

Federal and state governments could redesign and expand data systems and guidance tools to address these major changes and move into the roles now played by private-sector providers. As an alternative, they could help build an expanded public-private data infrastructure that could support a more open "applications marketplace" where both government and private-sector LMI providers could access this data infrastructure while protecting privacy and proprietary information. In exploring this public-private open applications marketplace approach, two major questions must be addressed. First, what are the major stakeholder needs and use cases that are critical in developing applications? Second, what are the most promising technical foundations for this expanded public-private data infrastructure that should be explored further?[4]

Major Stakeholder Needs and Use Cases for Improving Credentialing Markets

Government labor market information systems have been developed over decades to support macroeconomic policy, long-term higher education and workforce planning, and federal and state regulatory policies, as well as program administration and evaluation. They also have provided high-level and aggregated occupational information as well as consumer information for government-financed and -regulated credentials. Although government systems will still be needed to address these major functions, an expanded public-private data infrastructure for labor market information should address at least four major stakeholder needs and use cases.

Employer talent sourcing in open talent networks. From the demand side, employers should have better data to improve their end-to-end talent sourcing process within more open talent networks. This end-to-end employer talent sourcing process includes performance analytics of recent hires, employer signaling, talent outreach and engagement, applicant screening, on-boarding, development, and retention. This process will require better information on skills and credentials.

Pursuing career, education, and credentialing opportunities. From the supply side, students and workers should have better data to search for and pursue the full range of career, education, and credentialing opportunities. This includes developing online professional profiles, résumés, and portfolios; searching for career, education, and credentialing opportunities; applying for these opportunities; and managing ongoing professional development.

Developing new education and credentialing options. Also from the supply side, universities, colleges, and other talent service providers should have the data needed to improve service delivery to employers, students, and workers. This includes how to fill gaps in competencies and credentials between employer needs and student and worker profiles in a rapidly changing labor market.

Guiding, financing, and managing risks in education and credentialing investment. Students, workers, and public- and private-sector career advisors should have better information to guide prudent investment decisions in a constantly changing labor market. This includes information on the costs, risks, and expected returns from continuous investments in education and credentials over an entire career. A public-private data infrastructure and open applications marketplace also may enable greater investment and risk taking among government and private-sector investors and risk managers, since they could access better information for market-oriented government tools such as government student grants and loans and wage insurance, as well as similar private-sector investment tools and services such as income-sharing agreements (U.S. Chamber of Commerce Foundation 2017b).

Common to these four stakeholder use cases is the need for more comprehensive, real-time, and granular information to guide and manage the risks of short-term skills and credential investment decisions of employers, students, and workers in constantly changing national, state, and regional labor markets.

Promising Technical Foundations for This Expanded Data Infrastructure

Next, what are the implications of these stakeholder needs and use cases for developing an expanded public-private data infrastructure? Private-sector and government innovations provide lessons learned that can be applied to address these stakeholder use cases, including the need for public-private data standards and the potential power of Web 3.0 technologies as addressed in the U.S. Chamber of Commerce Foundation's T3 Innovation Network initiative (U.S. Chamber of Commerce Foundation 2018).

Public-private data standards. Private-sector innovations demonstrate the need to establish public-private data standards for describing the major features of jobs, credentials, credentialing organizations, and credential holders. These standards will leverage the power of the Web to promote transparency and promote the integration and interoperability of data systems as they manage and capture labor market transactions. Standards are critical in capturing the millions of transactions in the labor market necessary to generate ongoing labor market information.

Federal and state government reporting systems and regulatory policies have established definitions and vocabularies for credentials and credentialing organizations used in government policies and programs, but have not extended these efforts to the broader public-private credentialing marketplace. For example, federal and state agencies have made progress in aligning data standards across multiple government reporting systems through the Common Education Data Standards (CEDS). However, these efforts now should be expanded to develop public-private data standards through a comprehensive list of descriptors of jobs, credentials, credentialing organizations, and credential holders.

Establishing and managing public-private standards requires collaboration between multiple public and private technical standards organizations, as well as the input of employers, students, and workers; credentialing organizations; government; and private investors. One of the most difficult challenges is standardizing how competencies are communicated in employer job profiles, education and training program and credential descriptions, and credential holder profiles.

Future efforts to develop public-private data standards should build on current efforts by leading technical standards organizations, particularly the Credential Data Ecosystem Mapping Team initiative, which includes all the major standards organizations in the credentialing marketplace, including CEDS, Credential Engine, the HR Open Standards Consortium, the IMS Global Learning Consortium, and Postsecondary Electronic Standards Council (PESC).[5]

Web 3.0 technology utilization. Private-sector innovations as well as recent innovations in government also show the potential power of Web 3.0 technologies to support an expanded public-private data infrastructure. These Web 3.0 technologies include Semantic Web standards (e.g., Linked Data), distributed ledger technologies (e.g., blockchain), artificial intelligence, machine learning, and large-scale data analytics.[6]

Employers, education and training providers, students, and workers can increasingly use World Wide Web Consortium's (W3C) Semantic Web standards and related technologies to improve web search and discovery. On the demand side, search engines (e.g., Google), applicant tracking system vendors, and job-board vendors are leveraging Schema.org and other standards (e.g., the HR Open Standards Consortium) to improve the use of structured data in online job postings. The aforementioned U.S. Chamber of Commerce Foundation's job registry will build on these standards and applications to improve how employers communicate competency and credentialing requirements. On the supply side, Credential Engine is pioneering the use of Semantic Web standards in the development and use of its Credential Transparency Description Language (CTDL). Similar applications could improve how students and workers publish and use their professional profiles on the open web. Federal government agencies also are exploring how to use these standards to publish government statistics and related information. These federal government initiatives have major implications for how to use these standards to integrate government data into a larger public-private data infrastructure.

One of the most difficult challenges in building a new public-private data infrastructure for labor market information is how to provide access to employer, student, and worker transaction data while maintaining privacy and protecting proprietary information. The government collects records from employers on employment and wages, as well as individual-level data on government-financed and -regulated education, training, and credentials. However, access to government data is limited to specific purposes, primarily clustered around research and government program evaluation. Private-sector data providers also have millions of individual-level records, including résumé data, but often consider such records proprietary. Currently, neither government agencies nor private providers allow access to this data as part of an open applications marketplace.

Recent innovations in information technology now allow integration and use of these granular, individual-level data in open applications while managing the risks to the privacy and data security of employers, students, and workers. One promising approach is to utilize distributed ledger technologies (e.g., blockchain) in conjunction with smart contracts. Both the public and private sectors currently are exploring these technologies[7] for a variety of applications that require trust and privacy protection. Another opportunity for exploration is how semantic web and distributed ledger technologies can support artificial intelligence and machine learning applications as well as big data analytics applications.

CONCLUSIONS AND POLICY IMPLICATIONS

Government has historically provided labor market information, including information on credentials to improve the functioning of labor markets in the United States. Over the last few decades, government LMI systems have been focused on supporting macroeconomic policy and long-term government planning, program management, and funding allocation for a government-financed and -regulated credentialing marketplace. Recent changes in the credentialing marketplace are raising the stakes on investment in credentials by employers, students, workers, and government in a dynamic public-private credentialing marketplace. This has created the need for more comprehensive, granular, and real-time labor market information down to the regional labor market level. At the same time, recent advances in information technology and the rise of new private-sector LMI providers have generated new questions about the technical foundations of government data systems and about the role of public and private sectors in providing labor market information.

The time is right to explore an expanded public-private data infrastructure and an open applications marketplace that do two things: 1) provide labor market information designed to address changes in credentialing markets and 2) leverage recent advances in information technology and related private-sector innovations. This new public-private data infrastructure should incorporate public-private data standards and Web 3.0 technologies.

This proposed approach has a number of implications for government policy. First, although government should have the primary role in establishing core economic indicators for macroeconomic policy, the public sector should collaborate more with the private sector to develop data standards. Government policies should support current ongoing efforts to create these standards at a national and even international level. Second, current federal and state "open government" initiatives in the United States should focus more attention on publishing open-licensed data to the web based on Semantic Web standards and encouraging other private-sector partners to do the same. Federal and state governments also should work with private-sector partners to create a more comprehensive individual-level data infrastructure that can support an open applications marketplace while ensuring data security and privacy. Finally, government policy should ensure that the future open applications marketplace addresses the needs of all students and workers, including low-income and low-skilled workers seeking career advancement opportunities in the credentialing marketplace.

Notes

1. For more information about Credential Engine, see "Fixing the Credentialing Chaos: A National Tool and State Application" by Ken Sauer and Stephen Crawford in Volume 3 of this book.
2. These schemas and standards are referenced in U.S. Chamber of Commerce Foundation (2017a).
3. For more information, visit https://www.credentialengine.org/.
4. The following section is based on a review of public-private data standards initiatives and Web 3.0 technology applications in talent markets referenced in U.S. Chamber of Commerce Foundation (2018), from a joint project, the T3 Innovation Network, funded by the Lumina Foundation.
5. This initiative is referenced along with the full list of standardization organizations in U.S. Chamber of Commerce Foundation (2018).
6. This is based on a review of Web 3.0 technology applications in talent markets in the U.S. Chamber of Commerce Foundation (2018).
7. For public-sector applications, see Cheng et al. (2017).

References

Barnes, William R., and Larry C. Ledebur. 1997. *The New Regional Econo-mies: The U.S. Common Market and the Global Economy.* Thousand Oaks, CA: Sage.

Cappelli, Peter. 1999. *The New Deal at Work: Managing the Market-Driven Workforce.* Boston: Harvard Business School Press.

Carnevale, Anthony P., Nicole Smith, and Jeff Strohl. 2013. *Recovery: Job Growth and Education Requirements through 2020.* Washington, DC: Georgetown Public Policy Institute, Center on Education and the Work-force.

Cheng, Steve, Matthias Daub, Axel Domeyer, and Martin Lundqvist. 2017. "Using Blockchain to Improve Data Management in the Pub-lic Sector." McKinsey and Company, February. https://www.mckinsey .com/business-functions/digital-mckinsey/our-insights/using-blockchain -to-improve-data-management-in-the-public-sector (accessed June 5, 2018).

Credential Engine. 2018. *Counting U.S. Secondary and Postsecondary Cre-dentials.* Washington, DC: Credential Engine.

Moretti, Enrico. 2012. *The New Geography of Jobs.* New York: Houghton Mif-flin Harcourt.

Reamer, Andrew. 2015. *Information Resources to Facilitate Middle Skills Workforce Development.* Prepared for the National Academies Board on Science, Technology, and Economic Policy, Project on the Supply Chain for Middle-Skilled Jobs: Education, Training and Certification Pathways. Washington, DC: George Washington University.

U.S. Chamber of Commerce Foundation. 2017a. *Clearer Signals: Building an Employer-Led Job Registry for Talent Pipeline Management.* Washington, DC: U.S. Chamber of Commerce Foundation.

———. 2017b. *The Opportunity Project: A New Social Contract for a Chang-ing World.* Washington, DC: U.S. Chamber of Commerce Foundation.

———. 2018. *Improving the Talent Marketplace through the Application of Web 3.0 Technologies.* Washington, DC: United States Chamber of Com-merce Foundation.

World Economic Forum. 2016. *The Future of Jobs: Employment, Skills, and Workforce Strategy for the Fourth Industrial Revolution.* Global Challenge Insight Report. Geneva, Switzerland: World Economic Forum.

23

Credentialing Entrepreneurs

How and Why

Alejandro Crawford

REVERSING JOB-CREATOR LOSS

Start-ups drive job creation, and American start-up rates have declined for decades (Fikri, Lettieri, and Reyes 2017). A national credential for entrepreneurship could reverse this trend by reopening on-ramps to entrepreneurship and building bridges to other careers.

Every year, firms throughout the economy create and eliminate jobs, but new firms generate virtually all of the resulting *net* jobs (Wiens and Jackson 2015). From 1992 to 2014, start-ups created an average of 2.9 million net jobs annually, while established firms eliminated more jobs than they created.[1] Today, America's entrepreneurial job-creation engine is faltering: since the 1970s, start-up rates have *halved* (Fikri, Lettieri, and Reyes 2017). After the Great Recession of 2008–2010, the American economy entered unprecedented territory, as business deaths actually eclipsed business births. The ensuing recovery has created significantly fewer new businesses than have other recent recoveries (Haltiwanger, Miranda, and Jarmin 2013).

American entrepreneurship has not only diminished but also narrowed geographically. From 2010 to 2014, half of new firms came from just five metro areas: New York, Los Angeles, Houston, Dallas, and Miami.[2] Entrepreneurship remains demographically narrow as well. For example, although they represent almost half the workforce, women hold majority stakes in just over a third of small businesses and start fewer than 1 in 10 venture capital–financed, high-growth tech ventures (Raina 2016).[3]

The narrowness and decline of American entrepreneurship might seem counterintuitive. Nearly two-thirds of American adults see entrepreneurship as a good career choice, and three-quarters accord entre-preneurs high status (Singer, Herrington, and Menipaz 2018). More-over, today's aspiring entrepreneur can exploit breakthroughs that have lowered long-standing barriers. For example, new opportunities for fund-raising and prototyping, such as crowdfunding and 3D-printing hubs, abound.

At the same time, other trends may be driving talent away from entrepreneurship. For example, educational debt correlates negatively with small business formation, and both student debt and health-care costs have mushroomed in an era when incumbent firms offer attractive salaries, recruiting perks, and résumé-building experience (Ambrose, Cordell, and Ma 2015). Facing high opportunity costs, graduates may decide that entrepreneurship's risks outweigh its appeal. A recent grad-uate of a coding academy describes the barriers to entrepreneurship this way: "An emerging consensus amongst my generation [is] that millen-nials have some amazing ideas but feel hugely trapped by connected webs of constraint that reduce time for entrepreneurship. These webs of constraint include student loans and a need to be plugged into certain jobs for reliable income and access to necessities like health insurance."[4]

Starting a business has never been easy, but when the economy fails to replenish its ranks of entrepreneurs, overall job-creating capac-ity diminishes. Under such circumstances, would-be entrepreneurs need on-ramps and bridges. They require reasonable access to essen-tial resources—the "entrepreneurial ecosystem" described later in this chapter—and they need passable crossings to less risky endeavors. More than half of start-ups fail after 5 years, and about two-thirds after 10 (BLS 2016). The entrepreneur faces likely failure even if she creates jobs along the way, and she may well emerge struggling to translate the value of her experience to the wider market.

In a few enclaves such as Silicon Valley, entrepreneurship car-ries such prestige that future investors and employers often recognize strengths built through launching a venture, even if that venture ends in failure. Beyond such enclaves, should an entrepreneur wish to dem-onstrate her qualifications—whether to investors or employers—what recourse does she have? She can take a college course, enter a busi-ness plan competition, pitch her ideas at meet-ups, create profiles on Gust and AngelList, earn certificates through MOOCs, enroll in Gen-eral Assembly courses, or pursue a range of other fragmented activities. Many of these are valuable, but none cements her value the way a recognized credential would.

This chapter proposes a national entrepreneur's credential, building on the framework introduced in my recent report, *An Ecosystem Model for Credentialing Entrepreneurs* (Crawford 2017). A national credential could widen market recognition for entrepreneurial competencies and improve the risk calculus for entrepreneurship by serving as a kind of insurance for would-be entrepreneurs. From entry-level workers to midcareer professionals, more people could attempt ventures if, in the process, they established competencies that investors and employers recognize and value.

According to surveys, venture capitalists value managerial competence at least as much as idea generation, product development, or technology savvy (Gompers et al. 2016). Employers, for their part, rely on soft skills like problem solving, adaptability, collaboration, and communication, but struggle to select for such skills when hiring (Vozza 2018). An effective entrepreneur's credential would enable entrepreneurs to show they had demonstrated such skills. In other words, a national credential could serve as a market signal, conveying the value of entrepreneurial competencies to investors in new ventures, and to the wider market for talent. If a credential could deliver such a market signal, would it replenish the ranks of entrepreneurs? The possibility merits testing, since narrow and declining entrepreneurship chokes the economy's capacity to generate jobs.

ENTREPRENEUR AND ECOSYSTEM

Harvard's Howard Stevenson famously defined entrepreneurship as the "pursuit of opportunity beyond resources controlled" (Eisenmann 2013). To establish and scale their ventures, entrepreneurs draw resources from a rich "ecosystem." This ecosystem features both financial investors and those who provide the knowledge, resources, and opportunities on which ventures depend (Foster and Shimizu 2013). The strategy consulting firm Acceleration Group (for which I serve as managing director) organizes the entrepreneurial ecosystem into seven "CAPTURE" categories, which it calls the CAPTURE Framework:

- **Cash and capital**
- **Access to market**
- **Prototyping and production capacity**
- **Talent and training**
- **Users for testing and early adoption**
- **Regulatory licenses and permissions**
- **Economic guidance for developing a scalable business model**

Entrepreneurs "CAPTURE" resources from the ecosystem as they *build* their ventures, *showcase* these ventures' potential, and *connect* to investors in each category. Each step requires a reciprocal interaction between entrepreneur and ecosystem, as Table 23.1 shows. Entrepreneurs make the case for investing in their ventures, and investors across the CAPTURE categories (we will follow the practice of Acceleration Group and call them "CAPTURE investors") evaluate that case before making their knowledge, resources, and opportunities available.

If a national entrepreneur's credential could improve the basis for CAPTURE investors to identify capable early-stage entrepreneurs, it could expand market participation on both sides.[5] To develop such a credential in practice requires three major building blocks: 1) recognized standards and competencies, 2) accreditable demonstration opportunities, and 3) a common platform for establishing and assessing competencies. The following sections expand upon these requirements.

Recognized Standards and Competencies

First, a national entrepreneur's credential requires an entrepreneurial competency framework. Well-developed frameworks exist, including the National Content Standards for Entrepreneurship Education

Table 23.1 Assessable Ecosystem Interactions

Process	Entrepreneur	Ecosystem
Build	Model venture and make case	Vet solution
Showcase	Prove concept and validate market	Perform due diligence
Connect	Recruit resources and execute	Invest resources

SOURCE: Acceleration Group Inc.

(EntreEd),[6] the European Entrepreneurship Competence Framework (EntreComp),[7] and the Entrepreneurial Mindset Index (EMI).[8] Each of these frameworks emphasizes distinct competency types, including hard skills, soft skills, mindset attributes, and mobilization capabilities, as Table 23.2 illustrates. These competency types merit attention when designing a national credential, because the competencies required for entrepreneurship depart in important ways from those signaled by traditional business credentials.[9]

Table 23.2 Types of Entrepreneurial Competencies, with Examples

1. Hard skills	2. Soft skills	3. Mindset attributes	4. Mobilization capabilities
Business model	Critical thinking	Innovation and creativity	Recruiting talent and support
Market analysis	Communication	Adaptability and flexibility	Putting ideas into action
Product development	Collaboration	Initiative and resourcefulness	Accessing/ mobilizing resources

SOURCE: Acceleration Group Inc.

Each framework emphasizes one or more of the four competency types:

- The EntreEd framework divides entrepreneurial competencies into three types: 1) *entrepreneurial skills* (concept development and resourcing, as well as leadership and personal management), 2) *ready skills* (communication, digital, and financial literacies), and 3) *business functions* (comparable to the MBA tool kit in finance, operations, marketing, and strategy).[10]

- The EntreComp framework also divides entrepreneurial competencies into three types, but it moves beyond traditional categories of knowledge, skills, and ability. EntreComp emphasizes competencies built and demonstrated through ecosystem interaction: accessing and mobilizing resources, putting ideas into action, finding new opportunities, leveraging resources, and persuading others to support or join the venture.

- The Entrepreneurial Mindset Index emphasizes "mindset," breaking the entrepreneurial mindset down into "domains." These include communication and collaboration, critical thinking and problem solving, creativity and innovation, flexibility and adaptability, initiative and self-reliance, and opportunity recognition. These domains designate attitudes and soft skills critical not only for entrepreneurship but also more broadly for the "heuristic" work on which most job growth depends, work in which one must experiment to find the path to success (Gold and Rodríguez 2018).[11]

As this brief profile of distinct frameworks suggests, an entrepreneur's credential must reflect competencies beyond the situation analysis typically emphasized by MBA programs. The process for awarding this credential must assess entrepreneurs' capacity to recognize opportunities, mobilize resources, and adapt as they interact with the CAPTURE ecosystem. For evaluators to assess these kinds of dynamic entrepreneurial competencies, aspiring entrepreneurs need robust demonstration opportunities. Such demonstration opportunities constitute the second building block for a national entrepreneur's credential.

Accreditable Demonstration Opportunities

An entrepreneur's credential need not reflect extensive experience launching ventures, any more than a law degree attests to experience practicing law. Instead, the credential should open doors to further experience, based on focused demonstrations of entrepreneurial competency.

Entrepreneurial demonstration opportunities abound at colleges and other educational institutions, companies, community organizations, and capital providers (see the appendix for examples).[12] These opportunities allow entrepreneurs to build, showcase, and connect their ideas, while demonstrating their qualifications under pressure. Organizers of existing demonstration opportunities typically recruit judges to evaluate how well entrepreneurs perform. Some organizers develop demonstration opportunities within a given school or company, while others, such as the Network for Teaching Entrepreneurship (NFTE), Venture for America, and the National Science Foundation, offer forums across schools, companies, and regions.

Common demonstration opportunities include pitch competitions, accelerator selection processes, bottom-up-innovation programs, and entrepreneurial fellowships, as illustrated in the appendix. Even when participants exhibit valuable competencies, they typically emerge without standardized evidence of these competencies. A system for accrediting institutions that apply standardized criteria for submissions, evaluations, and awards could transform these demonstrations into "qualifying events." Entrepreneurs who succeed in these events would receive an entrepreneur's credential. Such tangible evidence, of competencies built and demonstrated through entrepreneurship, could lead more talent to view launching a start-up as a reasonable career move.

The credential should take the form of a professional certification, audited by a third party. Over time, the credential could encompass subcertifications by level, function (entrepreneurial marketing, finance, etc.), and stage. Accredited institutions should award the credential to entrepreneurs who demonstrate standardized competencies. An international credentialing body, such as the American National Standards Institute (ANSI), should oversee the standardization of entrepreneurs' challenges at qualifying events. This credentialing body should accredit institutions to award or deny official credentials on its behalf. To ensure inter-rater reliability, assessors from the credentialing body should review evaluator qualifications and assessment processes at awarding institutions.[13] This full-fledged accreditation process will take time to come to fruition. In the short term, therefore, foundations and relevant associations could endorse credential-awarding institutions as a starting point for quality assurance.

Accreditation should also require balanced, representative evaluator panels, in view of the correlation between evaluator homogeneity and success disparities for entrepreneurs. A 25-point gap separates the success rates (as measured by exits) of male- and female-founded start-ups, but "when startups are financed by VCs [venture capitalists] with female partners, that difference disappears" (Raina 2016, p. 3). This striking outcome underscores the importance of applying clear standards not only to the entrepreneur but also to the evaluator (Cutler 2015).

By standardizing existing demonstrations of entrepreneurial competency, accreditation could make such competency intelligible to the wider market. While this presents a major opportunity, it also introduces the logistical challenge of standardizing submission requirements and scoring across decentralized events. A shared library of entrepreneurs' challenges and scoring rubrics, available on a digital platform, could help address this challenge. Such a platform represents the third essential building block for a national entrepreneur's credential.

A Common Platform for Establishing and Assessing Competencies

As the aforementioned competency frameworks make clear, entrepreneurial competency goes beyond the mastery of learned content and the performance of algorithmic tasks. A meaningful credential must reflect entrepreneurs' performance in an array of dynamic challenges that test their capacity to recruit resources and adapt to market feedback.[14] An online library of challenges, for use in existing demonstration opportunities, could make it feasible to map performance to established entrepreneurial competencies.

Performance assessment should combine the kind of digital badging used in MOOC certifications, with awards from judges who rate performance in designated challenges.[15] As entrepreneurs undergo the challenges required to build, connect, and showcase their ventures, the digital platform should do the following:

- Capture the skills entrepreneurs build as they tackle specific challenges, from business model to brand positioning

- Rate performance based on business-case due diligence as entrepreneurs showcase their ventures in qualifying events

- Assign badges for resources recruited, adaptations made, and assumptions validated, as entrepreneurs connect with the ecosystem

Credentials should reflect these respective elements, as illustrated in Table 23.3, on the following page.

In this model, accredited institutions select from a library of standardized challenges, available through the platform, to use in qualified demonstration opportunities. These institutions—colleges (and other educational establishments), corporations, community organizations, and capital providers—select challenges relevant to their programs, goals, and events. Evaluators at accredited institutions assess entrepreneurs based on how well they perform in designated challenges.

Table 23.3 Forms of Assessment

Performance	Assessment
1 BUILD: Assessment of Competencies Demonstrated Through Challenges	Skills: Entrepreneurs demonstrate competencies through digital challenges such as: • Product design • Market validation • Brand development • User testing
2 SHOWCASE: "Due Diligence" Evaluation of Ventures	Ratings: Judges score entrepreneurs' demonstrations of respective competencies based on business-case due diligence criteria applied to ventures, which submit responses to challenges such as: • Business model • Market research • Go-to-market strategy • Operations • Financials
3 CONNECT: Resources Mobilized Through Successful Interactions	Badges: Entrepreneurs earn badges based on recruiting resources to the project from the CAPTURE ecosystem, including: • Capital from seed funders • Access through market gatekeepers • Production capacity through strategic partners • Talent through team members and supporters

SOURCE: RebelBase Inc.

Since ventures develop iteratively based on market feedback, challenges include robust mechanisms that enable entrepreneurs to elicit feedback from potential customers and stakeholders, as well as coaches, mentors, and evaluators. Evaluators assess the extent to which entrepreneurs incorporate market and community feedback into their venture strategies. Since successful ventures also depend upon collaboration between entrepreneurial team members who lead various functional areas of the venture, collaborators earn credit for their work commensurate with their contributions, based on models common for business school projects.[16]

The digital platform provides rubrics for evaluating entrepreneurs' performance as they complete the challenges, based on established entrepreneurial competency frameworks. This increases the legitimacy not only of participating entrepreneurs but also of the demonstration events themselves. These rubrics could include, for example, the following: viability of the business model, validation of the market opportunity, strategies for rolling out the product and taking it to market, preliminary operational demonstrations, and financial modeling. Criteria derive from real-world standards for business case due diligence. An international accreditation body reviews evaluator responses for accuracy in vetting solutions, valuing opportunities, and performing business case due diligence.[17]

CASE STUDY EXAMPLES

RebelBase Beta

The software-as-a-service (SaaS) platform RebelBase (developed by a team I lead) is testing the viability of providing standardized challenges, through a digital platform, to a range of organizations.[18] Students, employees, community members, and other potential innovators develop business models, validate markets, and make the case for new solutions, as they complete challenges with the help of dynamic hints and examples.

These users have the opportunity to showcase their capacities in a game-like format, in which they build recognition for their solutions as they undergo challenges such as designing solutions, creating brands, modeling cash flows, and pitching to investors. Entrepreneurs establish their competencies as they undergo each challenge, collaborate with team members, interface with stakeholders, and elicit feedback from a community of peers and advisors.

During beta testing, a variety of users, including executives at a nonprofit, students in entrepreneurship and innovation courses, and participants in a professional hackathon, tested the challenges selected for their purposes. Although the sample size was small, the beta test suggested that a library of entrepreneurial challenges available via a common digital platform can standardize criteria for assessment of entrepreneurial demonstration opportunities.[19]

Erasmus+

As this chapter has argued, a robust national entrepreneur's credential requires three elements: 1) an established entrepreneur's credentialing framework, 2) entrepreneurial demonstration opportunities, and 3) a library of standardized entrepreneurs' challenges for use in these demonstration opportunities. To illustrate how these three components could come together across institutions and even countries, it merits looking abroad at the European Union and affiliated countries' Erasmus+ network.[20] In February 2018, a consortium of 11 Erasmus+ national agencies, representing both EU and non-EU countries, launched the Youth@ Work initiative, focused on youth employability and entrepreneurship (Diroescu 2018).[21] This partnership explores uses of the EntreComp framework, mentioned above, to expand access to entrepreneurship and "make advancements in assessing entrepreneurial learning. . . . On this basis, guidelines can be developed on how to assess entrepreneurship as a competence" (Rebeccaw 2017).

Erasmus+ is assessing the feasibility of making a digital library of entrepreneurs' challenges and simulations accessible by means of a common platform, as outlined here. This initiative would apply a scoring system for performance in these challenges and map performance to competencies in the EntreComp framework. National agencies and partner universities would convene panels of judges for qualifying events, and Erasmus+ would accredit national agencies and their local partners to award an EU entrepreneur's credential.

An EU credential could foster opportunities for entrepreneurs to collaborate across borders to address unmet needs in the market and solve common problems. Armed with such a credential, young people would have high credibility when they approached CAPTURE investors in entrepreneurial ecosystems. Earning a credential while they try out entrepreneurship would allow them to build their employability in the process. An EU credential could play a crucial role in replenishing the ranks of job creators in countries facing both double-digit youth unemployment (Eurostat 2018) and overwhelming "skills gaps," where large percentages of employers see young hires as lacking the skills they require (European Centre for the Development of Vocational Training 2015).

CONCLUSION

Faced with declining entrepreneurship, the United States urgently needs to reallocate human capital to the new business start-ups that create virtually all net new jobs. A national entrepreneur's credential could stimulate entrepreneurial activity by enabling entrepreneurs to communicate their capabilities to the market.

Existing competency frameworks and demonstration opportunities constitute useful building blocks for such a credential. To convert these building blocks into a national credentialing system requires a common digital platform. Through a library of challenges, such a platform could standardize the assessment of entrepreneurial performance. An accreditation body could authorize organizations that offer entrepreneurial demonstration opportunities to award credentials based on performance in these challenges.

Such a platform would provide aspiring entrepreneurs crucial opportunities to build, showcase, and connect their ventures and innovations. It would also enable them to establish recognized competencies in the process. This would equip entrepreneurs to convey their capabilities to the market. If the market were to recognize this signal, it could change the risk calculus for attempting start-ups.

The U.S. economy cannot afford to wait for existing institutions to build market recognition for entrepreneurial competencies through a process of gradual evolution. Indeed, many institutions may prove too siloed, stratified, and slow moving to achieve the needed overhaul. It is time to connect innovation ecosystems across existing colleges, companies, community organizations, and capital providers, enabling a range of resource providers to identify, champion, and invest in talented entrepreneurs.

In an increasingly globalized economy, entrepreneurs need to work with team members and resource providers beyond their local ecosystems. Consequently, the longer-term solution must connect ecosystems across regions, industries, and even countries. Regional accreditation bodies should make their standards interoperable and recognize each other's credentials. Globally compatible entrepreneurs' credentials could provide a potent mechanism for broadening access to entrepreneurial experience, thus connecting entrepreneurs to a worldwide ecosystem of opportunities and resources.

Finally, researchers who study jobs and growth need to deepen their understanding of the "job-creator loss" that occurs when talent is diverted from entrepreneurship, and how to reverse this trend. A linked platform for entrepreneurial demonstrations could generate critical insights about the attributes and interactions that lead talent to launch ventures, and so could induce resource providers to invest in these ventures. Such data could in turn guide further efforts to expand access to entrepreneurship.

Notes

I would like to acknowledge Stephen Crawford and Roy Swift for expert guidance on framing the requirements for a practicable entrepreneur's credential; Daniel Ramírez-Raftree and Sonia Ganess of Acceleration Group for vital ideas, tireless revisions, and effective systems thinking; Tiffany Kwan, Tuba Erbil, and the RebelBase team for conceiving the architecture for a digital platform that enables entrepreneurs to establish their competencies through a library of challenges; Raluca Diroescu for insight into the Erasmus+ strategy for expanding youth entrepreneurship; Hunter Lovins and Kathy Hipple for invaluable insight in refining the Disrupt to Sustain challenge categories; and Milika Nevárez, Richard D. Crawford, Ashley Bozarth, and Ben Jones for their painstaking review of drafts. I would further like to acknowledge Peter Joyce, Eric Johnson, Branka Minic, Tom Gold, the Research Triangle Institute, and the members of the Global Center for Youth Employment (GCYE) for supporting the literature review and framework on which this chapter builds, and Joyce Moy, Brian Gurski, and Liu Fang for collaborating on the Entrepreneurship Pathways concept from which that framework emerged. All errors are my own.

1. Within the first five years, as new ventures fail, they destroy about 40 percent of the jobs they have created. However, those that survive grow faster than mature firms (Haltiwanger, Jarmin, and Miranda 2013).
2. This is a measure of the number of firms generated, not their rate of growth. The highest per-capita density of fast-growing firms on the 2017 Inc. 5000 list per capita can be found in Boulder, Colorado; Provo, Utah; Huntsville, Alabama; and Washington, D.C. (Hathaway 2018).

3. With entrepreneurship already concentrated by gender, restrictive immigration policy risks further limiting job creation. Immigrants are disproportionately entrepreneurial (Kauffman Foundation 2018), and without immigrants and their children, the Fortune 500 would dwindle to the "Fortune 284" (Florida 2017).

4. Brendan Hamill, e-mail message to author, February 20, 2018. Used with permission and edited for clarity.

5. In a two-sided market, better matching can facilitate market expansion (see Crawford [2017]).

6. Competencies represent illustrative examples, rather than an exhaustive list. For more information, see the web page http://www.entre-ed.org/natstandards/national-entrepreneurship-standards/standards-summary/ (accessed August 23, 2018), which lists the entrepreneurial skills, ready skills, and business functions that make up the National Consortium for Entrepreneurship Education's national content standards for entrepreneurial education and related tool kit.

7. As above, competencies represent illustrative examples rather than an exhaustive list. For more information, see McCallum et al. (2018).

8. Here again, domains represent illustrative examples rather than an exhaustive list. For more information, see World Economic Forum (2018).

9. Successful entrepreneurs think differently from the way conventional managers do. Managers are trained to apply "causal reasoning" by choosing the optimal path to a given end using established means. By contrast, entrepreneurs employ "effectuation," which "begins with a given set of means, and allows goals to emerge contingently over time from the varied imagination and diverse aspirations of the founders and the people they interact with" (Sarasvathy 2018).

10. See, for example, Goodstein and Richmond (2017).

11. As opposed to "algorithmic" activities, which entail following an established set of steps, heuristic activities constitute most job growth, writes Daniel Pink (2009): "The consulting firm McKinsey & Co. estimates that in the United States, only 30 percent of job growth now comes from algorithmic work, while 70 percent comes from heuristic work" (p. 30).

12. In practice, these institutional categories frequently overlap, through various forms of collaboration. A *New York Times* article called the growth of various forums at universities an "innovation arms race" (Singer 2015), and many corporations are engaged in similar opportunities.

13. "Inter-rater reliability" means that distinct panels of judges assign equivalent ratings to comparable demonstrations. Given the uncertainty of early-stage ventures, investors often disagree strenuously about the potential of a business but concur when it comes to the competencies and relative strengths demonstrated by members of respective start-up teams.

14. Psychologist Donald Schön (1983) calls such dynamic adaptation to feedback "reflection in action," citing the example of jazz performers, for whom "improvisation consists of varying, combining and recombining a set of figures within the schema which bounds and gives coherence to the performance" (p. 55).

15. For example, to award badges and certificates for its Massive Open Online Courses, or MOOCs, MIT partners with the learning platform GetSmarter. At the

end of a given program, assessments determine whether participants have completed module exercises. If so, they are awarded a digital certificate administered by the digital credential and badging platform Accredible. For more information on digital certificates and badging, see the company's website.

16. This could be supported by assessments emphasizing team interaction. For example, Andrea Bennardo of the human resource consulting firm RisorSe has developed innovative psychometric approaches that emphasize the *interaction* of various mindsets and competencies within entrepreneurial teams.

17. Such criteria can be made systematic and applied. For example, Acceleration Group has developed due diligence frameworks for angel investors and taught them to investors on behalf of an angel group.

18. For more information, see the company homepage, https://rebelbase.co/.

19. One of the test users, the Bard MBA in Sustainability's 2017 venture competition, serves to illustrate the use of the challenges. Participants performed the following assessable tasks, corresponding to digital challenges in the respective categories. Teams competed in one or more categories according to their preparation level, and judges reviewed posted challenge entries to score team performance.

    1. Innovation
       Solution: Define a product, service, or initiative that solves a critical problem.
       Business model: Lay out a viable business model.
       Impact model: Make the case that their innovation will have significant impact.

    2. Route to market
       Market: Identify an addressable market and understand its size and shape.
       Strategy: Lay out a persuasive go-to-market strategy.
       Scale: Show whether it can scale and how.

    3. Resources
       Rollout: Present a feasible model for going from minimum viable product to scale.
       Team: Clarify whom the team should include and why this team can pull it off.
       Resources: Identify resources in the ecosystem they'll need and how they'll access them.

    4. Financials
       Cash: Present a plausible cash-flow model, showing where the money will come from.
       Impact metrics: Lay out a way to prove this to stakeholders.
       Capital: Model scenarios for capital required, with plausible returns for investors.

    See "Disrupt to Sustain Competition Highlights," Acceleration Group (2017).

20. For information about Erasmus+, see European Commission (2018).

21. Youth@Work is an initiative of the Erasmus+ national agencies of Turkey, the United Kingdom, France, Italy, Spain, Poland, Hungary, Malta, the Republic of Macedonia, Greece, and Cyprus. See Diroescu (2018).

References

Acceleration Group. 2017. "Disrupt to Sustain Competition Highlights." Vimeo from Amy Kalafa. New York: Acceleration Group. http://acceleration group.net/insights/disrupt-to-sustain-competition-highlights/ (accessed June 29, 2018).

Ambrose, Brent W., Larry Cordell, and Shuwei Ma. 2015. "The Impact of Student Loan Debt on Small Business Formation." Federal Reserve Bank of Philadelphia Working Paper No. 15-26. Philadelphia: Federal Reserve Bank of Philadelphia.

Arbor Brothers. 2018. *Arbor Brothers: Engaged Philanthropy: Apply.* New York: Arbor Brothers. http://www.arborbrothers.org/apply/ (accessed March 18, 2018).

Barclays. 2018. *Social Innovation Facility.* London: Barclays. https://www .home.barclays/citizenship/access-to-financing/social-innovation.html (accessed June 29, 2018).

Bureau of Labor Statistics (BLS). 2016. *Business Employment Dynamics: Entrepreneurship and the U.S. Economy.* Washington, DC: Bureau of Labor Statistics. https://www.bls.gov/bdm/entrepreneurship/bdm_chart3 .htm (accessed April 16, 2018).

Butler, Timothy. 2017. "Hiring an Entrepreneurial Leader." *Harvard Business Review*, March–April. https://hbr.org/2017/03/hiring-an-entrepreneurial -leader (accessed March 18, 2018).

Cornell University. 2018. *Cornell Entrepreneur Network (CEN): Everything Cornell Entrepreneurs Need Now.* Ithaca, NY: Cornell University. https:// alumni.cornell.edu/connect/networking/cen/ (accessed August 24, 2018).

Crawford, Alejandro. 2017. *An Ecosystem Model for Credentialing Entrepreneurs.* Research Triangle Park, NC: Global Center for Youth Employment, RTI International.

Cutler, Kim-Mai. 2015. "Here's a Detailed Breakdown of Racial and Gender Diversity Data across U.S. Venture Capital Firms." *TechCrunch—Startup and Technology News*, October 6. https://techcrunch.com/2015/10/06/s23p -racial-gender-diversity-venture/ (accessed March 11, 2018).

Diroescu, Raluca. 2018. "Launching of Strategic Partnership on Youth Employability." Address to the International Symposium on Youth Employment Challenges (ISYEC), held in Kayseri, Turkey, February 27–March 1.

Eisenmann, Thomas R. 2013. "Entrepreneurship: A Working Definition." *Harvard Business Review*, January 10. https://hbr.org/2013/01/what-is -entrepreneurship (accessed September 10, 2016).

European Centre for the Development of Vocational Training. 2015. *Skill Shortages and Gaps in European Enterprises: Striking a Balance between*

Vocational Education and Training and the Labour Market. Thessaloniki, Greece: European Centre for the Development of Vocational Training. http://www.cedefop.europa.eu/en/publications-and-resources/publications/3071 (accessed April 16, 2018).

European Commission. 2018. *What Is Erasmus+?* Brussels: European Commission. https://ec.europa.eu/programmes/erasmus-plus/about_en (accessed June 29, 2018).

Eurostat. 2018. *Unemployment Statistics.* Luxembourg: Eurostat. http://ec.europa.eu/eurostat/statistics-explained/index.php/Unemployment_statistics (accessed April 16, 2018).

Fikri, Kenan, John Lettieri, and Angela Reyes. 2017. *Dynamism in Retreat: Consequences for Regions, Markets, and Workers.* Washington, DC: Economic Innovation Group. http://eig.org/wp-content/uploads/2017/07/Dynamism-in-Retreat-A.pdf (accessed March 11, 2018).

Florida, Richard. 2017. "Without Immigrants, the Fortune 500 Would Be the Fortune 284." *CityLab*, December 5. https://www.citylab.com/equity/2017/12/without-immigrants-the-fortune-500-would-be-the-fortune-284/547421/ (accessed March 18, 2018).

Foster, George, and Carlos Shimizu. 2013. *Entrepreneurial Ecosystems around the Globe and Company Growth Dynamics.* Report summary for the annual meeting of the New Champions 2013. Cologny, Switzerland: World Economic Forum.

Gold, Thomas, and Sophia Rodríguez. 2018. "Activating the Entrepreneurial Mindset in Youth: An Innovative, Evidence-Based Approach to Learning 21st Century Skills." Paper presented at the Eighth International Conference on the Future of Education, held in Florence, Italy, June 28–29.

Golden Seeds. 2018. *Apply for Funding.* New York: Golden Seeds. http://www.goldenseeds.com/entrepreneurs/apply-for-funding (accessed March 18, 2018).

Gompers, Paul, William Gornall, Steven N. Kaplan, and Ilya A. Strebulaev. 2016. "How Do Venture Capitalists Make Decisions?" NBER Working Paper No. 22587. Cambridge, MA: National Bureau of Economic Research. http://www.nber.org/papers/w22587.pdf (accessed June 28, 2018).

Goodstein, Eban, and Reagan Richmond. 2017. "Creating a Curriculum for Mission-Driven Business Education." Bard MBA in Sustainability Working Paper. Annandale-on-Hudson, NY: Bard College.

Haltiwanger, John, Ron S. Jarmin, and Javier Miranda. 2013. "Who Creates Jobs? Small versus Large versus Young." *Review of Economics and Statistics* 95(2): 347–361. https://www.mitpressjournals.org/doi/pdf/10.1162/REST_a_00288. (accessed April 14, 2018).

Haltiwanger, John, Javier Miranda, and Ron S. Jarmin. 2013. *Anemic Job Cre-*

ation and Growth in the Aftermath of the Great Recession: Are Home Prices to Blame? Business Dynamic Statistics Briefing. Kansas City, MO: Ewing Marion Kauffman Foundation. https://www.census.gov/ces/pdf/BDS _StatBrief8_Home_Prices.pdf (accessed April 16, 2018).

Hathaway, Ian. 2018. *High-Growth Firms and Cities in the U.S.: An Analysis of the Inc. 5000.* Washington, DC: Brookings Institution. https://www .brookings.edu/research/high-growth-firms-and-cities-in-the-us-an -analysis-of-the-inc-5000/ (accessed March 11, 2018).

Kauffman Foundation. 2018. *Immigration.* A report in the series State of the Field: Distilling the Universe of Entrepreneurship Research. Kansas City, MO: Ewing Marion Kauffman Foundation. https://www.kauffman .org/microsites/state-of-the-field/topics/background-of-entrepreneurs/ demographics/immigration (accessed June 28, 2018).

McCallum, Elin, Lisa McMullan, Rebecca Weicht, and Alison Price. 2018. *EntreComp into Action—Get Inspired, Make It Happen: A User Guide to the European Entrepreneurship Competence Framework.* EU Science Hub. Brussels: European Union. https://ec.europa.eu/jrc/en/publication/ eur-scientific-and-technical-research-reports/entrecomp-action-get-inspired -make-it-happen-user-guide-european-entrepreneurship-competence (accessed August 23, 2018).

New York University. 2018. *NYU/D-Prize Social Venture Competition: There Are Proven Ideas to Alleviate Poverty All across the Globe. Can You Distribute Them to the People Most in Need?* New York: New York University Social Entrepreneurship Program. https://www.nyu.edu/social -entrepreneurship/d-prize/ (accessed June 29, 2018).

Pink, Daniel H. 2009. *Drive: The Surprising Truth about What Motivates Us.* New York: Riverhead.

Quake Capital. 2018. *Apply to Our Accelerator.* New York: Quake Capital. https://www.quakecapital.com/apply (accessed March 18, 2018).

Raina, Sahil. 2016. "Research: The Gender Gap in Startup Success Disappears When Women Fund Women." *Harvard Business Review*, July 19. https:// hbr.org/2016/07/research-the-gender-gap-in-startup-success-disappears -when-women-fund-women (accessed March 11, 2018).

Rebeccaw. 2017. "EntreComp: From a Reference Framework to Educational Practice in Entrepreneurial Learning." *EntreAssess* (blog), April 7. http:// entreassess.com/2017/04/07/entrecomp-from-a-reference-framework-to -educational-practice-in-entrepreneurial-learning/ (accessed March 18, 2018).

Sarasvathy, Saras D. 2018. "What Makes Entrepreneurs Entrepreneurial?" Darden Case No. UVA-ENT-0065. Darden School of Business, University of Virginia. http://www.effectuation.org/sites/default/files/research _papers/what-makes-entrepreneurs-entrepreneurial-sarasvathy_0.pdf (accessed March 11, 2018).

Schön, Donald A. 1983. *The Reflective Practitioner: How Professionals Think in Action*. New York: Basic Books.

Singer, Natasha. 2015. "Universities Race to Nurture Start-Up Founders of the Future." *New York Times*, December 28. https://www.nytimes.com/2015/12/29/technology/universities-race-to-nurture-start-up-founders-of-the-future.html (accessed March 19, 2018).

Singer, Slavica, Mike Herrington, and Ehud Menipaz. 2018. *Global Report 2017/18*. London: Global Entrepreneurship Monitor (GEM). http://www.gemconsortium.org/report/50012 (accessed March 11, 2018).

Small Business Innovation Research Program (SBIR). 2018. *Applicants*. Washington, DC: SBIR. https://www.sbir.gov/applicants (accessed June 29, 2018).

Vozza, Stephanie. 2018. "These Are the Five Soft Skills Recruiters Want Most." *Fast Company*, January 26. https://www.fastcompany.com/40520691/these-are-the-five-soft-skills-recruiters-want-most (accessed March 11, 2018).

Wiens, Jason, and Chris Jackson. 2015. "The Importance of Young Firms for Economic Growth." *Entrepreneurship Policy Digest*, September 14. An Educational Policy Brief from the Ewing Marion Kauffman Foundation. https://www.kauffman.org/what-we-do/resources/entrepreneurship-policy-digest/the-importance-of-young-firms-for-economic-growth (accessed March 11, 2018).

World Economic Forum. 2018. *Entrepreneurship Mindset Index*. Submitted by Network for Teaching Entrepreneurship. Geneva, Switzerland: World Economic Forum. http://reports.weforum.org/disrupting-unemployment/entrepreneurship-mindset-index/ (accessed August 23, 2018).

Appendix 23A

Examples of Existing Demonstration Opportunities

Institutional category	User type	Purpose	Award
College/educational			
1. NYU/D-Prize Social Venture Competition[1] 2. Cornell + CofoundersLab[2] 3. SUNY (FIT) Entrepreneurship Practicum[3]	1. Competition or hack 2. Cofounder, adviser, or service provider 3. Educator	1. Filter entrants or structure challenges 2. Find collaborators or pitch services 3. Give and grade challenges	1. Award / funding 2. Contract 3. Grade / assessment
Corporate			
1. Barclays: Social Innovation Facility[4] 2. Google: Acquisition Database[5] 3. Neoway[6]	1. Corporate 2. Partner / acquiring firm 3. Employer	1. Stimulate intrapreneurial innovation[7] 2. Source innovation 3. Hire potential leaders	1. Recognition / funding 2. Partnering / acquisition 3. Job
Community			
1. RiseBoro Community Partnership[8] 2. SBIR/SSTR Seed Fund Opportunities[9]	1. Nonprofit 2. Grant maker	1. Seed initiative 2. Replace traditional application	1. Funding 2. Investment / funding
Capital providing			
1. Quake Capital[10] 2. Arbor Bros.[11] 3. Golden Seeds[12]	1. Accelerator 2. Engaged philanthropist 3. Angel group	1. Assess applicants 2. Assess applicants 3. Standardize deal flow	1. Acceptance 2. Investment / funding 3. Investment / funding

SOURCE: Acceleration Group Inc.

Appendix Table Notes

1. New York University (2018).
2. Cornell University (2018).
3. Fashion Institute of Technology (FIT), Entrepreneurship Program capstone course: EP 452—Entrepreneurship Practicum.
4. Barclays (2018).
5. See "Acquisitions" web page for Crunchbase at https://www.crunchbase.com/search/acquisitions/b167e0cce9ab4b6f29442f90a5a77f22bb373a60 (accessed August 23, 2018).
6. An entrepreneur's project profile on the RebelBase beta was used by me in a recent employment reference. For a discussion of how employers can select for entrepreneurial competencies when hiring, see Butler (2017).
7. The term *intrapreneurial*, used in the chart, refers to "internal" entrepreneurs who launch new initiatives within or spun off by existing organizations.
8. From an Acceleration Group internal document, *RiseBoro Due Diligence*, dated January 26, 2018.
9. SBIR (2018).
10. Quake Capital (2018).
11. Arbor Brothers (2018).
12. Golden Seeds (2018).

Part 5

Investing in Regional Workforce Development Systems

24
Coordinating Regional Workforce Development Resources

Stuart Andreason

What exactly makes up the workforce development system? Previous studies of the system, including one published in a previous Federal Reserve book on workforce development, suggest it is a patchwork quilt of programs, organizations, policies, and activities that help workers access skills and supports that get workers into jobs (Good and Strong 2015). In an effort to define it, former Federal Reserve Chair Janet Yellen described workforce development as a "catchall phrase to encompass different types of initiatives that help prepare people for jobs by providing them with training, placement assistance, and other support" (Yellen 2017).

The difficulty in framing a definition of the workforce development system is partially due to the large number of efforts engaged in preparing people for jobs by providing job seekers with training, placement, and other supports. Organizations ranging from those that help stabilize people's lives and provide basic supports like housing, health care, and transportation to those that provide highly specialized technical training are engaged in workforce development. Similarly, even "traditional" workforce development efforts are funded and administered through a number of different federal, state, and local agencies and organizations. Navigating this patchwork is a challenge for job seekers and businesses—and communities and organizations that are able to braid together the various support systems likely provide better services to both their job seeker and business clients.

Limited understanding of what organizations and supports are available can lead to job seekers dropping out of services at transition periods or workers never accessing services because they arrived at the "wrong front door" when they were searching for services. Similar challenges happen in engagement with businesses who do not understand why different efforts may or may not be able to support their needs, why there are different levels and types of administrative burdens and limited understanding of the goals of the different organizations involved in workforce development.

Many programs are developed and funded at the federal or state levels but are administered through some type of local government or regional entity. It makes intuitive sense that federal and state workforce development programs happen at the regional or local level, since workforce development and job seeking is something that is inherently based in place—labor markets and economic activities are local. Yet many of the organizations involved in this work, since they have different funding mechanisms and goals, have different definitions of what constitutes the local area or region. For example, workforce development boards, funded through the Workforce Innovation and Opportunity Act (WIOA), are defined as regions—but the core 10 counties of the Atlanta metropolitan area (which includes over 20 counties in total) have five WIOA-funded workforce development boards. Coordination between these boards is critical because workers and businesses seek jobs or offer goods and services across the entire local economy and may not understand the services they can receive from one of the boards versus another. Similarly, the job seeker or business may not understand why an organization not involved in the WIOA system can offer different services but never reaches as large a scale as other organizations, such as WIOA boards or community and technical colleges. The Atlanta example is not unique; similar challenges exist in communities across the nation.

The "patchwork quilt" of workforce development is seen as one singular system or entity by its job-seeker and business consumers, but there remain opportunities to improve the operations of the many disparate entities in the quilt. As workforce development becomes increasingly critical to local economic development efforts, investing in ways to make the system able to be more easily navigated and understood by businesses is critical to positioning workforce development organizations as key partners in economic development efforts and business services. Other chapters in this book explore how to demonstrate value to new partners like economic development organizations and businesses: investing in regional workforce development systems is really about positioning the workforce development industry, system, or patchwork quilt as a viable and high-quality partner.

While some may quickly turn to suggesting changes in the overall operation or policy environment of workforce development systems to make them less disparate, investing in coordination and navigation is often done under the premise that there is significant value in the work that is done at the various entities that make up the quilt. Smaller organizations can work within a community context and design interventions to fit those specific community needs. A local workforce development board can understand and catalyze local leadership, but the broader inefficiencies that exist because decentralized decision making has been incorporated into the workforce development policy arena need attention at a regional scale. This regional approach can help identify priorities, lift up local successes and bring them to full scale, raise awareness and market workforce development services, and create a singular "face" for workforce development partnership in a community.

Collective impact models focused on education policy are one example of how workforce development entities might coordinate efforts. Collective impact models like the Strive Partnership and other organizations in the Strive Together network are good examples of how multiple efforts can align, prioritize, and create a platform on which to discuss community priorities. A number of communities across the nation have pursued this work, particularly focused on workforce development—the Chicago Jobs Council is one of the longest-standing examples of this type of organization focused on workforce development, but certainly not the only. Collaboratives across the nation have begun to invest in regional coordination and collaboration because of the value that it may hold for job seekers and in economic development efforts. These groups help inform workforce development service providers and funders about important strategies that they may need to explore to be more effective. The following chapters elucidate some of those questions.

In a case study of the Atlanta workforce development system, Raphael Bostic and Ann Carpenter highlight challenges that job seekers face in accessing training. Although numerous researchers have studied housing and job "spatial mismatch," there have been fewer studies of a similar spatial mismatch involving housing and training, despite a regional workforce system collaborative in Atlanta having identified this as one of the major challenges that workforce development organizations face in recruiting participants. Bostic and Carpenter highlight this as a major challenge. Regional collaboratives focused on workforce development can help navigate these types of investigations and identify root causes of problems in the workforce and in local labor availability that go beyond what may be seen as simple skill or soft skill deficiencies.

Regional workforce development system collaboratives not only help identify root causes of challenges in the local labor pool, they also help keep workforce development organizations nimble, provide critical data and business intelligence to training organizations, and address hiring challenges in local industries. Tucker Plumlee describes how healthy regional workforce development collaboratives help collect both qualitative and quantitative information on business needs and economic trends. Both types of information provide critical information to training organizations—and collecting this information is often best administered through an intermediary organization, which can then share this with the multiplicity of workforce development organizations across a region. Similarly, these intermediary workforce organizations can help workers understand their career path in a local labor market—important information as workers and job seekers make decisions about training and careers they will pursue.

Many studies of workforce development policy and practice question whether it is an industry that can operate in either a "wholesale" or a "retail" business model. Local communities often discuss how to merge and combine organizations to create a more cohesive and singular workforce development organization or operator that can better interface with the demand side of the labor market. While there are often opportunities for mergers between workforce development organizations, absent a wholesale change of federal and state government policies on workforce development as well as significant shifts among the funding community, workforce development systems will often have a number of organizations all serving a local market. The appropriate question is how these organizations can collaborate to serve unique and local needs while scaling up to a level that is responsive to employers and that is also able to identify areas in which groups outside traditional workforce development organizations can help improve economic opportunities for workers. Many communities across the nation have embarked on this work, but in many places the efforts are still in the offing or are reaching a critical point where long-term success and sustainability of collaboration are uncertain. There are few definitive answers on how to sustain these efforts, but communities that are able to are likely to continue to attract investment from businesses and to expand opportunities for workers and job seekers.

References

Good, Larry, and Ed Strong. 2015. "Reimagining Workforce Policy in the United States." In *Transforming U.S. Workforce Development Policy for the 21st Century*, Carl Van Horn, Tammy Edwards, and Todd Greene, eds. Kalamazoo, MI: W.E. Upjohn Institute for Employment Research, pp. 13–43.

Yellen, Janet L. 2017. "Addressing Workforce Development Challenges in Low-Income Communities." Remarks by Janet L. Yellen, Chair, Board of Governors of the Federal Reserve System, at the 2017 annual conference of the National Community Reinvestment Coalition, "Creating a Just Economy," held in Washington, DC, March 28.

25

Cultivating Healthy Workforce Ecosystems

Tucker Plumlee

CULTIVATING THE WORKFORCE ECOSYSTEM

By now the training and education challenges facing workforce development in the United States education system are well-known. An online search for the term *skills gap* produces hundreds of thousands of results, including numerous articles from mainstream news outlets such as *Forbes*, *Bloomberg*, and the *Boston Globe*. The argument that U.S. workers are failing to keep pace with increasing skill demands continues to find support in periodic opinion polls of employers. As the total number of non-farm job openings reached a record high in 2017 (U.S. Bureau of Labor Statistics 2017), a survey of National Federation of Independent Business members found that 46 percent of employers reported having few or no qualified applicants for some open positions (Dunkelberg and Wade 2017).

Although some studies have questioned the extent of the "skills gap" and its role in preventing hiring (Abraham 2015; Cappelli 2015), what is clear is that our modern knowledge-based economy is being increasingly defined by rapidly changing demand for more advanced skills and postsecondary education. One analysis by the Pew Research Center found that the number of workers in occupations requiring average to above-average education, training, and experience increased by 68 percent between 1980 and 2015 (Pew Research Center 2016). Similarly, the Center for Education and the Workforce at Georgetown University found that 99 percent of the new jobs created in the post-Recession recovery required at least some postsecondary education (Carnevale, Jayasundera, and Gulish 2016). Just as workers must now be able to adapt to constantly shifting changes in demand for skills and education, our workforce systems must become more flexible and responsive in providing the ongoing training and reskilling they will need to respond to these changes.

However, our existing workforce system is often described by workforce professionals as a "patchwork quilt of programs," developed piecemeal from industry to industry and region to region and ill equipped to fully address these dynamic and rapidly shifting skill needs. Instead, the best models to address these challenges may be those that "spread the risk" of investing in new and innovative solutions across various stakeholders through collaborative systems building (Good and Strong 2015). In other words, the scale and complexity of the challenges we face in growing the workforce of the future requires the development of forward-thinking, collaborative systems focused on skill development aligned with industry and employer needs.

For over 40 years, the Council for Adult and Experiential Learning (CAEL) has partnered with employers, industry associations, economic development organizations, chambers of commerce, government agencies, and a wide array of other partners to better understand how to effectively link learning and work for greater economic vitality and prosperity. Through our consulting work in communities from California to Maine, we have come to understand effective workforce development efforts in terms of an ecosystem. A healthy *natural* ecosystem is one in which multiple interrelated and mutually dependent phenomena are constantly adjusting to changes elsewhere in the system to maintain balance. Correspondingly, a healthy *workforce* ecosystem is one in which a range of stakeholders understand, and are positioned to act upon, the interconnected and interdependent factors that ensure that education and training assets are well aligned with, and responsive to, shifting workforce demand for skills and learning. A well-aligned workforce ecosystem is one in which a wide range of regional stakeholders—K–12 systems, 2- and 4-year colleges and universities, employers, economic developers, workforce boards, state and local agencies, and many others—all play their part in understanding, revealing, and meeting the talent needs of the regional economy and work together to address complex issues that cannot be solved individually.

This chapter identifies and defines the various components and activities CAEL sees as necessary for building a healthy and well-aligned workforce ecosystem, one that addresses the challenges facing workers seeking meaningful and gainful employment, as well as employers and industries seeking qualified and productive employees. It also shares examples from our own work developing regionally implementable workforce ecosystem strategies to highlight the ways in which communities across the nation are coming together to create targeted solutions to their most pressing workforce needs.

UNDERSTANDING THE ECONOMIC LANDSCAPE

Developing an effective and well-aligned workforce ecosystem requires an understanding of the current and evolving needs of local employers and industries. Where are jobs being created that need to be filled (i.e., which industries or sectors are growing)? Are there enough workers with the necessary skills (whether developed through formal education or on-the-job learning) to fill these jobs? What additional skills will workers need to fill them? Do these jobs pay well and provide opportunities for career growth and advancement? Will the same industries that are growing now continue to grow 10 or 15 years into the future?

Answering these questions requires access to a wealth of quality labor market information (LMI). This information can come from traditional LMI sources such as Bureau of Labor Statistics data and growth projections, as well as newer sources such as real-time job-posting data. In addition to quantitative measures of job and wage growth, however, we have found qualitative information to be just as valuable in understanding local and regional workforce landscapes. Focus groups and surveys of employers, workers, and education partners can often reveal hidden trends and insights, particularly when used to validate or reflect on quantitative analysis.

Beyond this raw data, effective workforce systems must also have the capacity to synthesize quantitative and qualitative LMI, interpret short- and long-term trends, and identify which high-growth industries and occupations to target development efforts around. This process is also cyclical—jobs and skills needs constantly evolve, and workforce systems need to engage in an ongoing process of gathering, validating, and interpreting data from a wide array of sources. Doing so creates a reservoir of actionable workforce intelligence that stakeholders can draw on to inform alignment across the workforce system.

This kind of holistic and comprehensive LMI approach was employed by the Allegheny Conference on Community Development to identify the challenges and opportunities facing the workforce of the Pittsburgh region over the coming decade. In addition to drawing on traditional labor market data, CAEL partnered with Burning Glass Technologies to gather relevant job-postings data and conducted interviews and focus groups with more than 130 CEOs and human resource directors from 85 regional employers, as well as local leaders in K–12 and postsecondary education. The results of this analysis, as well as a methodology for gathering actionable workforce intelligence, was outlined in a May 2016 report (*Inflection Point: Supply, Demand and the Future of Work in the Pittsburgh Region*)[1] that will be used to focus and guide future workforce development efforts in the region.

Employ Milwaukee, a regional Workforce Investment Board (WIB) in Wisconsin, used a similar approach in developing a more effective regional/countywide workforce intelligence system. The goal of this work was not only to assess the quality and comprehensiveness of the WIB's own LMI, but to develop strategies of regional collaboration around its shared collection and use. The result was a detailed report and set of recommendations for improvement, including the establishment of a formalized shared data repository that draws on industry advisory boards as a source of ongoing employer information and publishes regular workforce intelligence reports. This dynamic databank of quantitative and qualitative LMI will provide workforce stakeholders across the Milwaukee region with a shared understanding of the region's shifting labor needs as they develop collaborative programs and initiatives to meet those changes head-on.

LOCATING AND DEVELOPING VALUABLE EDUCATION AND TRAINING CREDENTIALS

Understanding labor demand only deals with half of the healthy workforce equation—it is equally important to understand the unique education and training resources available locally or regionally. What postsecondary or vocational training institutions exist and what sorts of programs and credentials do they offer? Are these programs geared toward local needs; if not, which needs aren't being met? Are there unique programs or resources that aren't widely available in nearby regions (or even nationally)? Mapping available education and training resources is important not only for meeting local or regional demand, but also for attracting new businesses and industries to a community or region. Unique resources not only sustain economic vitality, they encourage further growth.

Understanding the landscape of local education and training offerings was the primary charge of a group in Kansas City known as GradForceKC, one of 75 local partnerships that participated in the Lumina Foundation's Community Partnerships for Attainment (CPA) initiative. The effort involved conducting an in-depth inventory of all the postsecondary credentials in the region that support skill development in targeted growth industries (previously identified through an LMI analysis conducted by one of GradForceKC's public-sector partners). The inventory identified potential gaps where critical industry skills were not being offered by existing programs by analyzing existing programs and credentials at 41 local postsecondary institutions—including public and private universities/colleges as well as vocational/career training programs. This initial work also established a standard methodology for the education inventory process that has allowed Kansas City partners (GradForceKS as well as college and university partners) to update the inventory regularly to reflect changing offerings and industry needs.[2]

To accurately identify potential gaps, however, an inventory of these types of resources must also address the quality or relevance of the programs and credentials being offered. Are the education and training credentials being offered recognized and valued by industry employers? Is the training and education being offered addressing skills (both soft and technical) that are in demand by employers? If the answer to these questions is no, the inventory should identify which skills are not being offered and whether a new program is necessary to develop them or existing programs should be revised to fill potential gaps.

For example, in Nashville (also a member of the Lumina CPA initiative), a similar regional inventory was conducted of education assets related to two growing industries identified by the Nashville Regional Chamber of Commerce (advanced manufacturing and information technology). The inventory was then tied back to in-demand occupations in each industry. By cross-walking individual education/training programs and credentials to specific occupations based on shared skills and employer-identified educational expectations for those occupations, training gaps or skill shortages could be more directly identified.

MAPPING PATHS FOR WORKERS AND JOBSEEKERS

To this point, our understanding of the talent landscape—which jobs and industries are in demand, the skills they require, and the education and training resources available to address those skills—is still relatively static. While a static approach may say much about the workforce as it currently exists as well as what will be needed to meet potential growth, it says little about how workers can navigate these two realities, moving between existing jobs and preparing for the jobs of the future by accessing education and training. The careers pathways model has gained significant traction by mapping the landscape of job and education/training opportunities within an industry or region and facilitating the effective movement of workers by raising awareness of these opportunities and how they are related.

Developing accurate and effective career pathways involves first understanding how in-demand jobs are related to other opportunities in the workforce based on their shared skills. Identifying the experience, education, training, or credentials necessary to move between these occupations (either by transfer or advancement) allows both employers and workers to better understand how existing resources can facilitate career movement. This dynamic understanding of industries and jobs provides additional insight into the ways in which systems might be better aligned to help facilitate a workforce that is mobile and adaptable.

The true value of the career pathways approach lies not only in its ability to facilitate a better understanding of workforce dynamics, but in its ability to communicate this information to job seekers and workers. As Randall W. Eberts has argued, "the next generation of workforce development programs will need to be smarter in providing information to customers" and "provide customers with [the] data essential to make informed [career] decisions" (Eberts 2015, p. 383). Career pathway tools equip workers with the critical ability to more easily understand and navigate their place within the workforce.

For example, multiple industry-specific career-pathing tools have been developed recently that provide access to actionable information in an easily navigable, interactive, online format. Funded by J.P. Morgan Chase & Co. and developed in partnership with a wide range of stakeholders, the site www.PetrochemWorks.com was created in response to the steady demand for workers in the petrochemical industry in the Houston/Texas Gulf Coast region. Built on LMI validated by industry and education partners, the website matches users to several in-demand industry occupations based on an interests/skills profile. The user is then able to explore how these occupations are related to others in the industry and plan potential career moves, as well as determine the education and skills they will need to make those transitions. Access to this kind of dynamic planning is particularly useful for workers in an industry where demand can change quickly depending on economic circumstances (such as the price of oil). A similar tool focused on the New York City financial services sector, www.BankingOnMyCareer .com, also recently launched.

However, access to the significant design and development resources necessary to build interactive web tools is not necessarily a barrier to developing useful, detailed, or attractive career pathway information and resources. Career pathway work in Tulsa began when the Tulsa Regional Chamber recognized that the region's high employment was not reaching all neighborhoods and members of the community, indicating a need for a better understanding and alignment of the region's workforce and education systems. After working with local employers and other partners to analyze regional growth projections and education assets, career pathways were outlined across nine of the region's target industries. As opposed to the single-industry focus of the prior examples, the purpose of this career-pathing project was to provide workers, employers, and other stakeholders with an understanding of career mobility across the entire regional workforce.[3]

UNIVERSAL ACCESS TO QUALITY EDUCATION

Still, open access to information regarding available career and skill-development opportunities is useful only if workers also have full access to the opportunities themselves. It is important not only for educational resources to be aligned with workforce needs, but also for these resources to be aligned with the needs of all learners. However, postsecondary education (especially higher education) systems have historically been built to primarily serve traditional (full-time, residential, aged 18–22) students, a population that increasingly makes up a shrinking portion of college enrollments (Kiley 2013). Using seat time (credit hours) as the default measure of credential completion not only privileges those with the time and ability to regularly sit in a classroom, it ignores (or even devalues) learning gained outside the classroom (Carnevale and Hanson 2015). For incumbent workers who may need to obtain a degree or pursue additional training to move up in their career, the ability to balance education with their current work through online, distance, or other alternative education options is vital.

Similarly, the ability to incorporate and officially recognize any relevant learning workers have acquired on the job into their education is not only practically useful—potentially allowing them to save time and money they would have otherwise spent on repetitive coursework—it can allow for a more integrated and engaging learning experience. Nontraditional education methods such as prior learning assessment (PLA)—in which prior workplace or life learning is evaluated and assessed for formal credit—provide one important avenue for addressing the needs of adults and working learners. While these models may not be appropriate to apply to all education or training programs, workforce development should include efforts to recalibrate how certain education programs and services are structured. This process also encourages greater communication between education systems and employers around the skills and learning outcomes sought from various programs.

The ECMC Foundation recently provided funding to four different communities (Philadelphia, Miami, Norfolk, and Seattle) to explore methods for better integrating PLA into existing workforce systems. The initiative is building on existing assets in each community, linking and strengthening relationships between local community colleges and WIBs and promoting increased use of PLA. This also involves the development of processes that facilitate the referral of interested WIB clients with significant workplace learning to community colleges where they can receive credit, through PLA, in pursuit of a relevant degree or credential.

Innovate Northeast Florida, a private/public sector initiative aimed at bolstering employment and asset growth in the Jacksonville metropolitan area, provides another example of coordinated efforts to integrate PLA initiatives into regional workforce development. As a part of its newly formed regional strategy to encourage growth in five different target industries (including aircraft and aviation, and health-care information technology), the partnership's "Back to College" campaign is working to encourage adults to pursue STEM (science, technology, engineering, and math) education. This will allow the area to develop a more direct and immediate pipeline to fill in-demand occupations in these target industries. This campaign has included working with education institutions in the region to promote and implement PLA more widely, allowing adults to more easily access postsecondary STEM programs.

FOSTERING LIFELONG LEARNING AND CONTINUOUS SKILL DEVELOPMENT

Inherent in each of the healthy workforce ecosystem components we have addressed so far is a key assumption regarding the relationship between learning and work. That is, for a truly healthy workforce ecosystem, "work and learning must happen simultaneously, not sequentially, allowing for learning to have experiential context and for work to be improved by learning" (Good and Strong 2015, p. 20). Developing a healthy workforce ecosystem is not only a matter of developing the knowledge, programs, and systems necessary to link workforce demand with educational and training resources; it also requires cultivating a culture that values and encourages lifelong, work-based learning.

Even mainstream economic thinkers are beginning to highlight the fundamental importance of lifelong learning in economic and workforce development. The *Economist* (2017) argued that "to remain competitive, and to give low- and high-skilled workers alike the best chance of success, economies need to offer training and career-focused education throughout people's working lives." Likewise, in a recent op-ed, Thomas Friedman advocated for a "permanent education-to-work-to-life-long-skill building pipeline" (Friedman 2017). At one level, the kind of workforce ecosystem we are describing reflects exactly this sort of pipeline: a system of integrated and mutually reinforcing programs, initiatives, and relationships that ensure workers are consistently aware of their place within the workforce as well as the development and advancement opportunities open to them. At a more fundamental level, a healthy ecosystem depends on a strong culture of lifelong learning, in which workers are not only aware of their existing skills and opportunities, but are motivated to constantly seek out the learning, education, and training necessary to refine these skills and develop new ones.

As an example, the Walmart Foundation's Opportunity Initiative is providing $100 million in grants over five years to a range of organizations and local initiatives focused on clarifying and developing opportunities for workers in the retail sector. FHI360 is using this funding to better understand the foundational and transferable skills developed through retail work as well as test communication strategies that communicate this value to incumbent workers and job seekers. This emphasis on helping workers understand how retail jobs—which are often considered "dead-end"—provide skills that can be developed and applied to other, higher-wage, in-demand jobs helps cultivate this cultural value around ongoing skill development and lifelong learning, regardless of industry or workplace context.

Similarly, EmployIndy, the local workforce development board for Marion County, Indiana, is helping workers laid off from a local manufacturer by developing tools and resources that counseling staff can use to show how the skills and competencies the workers have developed in their current positions can help them secure jobs in other local in-demand industries. These tools and resources also point toward local education and training resources that can help develop and refine any additional skills the workers will need to enter another field. Not only does this provide workers with immediate assistance in identifying and securing new jobs, it also highlights the value of understanding how ongoing skill development and learning can mitigate the effects of layoffs and other shifts in local labor markets.

DEVELOPING COLLABORATIVE PARTNERSHIPS FOR GROWTH

The real-world examples provided throughout this chapter—drawn from a wide variety of CAEL projects that have taken place in communities and regions nationwide—illustrate how the various components of a well-aligned, healthy workforce ecosystem build and depend on one another to create an environment that encourages lifelong learning and ongoing talent development around in-demand skills, occupations, and industries. These examples also illustrate the wide variety of stakeholders and partners involved in building the components necessary for a healthy workforce ecosystem. Because the workforce and talent alignment challenges facing communities now are far too complex for any one entity to address on their own, building collaborative partnerships between workforce stakeholders—particularly employers and education partners—in a community or region is critical to cultivating a healthy ecosystem.

Any one of these players—WIBs, economic development organizations (EDOs), community colleges, chambers of commerce, industry associations, state agencies, national organizations, and many others—may fill a variety of roles in developing this ecosystem (or many at the same time), depending on local context. For example, the responsibility and ability to gather and analyze relevant LMI may fall to a community college in one community or region, or be the primary role of an EDO in another. As a result, the development of a formal workforce strategy that outlines not only the roles and responsibilities of each partner, but also the overall goals and measures of success for true system alignment, is critical. Successful examples of these sorts of comprehensive regional workforce development strategies include those developed by the Charleston Metro Chamber of Commerce in 2014 for the Charleston, South Carolina area,[4] and the Centralina Council of Governments' 2012–2017 comprehensive economic development strategy (CEDS) for the Charlotte, North Carolina region.[5]

Even more important, however, is the ongoing process of fostering mutually beneficial, collaborative relationships between partners. This kind of relationship-building process is difficult to prescribe, as much of it depends on local history, the unique mix of relevant institutions within a community, and their power dynamics. However, we have often found that one or more partners taking on the central role of conveners or lead intermediaries is often useful for mitigating and coordinating these partnerships. Increasing opportunities for communication and collaboration between all stakeholders (through regional industry and education roundtables, for example) is also beneficial.

The model of sector partnerships—in which employer, education, and workforce stakeholders convene regularly to address ongoing workforce challenges in a specific industry—is at least one emerging model for developing collaborative workforce initiatives that has seen significant success (Holzer 2015). Recent work by the Iowa Department of Education to coordinate sector partnership efforts across the state provides testimony to this success. A focus on addressing long-term industry workforce challenges through better alignment of educational resources has led to more targeted information sharing and collaboration between employers and education institutions (Woolsey and Groves 2013). In the case of Iowa, this has facilitated the development of statewide career pathways (in the information technology and energy industries) with input and validation from a broad range of employers and industry associations. These partnerships also allow for coordinated, statewide strategies to deploy these pathways to a range of users and audiences.

CONCLUSION: INVESTING IN A WORKFORCE ECOSYSTEM APPROACH

Moving toward broad-based collaborative models for building comprehensive workforce ecosystems entails a necessary shift in how workforce development efforts are funded. Investing in cultivating a healthy workforce ecosystem requires investing in more than just the federally funded workforce system. Wide ranging public and private investments in regional workforce development must become the new normal. Not only does this mean moving to a shared federal, state, and local approach to public workforce funding (Good and Strong 2015), it also means engaging local employers, industry associations, chambers of commerce, and other private entities to invest in workforce development efforts.

Developing a healthy workforce ecosystem also requires investing in public policy goals that foster each of its components. This includes developing increased incentives for regional thinking among local governments (such as increased funds for regional councils of government or workforce intermediaries), as well as incentives to encourage employer investment in employee training and development. Implementing federal and state educational policies that allow for the development of more innovative and accessible instructional and learning approaches such as PLA (including the ability for students to use federal aid, such as Pell grants, to pay for these types of programs) will also be important. Finally, revitalizing work-based learning approaches (such as apprenticeship programs) can help foster the kinds of attitudes toward lifelong learning and skill development that allow workforce ecosystems to thrive.

More than shifts in funding and policy, however, a workforce ecosystem approach requires a fundamental shift in how we think about workforce development in the United States. Workforce development must be seen as an ongoing process, not a finished project. It is a constantly renewing network of collaborative relationships between invested stakeholders rather than just a series of discrete and individually targeted programs. Workforce development must constantly evolve to respond to the challenges of new economic realities, with constant realignment between shifting labor demand and ever-changing educational resources. Building healthy workforce ecosystems depends more on having the right players at the table than following a prescribed plan. Finally, it means integrating workforce development into all facets of our professional life and cultivating a culture of lifelong learning that sees ongoing skill development and career navigation as the nature of work, rather than as stages along the journey.

Notes

1. http://p4pittsburgh.org/pages/inflection-point-supply-demand-and-the-future-of -work-in-the-pittsburgh-region (accessed May 3, 2018).
2. The original inventory can be found here: http://www.kcworkforce.org/Assets/ reports/EducationAssetInventory2015.pdf. The most recent (updated) version can be found here: http://www.kcworkforce.com/EAI.pdfhttp://www.kcworkforce .com/EAI.pdf (accessed May 3, 2018).
3. https://tulsachamber.com/careerpathways (accessed May 3, 2018).
4. https://www.charlestonchamber.net/talent-demand-analysis-results (accessed May 3, 2018).
5. http://www.centralinaedc.org/CEDS.php (accessed May 3, 2018).

References

Abraham, Katharine G. 2015. "Is Skill Mismatch Impeding U.S. Economic Recovery?" *ILR Review* 68(2): 291–313.

Cappelli, Peter H. 2015. "Skill Gaps, Skill Shortages, and Skill Mismatches." *ILR Review* 68(2): 251–290.

Carnevale, Anthony P., and Andrew R. Hanson. 2015. "Learn and Earn: Connecting Education to Careers in the 21st Century." In *Transforming U.S. Workforce Development Policies for the 21st Century*, Carl Van Horn, Tammy Edwards, and Todd Greene, eds. Kalamazoo, MI: W.E. Upjohn Institute for Employment Research, pp. 77–103.

Carnevale, Anthony P., Tamara Jayasundera, and Artem Gulish. 2016. *America's Divided Recovery: College Haves and Have-Nots*. Washington, DC: Georgetown University, Center on Education and the Workforce.

Dunkelberg, William C., and Holly Wade. 2017. *NFIB Small Business Economic Trends Monthly Report: June 2017*. Washington DC: National Federation of Independent Business Research Foundation. http://www.nfib.com/ asscts/SBET-Junc-2017.pdf (acccsscd July 31, 2017).

Eberts, Randall W. 2015. "Toward a More Intelligent Workforce Development System." In *Transforming U.S. Workforce Development Policies for the 21st Century*, Carl Van Horn, Tammy Edwards, and Todd Greene, eds. Kalamazoo, MI: W.E. Upjohn Institute for Employment Research, pp. 383–410.

Economist. 2017. "Lifelong Learning Is Becoming an Economic Imperative." January 12. https://www.economist.com/news/special -report/21714169-technological-change-demands-stronger-and -more-continuous-connections-between-education (accessed January 25, 2017).

Friedman, Thomas L. 2017. "Smart Approaches, Not Strong-Arm Tactics, to Jobs." *New York Times,* January 25. https://www.nytimes.com/2017/01/25/opinion/smart-approaches-not-strong-arm-tactics-to-jobs.html   (accessed January 25, 2017).

Good, Larry, and Ed Strong. 2015. "Reimagining Workforce Policy in the United States." In *Transforming U.S. Workforce Development Policies for the 21st Century*, Carl Van Horn, Tammy Edwards, and Todd Greene, eds. Kalamazoo, MI: W.E. Upjohn Institute for Employment Research, pp. 13–43.

Holzer, Harry J. 2015. "The U.S. Approach to Higher Education and Workforce Development: Separate Parts in Search of a Whole." In *Transforming U.S. Workforce Development Policies for the 21st Century*, Carl Van Horn, Tammy Edwards, and Todd Greene, eds. Kalamazoo, MI: W.E. Upjohn Institute for Employment Research, pp. 105–127.

Kiley, Kevin. 2013. "The Pupil Cliff." *Inside Higher Ed*, January 11. https://www.insidehighered.com/news/2013/01/11/wiche-report-highlights-decline-high-school-graduates-and-growing-diversity (accessed July 31, 2017).

Pew Research Center. 2016. *The State of American Jobs*. Washington, DC: Pew Research Center. http://www.pewsocialtrends.org/2016/10/06/the-state-of-american-jobs/ (accessed July 21, 2017).

U.S. Bureau of Labor Statistics. 2017. *Job Openings and Labor Turnover–April 2017*. Washington, DC: U.S. Bureau of Labor Statistics. https://www.bls.gov/news.release/archives/jolts_06062017.pdf (accessed July 21, 2017).

Woolsey, Lindsey, and Garrett Groves. 2013. "State Sector Strategies Coming of Age: Implications for State Workforce Policymakers." Washington, DC: National Governors Association Center for Best Practices. fhttps://www.nga.org/files/live/sites/NGA/files/pdf/2013/1301NGASSSReport.pdf (accessed July 31, 2017).

26
Examining Spatial Mismatch and Mobility in the Workforce System

Raphael Bostic
Ann Carpenter

In the past few decades, income and wealth disparities in the United States have risen to unprecedented levels. Recent research has shown that economic mobility, defined here as one being able to earn more than previous generations of one's family, is the exception rather than the rule, particularly for individuals raised in the most disadvantaged zip codes in the country (Chetty et al. 2014). There are various explanations for this lack of economic mobility, including factors such as inadequate spending on social safety net programs and childhood exposure to the negative impacts of poverty.

Central to the notion of mobility is the idea that one should be able to gain access to higher-paying jobs. Yet barriers exist that make this difficult for some families. One such barrier has been the spatial pattern of urban development in the United States in the latter half of the twentieth century. This development resulted in sprawling, automobile-dependent metropolitan areas. Many employment centers, particularly retail and other services, moved to the more affluent suburbs.

The suburbanization of employment introduced the notion of "spatial mismatch," which is a phenomenon in which housing options affordable to lower-income families are physically distant from low- and middle-skill jobs. Spatial mismatch is most notable in metropolitan regions that feature greater housing segregation and less connectivity between urban housing and suburban employment centers, in part arising from there being more limited transportation options (Ihlanfeldt and Sjoquist 1998). A national survey of workers in 28 large metropolitan areas found that this imbalance was most pronounced in "hot" housing markets such as New York, Boston, Atlanta, and San Francisco (Cervero et al. 2006).

Spatial mismatch is important to the extent that prospective workers lack the means to get to the now-distant jobs. Transportation access and costs thus become important considerations, and the less extensive transportation networks that exist in many large metropolitan areas often mean that spatial mismatch equals an inability for lower-income workers to physically access promising jobs. The lack of accessibility of these job opportunities restricts job seekers' ability to identify openings and secure and maintain employment (Grengs 2010; Ihlanfeldt and Sjoquist 1998; Taylor and Ong 1995). In terms of equity outcomes, more compact, less sprawling areas with shorter commutes have been shown to produce higher rates of upward economic mobility, a finding that indicates spatial mismatch may also influence a child's later ability to achieve career success (Chetty et al. 2014).

The lack of connectivity between affordable housing and employment centers has a significant impact on regional economic development, especially in those metropolitan areas where public transit is less robust. In this chapter, we seek to understand whether a similar spatial mismatch pattern is evident between housing and workforce development opportunities, with a particular focus on data from the Atlanta metropolitan area. As a backdrop, evidence has found that the spatial mismatch of housing and jobs is a problem in Atlanta. Studies by the Brookings Institution highlighted the lack of transit access to jobs and found that Atlanta ranks 91st out of the largest 100 metropolitan areas in terms of the share of jobs accessible by public transit, considering the geographical breadth of its service coverage and its service schedule (Tomer 2012). Only 21.7 percent of jobs in the Atlanta metropolitan area are accessible within 90 minutes by transit, and only 3.4 percent of them are accessible within 45 minutes (Tomer et al. 2011). The situation is worse for jobs in the suburbs, where only 17.4 percent are accessible within 90 minutes by transit. And it is even quite low for jobs in the center city, where the percentage is 33.2 (Tomer et al.).

The existing housing/jobs spatial landscape makes the question of whether there is a spatial mismatch between housing and workforce development providers all the more important. If many lower-income and lower-wage families have very limited access to both jobs and training to make them competitive for jobs, then the possibility of economic mobility must be quite small. Understanding the spatial mismatch challenge in the context of workforce development is thus an important element for assessing the economic isolation of lower-income families and the broader health and inclusion of the regional economy.

This question is also important because the economic turmoil of the last decade has shed light on the need for workers to develop specialized skills in a transitional economy. Workers that lack these skills must acquire them if they are to have any hope of economic mobility. Workforce development programs can be a vehicle for this skill acquisition, which makes the issue of spatial mismatch as a potential barrier to the effectiveness of these programs relevant.

BACKGROUND

Evidence has shown that workforce development programs can positively affect employment outcomes and earnings among target populations. For example, evaluations of Cincinnati's workforce development system found that programs collectively increased regional earnings by $7.3 million per year and amounted to net benefits to employers of nearly $5,000 per employee because of higher retention and reduced recruitment costs (DiMario, Elvery, and Spence 2016).[1] Workforce development providers and intermediaries often serve as a pipeline to employment and provide disadvantaged community members with access to the social networks that underpin a knowledge-based economy (Chapple 2006). At a regional level, the development of human capital, including workforce skill levels, is also seen as important for economic growth (Glaeser and Saiz 2003) and provides opportunities for greater social inclusion and economic diversification (Lowe 2007).

Previous work by the Atlanta Fed and its partners has shown that transportation challenges, if not spatial mismatch, exist and have implications for workforce development program outcomes. According to a survey of 204 workforce development providers and intermediaries in the 10-county area served by the Atlanta Regional Commission, the second most significant barrier to utilizing services was lack of transportation options to access services, just after lack of knowledge of available services (Metro Atlanta eXchange for Workforce Solutions 2014). This was the case despite the fact that 47 percent of workforce development providers offer transportation subsidies as part of their

support services (Rich 2002). More than 7 out of 10 providers and intermediaries responded that transportation limitations prevent prospective
clients from accessing training as part of the Metro Atlanta eXchange
for Workforce Solutions (MAX) survey (see Figure 26.1). Of these, 28
percent felt it was the top barrier based on their experience in the region.

In a recent study on regional workforce development alignment
(Andreason and Carpenter 2015), access to transportation was also
raised as an issue during interviews with representatives of various
regional workforce development initiatives. For example, in Chicago,
public transportation day passes were critical for clients needing to
access training and work sites. When the Chicago Transit Authority
deployed a new credit card–based fare system, workforce development
providers were no longer able to distribute one-day transit subsidies,
which, until an administrative solution was found, had a significant
negative impact on the population served.

Concerns about spatial mismatch for workforce development programs are not new, and programs have been developed that specifically
provide transportation options to job seekers and lower-income workers to help them access workforce development programs. One such

**Figure 26.1 Barriers to Accessing Workforce Development Resources in
Metropolitan Atlanta**

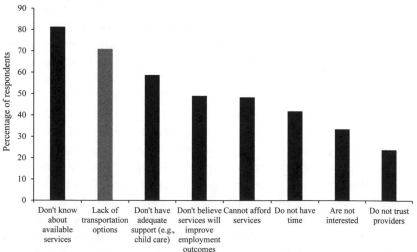

SOURCE: MAX survey of metropolitan Atlanta workforce development providers
(2014).

program at the federal level is the Jobs Access to Reverse Commuting (JARC) program.[2] JARC, which has been discontinued, was a U.S. Department of Transportation program funded by the 1998 Transportation Equity Act for the 21st Century. Designed to address access to jobs, particularly in suburban areas, it provided flexible transportation funds at a 50 percent match to states and metropolitan areas. Access to workforce development was a popular use of the funds. A study of clients served under California's JARC program found that the subjects were most interested in specialized transportation services for children and for accessing job training sites (Cervero and Tsai 2003).

Thakuriah et al. (2005) report on the findings from an analysis of JARC programs in 23 small and large metropolitan and rural areas. The analysis found that JARC transportation options included both fixed-route (for example, bus and rail) and demand-responsive (for example, paratransit and van pool) modes. The authors found that many demand-responsive services were attached to job training services, such as the King County Workforce Training Center in Seattle. The study included a survey of riders across these 23 metropolitan areas, which revealed that JARC users tend to have lower incomes than other commuters and that approximately 10 percent use JARC services for job-training or job-seeking purposes. Two important findings emerged from this work. First, almost two-thirds of survey respondents reported that they would not have been able to access their destination without the service, indicating that JARC opened up opportunities not just for employment but also for workforce development. Second, many users experienced higher earnings because of the services, and this was particularly true in large metropolitan areas.

Another study— this one focused on California—found that JARC activities included schedule extensions, new routes, user-side assistance, new shuttles, low-interest loans, and route extensions (Cervero and Tsai 2003). Specific examples included San Diego's All Congregation Together Comlink shuttle program and Santa Cruz's Connections Shuttle, both of which provided access to job training centers as part of their mission to connect residents with job opportunities. Twelve percent of trips taken on the Connections Shuttle were to job training centers. The Connections Shuttle also trained and employed job seekers to become drivers, thereby creating 100 jobs in the field over a short period. While the program gave precedence to public transportation projects, it also funded other modes, including private automobiles. For example, a San Mateo County program offered low-interest loans to purchase a car, which led to a 26 percent increase in attendance at job-related educational activities among participants.

ANALYSIS OF ATLANTA REGIONAL WORKFORCE DEVELOPMENT PROVIDERS AND INTERMEDIARIES

This analysis is an extension of the previous analysis of Atlanta's MAX program to help provide a better understanding of the landscape of workforce development providers at the regional level, with an eye toward the question of whether there is a spatial mismatch problem. The possibility of spatial mismatch in Atlanta is credible, given its sprawling urban footprint and economy. Atlanta's metropolitan region spans 29 counties and includes 135 primary cities and towns (Metro Atlanta Chamber 2018).[3]

As part of the regional MAX initiative, funders including the state, regional workforce investment boards, and foundations were asked to provide lists of the workforce programs that they fund in the 10-county metropolitan Atlanta region. Their combined input identified 536 physical locations, which were geocoded by the address they were operating from in December 2014. The compiled list included providers and intermediaries from the academic, nonprofit, and for-profit sectors. Examples include One-Stop Career Centers, technical colleges, private trade academies such as cosmetology schools, mission-oriented nonprofits such as Goodwill, high schools that offer career pathway programs, county agencies such as departments of family and children services, and many others. Each of the 536 offices received the MAX survey, and 204 (38 percent) responded.

We analyzed this database of intermediaries and providers to see if there was evidence of spatial mismatch. Based on Atlanta regional transit data on the location of stops, a majority of the offices (63 percent) were within a one-quarter-mile to one-mile radius of a transit stop.[4] As shown in Map 26.1, transit coverage is most dense in Fulton, DeKalb, and Clayton Counties. These three counties are served by the largest transit system in the region, the Metropolitan Atlanta Rapid Transit

Map 26.1 Atlanta Workforce Development Offices and Transit Coverage

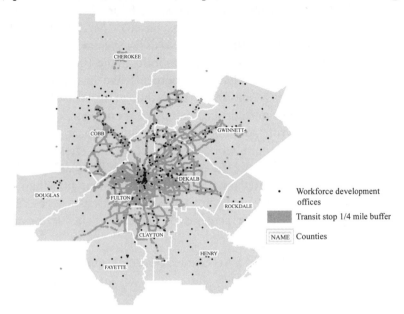

SOURCES: MAX survey of workforce development providers (2014); Atlanta Regional Commission General Transit Feed Specification (GTFS) data (2016).

Authority (MARTA). Three additional counties, Cherokee, Cobb, and Gwinnett, provide bus service independent from MARTA, with limited local service and links to commuter stations in the urban core areas of downtown and midtown Atlanta. The remaining four counties (Douglas, Fayette, Henry, and Rockdale) have no countywide public transportation system but have limited regional commuter bus service. As only three counties opted into the MARTA system, clearly regional transportation coverage and coordination is lacking.

This result—that most workforce development providers are located close to transit—is somewhat misleading, however. Although most workforce development offices are accessible from a transit stop, Atlanta's transit system is largely designed for downtown commuters; cross-regional trips (e.g., trips from southern suburban communities to northern suburban employment centers) can be incredibly time consuming. For example, a trip originating within a quarter-mile of a MARTA transit stop in south Clayton County and ending at one of the northernmost workforce development providers within a quarter-mile of a MARTA station would take between 2 hours 21 minutes and 2 hours 40 minutes to travel about 40 miles, based on MARTA's trip planner (see Map 26.2). Trips outside the MARTA system may take even longer or be impossible without an automobile. In the 10-county region, 1,658,801 working-age residents (50 percent) live in a census block group that lacks at least one transit stop, indicating lack of access to transit. These residents must depend on more expensive modes of transportation such as private automobiles, taxis, and rideshare services.

Not surprisingly, more workforce development sites in Fulton, DeKalb, and Clayton Counties (all part of the MARTA system, as stated above) are within a quarter-mile to a mile of a transit stop than sites in counties that have regional transit links or no transit access at all (see Figure 26.2). A small percentage (21 percent) of sites in the coun-

Map 26.2 Example of Transit-Accessible, Time-Consuming Trip from Home to Training Site

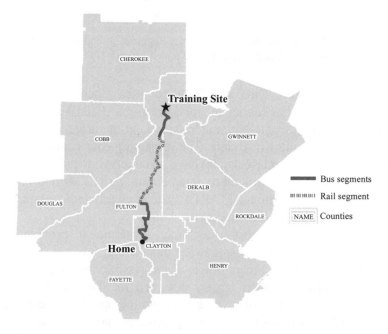

SOURCE: Fastest route from Hibiscus Court, Riverdale, Georgia, to Sun Valley Drive, Roswell, Georgia, determined using MARTA's trip planner (http://www.itsmarta.com/planatrip.aspx).

Figure 26.2 Share of Workforce Development Sites Accessible by Transit in Metro Atlanta Counties

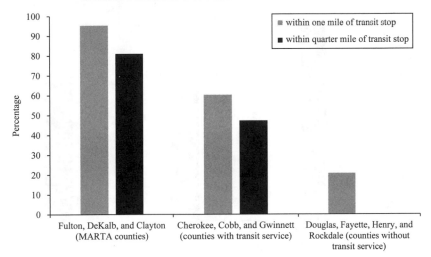

SOURCE: MAX survey of workforce development providers (2014); Atlanta Regional Commission GTFS data (2016).

ties without public transit systems are within one mile of a transit stop because of the presence of a state-run Xpress commuter bus stop, which serves the central business district and connects with MARTA. None of these sites are within a more walkable one-quarter-mile distance of a transit stop, and none of them offer intercounty connectivity or connectivity to adjacent suburban counties.

Poverty and unemployment rates are highest in the core counties of Fulton, DeKalb, and Clayton, the counties forming the MARTA system (see Figure 26.3). However, although the unemployment and poverty rates in the suburban counties with transit service are lower than in those without transit service, the unemployment and poverty rates in those counties are still significant. Furthermore, a recent analysis of the region by the United Way of Greater Atlanta shows that there are pockets of need in every county in the Atlanta Regional Commission's coverage area except one (United Way of Greater Atlanta 2017). This reality makes the case that there is an important need for greater accessibility to workforce development sites in counties without transit services.

While the above analysis does not analyze where particular populations served reside in relation to workforce development locations, the

Figure 26.3 Unemployment and Poverty Rates of Metro Atlanta Counties

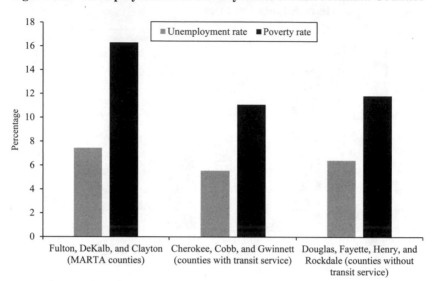

SOURCE: U.S. Census Bureau's American Community Survey five-year median household income estimates (2014).

map and descriptive statistics above suggest that many Atlanta households may indeed find it difficult to reach workforce development services from their respective residences. Nearly 200 offices (37 percent) are not located within a quarter-mile of a transit stop, and even those that are may not be accessible to a large number of households within a reasonable travel time. Furthermore, residents throughout the region may have trouble taking advantage of services provided by workforce development providers in outlying counties without transit service, because there are very limited transportation options for accessing these services.

DISCUSSION

The spatial mismatch between affordable housing and jobs has long been a concern for policymakers interested in promoting economic mobility, because mobility will be considerably more difficult for families that have challenges getting to good jobs. In this chapter, we have looked at the related issue of the spatial mismatch of housing and workforce development programs, which can also be important if prospective workers and lower-income people need to acquire skills in order to qualify for available jobs. Looking at Atlanta, we find evidence suggesting that spatial mismatch between housing and workforce development providers may be a significant problem for many Atlanta lower-income families. Our research, like others, highlights the important role that transportation networks, particularly the existence of public transit options, can play.

We close by offering possible strategies for mitigating the impact of spatial mismatch. One possible approach is to invest more in infrastructure, including transit services and affordable housing, as research has shown that this can increase workforce development participation and improve outcomes for job seekers (St.Clair 2017). In Atlanta, the recent addition of Clayton County, a relatively lower-income area of the region, to the MARTA system represents progress in this context. In 2001, Clayton County began operating an independent transit authority known as C-Tran, but it consistently required significant state subsidy. Without a permanent revenue stream, the service was discontinued in 2009, and transit-dependent residents were forced to move or commute on foot (often several miles) in order to keep their jobs (Karner and Duckworth 2017). In 2014, recognizing the significant economic disadvantage to its population, Clayton County held a ballot initiative to join MARTA, which voters approved by a three-to-one margin.[5] Clayton thus became the first new county to join MARTA since 1971.

Another approach to alleviating the spatial mismatch problem involves place-based economic and workforce development strategies that focus on employers located closer to communities than the often-distant suburban jobs. Local employers and industries could commit to training and employing the resident population, thereby providing critical opportunities for employment, particularly in underserved communities, and potentially increasing a firm's employee reliability and retention. Such efforts require relationship building between employers, residents, and often intermediaries. An example of this is Atlanta's Aerotropolis project, which aims to build a bridge between the airport, Atlanta's economic engine, and the lower-income, predominately African American neighborhoods surrounding it.

A third strategy is for workforce development intermediaries and providers to locate their services closer to the populations they are meant to serve or in more transit-accessible locations. This could involve relocating offices or providing satellite services near low-income housing or in central, transit-adjacent locations. Geographic information systems could be used to identify areas with high unemployment and then overlay them with transportation-system networks to ensure that new outreach facilities are easily accessible (Mabe, Powell, and Ruder 2015). Furthermore, better coordination of the workforce development, housing, and transportation sectors at the federal, state, and regional levels would allow agencies to leverage public funding and increase access to services for those that need them most. For example, federal programs such as the U.S. Department of Housing and Urban Development's Family Self-Sufficiency Program help coordinate job training for recipients of housing assistance in order to reduce reliance on subsidies. These facilities are often located in or close to communities that suffer from spatial mismatch and can potentially be leveraged by other workforce development providers.

Many programs have also focused on providing transportation subsidies to those seeking job training. The now defunct JARC program, mentioned above, was successful in providing access to workforce development in suburban areas through flexible funds that were adaptable to the needs and existing infrastructure of the area. Various studies have called for greater deployment of support services, including transportation and child care subsidies, in the provision of workforce development programs (Weigensberg et al. 2012). However, as noted in the Atlanta example, transit subsidies are often not fully available, and, perhaps more importantly, transit systems may be ill suited for seekers of job training. Indeed, some training programs have even required availability of a private vehicle to increase trainee attendance (Bell and Orr 2002). Some experts have suggested that private automobile ownership is the most effective solution for the poor to navigate a sprawling metropolitan environment (Giloth 2000). This indicates that the optimal strategy for using flexible funds to help improve workforce development outcomes might be tied to maximum flexibility in transportation. The city could achieve this by promoting access to private automobile ownership and usage in addition to providing transit subsidies, van pools, and other modes of group transportation.

Previous Atlanta Fed analysis found that workforce development program success is inhibited by system fragmentation, competition, and redundancies (Andreason and Carpenter 2015). Atlanta's MAX initiative was established to combat this tendency and coordinate resources across the system. MAX participants have discussed transit expansion options, realigned their training to better meet employer needs, and jointly implemented an online mapping portal to increase the visibility and connectivity between providers and their constituencies. The MAX portal could be further enhanced by coordinating relocation decisions and by including transportation access information as well as transit routes and trip planners. On balance, better regional coordination of and collaboration between providers has the potential to reduce transportation burdens and provide support services at scale.

Finally, new transportation technologies such as ride-sharing apps and self-driving or autonomous vehicles may provide future mobility solutions for workforce development participants. While these technologies are currently out of reach for many lower-income individuals, ride-share services have begun to explore partnerships with transit agencies and offer fixed-route and fixed-fare trips at reduced costs. As technologies improve, these modes may become increasingly affordable and accessible.

Our analysis constitutes only an initial examination of the role of potential spatial mismatch in the workforce development ecosystem in Atlanta. Policymakers and practitioners would benefit from the use of individual-level survey and administrative data on workforce development programs that could help provide a deeper understanding of the scope of the issue and more nuanced potential regional solutions. However, the role of transportation services generally and public transit specifically in workforce development should not be discounted. In order to ensure economic mobility at the regional level, job seekers must be able to physically access workforce development services.

As a final comment, we believe that the findings here are relevant for and can likely be generalized for metropolitan areas beyond Atlanta. Given that Atlanta's spatial layout resembles that of many southern and western cities in the United States that have experienced considerable growth since the mid-twentieth century, the patterns seen in Atlanta could signal similar challenges elsewhere. The analysis here and the prescriptions we offer may be relevant for a large number of other metropolitan areas, such as Charlotte, Houston, and Nashville. We encourage policymakers in these places and others like them to take time to understand the spatial mismatch realities regarding both jobs and workforce development providers and then consider implementing strategies to reduce the adverse effects of this spatial mismatch. Only with such an approach will economic mobility—and broader economic vitality—become more widespread.

Notes

1. While studies have shown mixed results with respect to certain federal workforce development programs (Doolittle et al. 1993), at an individual level, even the perception of a greater skill level affects employment participation (Blumenberg 2002).
2. Other programs include the U.S. Department of Transportation's Ladders of Opportunity Initiatives and the U.S. Department Housing and Urban Development's Welfare to Work and Bridges to Work demonstration programs.
3. See a map of the 29-county metropolitan statistical area of Atlanta at https://dch .georgia.gov/sites/dch.georgia.gov/files/Atlanta%20Service%20Area%20Map .pdf (accessed August 22, 2018).
4. Data on transit stops were obtained from the Atlanta Regional Commission Open Data and Mapping Group platform at http://opendata.atlantaregional.com/ datasets/transit-stops-2016 (accessed August 23, 2018).
5. The measure called for a one-penny increase in the sales-tax rate.

References

Andreason, Stuart, and Ann Carpenter. 2015. *Fragmentation in Workforce Development and Efforts to Coordinate Regional Workforce Development Systems: A Case Study of Challenges in Atlanta and Models for Regional Cooperation from across the Country.* Community and Economic Development Discussion Paper No. 2015-2. Atlanta, GA: Federal Reserve Bank of Atlanta.

Bell, Stephen H., and Larry L. Orr. 2002. "Screening (and Creaming?) Applicants to Job Training Programs: The AFDC Homemaker–Home Health Aide Demonstrations." *Labour Economics* 9(2): 279–301.

Blumenberg, Evelyn. 2002. "On the Way to Work: Welfare Participants and Barriers to Employment." *Economic Development Quarterly* 16(4): 314–325.

Cervero, Robert, Karen Chapple, John Landis, Martin Wachs, Michael Duncan, Patricia Lynn Scholl, and Evelyn Blumenberg. 2006. *Making Do: How Working Families in Seven U.S. Metropolitan Areas Trade Off Housing Costs and Commuting Times*. Berkeley: University of California, Berkeley, Institute of Transportation Studies.

Cervero, Robert, and Yu-Hsin Tsai. 2003. "Job Access and Reverse Commuting Initiatives in California: Review and Assessment." *Transportation Research Record* 1859(1): 78–86.

Chapple, Karen. 2006. "Networks to Nerdistan: The Role of Labor Market Intermediaries in the Entry-Level IT Labor Market." *International Journal of Urban and Regional Research* 30(3): 548–563.

Chetty, Raj, Nathaniel Hendren, Patrick Kline, and Emmanuel Saez. 2014. "Where Is the Land of Opportunity? The Geography of Intergenerational Mobility in the United States." *Quarterly Journal of Economics* 129(4): 1553–1623.

DiMario, Sharron M., Joel A. Elvery, and Christopher Spence. 2016. "Employers' Investment in Career Pathways Improves Retention and Enhances Employee Engagement in Cincinnati, Ohio." In *Developing Career-Based Training*, Stuart Andreason, ed. Atlanta, GA: Federal Reserve Bank of Atlanta, pp. 23–29.

Doolittle, Fred, Steve Bell, Howard Bloom, George Cave, James Kemple, Larry Orr, Linda Traeger, and John Wallace. 1993. *A Summary of the Design and Implementation of the National JTPA Study*. New York: Manpower Demonstration Research Corporation.

Giloth, Robert P. 2000. "Learning from the Field: Economic Growth and Workforce Development in the 1990s." *Economic Development Quarterly* 14(4): 340–359.

Glaeser, Edward L., and Albert Saiz. 2003. "The Rise of the Skilled City." NBER Working Paper No. 10191. Cambridge, MA: National Bureau of Economic Research.

Grengs, Joe. 2010. "Job Accessibility and the Modal Mismatch in Detroit." *Journal of Transport Geography* 18(1): 42–54.

Ihlanfeldt, Keith R., and David L. Sjoquist. 1998. "The Spatial Mismatch Hypothesis: A Review of Recent Studies and Their Implications for Welfare Reform." *Housing Policy Debate* 9(4): 849–892.

Karner, Alexander, and Richard Duckworth. 2017. *Opportunity Deferred: Race, Transportation, and the Future of Metropolitan Atlanta*. Atlanta, GA: Partnership for Southern Equity.

Lowe, Nichola J. 2007. "Job Creation and the Knowledge Economy: Lessons from North Carolina's Life Science Manufacturing Initiative." *Economic Development Quarterly* 21(4): 339–353.

Mabe, William, Scott Powell, and Alex Ruder. 2015. "Doing More with Less:

Leveraging Advances in Data Science to Support an Intelligent Workforce System." In *Transforming U.S. Workforce Development Policies for the 21st Century*, Carl Van Horn, Tammy Edwards, and Todd Greene, eds. Kalamazoo, MI: W.E. Upjohn Institute for Employment Research, pp. 441–469.

Metro Atlanta Chamber. 2018. *29-County Metropolitan Statistica Area (MSA)*. Atlanta, GA: Metro Atlanta Chamber. https://dch.georgia.gov/sites/dch .georgia.gov/files/Atlanta%20Service%20Area%20Map.pdf (accessed March 13, 2018).

Metro Atlanta eXchange for Workforce Solutions. 2014. *MAX Survey Data*. Atlanta, GA: Metro Atlanta eXchange for Workforce Solutions.

Rich, Michael J. 2002. *Workforce Development in the Atlanta Metropolitan Region: Findings from a Survey of Provider Organizations*. Report prepared for the United Way of Metropolitan Atlanta, Workforce Development Task Force. Atlanta, GA: United Way of Metropolitan Atlanta.

St.Clair, Noelle. 2017. *Investing in America's Workforce: Report on Workforce Development Needs and Opportunities*. Washington, DC: Federal Reserve System.

Taylor, Brian D., and Paul M. Ong. 1995. "Spatial Mismatch or Automobile Mismatch? An Examination of Race, Residence, and Commuting in U.S. Metropolitan Areas." *Urban Studies* 32(9): 1453–1473.

Thakuriah, Piyushimita Vonu, P. Sriraj, Siim Sööt, Yihua Liao, and Joost Berman. 2005. "Activity and Travel Changes of Users of Job Access Transportation Service: Analysis of a User Survey." *Transportation Research Record* 1927(1): 55–62.

Tomer, Adie. 2012. *Where the Jobs Are: Employer Access to Labor by Transit*. Washington, DC: Brookings Institution.

Tomer, Adie, Elizabeth Kneebone, Robert Puentes, and Alan Berube. 2011. *Missed Opportunity: Transit and Jobs in Metropolitan America*. Washington, DC: Brookings Institution.

United Way of Greater Atlanta. 2017. *Child Well-Being Overview*. Atlanta, GA: United Way of Greater Atlanta. https://www.unitedwayatlanta.org/ child-well-being-overview/ (accessed March 12, 2018).

Weigensberg, Elizabeth, Colleen Schlecht, Faith Laken, Robert Goerge, Matthew Stagner, Peter Ballard, and Jan DeCoursey. 2012. *Inside the Black Box: What Makes Workforce Development Programs Successful?* Chicago: Chapin Hall at the University of Chicago.

Appendix
Investing in America's Workforce

Report on Workforce Development
Needs and Opportunities

Noelle St.Clair

This report was originally published in 2017 as part of the Investing in America's Workforce Initiative.

This report is the result of a collaborative effort of the community development departments across the Federal Reserve System, including the 12 regional Reserve Banks and the Board of Governors. The Federal Reserve community development function would like to thank the attendees of all the regional listening sessions who generously shared their time, knowledge, and insights to inform this research. We would also like to acknowledge the System working group responsible for hosting the regional listening sessions:

Ruben Ahedo, Federal Reserve Bank of Dallas
Stuart Andreason, Federal Reserve Bank of Atlanta
Jeanne Milliken Bonds, Federal Reserve Bank of Richmond
Tony Davis, Federal Reserve Bank of New York
Peter Dolkart, Federal Reserve Bank of Richmond
Michael Eggleston, Federal Reserve Bank of St. Louis
Kyle Fee, Federal Reserve Bank of Cleveland
Jen Giovannitti, Federal Reserve Bank of Richmond
Rob Grunewald, Federal Reserve Bank of Minneapolis
Jason Keller, Federal Reserve Bank of Chicago
Whitney Mancuso, Federal Reserve Bank of Atlanta
Lupe Mares, Federal Reserve Bank of Dallas
Craig Nolte, Federal Reserve Bank of San Francisco
Andrew Pack, Federal Reserve Bank of St. Louis
Carmen Panacopoulos, Federal Reserve Bank of Boston
Edison Reyes, Federal Reserve Bank of New York

Chris Shannon, Federal Reserve Bank of Boston
Steven Shepelwich, Federal Reserve Bank of Kansas City
Noelle St.Clair, Federal Reserve Bank of Philadelphia

Thank you to Eileen Divringi and Asia King who supported this research through transcript coding and Keith Wardrip and Theresa Y. Singleton for their guidance. Also, thank you to the Federal Reserve Bank of Richmond for editing, design and printing. Lastly, thank you to Todd Greene for his leadership of this Federal Reserve System initiative.

The views expressed in this report are those of the listening session participants, as summarized by the author, and do not necessarily reflect the views of the Federal Reserve Bank of Philadelphia or the Federal Reserve System.

INTRODUCTION

Why Invest in Workforce Development?

The dual mandate of the Federal Reserve is to foster economic conditions that achieve both stable prices and maximum employment. In April 2017, the U.S. Department of Labor reported six million job openings, the highest recorded level since it started tracking in 2000. Yet, the share of Americans participating in the labor force is trending near a four-decade low.[1] Furthermore, a significant share of companies report difficulties filling job openings (ManpowerGroup 2016). These labor market challenges negatively impact workers, employers, and the broader economy as a whole. In a recent speech, Federal Reserve Chair Janet Yellen stated that "significant job market changes in recent years, brought about by global competition and technological advances—and the new shifting skills these changes demand—make workforce development more important than ever" (Yellen 2017).

The U.S. can reach its economic potential only through strong alignment between employer needs and a skilled workforce. Despite an improving economy and numerous programs, significant labor market challenges persist for both workers and employers. Reframing and reimagining workforce development efforts as investments—not just social services—can lead to larger-scale solutions and more accountable outcomes. Investing in workforce development can yield exponential returns because a stronger workforce supports a stronger economy.

Businesses, government, nonprofit, and philanthropic organizations have an opportunity to partner and rethink policy and investments, attract new resources, and improve economic mobility for workers. Investing in workforce development can bolster the efficient use of resources. It can lead to better outcomes for individuals as well as more competitive businesses and regional economic growth. And it can help us unlock the potential of America's workforce.

About Investing in America's Workforce: Improving Outcomes for Workers and Employers

"Investing in America's Workforce: Improving Outcomes for Workers and Employers" is a Federal Reserve System initiative in collaboration with the John J. Heldrich Center for Workforce Development at Rutgers University, the Ray Marshall Center for the Study of Human Resources at the University of Texas at Austin, and the W.E. Upjohn Institute for Employment Research. Led by the community development function of the Federal Reserve System,[2] this initiative aims to:

- Explore regional aspects of improving workforce outcomes and investments through a series of regional forums to gather information and ideas from people working at the intersection of training, recruitment, and finance. The findings from these forums are presented herein.

- Present promising approaches introduced at a national conference in Austin, Texas, in October 2017.

- Share research, best practices, and resources for workforce development, as compiled in this book.

- Create and implement a training curriculum for Community Reinvestment Act bank examiners regarding qualifying workforce investments under new Interagency Q&A clarifications of the regulation.[3]

The Investing in America's Workforce initiative ultimately seeks to create a foundation from which a new era of investment in America's workforce can grow.

METHODOLOGY

Regional Listening Sessions

To gain insights into the regional aspects of improving workforce outcomes and investments, the community development departments at each of the Federal Reserve Banks organized listening sessions during the first half of

2017. Through these regional listening sessions, Federal Reserve staff aimed to identify new approaches, opportunities, and challenges in investing and evaluating outcomes in workforce development across the country. Key workforce leaders from their respective regions were invited to each meeting. Participants represented training providers, regional industry employers, financial institutions, philanthropy, policymakers, and academic institutions. A total of 52 listening sessions were held across 32 states and Puerto Rico, and a total of 983 leaders participated by sharing their experience and insights. The two key questions asked of participants at the meetings were:

1) What opportunities for investment in workforce development exist and what would make workforce development more investable?

2) How can workforce development efforts be better evaluated?

Analysis

Twenty-nine of the regional listening sessions were recorded, transcribed verbatim, and entered into MaxQDA qualitative data analysis software. Notes from an additional 23 listening sessions were also entered.[4] Using the software, transcripts and notes were coded to identify themes that emerged regarding the challenges and opportunities for improving workforce investments and outcomes.[5]

A priori codes were developed to correspond with questions posed at the meetings. Additional codes were developed after the initial transcripts and notes were reviewed. This process allowed for the analysis and synthesis of a large amount of qualitative data that otherwise would have been difficult to manage.

Ten of the 52 transcripts were coded independently by two members of the study team and checked for intercoder reliability. This rigorous and collaborative qualitative approach allowed the analysis to move beyond anecdotal insights. Code analysis through full and repeated immersion in the data led to the identification of several meaningful themes, which are explored herein.

The views expressed in this report are the perceptions and opinions of the key informants who participated in the listening sessions, as summarized by the author, and do not necessarily represent the views of the author nor are they necessarily empirically supported facts. Direct quotes from participants are shared when they help support and illustrate summary statements, and, where appropriate, referrals to relevant resources are provided in an endnote.

CURRENT CHALLENGES

Surveys indicate that difficulties filling vacant positions are common across industries and up and down the skills spectrum (Society for Human Resource Management 2016; ManpowerGroup 2016). Additionally, low labor market participation is a challenge that, without intervention, will continue to hamper economic growth. By 2014, more than 16 percent of U.S. men between the ages of 25 and 54 with a high school education or less had dropped out of the workforce completely (White House 2016). Listening session participants, to frame a conversation around promising solutions and opportunities for investing in America's workforce, first described some of the current challenges contributing to these trends.

Skills Gap

A gap between the skills possessed by the local labor force and those demanded by local employers was a theme that emerged in every listening session held. Various potential causes of this skills gap were explored, including a lack of traditional educational attainment as well as a stigma attached to alternative educational paths such as career and technical education. There was a shared sentiment that outdated perspectives regarding opportunities in certain industries need to be revised to encourage more young people to pursue careers in fields with promising prospects.

> *Well, what's going on is all students are going to college, but they're not understanding some of the career opportunities that we need to fill middle-skill jobs. We have people that don't understand the gap — that don't understand that these are good career options that move people into the middle class.*
>
> *So, we talk about plumbers. Plumbers in Wisconsin make $68,000 a year on average. PhDs make $66,000. We don't get that message to parents and to teachers. And we need to get the facts in front of them so that they understand and can make better decisions.*

Some participants felt that a poor K–12 educational infrastructure is responsible for the skills gap. Inadequate services offered by guidance counselors and a focus on Advanced Placement (AP) classes rather than technical classes were examples that were cited of ways that some high schools push most students toward four-year degrees without exploring other options that may be more suitable to their personal interests and goals. Some participants noted that schools are trying to promote career exploration but either do not have adequate funding or have insufficient time because they must "teach to the test." Some expressed a need for career counseling in high school to inform career choices, which could help students with career aspirations that do not require a college degree and student loan debt. Participants lamented the apparent disconnect between the way our K–12 educational system prepares students for careers and the needs of the broader economy.

> *I taught in the apprenticeship program for 10 years, and a good percentage of the people coming in had gone to college for two to four years, gotten a degree, gotten a job, and said this isn't what I want to be. I want to do something with my hands. There's a percentage of the population that that's what they're built for. That's what they want to do. And the flip side of that, we need those people. When you flip the switch, the light should come on. You should be warm. You should be cool. It's not magic. There's work behind all of this that is noble work, and it's good work.*

The quality of K–12 basic education was another commonly cited cause when discussing the perceived skills gap. High levels of illiteracy, low math skills, and a lack of soft skills were frequently mentioned hindrances. Additionally, participants relayed that many immigrants struggle to obtain work, in part, because they lack English as a Second Language training. Lastly, it was noted that while training programs exist to support people in securing stable employment, awareness of these opportunities is limited. Participants stated that people seem to be aware of how to obtain unemployment benefits but not how to access training to return to the workforce.

Nonskills Barriers to Employment

While job-related skills training is critical, listening session participants pointed out many nonskills barriers that contribute to unemployment and low labor market participation for some populations. It was also noted that for those able to successfully access training programs, life factors, external to the training or education program, can get in the way of successful program completion or obtaining stable employment thereafter. Examples of these barriers that were cited include insufficient child care, limited disposable income to weather unexpected shocks, and unstable housing or transportation situations.

> *We need staff to manage the barriers that participants experience so that they can continue on with the program. Oftentimes there are instances that come up that prevent their ability to focus on the program itself. It could be that their utilities were shut off that morning and it's difficult to focus in an eight-hour training that day.*

But the recognition that life happens is so important to particularly vulnerable populations because they may be the only one in their environment who's going to work every day. And it is a struggle. When your children are sick, it's a struggle for us who have support systems. So, you couple that with you are new on the job, you have children, you have a car that may or may not start. People need that long-term follow-up.

Participants in several listening sessions mentioned deeply ingrained mind sets resulting from intergenerational poverty and limiting beliefs that are perpetuated in communities that have experienced generations of limited opportunities. The lack of role models, mentors, or supportive figures instilling a sense of confidence in oneself and one's ability were frequently mentioned barriers. Some job seekers are experiencing homelessness, recovering from addiction, or transitioning back from jail or prison. Participants relayed that these issues present barriers to employment when application processes request a home address, drug testing, or a background check to screen out those with past convictions. They also noted that some veterans struggle with post-traumatic stress disorder or other behavioral health issues, which can become a barrier to work if not adequately treated. Participants stated that these issues can lead individuals to drop out of the labor force and further perpetuate intergenerational poverty in some communities.

It's not only that they don't have the skills. It may be all the other barriers that people have in certain kinds of communities. So, we have tons of truck driver positions open. That's fairly easy to get into a truck driving position if you take the right courses and you pass them. You get the license, right? Should be a simple fit. It's not, because they have convictions or past driving records or they can't pass a drug test—and these are the things that are stopping people from getting the jobs. I'm not saying it's right or wrong. I'm just saying those are the things that you start to face when you're trying to take a labor force and match them with a job. It's not just give them a skill and go to work, and everyone's happy. It doesn't quite work that way.

Technological Advancement and Automation's Impact on Employer Demands

Automation's potential impact on the number of middle-skills jobs was a common theme across listening sessions. For the jobs that remain, the changing nature of work and the skills required to keep pace with technological advancements was a frequently cited concern among participants.[6] For example, one listening session concluded that twenty-first century literacy requires tech savviness. This was described as meaning that a skill such as memorization, often still stressed in K–12 education, is becoming less important than the ability to research, synthesize, and process information. Participants stated that educational institutions and training programs will need to keep up with these changing skill requirements so the labor force meets the demands of employers and remains competitive globally.

> *The whole economy has shifted in ways that we need to be thinking about. How will employment change in the years to come? One of the ways is that some jobs are becoming obsolete because of the technology and robotics and so forth. Many of these are good paying jobs. So how do we anticipate that and try to address that kind of issue and still prepare enough people to hold onto good jobs?*

Quality of Available Jobs Impeding Opportunities for Economic Mobility

While job growth in recent years has been robust, listening session participants observed that new jobs today either require a high level of skill or offer workers stagnant incomes, volatile schedules, and few benefits. They stated that lower paid jobs tend to be in the service sector, such as home health aides and food service positions. It was relayed that while these jobs are not at immediate risk of being lost to automation, their quality in terms of pay, benefits, and flexibility to accommodate competing priorities, such as family obligations, make economic mobility difficult even for those working multiple full-time positions. Participants explained that as job creation occurs at both ends of the employment spectrum, income stagnation for lower-income workers is exacerbating inequality and perpetuating the nonskills barriers to work described earlier.[7]

Additionally, many sessions included conversations about government benefits programs that often reduce or eliminate benefits when income rises, causing a net decrease in household income. Many participants referred to this "benefits cliff" as a disincentive to work. In rural listening sessions specifically, participants shared that a lack of quality jobs has led to a dramatic increase in disability claims.[8] The perception was that some workers choose to continue to receive government benefits rather than see their income reduced by taking a low-wage job.

Despite these challenges, participants discussed several promising strategies to connect job seekers with well-paying jobs that provide opportunities for career advancement.

PROMISING STRATEGIES

While educational systems lay the foundation for skills development, and educational attainment is an important factor in employability, the promising strategies identified in this research focus on current workers and job seekers rather than the future workforce (i.e., today's students). Although it is not included in this analysis, it goes without saying that a strong general education system is among the most important long-term workforce development strategies (Yellen 2017).

Participants in the regional listening sessions emphasized that, to make meaningful progress on solving current labor market challenges, it is important to identify not only opportunities for financial capital investment but also opportunities for investment in social capital. They stated that the following promising strategies require the collective will to alter current behaviors in the workforce development ecosystem, more than they require additional funding. It was noted that best practices should be both scalable and replicable, if possible, though consideration should go into the replicability of promising strategies across geographies.

Better Alignment of Workforce Development and Economic Development Efforts Using Sector Strategies

Listening session participants stated that economic and workforce development strategies need to be more closely aligned so that training providers can understand employers' current needs and anticipate changes that will alter those needs over time. Many regions shared that the main focus of economic development efforts is on business attraction and retention. In some regions, however, jobs are being created, but the local labor force does not have the skills to adequately fill those jobs. It was stated that without addressing these labor market challenges, localities run the risk of losing both the available jobs and the companies creating them.

Any time workforce representatives are sitting at the table with economic development, it's a win. Because we're in on the front side of that business expansion or the business moving to our state and we get an opportunity to sit with them in a planning cycle and prepare their workforce.

Through this lens, investing in a region's workforce has the potential to be a powerful economic development strategy that is "stickier" than the incentives often offered to attract and retain businesses, since even greater incentives can be extended by competing localities.[9] It may also have a higher return on investment because the benefits of improved economic mobility can lead to increased consumer purchasing power and potential neighborhood revitalization, as well as cost savings from reduced utilization of and demand for certain social services and public benefits programs.

> *From a business point of view, workforce is always one of the first questions. So, getting the business to relocate to an area, there's an adage now that businesses are going to where the workers are. Twenty years ago, workers would graduate from school and move to wherever the business that they wanted to work for was. It's changed. The dynamic is different. You'll see businesses that are relocating to urban areas or moving back into downtowns or moving to areas where there's a perception that the talent is available even if they have to pay a higher cost to be there because that's what they need. So, from a municipality's point of view like ours, the first question we get from a business that's looking to locate is what is the status of our workforce? Do those workers exist today?*

Listening session participants stressed that training providers should engage with employers to understand their hiring needs and to receive feedback on program design. The Workforce Innovation and Opportunity Act (WIOA), which was passed in 2014, requires the formation of boards led by private sector stakeholders to inform local workforce needs and craft partnerships across sectors. Workforce development boards actively set goals and develop strategies at both the state and local levels and manage comprehensive one-stop centers that provide a variety of WIOA-mandated services.[10] Despite this progress, several participants shared that local employers are often unaware of the programs and training services available in their area. It was stated that better marketing for workforce training providers and strategic connections between employers and organizations serving job seekers, including the public workforce system, should be encouraged.

> *I think a lot of times in the public workforce arena, we begin assuming we know what the business needs for training. And we use our best knowledge that we can to develop that training, and then we oftentimes create a mismatch with the business community in terms of value.*

Additionally, some voiced the need to move beyond partnerships between a single educational or training provider and a single employer to more systemic collaboration that could benefit a much broader group of employers and job seekers. Participants mentioned the use of "sector strategies," which are regional approaches to workforce and economic development that focus resources on the needs of a defined industry important to the local economy. Sector partnerships include various stakeholders—from local and regional employers to academic institutions and training providers—coming together to analyze an industry's current and future skill requirements. Essential skills can be compared with the skills available in the local labor market in order to identify skills gaps and inform a plan to close those gaps. Strategies often include the creation or promotion of industry-accepted credentials, building career pathways to higher-skilled jobs within the industry, and creating or informing program training (National Skills Coalition 2017a). Participants noted that these types of economic development strategies take a systemic rather than transactional view and have the potential to yield a trained workforce that not only supports business attraction and retention but also creates local opportunities for unemployed and underemployed residents.

Apprenticeships and Other Work-Based Training Models

Many listening session participants stressed that since vulnerable populations face significant financial strain, people need to be compensated for their time in training programs. Apprenticeships and other types of work-based learning models that allow people to both "earn and learn" were encouraged in nearly every listening session. These programs allow trainees to support themselves and their families while earning a license or industry credential through on-the-job training. They also allow employers to provide customized training for positions that may be difficult to fill or may soon be vacated by a growing number of retiring workers.[11]

> *Many of our resources in the public workforce system are dedicated to classroom training and not on-the-job training or apprenticeships. However, with this group of individuals at the very bottom of the rung, classroom training is not an option for them. They're looking to pay the rent this month to have a place to live next month and looking to pay a car payment this week in order to keep their car. So, when we have our resources so focused on classroom training, it's not an option for those folks. They can't afford to go to training and not work. And so much of the classroom training isn't flexible to where they could adjust their hours to accommodate their work.*

The apprenticeship model can be adapted for young people who can benefit from having on-the-job experience while in high school. Many listening session participants agreed that partnerships between employers, high schools, and postsecondary institutions that support internships, apprenticeships, coops, and career and technical education should be encouraged so that students gain important skills that will inform their career choices and lead to more success in the labor market.

> *So, the idea of not getting a degree, not going to college is just absolutely not what we talk about at the table. But we have to do a better job to get people to understand that in the twenty-first century, it is really about skill as well, and that the skills that people need can be received—can actually be delivered in a different form, in a different way, both on the job and in traditional settings.*

Increased Employer Training for Incumbent Workers to Foster Career Pathways and Create Access to Entry-Level Jobs

Several participants expressed the view that the private sector has increasingly come to rely on nonprofit or public agencies for training needs. Participants shared the concern that employer training tends to predominantly focus on employees with higher skills and levels of educational attainment.[12] However, it was noted that some employers are making a concerted effort to train more incumbent workers, allowing progression within a career while improving job access for local job seekers by creating vacancies in entry-level positions. According to listening session participants, this strategy, known as "upskilling and backfilling," has the potential to not only create new opportunities for job seekers but also increase the productivity of existing staff.[13]

> *Companies figuring out how they can reinvest in their employees is promising. Many of the companies in our area are investing in their incumbent workers. We do a great deal of incumbent worker training, but it's still not nearly enough. And I think companies have to look at it from building their own workforce from within too.*

Listening session participants frequently mentioned the need to foster career pathways or programs that "offer a clear sequence, or pathway, of education coursework and/or training credentials aligned with employer-validated work readiness standards and competencies," with the expectation that such training will lead to higher-skilled job opportunities and higher wages (USDOLETA 2016, p. 6). Participants shared that this strategy requires collaboration and cooperation between employers and training providers. Assistance with résumé writing and interview skills may enable job seekers to gain initial employment, whereas mentorship can advance career mobility. Stackable credentials may be obtained to show that an individual possesses the skills necessary to advance in the field. Aside from the services and programs offered by training providers and educational institutions, employers can support career pathways by providing opportunities for in-house training and promotion.

We don't disparage those low skill jobs. We need a lot of them. I think our strategy is not to get rid of them but to make sure that they're not the only job that somebody has. So, our strategy is to try to facilitate pathways from those entry-level low paying jobs into something that represents a living wage. And what's interesting, it's not that businesses don't want to do this. They've just got so much competitive pressure and so we want to make sure that they can remain cost-effective in their growth. It's understanding what allows those businesses to be competitive and still invest in their workforce.

Increased Coordination among Service Providers and with Funders

Working together to successfully move job seekers into stable employment can prove challenging due to resource constraints, a competitive funding environment, and differences in organizational cultures and operating models. Nevertheless, the need for coordination and collaboration was a theme that emerged in nearly every listening session and is supported by recent industry research. Among the three most challenging areas of activity for workforce development organizations is "developing and maintaining strategic partnerships with other organizations" (Jain, Newman, and Montes 2017, p. 3).

Coordination among service providers is essential for client success. Increased awareness of programs offered by other service providers allows for appropriate referrals to be made. Strong alignment also decreases the chances for duplication of efforts (for example, constantly surveying the same sets of businesses).[14] Listening session participants cited collective impact models,[15] data sharing, and centralized intake processes with a single point of entry as strategies to foster this collaboration.

Shared vision, mission, and expectations between training providers and their funders was also cited by participants as being essential. It was stated that overly restrictive funding streams can, in some cases, prevent training providers from successfully meeting the demands of both job seekers and employers. Participants mentioned that unrestricted funding is critical for organizations to deliver the outcomes that both their clients and their funders expect. Additionally, it was shared that overly rigid reporting requirements can distort what is measured and prioritized, so these indicators should be developed in partnership with the direct service providers.

How can we send this person with resources to that partner to make sure that they get the certificate or the additional training that they need so that all of our work kind of becomes exponentially powerful by really coordinating together on what happens next and making sure that we don't just check our individual box and then have the person fall off the bridge on the next part of their journey? So that investment in collaboration and connectivity, in getting us to truly become partners and not just referral sources to each other, but really strategic partners, is key to us reaching a whole different level of effectiveness.

Changes in Employer Behavior That Improve Job Access and Quality

Listening session participants expressed that when assessing candidates for open positions, most employers focus on educational attainment or personal connections, which puts low-income job seekers at a disadvantage. A promising strategy that emerged from the listening sessions is the adoption of skills-based hiring by employers to remove what, in some cases, may be an artificial barrier to employment.[16] Further, it was noted that alternative forms of training and credentialing, such as boot camps and digital badging, are being developed that reflect competencies rather than more traditional education and degree attainment. These credentials directly tell employers what a potential employee is capable of, whereas, listening session participants felt a college degree might serve as a signal or proxy for soft skills, such as work ethic, rather than as an indicator of actual ability.[17] Whether through industry-accepted credentials, certificates, or proven work experience, participants encouraged employers to give more weight to competencies than to traditional educational attainment, which could level the playing field for those from lower-income backgrounds. Additionally, they stated that hiring from reputable training providers can offset not only direct training costs for employers but also recruiting and screening costs as well.

Employers need to look at how they're contributing to the shortage in the workforce, if you will, from the perspective of how they define what skills and what experience and education they need for the positions that they have. Employers don't tend to go back and reevaluate that. We hire certain positions, and we've always identified those as requiring a four-year college degree. Well, really, do they?

Participants also stressed that, to increase workers' chances for economic mobility, employers should be encouraged to improve job quality, especially for entry-level positions. Job quality is measured not only in terms of wages but also by practices such as consistent and predictable scheduling, the availability of basic benefits such as retirement accounts, parental leave, and paid sick time, and career and wealth building opportunities. These practices may also contribute to business productivity through a more stable work environment (Brett and Woelfel 2016). Participants noted that the efforts by "high-road employers" to "raise the floor" recognize that while skill development is important, it is not sufficient to ensure economic security.[18]

OPPORTUNITIES FOR INVESTMENT

Considering the labor market challenges identified and the promising strategies discussed, listening session participants were asked to explore specific opportunities for investing in America's workforce. The following investment themes were identified as areas in which additional financial capital could improve outcomes. Participants offered that these investments could contribute to both preparing workers for and connecting them to stable, quality employment.

Invest in Core Programs and Services That Prepare Workers for Jobs

Participants shared that although numerous basic and technical skills training programs exist, these programs often address the needs of some job seekers but cannot fully meet demand. Furthermore, research has found that when faced with reduced public funding, workforce training providers are forced to "reduce the number of workers served, change the mix of services participants receive, or alter the methods of service provision to ones that may not be as effective" (Wandner 2015, p. 132). Participants also noted that investing in workforce training providers, including community colleges and educational institutions offering career and technical education, would allow more workers to receive in-demand skills training.

Listening session discussions revealed that additional funding and financing is also needed to deliver relevant job training in fast-changing industries. Training providers and career and technical education institutions are tasked with preparing workers with the skills that they need today and will need tomorrow, and to do that successfully, the latest technology is required. Funding or affordably and flexibly financing the latest equipment and technology is an opportunity for investment that listening session participants voiced is necessary for training providers to adequately meet the labor demands of employers.

If you are chasing technical profession workforce training in high demand industries, equipment is very expensive because we pro-

vide industry mirroring classrooms, which means that we have to use equipment that we aren't turning a profit on. The reason that industry can afford it is because they can calculate mathematically how long that machine needs to operate. They will get all of that money back. And we can't do that because it's a training environment and so it's just a little bit different ballgame and I think on behalf of our technical colleges for sure, because that's all we do, the investment in equipment is a major need. It's very challenging for us to keep up with.

Participants conveyed the importance of unrestricted capital from funders. They stated that the ability to adapt and refine operational strategies in response to organizational learnings and environmental changes allows workforce organizations to effectively meet the needs of both job seekers and employers.

I feel like there's not an understanding of what it takes to do this work. And that means the cost associated with it, the time associated with it, realistic outcomes associated with that. So, it's just like hurry up and do really well, and do with large numbers. There's just not an understanding of the reality of that. And organizations are severely under-resourced to do what should be done for young people, for adults.

Invest in Workforce Intermediaries That Connect Workers to Jobs

Workforce intermediaries that connect employers with a supply of skilled labor from training providers take a dual customer approach, meeting the needs of both workers and employers. Participants expressed that investing in these entities is essential because they can "speak the language" of businesses and develop relationships in a way that may be difficult for training providers focused on holistically meeting the needs of job seekers. Workforce intermediaries can also serve to educate training providers about the skills demanded by local employers.

I think their goal is really to try to broker agreements between employers and job seekers. And it is really tough on both sides I think to navigate that system. But I also don't know if they frankly have the resources to do that. And so, investment in intermediary is best—a lot of people don't want to invest in that because it's not direct service. But in order to have people navigate the system on both sides, I think we need that.

Participants in several listening sessions explained that workforce development agency efforts and programs were largely designed for midsized and large employers. Yet, the clear majority of employment in their areas is by small businesses. They further suggested that small employers are more impacted by not being able to find the right skills mix or to influence the design and development of local and regional workforce efforts, often due to the need to focus on their business rather than engage in lengthy meetings with workforce development service providers. They also identified difficulty in navigating the various workforce development provider services. Several participants mentioned that workforce intermediaries could address the challenges small businesses face in meeting their talent needs.

> *If there could be an investment in some kind of intermediary entity that could assist to aggregate many of these small businesses and medium-sized businesses into the industries that match up to these programs to help them access and inform the available services, that would be important.*

Invest in Early Childhood Education

Though this research did not focus on education per se, early childhood education was identified by participants as an effective two-generation approach. Participants noted that investments in quality early childhood education centers can yield both short- and long-term impacts. High-quality early childhood education not only seeks to lay the foundation for a productive future workforce, but it also can allow the current workforce (i.e., the parents) to maintain employment, knowing that their children are adequately cared for while learning skills needed to thrive in the future. A lack of affordable, accessible child care options was a frequently cited barrier to employment in the listening sessions. Participants stated that by addressing the needs of both parent and child, improved outcomes can be achieved for the family, contributing to economic mobility and reducing the likelihood of intergenerational poverty.

> *And the other thing I see about workforce development—it really starts at the pre-K level.*

> *We frequently in our world talk about executive function skills and social and emotional skills. And those are developed frequently in early ed, okay. And that's where the window is.*

> *We can't manage child care. So, in states where employment and training has been really successful, the states have funded childcare services fully through until someone completes 90 days of employment, so all the way through every transition—stable child care. It's the biggest predictor of success.*

Invest in Community Infrastructure Including Transportation Systems and Affordable Housing

In listening sessions hosted in rural areas, it was noted that access to transportation is crucial because many rural residents may have to travel long distances for work and training programs. Even in more urbanized areas, insufficient access to public transportation was cited as a common employment barrier. Participants stated that lack of affordable, accessible housing options is a challenge because housing instability decreases the likelihood that a worker will retain employment. It was additionally noted that shortages in affordable housing may hinder economic development efforts to attract and retain businesses. Participants stated that without sufficient housing options for their workforce, businesses may choose a competing locality to locate or expand, thereby reducing the availability of jobs for job seekers in that market. Though these investments are more place based in nature, it was noted that they are important to foster a holistic strategy for developing and deploying human capital. Participants stressed the need to adopt a new strategy that invests not only in human capital but also in the built environment, with the goal of increasing the supply of affordable housing, accessible transportation, community facilities, and high-quality child care options.

> *No matter what the program is, it has to be a holistic approach. You have to worry about not just getting the skills, but the education. You have to worry about transportation. You have to worry about the day care. Otherwise they're not going to be successful. And housing is a big issue, and first time loans for individuals and tenants that want to improve and move ahead. Some people are living in places where they should not be living because they can't get that first loan and their kids are growing up in areas where they shouldn't be housed. And so they can't even get to the point where they want to get their skills because their basic needs aren't met, and that's a huge issue.*

Invest in Comprehensive Supportive Services

As was discussed regarding current challenges, there are many nonskills barriers to employment. Participants in nearly every listening session mentioned that investments in comprehensive supportive services are essential for ensuring client success in any workforce program. Recent research confirmed this sentiment: "By providing support services such as counseling, case management, and connections to public benefits such as transportation, child care, and medical and housing assistance . . . grantees helped their participants succeed in and beyond training programs. However, finding funds to pay for supportive services in the resources typically available for workforce programming is challenging because much of the funding that is available cannot be used to provide the types of comprehensive and ongoing support necessary to help participants achieve stable, long-term employment" (Jain, Newman, and Montes 2017, p. 6). Whereas the preceding investment opportunity focuses on improvements in the physical infrastructure of a community (e.g., public transit system or affordable housing stock), participants expressed that investments in supportive services would provide the resources for those connected to the workforce system to access this infrastructure investment and to benefit from other essential services targeting those dealing with addiction or transitioning from jail or prison, for example. Postemployment support services are equally important, allowing clients to not only obtain but maintain employment.

> *Our biggest challenge is that we do coordinate with a lot of other agencies on funding, but there are huge gaps that we cannot fill with the funding we get. We cannot provide the support that people need to transition from employment services into jobs, from the first job and stabilization to the next. There is no support for that. We have huge gaps in the funding that we're struggling with to really move. We can't move the needle on equity and poverty if we don't change the way we support people in getting where they need to go.*

Invest in Efforts to Increase Job Access and Quality

Self-employment can be a viable option for some trying to enter the workforce, though entrepreneurship has been on the decline and the failure rate among startup businesses is high (Haltiwanger 2015; Griffith 2014). If successful, however, entrepreneurs who operate small businesses in low- and moderate-income communities are a source of job creation in those communities and tend to hire locally. Some participants identified entrepreneurial support services for residents of low-income areas or those facing barriers to employment as an opportunity for investment. Others expressed a need for investing in small business capacity building,[19] including engaging businesses around job quality efforts and using innovative financial products to incentivize behaviors that increase access to jobs for those facing employment barriers. For example, several participants mentioned that reduced interest rates on small business loan products could be used to incentivize businesses to adopt these behaviors.

Social enterprises, which are organizations that address a basic unmet need or solve a social problem through a market-driven approach, were also identified as an opportunity for investing in workforce development.[20] Social enterprises generate their own revenue as they address a societal problem, which reduces or eliminates the need for traditional fund-raising. By providing on-the-job experience and training, for-profit and nonprofit social enterprises can use private sector business models for the social purpose of expanding employment opportunities and outcomes for traditionally difficult-to-employ populations. The most well-known example may be Goodwill, which has not only become a household name but also in 2016 helped more than 313,000 individuals "train for careers in industries such as banking, IT, and health care, to name a few—and get the supporting services they needed to be successful—such as English language training, additional education, or access to transportation and child care."[21] In addition to investing directly in social enterprises, several participants mentioned that there are opportunities to invest in incubators and accelerators that support social enterprises focused on job access and quality.

> *And so, we ended up starting a pilot to create an opportunity for investment across multiple layers of outcomes. So, we started a construction company that would hire people who had barriers to employment, usually a criminal record in the case of our pilot, to do rehab and lead remediation work for the city. There are currently only two for-profit subcontractors who are even interested in being on the lead remediation list for the city. Because we're a nonprofit, we don't need to make money off of this. We need to pay these men a living wage so we can afford to compete and make that something that's sustainable.*

HOW TO MAKE WORKFORCE DEVELOPMENT MORE INVESTABLE

One of the main goals of the Investing in America's Workforce Initiative is to re-envision workforce solutions as investments in the national economy, not as social services. Once the previously discussed opportunities for investment were identified, participants reflected on ways to drive more capital to those opportunities. Listening session participants were asked for ideas to make workforce development more investable, which led to the following insights.

Classify Workers as Assets, Not Expenses

Several listening sessions referenced the work of Zeynep Ton of MIT, who has done considerable research on the reclassification of employees as assets to be invested in as opposed to a line item labor cost to be reduced. This shift in perspective may encourage employers to improve job quality and make direct investments in skills training and professional development. It also has been empirically shown (in retail settings) to increase productivity and business performance, yielding a high return on investment for workers and employers alike.[22]

From this perspective, third-party investors may also be interested in investing in the asset of human capital, which has led to the emergence of income share agreements (ISAs). ISAs are a financial product through which a student receives capital to cover education or training expenses in exchange for an agreement to pay a percentage of their future income for a set period. Though ISA proponents typically discuss this financial innovation to limit student loan debt associated with traditional higher education expenses, ISAs have also been used to fund the education of community college students and trainees attending short-term career boot camps. Participants said that while ISAs bring innovation in education and training finance, further experience and research are needed to determine their efficacy for students and workers.[23]

Maximize Efficiency of Existing Funding Streams While Exploring Potential New Resources

Though the public workforce system is an essential component of a successful workforce development strategy, federal support for workforce development programs has declined more than 20 percent since 2010 (National Skills Coalition 2017b). Participants expressed that existing federal and state funding streams that support workforce training programs, including the Workforce Innovation and Opportunity Act (WIOA), Supplemental Nutrition Assistance Program (SNAP), Employment and Training, and Temporary Assistance for Needy Families (TANF) should be at least maintained, if not expanded. Accessing dormant public accounts for impact investing purposes, such as using forfeiture funds to cover the cost of reentry programs, was also mentioned.[24] Additionally, a few participants noted that requiring increased transparency regarding job quality standards by public companies in SEC disclosures could arm shareholders with information needed to drive capital to employers offering quality jobs and investing in their workers.

> And so, one of the things that I've been pushing is to allow us to tap into forfeiture funds as a way to fund reentry programs to put people into employment. There's millions of dollars in the federal forfeits funds just sitting there and we're not accessing that for programs.

Government investments in workforce development initiatives could also take the shape of tax credits or subsidies explicitly intended to encourage employer behavior change, such as the adoption of an apprenticeship program.

As noted above, however, federal support for workforce development has been steadily declining. Perhaps unsurprisingly, participants relayed that employers represent the most important stakeholder group when it comes to investing in America's workforce. It was also mentioned that aside from investing in in-house training, when serving as a purchaser of training programs and services, employers become an important source of earned revenue for workforce organizations, decreasing the need for public investment.

> *Private sector investment is going to be critical. Because the federal government is putting less and less money into workforce development. We're seeing less funding year in, year out. So, it is going to be critical. Either the federal government is going to have to start looking at the importance of workforce development and putting that investment back in it or we're going to have to look for other sources of funding.*

Several participants suggested that private sector leverage strategies should be utilized to make public tax payer dollars go further. Local, state, and federal governments can use small amounts of public capital to leverage large amounts of private investment. Since foundations are often called upon to make up for shortfalls in public funding, philanthropy may want to consider financial tools that allow for leveraging private capital. While grants can yield significant impact, some foundations are also exploring the use of other forms of capital such as investments out of endowments as well as credit enhancements in the form of guarantees or loan loss reserves (Schiff and Dithrich 2017). Recent guidance on the CRA, which requires lenders to meet the credit needs of low- and moderate-income communities and people in their service areas, clarified that "economic development initiatives" eligible for CRA credit "include provisions for creating or improving access by low- or moderate-income persons to jobs or to job training or workforce development programs" (Sobel Blum and Shepelwich 2017, p. 1). It was noted that this clarification provides an opportunity to deepen engagement with financial institutions around opportunities for investing in workforce development efforts. Participants also mentioned pension funds as a potential new source of capital for investments in workforce development efforts.

Offer Financial Products That Allow Organizations to Increase Capacity and Scale

Listening session participants stated that many of the organizations that are best positioned to develop human capital lack the financial resources to deliver effective services at scale. Additionally, some sources of capital are too restrictive to allow organizations the flexibility they need to meet various program goals. It was emphasized that as organizations are faced with potential cuts in government spending, innovative uses of private capital should be explored. They cautioned, however, that financing should not be confused with funding. Though there will always be a great need for traditional philanthropic grants and public subsidy, better access to and use of flexible debt financing could help suitable nonprofits more effectively manage working capital and serve more clients (Avivar Capital 2016). Participants said that there are opportunities to support organizational growth by providing working capital, bridge loans, facility financing, or equipment loans that are more flexible, longer term, more risk tolerant, or more affordable than what is currently available.

> *But there is a big barrier there because of lack of capital, so they have resorted to going to private lenders who are earning on a weekly basis more than what four or five jobs would require in pay—much more than that. I mean it's 10 times—10 jobs could've been funded with the interest that they're paying on this loan.*

Address Funding Needs Using Outcomes-Based Funding Models

While some organizations generate earned revenue that would allow them to take on below-market-rate debt or other forms of loans or investment to support growth, other programs, interventions, and organizations may require pure grant funding. Several listening session participants mentioned the emerging field of outcomes-based funding that allows for the monetization of social impact, thereby creating investment opportunities. In a typical outcomes-based funding model, such as a social impact bond, a back-end payer, typically a government entity, agrees to pay a specific price for an intended outcome, while an investor or group of investors provides the up-front capital to the service provider.[25] Because the capital is provided at the outset and the investor is repaid only if the agreed-upon outcomes are achieved, this model provides funding that operates like a grant for the recipient and an investment for the source of capital.

> *There are social impact bonds and other instruments that are now coming to the fore to allow us to make investments in these kinds of issues.*

Participants stressed the need for flexibility from their funders to be able to adapt over time and employ processes that best meet the holistic needs of the clients they serve. Oftentimes, the prescriptive nature of funding streams prevents organizations from making strategic decisions about how best to serve their clients. One positive aspect of outcomes-based financing is that the funder is essentially purchasing outcomes, which improves accountability while leaving the process required to achieve those outcomes in the hands of the provider. This allows organizations to build upon lessons learned and change strategic direction over time without the fear of losing funding.

Use Philanthropic Capital to Promote Innovation, Collaboration, and Capacity Building

Research shows that between 2008 and 2014, grants made by the largest U.S. foundations to support workforce development totaled roughly $2.6 billion, or about $370 million annually.[26] This represented an average of less than 2 percent of total grant making annually over the study period (Wardrip and de Zeeuw 2018). Participants expressed that since foundation grants represent the most flexible source of funding, philanthropic capital should be used strategically to foster innovation, collaboration, and field building among multiple stakeholders.

Innovation grants and seed funding can support promising strategies that either do not have the potential for revenue generation and thus cannot attract return-seeking capital, or that first need proof of concept to become investable. Several participants noted that often the main constraint is not one of capital but of risk tolerance. They stated that foundation support can lend credibility to new programs or interventions.

> There is a need for risk capital of pilot programs, the value of bringing people together to run pilots to try things differently. Because that risk capital pilot program then de-risks the change eventually. And it takes a while. As this project moves forward, the information needs to be brought forward to philanthropy, to government, in order to pool resources to run pilots. I love pilots. Because you know what? Fast failure then. Doesn't work, kill it. If it works, let's build it out and it'll help people see success.

Many listening session discussions also focused on the need to combine capital with capacity building to foster collaboration and local leadership. As one example of the ways in which foundations can promote collaboration, the Bridgespan Group recommends that philanthropy "fund and facilitate deep regional partnerships between high schools, higher education institutions, employers, and other community partners to align public education systems with pathways to careers, including market-aligned curricula and work-based learning opportunities" (Ross et al. 2016, p. 16). This sentiment was reiterated in many of the listening sessions.

At a systemic level, workforce solutions are an untapped opportunity for investment and would likely need funding from philanthropy for capacity and field building to reach scale. As previously mentioned, the field of human capital investment has already been taking shape with the emergence of social impact bonds and other outcomes-based financing models that track outcomes (i.e., human capital improvements) rather than outputs (i.e., number of people served). Participants said that grants to support future field building work could prove to make workforce solutions more investable over time.

Create Financial Intermediaries

Many participants relayed that developing local and regional intermediaries to attract and deploy capital could increase the involvement of a broader range of potential investor types that may be unable or unwilling to invest directly in workforce enterprises. A financial intermediary can blend public, private, and philanthropic capital in creative ways to meet the risk-adjusted return appetites of each stakeholder group. Intermediaries also serve to reduce transaction costs for investors by offering customized underwriting to assess risks that may be unfamiliar to those investors. Additionally, regarding the size and duration of the investment, intermediaries can provide capital on terms suitable to the recipient but in short supply today (Next Street 2016). Participants in the listening sessions noted that regional intermediaries focused on raising and disbursing capital could allow staff at organizations to focus more on program delivery and less on navigating the often-complicated landscape of potential funding sources. It should be noted, however, that the intermediary's expenses would need to be weighed against the efficiencies achieved.

> *On the investment side, it's the investment in some of the CDFIs. We have partnered with CDFIs, where we basically participate in a loan or two with them. When they can't quite do it on their own, we come in with the other piece of it. So, we're participating with your CDFIs on some of the lending, but also investing in their capital, so that they can go out and lend in the community.*

IMPACT MEASUREMENT AND EVALUATION

Reframing workforce development efforts as investments requires a reexamination of how success is evaluated. In other words, how is return on investment in workforce development efforts being measured? What outcomes are prioritized over others? Are there conflicts between short-term and long-term goals? How does the choice of indicators alter incentives and behaviors of training providers, participants, and funders?

As these questions were posed and pondered, many listening session participants noted that while impact measurement is required of their organization, funders (both public and philanthropic) may not appreciate the cost of this requirement in terms of systems, time, and staff capacity needed. Despite this frustration and the challenges inherent in impact measurement generally, several best practices were identified.

Measure Both Short-Term and Long-Term Results

Participants stressed the need to measure both short-term outputs and long-term outcomes rather than prioritizing the former over the latter. They stated that a short-term indicator such as job placement should be complemented by longer-term indicators such as job retention and wage growth, while a longer time horizon requires patience and additional resources dedicated to evaluation efforts. Participants mentioned that administrative data, wage data, and data from the Bureau of Labor Statistics can be utilized and shared across entities to track program participants' outcomes longitudinally. Intermediate outcomes can also be shared to encourage continuous momentum around a program or service.

> So really looking at what career placement means, because to me, success and outcomes would be on retention and a career pathway that leads to financial stability, which means they can afford a house and child care. We're talking basic needs here. But just to get someone a job and put them in a low-wage job—that doesn't benefit them in the long term. We have to ask the right questions and be patient in our outcomes. I've had many training studies where after a year-and-a-half there was nothing going on. It looked like the programs were showing no outcomes whatsoever. And at year two, even year three and four, we started to see the impact from those seeds that were sown. So, we have to be very patient and set up your theory of change so that you can measure milestones along the way. Get them early successes like increas-

ing training completion. That's a big one right there. It's hard for people to balance work and family and complete training, etc.; so, set up those, what we call intermediate outcomes, but be patient. The funding community and government has to understand that these programs take three to four years to really show their yield in so many cases. So, we'd stress the need to be patient and also ask the right questions.

Coordinate Data and Standardize Metrics across Entities

Listening session participants stressed the need for data sharing and called on funders to agree on a uniform set of metrics where impact evaluations are concerned. Regarding the former, some participants mentioned that local efforts to house public assistance services and workforce programs under one roof in one-stop centers have allowed for beneficiaries' needs to be addressed holistically. They noted that data sharing among colocated program staff could create an opportunity to analyze how the workforce development system affected the receipt of public assistance. Participants also shared that workforce development agencies and intermediaries have an opportunity to better use local and regional labor market data to inform their work, including matching their efforts to local current and future demand from employers. Additionally, participants mentioned that coordination is needed on the part of funders so that organizations are not overly burdened by different reporting requirements for each source of funds.

So, it's become critical that we share data—that we look at it in more of a three-dimensional way. We're really looking at more short-, medium-, and long-term outcomes for the people we serve, and being able to follow them over a longer arch to show we didn't just place them in a job—that they persisted and they stayed in that job for this many years and that turned into a career. And so, the inner connectivity of our data would allow us to continue to help each other to track those long-term successes and what that generates in revenue for our communities and saves our communities in terms of tax dollars being used for social support and other things.

The Workforce Data Quality Campaign, a project of the National Skills Coalition, calls for "longitudinal data systems that connect workforce training and other postsecondary education data with employment and social services data" to more effectively measure and evaluate impact as people move through and utilize a variety of programs and services.[27] Many participants felt that these systems could be used to inform better decision making, but cautioned that such systems require extensive collaboration and the identification of mutual interests and goals among various stakeholders willing to share data. Coordinated data systems also require significant effort to develop and funding to sustain (Pena 2017). Some listening session participants noted, however, that aggregating disparate data among actors such as local chambers of commerce, community and vocational colleges, universities, workforce training providers, and others will allow a community to more comprehensively view their local labor market issues and appropriately assess demand.

Rethink Return on Investment

While some participants believed that the ability to scale and offer services to more people was essential, others thought that the focus should be on the quality of service as measured by the outcome achieved. Some expressed that shifting the focus to the cost of achieving outcomes, rather than the cost of delivering services, could equip organizations with the investments needed to achieve their goals while improving accountability to funders and investors.

One of the things that funders want is volume. And as a nonprofit, volume is great, but I'm not always positive that volume leads to long-term impact. So, we had a big success last year. We got four people hired and that cost us about $11,000 per person. And I'm really proud of it because they have jobs, hopefully, for life. As a nonprofit, I always hear you have to serve people, you have to serve more people. And you know what? I'll serve more people, but they'll be looking for a job in 90 days. So I just think a little bit more pragmatism around how financial institutions fund to realize that one person needs a lot of work to get a job for life.

Some participants felt that the focus of an impact evaluation should be on the value that a given program adds to a participant's outcomes in the labor market as compared with the outcomes if the client had not received any services. This slight nuance of measuring added value from a specific intervention considers the heterogeneity of clients and their skills and abilities when they begin their training. Similar to extending the time frame for evaluation in longitudinal methodologies, increasing evaluation sophistication to account for the diversity of client populations will inevitably add time and cost in addition to increased rigor. For example, participants mentioned that the most sophisticated impact evaluations use randomized controlled trials, but this is also the most costly and time-consuming methodology.

There's lots of ways of measuring what works, but the way we look at what works is by looking at value-added over what would have happened. And how do we know that? We know that by creating some kind of comparison first. We try to always do that in all of our studies because we know from the past that outcomes are really unreliable as a way of measuring, just looking at outcomes alone. A lot of our studies have shown that those who come into programs with lower outcomes have larger impacts. So, we always want to know, what would have happened had this program not operated.

Several participants mentioned that measuring business satisfaction might also be a useful indicator of success for workforce training providers.

I think another way that I know we're struggling to quantify our efforts is the return on investment to employers when we're partnering with them. So, do they have lower recruitment costs? Do they have lower costs around turnover, or higher productivity of workers who come through some of our training programs?

Participants noted that not all outcomes of a program are quantifiable. For example, any improvements that an initiative brings to the broader workforce system are often missing from the typical evaluation. "Progress in this work can be challenging to measure and is not always quantifiable. Typical performance measures used to assess progress focus on training completion, certifications earned, job placement, wage rates, and short-term employment retention. While these indicators certainly point to important participant milestones, they fail to document the ongoing work of relationship building and employer engagement that is required to design and deliver effective workforce development services" (Jain, Newman, and Montes 2017, p. 9). Several listening session participants expressed that process improvements should be included in the assessment of return on investment, although their inclusion would likely have to be qualitative rather than quantitative.

CONCLUSIONS

Listening session participants frequently spoke to the industry-accepted need for broad systems change. "We often believe that one new part—one more proven 'best practice' or policy change—will generate improved results unattended. The law is passed, the randomized control trial completed, and it is onto the next challenge. We consistently forget that these are only the first steps in initiating true systems change" (Dawson 2016, p. 2). Similarly, convening, researching, and sharing potential solutions are important steps, but to make meaningful progress on the challenges identified, a broad shift will need to occur. This shift requires stakeholders from across the public, private, nonprofit, and philanthropic sectors to view workforce solutions as long-term investments in our nation's economic potential. But how can these opportunities for investment be actualized?

This collaborative research, which includes insights from nearly 1,000 experts from across the country, points to the current challenges and promising strategies for improving the human capital of America's labor force. It also outlines strategies for making these opportunities more investable by attracting new sources of capital and using existing sources more efficiently. Insights from the listening sessions point to the fact that these challenges cannot be solved by the public or nonprofit sectors alone. Challenges of this magnitude require public-private partnership and the collaboration of various stakeholder groups.

Albert Einstein famously made the claim that problems cannot be solved with the same level of thinking that created them. Though the challenges are vast, promising solutions call for the ability to see not only the market failures that have resulted from disinvestment over time, but also the market opportunities latent in this country's vast store of human capital. This requires a paradigm shift in which those involved begin to think like investors. Unlike lenders who must rely on healthy skepticism to avoid taking unnecessary risk, investors tend to be optimistic and future-oriented profit maximizers. Investors are not simply interested in the ability of a borrower to repay but are interested in the overall success of the investee. Just as investors succeed when the companies they invest in succeed, the U.S. economy will strengthen when investments in its workforce allow people to move out of poverty and into stable, family-sustaining employment.

Financial systems tend to focus on and incentivize quarterly earnings, but wealth building requires thinking in long-term investment horizons. Similarly, investments in America's workforce should be considered both for their initial outcomes for those struggling to obtain work now and for their long-term effects on economic mobility, neighborhood revitalization, and economic growth. Workforce investments have the potential to increase labor market participation, business productivity, and consumer spending—while at the same time, lowering costs associated with unemployment, disinvestment, and intergenerational poverty. Maximizing the potential of the U.S. workforce is an opportunity with high potential return on investment for workers, employers, and the national economy.

Notes

1. Author's analysis of labor force participation rate data from the U.S. Bureau of Labor Statistics, Current Population Survey, Series LNS11300000, accessed on August 4, 2017.
2. For information on the Community Development function of the Federal Reserve System, visit https://www.fedcommunities.org (accessed September 14, 2018).
3. The Interagency Questions and Answers Regarding Community Reinvestment (Questions and Answers) can be found at https://www.gpo.gov/fdsys/pkg/FR-2016-07-25/pdf/2016-16693.pdf (accessed September 14, 2018).
4. These listening sessions were not transcribed either because the host Reserve Bank chose not to record the session or because the sound quality of the recording was poor. See Table A.1 for a list of the listening sessions and details regarding which were recorded and which were summarized via notes.
5. See Table A.2 for the codebook containing the list of themes.
6. For a discussion of automation's effects on employment, see Autor (2015); Manyika et al. (2017).
7. See Autor (2010) for more on this subject.
8. For a discussion of the interrelationship between disability claims and employment, see McCoy (2017) and Autor et al. (2013).
9. For a discussion of economic development that includes workforce development, see Liu (2016).
10. An overview of the Workforce Innovation and Opportunity Act is available at https://www.doleta.gov/wioa/Overview.cfm (accessed September 14, 2018).
11. For more information on apprenticeships, see https://www.philadelphiafed.org/community-development/publications/special-reports/apprenticeship-guide (accessed September 14, 2018).
12. For research on this topic, see Lerman et al. (2004).
13. Findings from a survey of employers that pursued grant-funded upskill/backfill strategies can be found in Shanbacker and Woolsey (2014).
14. For case studies of successful regional workforce development models, see Andreason and Carpenter (2015).
15. For more on collective impact, visit https://www.collectiveimpactforum.org (accessed September 14, 2018).
16. More information on skills-based hiring can be found in Ross et al. (2016); Canner et al. (2015); Bilvin and Wallerstein (2016).
17. Fuller et al. (2014) discuss employers' use of a college degree as a proxy for soft skills during the hiring process.
18. For case studies of this strategy, see the Hitachi Foundation's Pioneer Employers Initiative at http://hitachifdn.nonprofitsoapbox.com/our-work-good-companies-at-work/pioneer-employers (accessed September 14, 2018).
19. For more information on the credit needs of small employer firms, see the Small Business Credit Survey, a national collaboration of the Federal Reserve System available at https://www.newyorkfed.org/medialibrary/media/smallbusiness/2016/SBCS-Report-StartupFirms-2016.pdf (accessed September 14, 2018).

20. This is the definition provided by the Social Enterprise Alliance. To learn more, visit https://socialenterprise.us/about/social-enterprise/ (accessed September 14, 2018).

21. For more information on Goodwill Industries International, visit http://www .goodwill.org/about-us/ (accessed September 14, 2018).

22. Read more about Zeynep Ton's "good jobs strategy" here: https://hbr.org/2012/01/ why-good-jobs-are-good-for-retailers.

23. For more on income share agreements, see "Capital for Communities: Financing Human Capital through Income Share Agreements" at https://www.philadelphiafed .org/community-development/publications/cascade/92/03_capital-for-communities (accessed September 14, 2018).

24. For more on the U.S. Federal Forfeiture Fund, see https://www.justice.gov/afp/ fund. In the U.K., Big Society Capital has also used dormant federal accounts for impact investing purposes. For more information see https://www.bigsociety capital.com/latest/type/news/%C2%A331-million-dormant-bank-accounts -invested-big-society-projects (accessed September 14, 2018).

25. For more on outcomes-based financing, see https://www.investinresults.org (accessed September 14, 2018).

26. This is a conservative calculation, as the data set used in this research includes only grants of at least $10,000 made by the largest U.S. foundations.

27. For more information on the Workforce Data Quality Campaign, see https://www .nationalskillscoalition.org/national-initiatives/workforce-data-quality-campaign (accessed September 14, 2018).

Table A.1 List of Listening Sessions

Reserve bank	Location	Date	Recorded and transcribed	Summary notes provided
Atlanta	Atlanta, Ga.	10-April	X	
	Melbourne, Fla.	11-April	X	
	Jacksonville, Fla.	28-April	X	
	Starkville, Miss. (w/ St. Louis)	28-Feb.		X
	Valdosta, Ga.	27-April	X	
	Miami, Fla.	28-March		X
	Nashville, Tenn.	24-March		X
	New Orleans, La.	13-April		X
Boston	Boston, Mass.	11-April	X	X
	Hartford, Conn.	12-April	X	X
Chicago	Springfield, Ill. (2)	9-March	X	
	Milwaukee, Wis.	17-March	X	
	Des Moines, Iowa	28-March	X	
	Fort Wayne, Ind.	13-April	X	
Cleveland	Cleveland, Ohio	15-March		X
	Cincinnati, Ohio	24-April		X
	McHenry, Md. - partnered with Richmond Fed	9-March		X
Dallas	Houston, Texas	21-Feb.	X	
	El Paso, Texas	16-March	X	
	Dallas, Texas	1-March		X
	San Antonio, Texas	25-April	X	
Kansas City	Kansas City, Mo.	20-April		X
	Denver, Colo.	21-March		X
	Kearney, Neb.	22-March		X
	Omaha, Neb.	23-March		X
	Albuquerque, N.M.	4-April		X
	Tahlequah, Okla.	26-April		X
	Oklahoma City, Okla.	27-April		X
Minneapolis	Minneapolis, Minn.	18-Apr		X
	Minneapolis, Minn.	17-May	X	X
New York	New York, N.Y.	2-Feb.	X	
	San Juan, Puerto Rico	3-March	X	X
	Buffalo, N.Y.	27-March	X	
	Newark, N.J.	3-May	X	

(continued)

Table A.1 (continued)

Reserve bank	Location	Date	Recorded and transcribed	Summary notes provided
Philadelphia	Philadelphia, Pa.	15-Feb.	X	
	Vineland, N.J.	1-March	X	
	Lancaster, Pa.	24-March	X	
Richmond	Baltimore, Md.	2-March		X
	McHenry, Md. – partnered with Cleveland Fed	9-March		
	Raleigh, N.C.	31-May		X
	Columbia, S.C.	14-June		X
	Richmond, Va.	29-Sep.		X
San Francisco	Yakima, Wash.	16-March	X	X
	Tacoma, Wash.	28-March	X	X
	Spokane, Wash.	30-March	X	X
	Los Angeles, Calif.	3-May		X
	Salt Lake City, Utah	4-May	X	X
	Las Vegas, Nev.	18-May	X	X
	Bend, Ore.	1-June	X	
	Lincoln City, Ore.	2-June	X	
	Vancouver, Wash.	10-April	X	X
St. Louis	St. Louis, Mo.	7-April	X	
	Starkville, Miss. (w/ Atlanta)	28-Feb.		X

Table A.2   Codebook

Current challenges
    stigma/lack of awareness of alternative career paths
    job loss due to automation
    job quality
    lack of coordination/fragmentation
    funding restrictions/requirements
    resource constraints
    skills gap
      soft skills
    best practices mobility
    nonskill-related barriers to work
      housing
      drug screen/background check
      benefit cliff/mindset
      family relations
      transportation
      childcare
Outcome measurement/evaluation
    longitudinal study/retention rates
    coordinate data
    standardize metrics
    process vs. outcome vs. impact
    qualitative data
    ROI
    value added
    RCT
    learn from past work
    intermediate outcomes
    story telling/marketing
    quick cheap evaluation
Strategies
    entrepreneurship/small business development
    social enterprises
    connect workforce and econ dev
      research on needs
    education
      higher ed
        bachelors
        associates
      financial education
      vocational education/CTE
      youth education
        academic and career planning
        early childhood education

(continued)

Table A.2 Codebook (continued)

   employer offered training for incumbent workers
   work-based learning
   retraining
   credentialing/certification
   career pathways
   collaboration and communication
   scale/replicate models
Opportunity for investment
   intermediation
Entities/players
   policymakers/government
   elementary and high schools
   colleges/universities
   community colleges
   CDFIs
   CDCs/CBOs
   financial institutions
   workforce system
   employers/corporations
Funding sources
     public
       local
       state
       federal
     private
       social impact bonds
       CRA
       philanthropy
Client subpopulations
   people in poverty or experiencing homelessness
   immigrants
   older workers
   veterans
   people with disabilities
   opportunity youth and millennials
   formerly incarcerated

References

Andreason, Stuart, and Ann Carpenter. 2015. *Fragmentation in Workforce Development Efforts to Coordinate Regional Workforce Development Systems,* Atlanta, GA: Federal Reserve Bank of Atlanta.

Autor, David H. 2010. *The Polarization of Job Opportunities in the U.S. Labor Market: Implications for Employment and Earnings.* Washington, DC: Center for American Progress and The Hamilton Project.

———. 2015. "Why Are There Still So Many Jobs? The History and Future of Workplace Automation." *Journal of Economic Perspectives* 29(3): 3–30.

Autor, David H., David Dorn, and Gordon H. Hanson.. 2013. "The China Syndrome: Local Labor Market Effects of Import Competition in the United States." *American Economic Review* 103(6): 2121–2168.

Avivar Capital. 2016. *Driving Postsecondary Success with Impact Investing.* Los Angeles: Avivar Capital.

Bilvin, Jamai, and Ben Wallerstein. 2016. *Shift Happens: The Entrepreneurs, Wonks, and Investors Revolutionizing the Learning-to-Employment Landscape*: Santa Fe, NM, Washington, DC: Innovate+Educate, Whiteboard Advisors.

Brett, Daniel, and Tom Woelfel. 2016. *Moving beyond Job Creation: Defining and Measuring the Creation of Quality* Jobs. San Francisco, CA: Pacific Community Ventures.

Canner, Niko, Abigail Carlton, Guy Halfteck, and John Irons. 2015. *Impact Hiring: How Data Will Transform Youth Employment,* New York, NY, San Francisco, CA: Rockefeller Foundation, Incandescent, Knack.

Dawson, Steven L. 2016. "Targeting Workforce Dollars: You Don't Get What You Don't Pay For." *The Pinkerton Papers* Job Quality Series No. 3. New York: Pinkerton Foundation.

Fuller, Joseph, Jennifer Burrowes, Manjari Raman, Dan Restuccia, and Alexis Young. 2014. *Bridge the Gap: Rebuilding America's Middle Skills.* Cambridge, MA: Harvard Business School.

Griffith, Erin. 2014. "Why Startups Fail, According to their Founders. *Fortune,* September 25.

Haltiwanger, John. 2015. "Top Ten Signs of Declining Business Dynamism and Entrepreneurship in the U.S." Paper prepared for the Kauffman Foundation New Entrepreneurial Growth Conference held June 17–19 in Amelia Island, FL.

Jain, Ranita, Amanda Newman, and Marcela Montes. 2017. *Investing in Workforce Program Innovation: A Formative Evaluation of Five Workforce Organizations' Experiences during the Human Capital Innovation Fund Initiative.* New York: The Aspen Institute.

Lerman, Robert I., Signe-Mary McKernan, and Stephanie Reigg. 2004. "The Scope of Employer Provided Training in the United States: Who, What, Where, and How Much?" In *Job Training Policy in the United States*, Christopher J.

O'Leary, Robert A. Straits, and Stephen A. Wandner, eds. Kalamazoo, MI: W.E. Upjohn Institute for Employment Research, pp. 211–244.

Liu, Amy. 2016. *Remaking Economic Development: The Markets and Civics of Continuous Growth and Prosperity*. Washington, DC: The Brookings Institution, Metropolitan Policy Program.

ManpowerGroup. 2016. *U.S. Talent Shortage Survey*. Milwaukee, WI: ManPowerGroup.

Manyika, James, Michael Chui, Mehdi Miremadi, Jacques Bughin, Katy George, Paul Willmott, and Martin Dewhurst. 2017. *A Future That Works: Automation, Employment, and Productivity*. New York: McKinsey & Company, McKinsey Global Institute.

McCoy, Terrence. 2017. "Disabled, or Just Desperate? Rural Americans Turn to Disability as Jobs Dry Up." *Washington Post*, March 30. http://www.washingtonpost.com/sf/local/2017/03/30/disabled-or-just-desperate/?utm_term=.1b2d6433ffd7 (accesssed May 25, 2018).

National Skills Coalition. 2017a. "Congess Should Invest in Workforce Education and Training Programs." Washington, DC: National Skills Coalition. http://www.nationalskillscoalition.org/resources/publications/file/Why-Congress-should-invest-in-workforce-education-and-training-programs.pdf (accessed July 28, 2017).

———. 2017b. *Building America's Infrastructure Workforce: Partnering with Industry to Meet the Demand for Skilled Workers*. Washington, DC: National Skills Coalition.

Next Street. 2016. *Bridging the Gap: Impact Investing Supply and Demand in the Chicago Region,* Chicago: MacArthur Foundation and The Chicago Community Trust.

Pena, Cristina. 2017. *From Patchwork to Tapestry: Collaborating to Maximize Data Utility*. Washington DC: National Skills Coalition.

Ross, Michaela, Reilly Kiernan, Devin Murphy, and Debby Bielak. 2016. *"Billion Dollar Bets" to Establish Pathways to Careers: Creating an Economic Opportunity for Every American*. Boston: Bridgespan Group.

Schiff, Hannah, and Hannah Dithrich. 2017. *Scaling the Use of Guarantees in U.S. Community Investing*. New York: Global Impact Investing Network.

Shanbacker, Elise, and Lindsey Woolsey. 2014. *Upskill/Backfill Strategies: Advancing Incumbent Workers and Opening Opportunities for Job Seekers*. Washington, DC: National Governors Association.

Sobel Blum, Elizabeth, and Steve Shepelwich. 2017. *Engaging Workforce Development: A Framework for Meeting CRA Obligations*. Dallas and Kansas City: Federal Reserve Banks of Dallas and Kansas City.

Society for Human Resources Management. 2016. *The New Talent Landscape: Recruiting Difficulty and Skills Shortages*. Alexandria, VA: Society for Human Resources Management.

U.S. Department of Labor, Employment and Training Administration (USDOLETA). 2016. *Career Pathways Toolkit: A Guide for System Develop-*

ment. Washington, DC: U.S. Department of Labor, Employment, and Training Administration.

Wandner, Stephen A. 2015. "The Future of the Public Workforce System in a Time of Dwindling Resources." In *Transforming U.S. Workforce Development Policies*, Carl Van Horn, Tammy Edwards, and Todd Greene, eds. Kalamazoo, MI: W.E. Upjohn Institute for Employment Research, pp. 129–163.

Wardrip, Keith, and Mels de Zeeuw. 2018. "Nimble Capital for an Agile Workforce." In *Investing in America's Workforce: Improving Outcomes for Workers and Employers*. Vol. 3, *Investing in Systems for Employment Opportunity*, Carl E. Van Horn, Todd Greene, Heath Prince, and Stuart Andreason, eds. Kalamazoo, MI: W.E. Upjohn Institute for Employment Research, pp. 29–47.

White House. 2016. *The Long Term Decline in Prime-Age Male Labor Force Participation*. Washington, DC: The White House.

Yellen, Janet L. 2017. "Addressing Workforce Development Challenges in Low-Income Communities." Remarks delivered at "Creating a Just Economy," the 2017 annual conference of the National Community Reinvestment Coalition, held March 28 in Washington, DC. https://www.federalreserve.gov/newsevents/speech/yellen20170328a.htm (accessed May 25, 2018).

Authors

Evan Amoroso served as a research associate at the U.S. Conference of Mayors and is an undergraduate student at James Madison University.

Kathy Amoroso is assistant executive director for education and workforce at the U.S. Conference of Mayors.

Stuart Andreason is the director of the Center for Workforce and Economic Opportunity at the Federal Reserve Bank of Atlanta.

Michael Bartlett is a senior policy analyst with the Postsecondary Education Program in the Economic Opportunity Division at the National Governors Association Center for Best Practices.

Jordana Barton is senior advisor in Community Development at the Federal Reserve Bank of Dallas.

Josh Bersin is a global human resources and workforce industry analyst and founder of Bersin™ by Deloitte.

Elizabeth Sobel Blum is senior community development advisor at the Federal Reserve Bank of Dallas.

Raphael Bostic is the president and chief executive officer of the Federal Reserve Bank of Atlanta.

Ann Carpenter is a senior community and economic development adviser at the Federal Reserve Bank of Atlanta.

Richard Cave is a principal with IBM Market Development and Insights. He conducts research and creates insight into business and technology trends.

Yvette Chocolaad is policy director for Employment and Training Programs, and Labor Market Information, at the National Association of State Workforce Agencies.

Alejandro Crawford is managing director of Acceleration Group, chief executive officer of RebelBase, and professor of entrepreneurship at the Bard MBA in Sustainability.

Stephen Crawford is a research professor at George Washington University's George Washington Institute of Public Policy.

Mels de Zeeuw is a senior research analyst in the Community and Economic Development Department at the Federal Reserve Bank of Atlanta.

Lauren Eyster is a senior fellow at the Urban Institute, focusing on workforce development research and evaluation.

Mike Foden is a consultant with IBM Market Development and Insights and has 20 years' experience in analysis in information technology, retail, and consumer behavior.

John Hagel is founder and chairman of the Deloitte Center for the Edge, a research center based in Silicon Valley.

Richard A. Hobbie is a visiting scholar at the John. J. Heldrich Center for Workforce Development at Rutgers University and retired from full-time work.

Michael King is the worldwide leader for the IBM Education Industry with responsibility for strategy, marketing, and sales.

Chauncy Lennon is a managing director in global philanthropy at JPMorgan Chase & Co.

Demetra Smith Nightingale is an Institute fellow at the Urban Institute, where her research focuses on social, economic, and labor policy issues.

Miguel Palacios is assistant professor of finance at the Haskayne School of Business, University of Calgary, and co-founder of Lumni Inc., a company that offers income-contingent financing to students.

Tucker Plumlee is a former research associate at the Council for Adult and Experiential Learning, and is now a research analyst at Northern Virginia Community College.

Heath Prince is a research scientist and the director of the Ray Marshall Center at the University of Texas's Lyndon B. Johnson School of Public Affairs.

Celeste Richie is a public policy professional with more than a decade of experience working in federal, state, and local government.

Alexander Ruder is a senior policy advisor in community and economic development at the Federal Reserve Bank of Atlanta.

Ken Sauer is senior associate commissioner and chief academic officer for the Indiana Commission for Higher Education, executive director of the Indiana Commission for Proprietary Education, and vice chair of the Midwestern Higher Education Compact.

Jeff Schwartz is a principal with Deloitte Consulting LLP, the global leader for human capital marketing and eminence, and Deloitte's U.S. leader for the future of work.

Nirav Shah is a vice president on the social investment team at Social Finance.

Steven Shepelwich is a senior community development advisor at the Federal Reserve Bank of Kansas City.

Robert Sheets is a research professor at the George Washington Institute of Public Policy.

Martin Simon is acting director for the Economic Opportunity Division at the National Governors Association, Center for Best Practices.

Noelle St.Clair is community development advisor and outreach manager at the Federal Reserve Bank of Philadelphia.

Sarah Steinberg is vice president of global philanthropy at JPMorgan Chase & Co.

Matthew Stent is a manager in IBM's Market Development and Insights team and has a long-held passion for championing market insights within IBM.

Jason A. Tyszko is vice president of the Center for Education and Workforce at the U.S. Chamber of Commerce Foundation.

Carl E. Van Horn is distinguished professor of public policy at Rutgers University, and director of the Heldrich Center for Workforce Development.

Andy Van Kleunen is the founding chief executive officer of National Skills Coalition.

Stephen Wandner is a fellow at the Urban Institute, the W.E. Upjohn Institute for Employment Research, and the National Academy of Social Insurance.

Keith Wardrip is the community development research manager at the Federal Reserve Bank of Philadelphia.

Bryan Wilson is director of Workforce Data Quality Campaign at National Skills Coalition.

Rachel Zinn is a senior budget management analyst for the city of Baltimore.